W9-BYL-142

Contents

OpenGL® ES 2.0
Programming Guide

OpenGL® Series

★ Addison-Wesley

Visit **informit.com/opengl** for a complete list of available products

---

The OpenGL graphics system is a software interface to graphics hardware. ("GL" stands for "Graphics Library.") It allows you to create interactive programs that produce color images of moving, three-dimensional objects. With OpenGL, you can control computer-graphics technology to produce realistic pictures, or ones that depart from reality in imaginative ways.

The **OpenGL Series** from Addison-Wesley Professional comprises tutorial and reference books that help programmers gain a practical understanding of OpenGL standards, along with the insight needed to unlock OpenGL's full potential.

OpenGL® ES 2.0
Programming Guide

Aaftab Munshi
Dan Ginsburg
Dave Shreiner

✦ Addison-Wesley

Upper Saddle River, NJ • Boston • Indianapolis • San Francisco
New York • Toronto • Montreal • London • Munich • Paris • Madrid
Capetown • Sydney • Tokyo • Singapore • Mexico City

Many of the designations used by manufacturers and sellers to distinguish their products are claimed as trademarks. Where those designations appear in this book, and the publisher was aware of a trademark claim, the designations have been printed with initial capital letters or in all capitals.

The authors and publisher have taken care in the preparation of this book, but make no expressed or implied warranty of any kind and assume no responsibility for errors or omissions. No liability is assumed for incidental or consequential damages in connection with or arising out of the use of the information or programs contained herein.

The publisher offers excellent discounts on this book when ordered in quantity for bulk purchases or special sales, which may include electronic versions and/or custom covers and content particular to your business, training goals, marketing focus, and branding interests. For more information, contact:

U.S. Corporate and Government Sales, (800) 382-3419, corpsales@pearsontechgroup.com

For sales outside the United States please contact:

International Sales, international@pearson.com

Visit us on the Web: informit.com/aw

This Book Is Safari Enabled

The Safari® Enabled icon on the cover of your favorite technology book means the book is available through Safari Bookshelf. When you buy this book, you get free access to the online edition for 45 days.

Safari Bookshelf is an electronic reference library that lets you easily search thousands of technical books, find code samples, download chapters, and access technical information whenever and wherever you need it.

To gain 45-day Safari Enabled access to this book:

- Go to informit.com/onlineedition
- Complete the brief registration form
- Enter the coupon code F1GR-7SFI-LPRP-Q2ID-HBCC

If you have difficulty registering on Safari Bookshelf or accessing the online edition, please e-mail customer-service@safaribooksonline.com.

Library of Congress Cataloging-in-Publication Data

Munshi, Aaftab.
  The OpenGL ES 2.0 programming guide / Aaftab Munshi, Dan Ginsburg, Dave Shreiner.
      p.   cm.
  Includes index.
  ISBN-13: 978-0-321-50279-7 (pbk. : alk. paper)
  ISBN-10: 0-321-50279-5 (pbk. : alk. paper) 1. OpenGL. 2. Computer graphics—Specifications. 3. Application program interfaces (Computer software) 4. Computer programming. I. Ginsburg, Dan. II. Shreiner, Dave. III. Title.

  T385.M863 2009
  006.6'6—dc22   2008016669

ISBN-13: 978-0-321-50279-7
ISBN-10:   0-321-50279-5
Text printed in the United States on recycled paper at Courier Stoughton in Stoughton, Massachusetts.
4th Printing February 2011

List of Figures

List of Examples

List of Tables

Foreword

Over the years, the "Red Book" has become the authoritative reference for each new version of the OpenGL API. Now we have the "Gold Book" for OpenGL ES 2.0—a cross-platform open standard ushering in a new era of shader programmability and visual sophistication for a wide variety of embedded and mobile devices, from game consoles to automobiles, from set top boxes to mobile phones.

Mobile phones, in particular, are impacting our everyday lives, as the devices we carry with us are evolving into full mobile computers. Soon we will be living in a world where most of us get our pixels delivered on these personal, portable devices—and OpenGL ES will be at the center of this handheld revolution. Devices such as the Apple iPhone already use OpenGL ES to drive their user interface, demonstrating how advanced graphics acceleration can play an important role in making a mobile phone fun, intuitive, and productive to use. But we have only just started the journey to make our handheld computers even more visually engaging. The shader programmability of the new generation of mobile graphics, combined with the portability and location awareness of mobile devices, will forever change how we interact with our phones, the Internet, and each other.

OpenGL ES 2.0 is a critical step forward in this mobile computing revolution. By bringing the power of the OpenGL ES Shading Language to diverse embedded and mobile platforms, OpenGL ES 2.0 unleashes enormous visual computing power, but in a way that is engineered to run on a small battery. Soon after this graphics capability is used to deliver extraordinary user interfaces, it will be leveraged for a wide diversity of visually engaging applications—compelling games, intuitive navigation applications, and more—all in the palm of your hand.

However, these applications will only be successful if enabled by a complete ecosystem of graphics APIs and authoring standards. This is the continuing mission of the Khronos Group—to bring together industry-leading companies and individuals to create open, royalty-free standards that enable the software community to effectively access the power of graphics and media acceleration silicon. OpenGL ES is at the center of this ecosystem, being developed alongside OpenGL and COLLADA. Together, they bring a tremendous cross-standard and multi-platform synergy to advanced 3D on a wide variety of platforms. Indeed, community collaboration has become essential for realizing the potential of OpenGL ES 2.0. The sophistication of a state-of-the-art programmable 3D API, complete with shading language, an effects framework, and authoring pipeline, has required hundreds of man years of design and investment—beyond any single company's ability to create and evangelize throughout the industry.

As a result of the strong industry collaboration within Khronos, now is the perfect time to learn about this new programmable 3D API as OpenGL ES 2.0–capable devices will soon be appearing in increasing volumes. In fact, it is very possible that, due to the extraordinary volume of the mobile market, OpenGL ES 2.0 will soon be shipping on more devices than any previous 3D API to create an unprecedented opportunity for content developers.

This level of successful collaboration only happens as the result of hard work and dedication of many individuals, but in particular I extend a sincere thanks to Tom Olson, the working group chair that brought OpenGL ES 2.0 to market. And finally, a big thank you to the authors of this book: You have been central to the creation of OpenGL ES 2.0 within Khronos and you have created a great reference for OpenGL ES 2.0—truly worthy of the title "Gold Book."

Neil Trevett
Vice President Mobile Content, NVIDIA
President, Khronos Group
April 2008

Preface

OpenGL ES 2.0 is a software interface for rendering sophisticated 3D graphics on handheld and embedded devices. OpenGL ES 2.0 is the primary graphics library for handheld and embedded devices with programmable 3D hardware including cell phones, PDAs, consoles, appliances, vehicles, and avionics. With OpenGL ES 2.0, the full programmability of shaders has made its way onto small and portable devices. This book details the entire OpenGL ES 2.0 API and pipeline with detailed examples in order to provide a guide for developing a wide range of high-performance 3D applications for handheld devices.

Intended Audience

This book is intended for programmers interested in learning OpenGL ES 2.0. We expect the reader to have a solid grounding in computer graphics. We will explain many of the relevant graphics concepts as they relate to various parts of OpenGL ES 2.0, but we do expect the reader to understand basic 3D concepts. The code examples in the book are all written in C. We assume that the reader is familiar with C or C++ and will only be covering language topics where they are relevant to OpenGL ES 2.0.

This book covers the entire OpenGL ES 2.0 API along with all Khronos-ratified extensions. The reader will learn about setting up and programming every aspect of the graphics pipeline. The book details how to write vertex and fragment shaders and how to implement advanced rendering techniques such as per-pixel lighting and particle systems. In addition, the book provides performance tips and tricks for efficient use of the API and hardware. After finishing the book, the reader will be ready to write OpenGL ES 2.0 applications that fully harness the programmable power of embedded graphics hardware.

Organization of the Book

This book is organized to cover the API in a sequential fashion, building up your knowledge of OpenGL ES 2.0 as we go.

Chapter 1—Introduction to OpenGL ES 2.0

This chapter gives an introduction to OpenGL ES, followed by an overview of the OpenGL ES 2.0 graphics pipeline. We discuss the philosophies and constraints that went into the design of OpenGL ES 2.0. Finally, the chapter covers some general conventions and types used in OpenGL ES 2.0.

Chapter 2—Hello Triangle: An OpenGL ES 2.0 Example

This chapter walks through a simple OpenGL ES 2.0 example program that draws a triangle. Our purpose here is to show what an OpenGL ES 2.0 program looks like, introduce the reader to some API concepts, and describe how to build and run an example OpenGL ES 2.0 program.

Chapter 3—An Introduction to EGL

This chapter presents EGL, the API for creating surfaces and rendering contexts for OpenGL ES 2.0. We describe how to communicate with the native windowing system, choose a configuration, and create EGL rendering contexts and surfaces. We teach you enough EGL so that you can do everything you will need to do to get up and rendering with OpenGL ES 2.0.

Chapter 4—Shaders and Programs

Shader objects and program objects form the most fundamental objects in OpenGL ES 2.0. In this chapter, we describe how to create a shader object, compile a shader, and check for compile errors. The chapter also covers how to create a program object, attach shader objects to it, and link a final program object. We discuss how to query the program object for information and how to load uniforms. In addition, you will learn about the difference between source and binary shaders and how to use each.

Chapter 5—OpenGL ES Shading Language

This chapter covers the shading language basics needed for writing shaders. The shading language basics described are variables and types, constructors, structures, arrays, attributes, uniforms, and varyings. This chapter also describes some more nuanced parts of the language such as precision qualifiers and invariance.

Chapter 6—Vertex Attributes, Vertex Arrays, and Buffer Objects

Starting with Chapter 6 (and ending with Chapter 11), we begin our walk through the pipeline to teach you how to set up and program each part of the graphics pipeline. This journey begins by covering how geometry is input into the graphics pipeline by discussing vertex attributes, vertex arrays, and buffer objects.

Chapter 7—Primitive Assembly and Rasterization

After discussing how geometry is input into the pipeline in the previous chapter, we then cover how that geometry is assembled into primitives. All of the primitive types available in OpenGL ES 2.0, including point sprites, lines, triangles, triangle strips, and triangle fans, are covered. In addition, we describe how coordinate transformations are performed on vertices and introduce the rasterization stage of the OpenGL ES 2.0 pipeline.

Chapter 8—Vertex Shaders

The next portion of the pipeline that is covered is the vertex shader. This chapter gives an overview of how vertex shaders fit into the pipeline and the special variables available to vertex shaders in the OpenGL ES Shading Language. Several examples of vertex shaders, including computation of per-vertex lighting and skinning, are covered. We also give examples of how the OpenGL ES 1.0 (and 1.1) fixed-function pipeline can be implemented using vertex shaders.

Chapter 9—Texturing

This chapter begins the introduction to the fragment shader by describing all of the texturing functionality available in OpenGL ES 2.0. This chapter covers all the details of how to create textures, how to load them with data, and how to render with them. The chapter details texture wrap modes, texture filtering, and mipmapping. In addition, you will learn about the various functions for compressed texture images as well as how to copy texture data from the color buffer. This chapter also covers the optional texture extensions that add support for 3D textures and depth textures.

Chapter 10—Fragment Shaders

Chapter 9 focused on how to use textures in a fragment shader. This chapter covers the rest of what you need to know to write fragment shaders. We give an overview of fragment shaders and all of the special built-in variables available to them. We show how to implement all of the fixed-function techniques that were available in OpenGL ES 1.1 using fragment shaders. Examples of multitexturing, fog, alpha test, and user clip planes are all implemented in fragment shaders.

Chapter 11—Fragment Operations

This chapter discusses the operations that can be applied either to the entire framebuffer, or to individual fragments after the execution of the fragment shader in the OpenGL ES 2.0 fragment pipeline. These operations include scissor test, stencil test, depth test, multi-sampling, blending, and dithering. This is the final phase in the OpenGL ES 2.0 graphics pipeline.

Chapter 12—Framebuffer Objects

This chapter discusses the use of framebuffer objects for rendering to off-screen surfaces. There are several uses of framebuffer objects, the most common of which is for rendering to a texture. This chapter provides a complete overview of the framebuffer object portion of the API. Understanding framebuffer objects is critical for implementing many advanced effects such as reflections, shadow maps, and post-processing.

Chapter 13—Advanced Programming with OpenGL ES 2.0

This is the capstone chapter, tying together many of the topics presented throughout the book. We have selected a sampling of advanced rendering techniques and show examples that demonstrate how to implement these features. This chapter includes rendering techniques such as per-pixel lighting using normal maps, environment mapping, particle systems, image post-processing, and projective texturing. This chapter attempts to show the reader how to tackle a variety of advanced rendering techniques.

Chapter 14—State Queries

There are a large number of state queries available in OpenGL ES 2.0. For just about everything you set, there is a corresponding way to get what the current value is. This chapter is provided as a reference for the various state queries available in OpenGL ES 2.0.

Chapter 15—OpenGL ES and EGL on Handheld Platforms

In the final chapter, we divert ourselves a bit from the details of the API to talk about programming with OpenGL ES 2.0 and EGL in the real world. There are a diverse set of handheld platforms in the market that pose some interesting issues and challenges when developing applications for OpenGL ES 2.0. We cover topics including an overview of handheld platforms, C++ portability issues, OpenKODE, and platform-specific shader binaries.

Appendix A—GL_HALF_FLOAT_OES

This appendix details the half-float format and provides a reference for how to convert from IEEE floating-point values into half-float (and back).

Appendix B—Built-In Functions

This appendix provides a reference for all of the built-in functions available in the OpenGL ES Shading Language.

Appendix C—Shading Language Grammar

This appendix provides a reference for OpenGL ES Shading Language grammar.

Appendix D—ES Framework API

This appendix provides a reference for the utility framework we developed for the book and describes what each function does.

Appendix E—OpenGL ES 2.0 on the iPhone 3GS

This appendix provides information on developing OpenGL ES 2.0 applications for the iPhone 3GS. Included in the appendix is information on how to build the sample code for the iPhone 3GS. In addition, it covers some of the platform specifics of developing OpenGL ES 2.0 applications with the iPhone SDK 3.0, including the use of Objective C, initializing a rendering surface, and transitioning from OpenGL ES 1.1 to OpenGL ES 2.0.

Examples Code and Shaders

This book is filled with example programs and shaders. You can download the examples from the book Web site at www.opengles-book.com.

The examples are all targeted to run on Microsoft Windows XP or Vista with a desktop GPU supporting OpenGL 2.0. The example programs are provided in source code form with Microsoft Visual Studio 2005 project solutions. The examples build and run on the AMD OpenGL ES 2.0 Emulator. Several of the advanced shader examples in the book are implemented in RenderMonkey, a shader development tool from AMD. The book Web site provides links on where to download any of the required tools. The OpenGL ES 2.0 Emulator and RenderMonkey are both freely available tools. For readers who do not own Visual Studio, you can use the free Microsoft Visual Studio 2008 Express Edition available for download at www.microsoft.com/express/.

Errata

If you find something in the book which you believe is in error, please send us a note at errors@opengles-book.com. The list of errata for the book can be found on the book's Web site at opengles-book.com/errata.html.

Acknowledgements

It was a real privilege working with Dan and Dave on this book. I want to thank them for all their hard work on this book. Their valuable insight and feedback were extremely helpful in improving the quality of the chapters I worked on.

Thanks go to my daughters, Hannah and Ellie, who are a constant reminder of what is most important in life. Their laughs, hugs, kisses, and especially zerbets were a much needed help in writing this book. And to the love of my life, Karen, I am always in awe of what an amazing wife you are. Without your patience, support, and love, this book would not be possible.

— *Aaftab Munshi*

I would like to thank the many colleagues that I have worked with over the years that have helped in my education on computer graphics, OpenGL, and OpenGL ES. There are too many people to list all of them, but a special thanks to Shawn Leaf, Bill Licea-Kane, Maurice Ribble, Benj Lipchak, Roger Descheneaux, David Gosselin, Thorsten Scheuermann, John Isidoro, Chris Oat, Jason Mitchell, and Evan Hart. I would like to thank AMD for its support in writing this book and my manager Callan McInally for encouraging me to write it.

I would like to extend a special thanks to Sofia af Petersens for her support while I worked on this book. I would also like to extend my unending gratitude to my parents for all that they've done for me. Finally, I would like to thank my friends and the many great teachers I have been fortunate to have over my life.

— *Dan Ginsburg*

First, I'd like to thank Affie and Dan for making this a fun and educational project. Additionally, many thanks go to my colleagues at ARM with special note of the assistance of Ed Plowman, Edvard Sørgård, Remi Pedersen, and Mario Blazevic.

Finally, projects like this would never occur without the unwavering patience and encouragement of my family: Vicki, Bonnie, Bob, and Phantom. Thanks for your love and support.

— *Dave Shreiner*

We all want to thank Neil Trevett for writing the Foreword and getting approval from the Khronos Board of Promoters to allow us to use text from the OpenGL ES specification in the Appendices. A special thank you and debt of gratitude to the reviewers—Brian Collins, Chris Grimm, Jeremy Sandmel, Tom Olson, and Adam Smith.

This book would also not have happened without the support of the folks at Addison-Wesley: Debra Williams Cauley and Curt Johnson.

A big thank you to the OpenGL ARB, the OpenGL ES working group and everyone that contributed to the development of OpenGL ES.

About the Authors

Aaftab Munshi

Affie has been architecting GPUs for more than a decade. At ATI (now AMD), he was a Senior Architect in the Handheld Group. He is the spec editor for the OpenGL ES 1.1 and OpenGL ES 2.0 specifications. He currently works at Apple.

Dan Ginsburg

Dan has been working on developing 3D computer graphics software for more than ten years. He is currently a software engineer at Still River Systems, where he is developing OpenGL-based image registration software for the Monarch250 proton beam radiotherapy system. Before joining Still River Systems, Dan was a Senior Member of Technical Staff at AMD, where he worked in a variety of roles, including the development of OpenGL drivers, the creation of desktop and handheld 3D demos, and leading the development of handheld GPU developer tools. Prior to working for AMD, he worked for n-Space, Inc., an Orlando-based game development company. Dan holds a B.S. in Computer Science from Worcester Polytechnic Institute and an MBA from Bentley College.

Dave Shreiner

Dave's been working with OpenGL for almost two decades, and more recently with OpenGL ES. During that time, he authored the first commercial training course on OpenGL while working at Silicon Graphics Computer Systems (SGI), and has worked as an author on the OpenGL Programming Guide. He's presented introductory and advanced courses on OpenGL programming worldwide at numerous conferences, including SIGGRAPH.

Dave is now a Media Systems Architect at ARM, Inc. He holds a B.S. in Mathematics from the University of Delaware.

Chapter 1

Introduction to OpenGL ES 2.0

What Is OpenGL ES?

OpenGL ES is an application programming interface (API) for advanced 3D graphics targeted at handheld and embedded devices such as cell phones, personal digital assistants (PDAs), consoles, appliances, vehicles, and avionics. OpenGL ES is one of a set of APIs created by the Khronos Group. The Khronos Group, founded in January 2000, is a member-funded industry consortium that is focused on the creation of open standard and royalty-free APIs for handheld and embedded devices.

In the desktop world there are two standard 3D APIs, DirectX and OpenGL. DirectX is the de facto standard 3D API for any system running the Microsoft Windows operating system and is used by the majority of 3D games on that platform. OpenGL is a cross-platform standard 3D API for desktop systems running Linux, various flavors of UNIX, Mac OS X, and Microsoft Windows. It is a widely accepted standard 3D API that has seen significant real-world usage. The API is used by games such as the Doom and Quake series, user interfaces as in Mac OS X, workstation computer-aided design (CAD) applications like CATIA, and digital content creation applications such as Maya and SoftImage|XSI.

Due to the widespread adoption of OpenGL as a 3D API, it made sense to start with the desktop OpenGL API in developing an open standard 3D API for handheld and embedded devices and modifying it to meet the needs and constraints of the handheld and embedded device space. The device constraints that OpenGL ES addresses are very limited processing capabilities and memory availability, low memory bandwidth, sensitivity to power consumption, and lack of floating-point hardware. The working group used the following criteria in the definition of the OpenGL ES specification(s):

- The OpenGL API is very large and complex and the goal of the OpenGL ES working group was to create an API suitable for constrained devices. To achieve this goal, the working group removed any redundancy from the OpenGL API. In any case where there was more than one way of performing the same operation, the most useful method was taken and the redundant techniques were removed. A good example of this is specifying geometry, where in OpenGL an application can use immediate mode, display lists, or vertex arrays. In OpenGL ES, only vertex arrays exist and immediate mode and display lists were removed.

- Removing redundancy was an important goal, but maintaining compatibility with OpenGL was also important. As much as possible, OpenGL ES was designed such that applications that were written to the embedded subset of functionality in OpenGL would also run on OpenGL ES. The reason this was an important goal is it allows developers to leverage both APIs and develop applications and tools that use the common subset of functionality. Although this was an important goal, there are cases where it has deviated, especially with OpenGL ES 2.0. This is discussed in detail in later chapters.

- New features were introduced to address specific constraints of handheld and embedded devices. For example, to reduce the power consumption and increase the performance of shaders, precision qualifiers were introduced to the shading language.

- The designers of OpenGL ES aimed to ensure a minimum set of features for image quality. Most handheld devices have limited screen sizes, making it essential that the quality of the pixels drawn on the screen is as good as possible.

- The OpenGL ES working group wanted to ensure that any OpenGL ES implementation would meet certain acceptable and agreed-on standards for image quality, correctness, and robustness. This is done by developing appropriate conformance tests that an OpenGL ES implementation must pass to be considered compliant.

There are three OpenGL ES specifications that have been released by Khronos so far: the OpenGL ES 1.0 and ES 1.1 specifications (referred to jointly as OpenGL ES 1.x in this book) and the OpenGL ES 2.0 specification. The OpenGL ES 1.0 and 1.1 specifications implement a fixed function pipeline and are derived from the OpenGL 1.3 and 1.5 specifications, respectively.

The OpenGL ES 2.0 specification implements a programmable graphics pipeline and is derived from the OpenGL 2.0 specification. Being derived from a revision of the OpenGL specification means that the corresponding OpenGL specification was used as the baseline for determining the feature set in the particular revision of OpenGL ES. A difference specification was then created that described the changes and additions to OpenGL ES versus the OpenGL specification from which it is derived.

As OpenGL ES 2.0 is derived from the powerful OpenGL 2.0 API, it enables extremely rich programmable game content. For example, the image in Color Plate 1 (see the center of this book) is from a demo of a pinball game targeted at OpenGL ES 2.0 and it uses shaders for advanced effects such as environment mapping and per-fragment lighting. This example demonstrates the kinds of effects that will be commonplace in OpenGL ES 2.0 applications. With OpenGL ES 2.0, much of the programmable graphics capabilities of desktop hardware are now available on embedded devices.

In the sections that follow we give an introduction to the OpenGL ES 2.0 pipeline.

OpenGL ES 2.0

OpenGL ES 2.0 is the API that we cover in this book. Our goal is to cover the OpenGL ES 2.0 specification in thorough detail (both the core specification and Khronos approved OpenGL ES 2.0 extensions), give specific examples of how to use the features in OpenGL ES 2.0, and discuss various performance optimization techniques. After reading this book, you should have an excellent grasp of the OpenGL ES 2.0 API, be able to easily write compelling OpenGL ES 2.0 applications, and not have to worry about reading multiple specifications to understand how a feature works.

OpenGL ES 2.0 implements a graphics pipeline with programmable shading and consists of two specifications: the **OpenGL ES 2.0 API specification** and the **OpenGL ES Shading Language Specification (OpenGL ES SL)**. Figure 1-1 shows the OpenGL ES 2.0 graphics pipeline. The shaded boxes in Figure 1-1 indicate the programmable stages of the pipeline in OpenGL ES 2.0. An overview of each stage in the OpenGL ES 2.0 graphics pipeline is presented next.

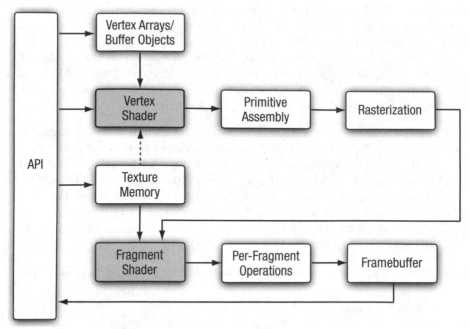

Figure 1-1   OpenGL ES 2.0 Graphics Pipeline

Vertex Shader

This section gives a high-level overview of what a vertex shader is. Vertex and fragment shaders are covered in depth in later chapters.

The vertex shader implements a general purpose programmable method for operating on vertices.

The inputs to the vertex shader consist of the following:

- Attributes—Per-vertex data supplied using vertex arrays.

- Uniforms—Constant data used by the vertex shader.

- Samplers—A specific type of uniforms that represent textures used by the vertex shader. Samplers in a vertex shader are optional.

- Shader program—Vertex shader program source code or executable that describes the operations that will be performed on the vertex.

The outputs of the vertex shader are called varying variables. In the primitive rasterization stage, the varying values are calculated for each generated fragment and are passed in as inputs to the fragment shader. The mechanism used to generate a varying value for each fragment from the varying values assigned to each vertex of the primitive is called interpolation. The inputs and outputs of the vertex shader are diagramed in Figure 1-2.

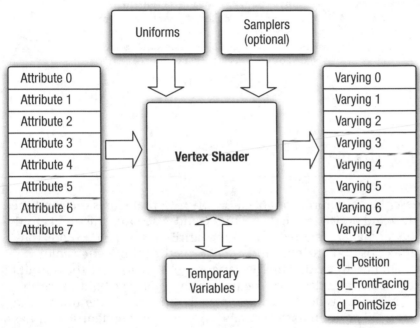

Figure 1-2   OpenGL ES 2.0 Vertex Shader

Vertex shaders can be used for traditional vertex-based operations such as transforming the position by a matrix, computing the lighting equation to generate a per-vertex color, and generating or transforming texture coordinates. Alternately, because the vertex shader is specified by the application, vertex shaders can be used to do custom vertex transformations.

Example 1-1 shows a vertex shader written using the OpenGL ES shading language. We explain vertex shaders in significant detail later in the book. We show this shader now just to give you an idea of what a vertex shader looks like. The vertex shader in Example 1-1 takes a position and its associated color data as input attributes, transforms the position by a 4 × 4 matrix and outputs the transformed position and color.

Example 1-1   A Vertex Shader Example

```
1.  // uniforms used by the vertex shader
2.  uniform mat4    u_mvpMatrix; // matrix to convert P from model
3.                               // space to normalized device space.
4.
5.  // attributes input to the vertex shader
6.  attribute vec4    a_position; // position value
7.  attribute vec4    a_color;    // input vertex color
8.
9.  // varying variables - input to the fragment shader
10. varying vec4      v_color;    // output vertex color
11.
12. void
13. main()
14. {
15.     v_color = a_color;
16.     gl_Position = u_mvpMatrix * a_position;
17. }
```

Line 2 describes a uniform variable u_mvpMatrix that stores the combined model view and projection matrix. Lines 6 and 7 describe the inputs to the vertex shader and are referred to as vertex attributes. a_position is the input vertex position attribute and a_color is the input vertex color attribute. On line 10 we declare the varying v_color to store the output of the vertex shader that describes the per-vertex color. The built-in varying called gl_Position is declared automatically, and the shader must write the transformed position to this variable. A vertex or fragment shader has a single entry point called the main function. Lines 12–17 describe the vertex shader main function. In line 15, we read the vertex attribute input a_color and write it as the vertex output color v_color. In line 16, the transformed vertex position is output by writing it to gl_Position.

Primitive Assembly

After the vertex shader, the next stage in the pipeline is primitive assembly. A primitive is a geometric object that can be drawn using appropriate drawing commands in OpenGL ES. These drawing commands specify a set of vertex attributes that describes the primitive's geometry and a primitive type. Each vertex is described with a set of vertex attributes. These vertex attributes contain information that the vertex shader uses to calculate a position and other information that can be passed to the fragment shader such as its color and texture coordinates.

In the primitive assembly stage, the shaded vertices are assembled into individual geometric primitives that can be drawn such as a triangle, line, or point-sprite. For each primitive, it must be determined whether the primitive lies within the view frustum (the region of 3D space that is visible on the screen). If the primitive is not completely inside the view frustum, the primitive might need to be clipped to the view frustum. If the primitive is completely outside, it is discarded. After clipping, the vertex position is converted to screen coordinates. A culling operation can also be performed that discards primitives based on whether they face forward or backward. After clipping and culling, the primitive is ready to be passed to the next stage of the pipeline, which is the rasterization stage.

Rasterization

The next stage, shown in Figure 1-3, is the rasterization phase where the appropriate primitive (point-sprite, line, or triangle) is drawn. Rasterization is the process that converts primitives into a set of two-dimensional fragments, which are processed by the fragment shader. These two-dimensional fragments represent pixels that can be drawn on the screen.

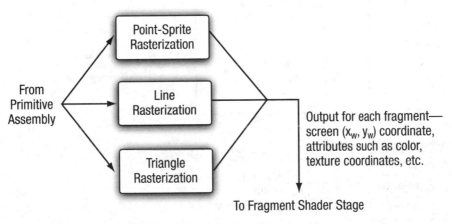

Figure 1-3   OpenGL ES 2.0 Rasterization Stage

Fragment Shader

The fragment shader implements a general-purpose programmable method for operating on fragments.

The fragment shader, as shown in Figure 1-4, is executed for each generated fragment by the rasterization stage and takes the following inputs:

- Varying variables—Outputs of the vertex shader that are generated by the rasterization unit for each fragment using interpolation.

- Uniforms—Constant data used by the fragment shader.

- Samplers—A specific type of uniforms that represent textures used by the fragment shader.

- Shader program—Fragment shader program source code or executable that describes the operations that will be performed on the fragment.

The fragment shader can either discard the fragment or generate a color value referred to as gl_FragColor. The color, depth, stencil, and screen coordinate location (x_w, y_w) generated by the rasterization stage become inputs to the per-fragment operations stage of the OpenGL ES 2.0 pipeline.

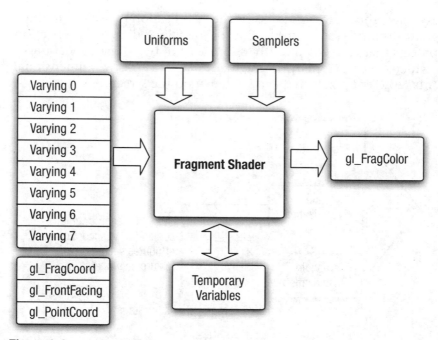

Figure 1-4   OpenGL ES 2.0 Fragment Shader

Example 1-2 describes a very simple fragment shader that can be coupled with the vertex shader described in Example 1-1 to draw a gouraud shaded triangle. Again, we will go into much more detail on fragment shaders later in the book. We present this just to give you a basic idea of what a fragment shader looks like.

Example 1-2   A Fragment Shader Example

```
1. precision mediump float;
2.
3. varying vec4   v_color;   // input vertex color from vertex shader
4.
5.
6. void
7. main(void)
8. {
9.     gl_FragColor = v_color;
10.}
```

Line 1 sets the default precision qualifier, which is explained in detail in Chapter 4, "Shaders and Programs." Line 3 describes the input to the fragment shader. The vertex shader must write the same set of varying variables that are read by the fragment shader. Lines 6–10 describe the fragment shader `main` function. Note that no output is declared in the fragment shader. This is because the only output variable is `gl_FragColor`, which in this example is set to input color to the fragment shader given by `v_color` in line 9.

Per-Fragment Operations

After the fragment shader, the next stage is per-fragment operations. A fragment produced by rasterization with (x_w, y_w) screen coordinates can only modify the pixel at location (x_w, y_w) in the framebuffer. Figure 1-5 describes the OpenGL ES 2.0 per-fragment operations stage.

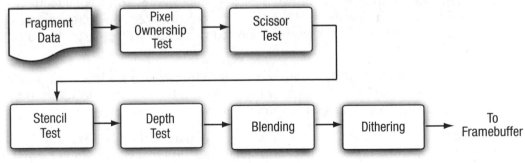

Figure 1-5   OpenGL ES 2.0 Per-Fragment Operations

The per-fragment operations stage performs the following functions (and tests) on each fragment, as shown in Figure 1-5:

- Pixel ownership test—This test determines if the pixel at location (x_w, y_w) in the framebuffer is currently owned by OpenGL ES. This test allows the window system to control which pixels in the framebuffer belong to the current OpenGL ES context. For example, if a window displaying the OpenGL ES framebuffer window is obscured by another window, the windowing system may determine that the obscured pixels are not owned by the OpenGL ES context and therefore might not be displayed at all.

- Scissor test—The scissor test determines if (x_w, y_w) lies within the scissor rectangle defined as part of the OpenGL ES state. If the fragment is outside the scissor region, the fragment is discarded.

- Stencil and depth tests—These perform tests on the stencil and depth value of the incoming fragment to determine if the fragment should be rejected or not.

- Blending—Blending combines the newly generated fragment color value with the color values stored in the framebuffer at location (x_w, y_w).

- Dithering—Dithering can be used to minimize the artifacts that can occur from using limited precision to store color values in the framebuffer.

At the end of the per-fragment stage, either the fragment is rejected or a fragment color, depth, or stencil value is written to the framebuffer at location (x_w, y_w). The fragment color, depth, and stencil values are written depending on whether the appropriate write masks are enabled or not. Write masks allow finer control over the color, depth, and stencil values written into the appropriate buffers. For example, the write mask for the color buffer could be set such that no red values get written into the color buffer.

In addition, OpenGL ES 2.0 also provides an interface to read back the pixels from the framebuffer. Note that only pixels can be read back from the color buffer. The depth and stencil values cannot be read back.

Note: Alpha test and LogicOp are no longer part of the per-fragment operations stage. These two stages exist in OpenGL 2.0 and OpenGL ES 1.x. The alpha test stage is no longer needed because the fragment shader can discard fragments and therefore the alpha test can be performed in the fragment shader. In addition, LogicOp is removed as it is very infrequently used by applications and the OpenGL ES working group did not get requests from independent software vendors (ISVs) to support this feature in OpenGL ES 2.0.

OpenGL ES 2.0 and OpenGL ES 1.x Backward Compatibility

OpenGL ES 2.0 is not backward compatible with OpenGL ES 1.x. It does not support the fixed function pipeline that OpenGL ES 1.x supports. The OpenGL ES 2.0 programmable vertex shader replaces the fixed function vertex units implemented in OpenGL ES 1.x. The fixed function vertex units implement a specific vertex transformation and lighting equation that can be used to transform the vertex position, transform or generate texture coordinates, and calculate the vertex color. Similarly, the programmable fragment shader replaces the fixed function texture combine units implemented in OpenGL ES 1.x. The fixed function texture combine units implement a texture combine stage for each texture unit. The texture color is combined with the diffuse color and the output of previous texture combine stage with a fixed set of operations such as add, modulate, subtract, and dot.

This is a departure from OpenGL 2.0, which implements a programmable pipeline but also provides full backward compatibility to older versions of OpenGL that implement a fixed function pipeline.

The OpenGL ES working group decided against backward compatibility for the following reasons:

- Supporting the fixed function pipeline in OpenGL ES 2.0 implies that the API would support more than one way of implementing a feature, in violation of one of the criteria used by the working group in determining what features should be supported. The programmable pipeline allows applications to implement the fixed function pipeline using shaders, so there is really no compelling reason to be backward compatible with OpenGL ES 1.x.

- Feedback from ISVs was that most games do not mix programmable and fixed function pipelines. They are either written for a fixed function pipeline or for a programmable pipeline. Once you have a programmable pipeline, there is no reason to use a fixed function pipeline as you have a lot more flexibility in the effects you want to render.

- The OpenGL ES 2.0 driver's memory footprint would be much larger if it had to support both the fixed function and programmable pipelines. For the devices targeted by OpenGL ES, minimizing memory footprint is an important design criteria. By separating the fixed function support into the OpenGL ES 1.x API and placing the programmable shader support into the OpenGL ES 2.0 API, vendors that do not require OpenGL ES 1.x support no longer need to include this driver at all.

Also note, unlike OpenGL ES 1.x, there are no profiles or "mandatory extensions" for OpenGL ES 2.0.

EGL

OpenGL ES commands require a rendering context and a drawing surface. The rendering context stores the appropriate OpenGL ES state. The drawing surface is the surface to which primitives will be drawn. The drawing surface specifies the types of buffers that are required for rendering such as a color buffer, depth buffer, and stencil buffer. The drawing surface also specifies the bit depths of each of the required buffers.

The OpenGL ES API does not mention how a rendering context is created or how the rendering context gets attached to the native windowing system. EGL is one interface between the Khronos rendering APIs such as OpenGL ES and the native window system. There is no requirement to provide EGL when implementing OpenGL ES. Developers should refer to the platform vendor's documentation to determine which interface is supported.

Any OpenGL ES application will need to do the following using EGL before any rendering can begin:

- Query the displays that are available on the device and initialize them. For example, a flip phone might have two LCD panels and it is possible that we can render using OpenGL ES to surfaces that can be displayed on either or both panels.

- Create a rendering surface. Surfaces created in EGL can be categorized as on-screen surfaces or off-screen surfaces. On-screen surfaces are attached to the native window system, whereas off-screen surfaces are pixel buffers that do not get displayed but can be used as rendering surfaces. These surfaces can be used to render into a texture and can be shared across multiple Khronos APIs.

- Create a rendering context. EGL is needed to create an OpenGL ES rendering context. This context needs to be attached to an appropriate surface before rendering can actually begin.

The EGL API implements the features just described and additional functionality such as power management, support for multiple rendering contexts in a process, sharing objects (such as textures or vertex buffers) across rendering contexts in a process, and a mechanism to get function pointers to EGL or OpenGL ES extension functions supported by a given implementation.

The latest version of the EGL specification is EGL version 1.4.

Programming with OpenGL ES 2.0

To write any OpenGL ES 2.0 application, you will need to know which header files need to be included and with which libraries your application needs to link. It is also useful to understand the syntax used by the EGL and GL command names and command parameters.

Libraries and Include Files

OpenGL ES 2.0 applications will need to link with the following libraries: the OpenGL ES 2.0 library named libGLESv2.lib and the EGL library named libEGL.lib.

OpenGL ES 2.0 applications will need to include the appropriate ES 2.0 and EGL header files. The following include files must be included by any OpenGL ES 2.0 application:

```
#include <EGL/egl.h>
#include <GLES2/gl2.h>
#include <GLES2/gl2ext.h>
```

egl.h is the EGL header file, gl2.h is the OpenGL ES 2.0 header file, and gl2ext.h is the header file that describes the list of Khronos-approved extensions for OpenGL ES 2.0.

The header file and library names are platform dependent. The OpenGL ES working group has tried to define the library and header names and how they should be organized but this might not be the case for all OpenGL ES platforms. Developers should, however, refer to the platform vendor's documentation for information on how the libraries and include files are named and organized.

EGL Command Syntax

All EGL commands begin with the prefix `egl` and use an initial capital letter for each word making up the command name (e.g., `eglCreateWindowSurface`). Similarly, EGL data types also begin with the prefix `EGL` and use an initial capital letter for each word making up the type name except for `EGLint` and `EGLenum`.

Table 1-1 gives a brief description of EGL data types used.

Table 1-1   EGL Data Types

Data Type	C-Language Type	EGL Type
32-bit integer	`int`	`EGLint`
32-bit unsigned integer	`unsigned int`	`EGLBoolean`, `EGLenum`
32-bit pointer	`void *`	`EGLConfig`, `EGLContext`, `EGLDisplay`, `EGLSurface`, `EGLClientBuffer`

OpenGL ES Command Syntax

All OpenGL ES commands begin with the prefix `gl` and use an initial capital letter for each word making up the command name (e.g., `glBlendEquation`). Similarly, OpenGL ES data types also begin with the prefix `GL`.

In addition, some commands might take arguments in different flavors. The flavors or types vary by the number of arguments taken (one to four arguments), the data type of the arguments used (byte [b], unsigned byte [ub], short [s], unsigned short [us], int [i], fixed [x], and float [f]), and whether the arguments are passed as a vector (v) or not. A few examples of command flavors allowed in OpenGL ES follow.

The following two commands are equivalent except one specifies the uniform value as floats and the other as integers.

```
glUniform2f(location, 1.0f, 0.0f);
glUniform2i(location, 1, 0)
```

The following lines describe commands that are also equivalent but one passes command arguments as a vector and the other does not.

```
GLfloat   coord[4] = { 1.0f, 0.75f, 0.25f, 0.0f };
glUniform4fv(location, coord);
glUniform4f(location, coord[0], coord[1], coord[2], coord[3]);
```

Table 1-2 gives a description of the command suffixes and argument data types used in OpenGL ES.

Table 1-2 OpenGL ES Command Suffixes and Argument Data Types

Data Type	Data Type	C-Language Type	GL Type
b	8-bit signed integer	signed char	GLbyte
ub	8-bit unsigned integer	unsigned char	GLubyte, GLboolean
s	16-bit signed integer	short	GLshort
us	16-bit unsigned integer	unsigned short	GLushort
i	32-bit signed integer	int	GLint
ui	32-bit unsigned integer	unsigned int	GLuint, GLbitfield, GLenum
x	16.16 fixed point	int	GLfixed
f	32-bit floating point	float	GLfloat, GLclampf

Finally, OpenGL ES defines the type GLvoid. This is used for OpenGL ES commands that accept pointers.

In the rest of this book, OpenGL ES commands are referred to by their base names only and an asterisk is used to indicate that this refers to multiple flavors of the command name. For example, glUniform*() stands for all variations of the command you use to specify uniforms and glUniform*v() refers to all the vector versions of the command you use to specify uniforms. If a particular version of a command needs to be discussed, we use the full command name with the appropriate suffixes.

Error Handling

OpenGL ES commands incorrectly used by applications generate an error code. This error code is recorded and can be queried using glGetError. No other errors will be recorded until the application has queried the first error code using glGetError. Once the error code has been queried, the current error code is reset to GL_NO_ERROR. The command that generated the error is ignored and does not affect the OpenGL ES state except for the GL_OUT_OF_MEMORY error described later in this section.

The `glGetError` command is described next.

GLenum	**glGetError**(void)

Returns the current error code and resets the current error code to
GL_NO_ERROR. If GL_NO_ERROR is returned, there has been no detectable
error since the last call to glGetError.

Table 1-3 lists the basic error codes and their description. There are other
error codes besides the basic error codes listed in Table 1-3 that are described
in the chapters that cover OpenGL ES commands that generate these specific errors.

Table 1-3   OpenGL ES Basic Error Codes

Error Code	Description
GL_NO_ERROR	No error has been generated since the last call to glGetError.
GL_INVALID_ENUM	A GLenum argument is out of range. The command that generated the error is ignored.
GL_INVALID_VALUE	A numeric argument is out of range. The command that generated the error is ignored.
GL_INVALID_OPERATION	The specific command cannot be performed in the current OpenGL ES state. The command that generated the error is ignored.
GL_OUT_OF_MEMORY	There is insufficient memory to execute this command. The state of the OpenGL ES pipeline is considered to be undefined if this error is encountered except for the current error code.

Flush and Finish

The OpenGL ES 2.0 API inherits the OpenGL client–server model. The application, or client, issues commands, and these commands are processed by
the OpenGL ES implementation or server. In OpenGL, the client and server
can reside on different machines over a network. OpenGL ES also allows the
client and server to reside on different machines but because OpenGL ES
targets handheld and embedded platforms, the client and server will typically be on the same device.

In the client–server model, the commands issued by the client do not necessarily get sent to the server immediately. If the client and server are over a network, it will be very inefficient to send individual commands over the network. Instead, the commands can be buffered on the client side and then issued to the server at a later point in time. As a result, there needs to be a mechanism that lets the client know when the server has completed execution of previously submitted commands. Consider another example where multiple OpenGL ES contexts (each current to a different thread) are sharing objects. To synchronize correctly between these contexts, it is important that commands from context A be issued to the server before context B that depends on OpenGL ES state modified by context A. The glFlush command is used to flush any pending commands in the current OpenGL ES context and issue them to the server. Note that glFlush only issues the commands to the server and does not wait for them to complete. If the client requires that the commands be completed, the glFinish command should be used. We, however, do not recommend using glFinish unless absolutely necessary. Because glFinish does not return until all queued commands in the context have been completely processed by the server, calling glFinish can adversely impact performance by forcing the client and server to synchronize their operations.

```
void    glFlush(void)
void    glFinish(void)
```

Basic State Management

Figure 1-1 showed the various pipeline stages in OpenGL ES 2.0. Each pipeline stage has state that can be enabled or disabled and appropriate state values that are maintained per context. Examples of state are blending enable, blend factors, cull enable, and cull face. This state is initialized with default values when an OpenGL ES context (EGLcontext) is initialized. The state enables can be set using the glEnable and glDisable commands.

```
void    glEnable(GLenum cap)
void    glDisable(GLenum cap)
```

glEnable and glDisable enable and disable various capabilities. The initial value for each capability is set to GL_FALSE except for GL_DITHER which is set to GL_TRUE. The error code GL_INVALID_ENUM is generated if cap is not a valid state enum.

The chapters that follow will describe the specific state enables for each pipeline stage shown in Figure 1-1. You can also check if a state is currently enabled or disabled by using the `glIsEnabled` command.

GLboolean   **glIsEnabled**(GLenum cap)

Returns `GL_TRUE` or `GL_FALSE` depending on whether the state being queried is enabled or disabled. Generates the error code `GL_INVALID_ENUM` if cap is not a valid state enum.

Specific state values such as blend factor, depth test values, and so on can also be queried using appropriate `glGet***` commands. These commands are described in detail in Chapter 14, "State Queries."

Further Reading

The OpenGL ES 1.0, 1.1, and 2.0 specifications can be found at www.khronos.org/opengles/. In addition, the Khronos Web site (www.khronos.org) has the latest information on all Khronos specifications, developer message boards, tutorials, and examples.

1. Khronos OpenGL ES 1.1 Web site: www.khronos.org/opengles/1_X/

2. Khronos OpenGL ES 2.0 Web site: www.khronos.org/opengles/2_X/

3. Khronos EGL Web site: www.khronos.org/egl/

Chapter 2

Hello Triangle: An OpenGL ES 2.0 Example

To introduce the basic concepts of OpenGL ES 2.0, we begin with a simple example. In this chapter, we show what is required to create an OpenGL ES 2.0 program that draws a single triangle. The program we will write is just about the most basic example of an OpenGL ES 2.0 application that draws geometry. There are number of concepts that we cover in this chapter:

- Creating an on-screen render surface with EGL.

- Loading vertex and fragment shaders.

- Creating a program object, attaching vertex and fragment shaders, and linking a program object.

- Setting the viewport.

- Clearing the color buffer.

- Rendering a simple primitive.

- Making the contents of the color buffer visible in the EGL window surface.

As it turns out, there are quite a significant number of steps required before we can start drawing a triangle with OpenGL ES 2.0. This chapter goes over the basics of each of these steps. Later in the book, we fill in the details on each of these steps and further document the API. Our purpose here is to get you running your first simple example so that you get an idea of what goes into creating an application with OpenGL ES 2.0.

Code Framework

Throughout the book, we will be building up a library of utility functions that form a framework of useful functions for writing OpenGL ES 2.0 programs. In developing example programs for the book, we had several goals for this code framework:

1. It should be simple, small, and easy to understand. We wanted to focus our examples on the relevant OpenGL ES 2.0 calls and not on a large code framework that we invented. Rather, we focused our framework on simplicity and making the example programs easy to read and understand. The goal of the framework was to allow you to focus your attention on the important OpenGL ES 2.0 API concepts in each example.

2. It should be portable. Although we develop our example programs on Microsoft Windows, we wanted the sample programs to be easily portable to other operating systems and environments. In addition, we chose to use C as the language rather than C++ due to the differing limitations of C++ on many handheld platforms. We also avoid using global data, something that is also not allowed on many handheld platforms.

As we go through the examples in the book, we introduce any new code framework functions that we use. In addition, you can find full documentation for the code framework in Appendix D. Any functions you see in the example code that are called that begin with es (e.g., esInitialize()) are part of the code framework we wrote for the sample programs in this book.

Where to Download the Examples

You can download the examples from the book Web site at www.opengles-book.com.

The examples are all targeted to run on Microsoft Windows XP or Microsoft Windows Vista with a desktop graphics processing unit (GPU) supporting OpenGL 2.0. The example programs are provided in source code form with Microsoft Visual Studio 2005 project solutions. The examples build and run on the AMD OpenGL ES 2.0 emulator. Several of the advanced shader examples in the book are implemented in RenderMonkey, a shader development tool from AMD. The book Web site provides links on where to download any of the required tools. The OpenGL ES 2.0 emulator and RenderMonkey are both freely available tools. Readers who do not own Visual Studio can use the free Microsoft Visual Studio 2008 Express Edition available for download at www.microsoft.com/express/.

Hello Triangle Example

Let's take a look at the full source code for our Hello Triangle example program, which is listed in Example 2-1. For those readers familiar with fixed function desktop OpenGL, you will probably think this is a lot of code just to draw a simple triangle. For those of you not familiar with desktop OpenGL, you will also probably think this is a lot of code just to draw a triangle! Remember though, OpenGL ES 2.0 is fully shader based, which means you can't draw any geometry without having the appropriate shaders loaded and bound. This means there is more setup code required to render than there was in desktop OpenGL using fixed function processing.

Example 2-1   Hello Triangle Example

```
#include "esUtil.h"

typedef struct
{
   // Handle to a program object
   GLuint programObject;

} UserData;

///
// Create a shader object, load the shader source, and
// compile the shader.
//
GLuint LoadShader(GLenum type, const char *shaderSrc)
{
   GLuint shader;
   GLint compiled;

   // Create the shader object
   shader = glCreateShader(type);

   if(shader == 0)
      return 0;

   // Load the shader source
   glShaderSource(shader, 1, &shaderSrc, NULL);

   // Compile the shader
   glCompileShader(shader);

   // Check the compile status
   glGetShaderiv(shader, GL_COMPILE_STATUS, &compiled);
```

```c
      if(!compiled)
      {
         GLint infoLen = 0;

         glGetShaderiv(shader, GL_INFO_LOG_LENGTH, &infoLen);

         if(infoLen > 1)
         {
            char* infoLog = malloc(sizeof(char) * infoLen);

            glGetShaderInfoLog(shader, infoLen, NULL, infoLog);
            esLogMessage("Error compiling shader:\n%s\n", infoLog);
            free(infoLog);
         }

         glDeleteShader(shader);
         return 0;
      }

      return shader;

}

///
// Initialize the shader and program object
//
int Init(ESContext *esContext)
{
   UserData *userData = esContext->userData;
   GLbyte vShaderStr[] =
      "attribute vec4 vPosition;    \n"
      "void main()                  \n"
      "{                            \n"
      "   gl_Position = vPosition;  \n"
      "}                            \n";

   GLbyte fShaderStr[] =
      "precision mediump float;                    \n"
      "void main()                                 \n"
      "{                                           \n"
      "  gl_FragColor = vec4(1.0, 0.0, 0.0, 1.0);  \n"
      "}                                           \n";

   GLuint vertexShader;
   GLuint fragmentShader;
   GLuint programObject;
   GLint linked;
```

```c
// Load the vertex/fragment shaders
vertexShader = LoadShader(GL_VERTEX_SHADER, vShaderStr);
fragmentShader = LoadShader(GL_FRAGMENT_SHADER, fShaderStr);

// Create the program object
programObject = glCreateProgram();

if(programObject == 0)
   return 0;

glAttachShader(programObject, vertexShader);
glAttachShader(programObject, fragmentShader);

// Bind vPosition to attribute 0
glBindAttribLocation(programObject, 0, "vPosition");

// Link the program
glLinkProgram(programObject);

// Check the link status
glGetProgramiv(programObject, GL_LINK_STATUS, &linked);

if(!linked)
{
   GLint infoLen = 0;

   glGetProgramiv(programObject, GL_INFO_LOG_LENGTH, &infoLen);

   if(infoLen > 1)
   {
      char* infoLog = malloc(sizeof(char) * infoLen);

      glGetProgramInfoLog(programObject, infoLen, NULL, infoLog);
      esLogMessage("Error linking program:\n%s\n", infoLog);

      free(infoLog);
   }

   glDeleteProgram(programObject);
   return FALSE;
}

// Store the program object
userData->programObject = programObject;

glClearColor(0.0f, 0.0f, 0.0f, 1.0f);
return TRUE;
}
```

```
///
// Draw a triangle using the shader pair created in Init()
//
void Draw(ESContext *esContext)
{
   UserData *userData = esContext->userData;
   GLfloat vVertices[] = {0.0f,  0.5f, 0.0f,
                          -0.5f, -0.5f, 0.0f,
                          0.5f, -0.5f,  0.0f};

   // Set the viewport
   glViewport(0, 0, esContext->width, esContext->height);

   // Clear the color buffer
   glClear(GL_COLOR_BUFFER_BIT);

   // Use the program object
   glUseProgram(userData->programObject);

   // Load the vertex data
   glVertexAttribPointer(0, 3, GL_FLOAT, GL_FALSE, 0, vVertices);
   glEnableVertexAttribArray(0);

   glDrawArrays(GL_TRIANGLES, 0, 3);

   eglSwapBuffers(esContext->eglDisplay, esContext->eglSurface);
}


int main(int argc, char *argv[])
{
   ESContext esContext;
   UserData  userData;

   esInitialize(&esContext);
   esContext.userData = &userData;

   esCreateWindow(&esContext, "Hello Triangle", 320, 240,
                  ES_WINDOW_RGB);

   if(!Init(&esContext))
      return 0;

   esRegisterDrawFunc(&esContext, Draw);

   esMainLoop(&esContext);
}
```

Building and Running the Examples

The example programs developed in this book all run on top of AMD's OpenGL ES 2.0 emulator. This emulator provides a Windows implementation of the EGL 1.3 and OpenGL ES 2.0 APIs. The standard GL2 and EGL header files provided by Khronos are used as an interface to the emulator. The emulator is a full implementation of OpenGL ES 2.0, which means that graphics code written on the emulator should port seamlessly to real devices. Note that the emulator requires that you have a desktop GPU with support for the desktop OpenGL 2.0 API.

We have designed the code framework to be portable to a variety of platforms. However, for the purposes of this book all of the examples are built using Microsoft Visual Studio 2005 with an implementation for Win32 on AMD's OpenGL ES 2.0 emulator. The OpenGL ES 2.0 examples are organized in the following directories:

Common/—Contains the OpenGL ES 2.0 Framework project, code, and the emulator.

Chapter_X/—Contains the example programs for each chapter. A Visual Studio 2005 solution file is provided for each project.

To build and run the Hello Triangle program used in this example, open Chapter_2/Hello_Triangle/Hello_Triangle.sln in Visual Studio 2005. The application can be built and run directly from the Visual Studio 2005 project. On running, you should see the image shown in Figure 2-1.

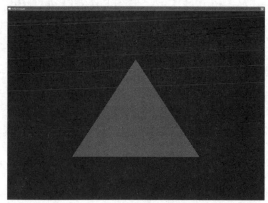

Figure 2-1   Hello Triangle Example

Note that in addition to providing sample programs, later in the book we provide several examples with a free shader development tool from AMD called RenderMonkey v1.80. RenderMonkey workspaces are used where we want to focus on just the shader code in an example. RenderMonkey provides a very flexible integrated development environment (IDE) for developing shader effects. The examples that have an .rfx extension can be viewed using RenderMonkey v1.80. A screenshot of the RenderMonkey IDE with an OpenGL ES 2.0 effect is shown in Color Plate 2.

Using the OpenGL ES 2.0 Framework

In the `main` function in Hello Triangle, you will see calls into several ES utility functions. The first thing the `main` function does is declare an `ESContext` and initialize it:

```
ESContext esContext;
UserData  userData;

esInitialize(&esContext);
esContext.userData = &userData;
```

Every example program in this book does the same thing. The `ESContext` is passed into all of the ES framework utility functions and contains all of the necessary information about the program that the ES framework needs. The reason for passing around a context is that the sample programs and the ES code framework do not need to use any global data.

Many handheld platforms do not allow applications to declare global static data in their applications. Examples of platforms that do not allow this include BREW and Symbian. As such, we avoid declaring global data in either the sample programs or the code framework by passing a context between functions.

The `ESContext` has a member variable named `userData` that is a `void*`. Each of the sample programs will store any of the data that are needed for the application in `userData`. The `esInitialize` function is called by the sample program to initialize the context and the ES code framework. The other elements in the `ESContext` structure are described in the header file and are intended only to be read by the user application. Other data in the `ESContext` structure include information such as the window width and height, EGL context, and callback function pointers.

The rest of the `main` function is responsible for creating the window, initializing the draw callback function, and entering the main loop:

```
esCreateWindow(&esContext, "Hello Triangle", 320, 240,
               ES_WINDOW_RGB);

if(!Init(&esContext))
    return 0;

esRegisterDrawFunc(&esContext, Draw);

esMainLoop(&esContext);
```

The call to `esCreateWindow` creates a window of the specified width and height (in this case, 320 × 240). The last parameter is a bit field that specifies options for the window creation. In this case, we request an RGB framebuffer. In Chapter 3, "An Introduction to EGL," we discuss what `esCreateWindow` does in more detail. This function uses EGL to create an on-screen render surface that is attached to a window. EGL is a platform-independent API for creating rendering surfaces and contexts. For now, we will simply say that this function creates a rendering surface and leave the details on how it works for the next chapter.

After calling `esCreateWindow`, the next thing the main function does is to call `Init` to initialize everything needed to run the program. Finally, it registers a callback function, `Draw`, that will be called to render the frame. The final call, `esMainLoop`, enters into the main message processing loop until the window is closed.

Creating a Simple Vertex and Fragment Shader

In OpenGL ES 2.0, nothing can be drawn unless a valid vertex and fragment shader have been loaded. In Chapter 1, "Introduction to OpenGL ES 2.0," we covered the basics of the OpenGL ES 2.0 programmable pipeline. There you learned about the concepts of a vertex and fragment shader. These two shader programs describe the transformation of vertices and drawing of fragments. To do any rendering at all, an OpenGL ES 2.0 program must have both a vertex and fragment shader.

The biggest task that the `Init` function in Hello Triangle accomplishes is the loading of a vertex and fragment shader. The vertex shader that is given in the program is very simple:

```
GLbyte vShaderStr[] =
   "attribute vec4 vPosition;      \n"
   "void main()                    \n"
   "{                              \n"
   "   gl_Position = vPosition;    \n"
   "};                             \n";
```

This shader declares one input `attribute` that is a four-component vector named `vPosition`. Later on, the `Draw` function in Hello Triangle will send in positions for each vertex that will be placed in this variable. The shader declares a `main` function that marks the beginning of execution of the shader. The body of the shader is very simple; it copies the `vPosition` input attribute into a special output variable named `gl_Position`. Every vertex shader must output a position into the `gl_Position` variable. This variable defines the position that is passed through to the next stage in the pipeline. The topic of writing shaders is a large part of what we cover in this book, but for now we just want to give you a flavor of what a vertex shader looks like. In Chapter 5, "OpenGL ES Shading Language," we cover the OpenGL ES shading language and in Chapter 8, "Vertex Shaders," we specifically cover how to write vertex shaders.

The fragment shader in the example is also very simple:

```
GLbyte fShaderStr[] =
   "precision mediump float;                  \n"
   "void main()                               \n"
   "{                                         \n"
   "   gl_FragColor = vec4(1.0, 0.0, 0.0, 1.0); \n"
   "}                                         \n";
```

The first statement in the fragment shader declares the default precision for float variables in the shader. For more details on this, please see the section on precision qualifiers in Chapter 5. For now, simply pay attention to the `main` function, which outputs a value of (1.0, 0.0, 0.0, 1.0) into the `gl_FragColor`. The `gl_FragColor` is a special built-in variable that contains the final output color for the fragment shader. In this case, the shader is outputting a color of red for all fragments. The details of developing fragment shaders are covered in Chapter 9, "Texturing," and Chapter 10, "Fragment Shaders." Again, here we are just showing you what a fragment shader looks like.

Typically, a game or application would not inline shader source strings in the way we have done in this example. In most real applications, the shader would be loaded from some sort of text or data file and then loaded to the API. However, for simplicity and having the example program be self-contained, we provide the shader source strings directly in the program code.

Compiling and Loading the Shaders

Now that we have the shader source code defined, we can go about loading the shaders to OpenGL ES. The LoadShader function in the Hello Triangle example is responsible for loading the shader source code, compiling it, and checking to make sure that there were no errors. It returns a *shader object*, which is an OpenGL ES 2.0 object that can later be used for attachment to a *program object* (these two objects are detailed in Chapter 4, "Shaders and Programs").

Let's take a look at how the LoadShader function works. The shader object is first created using glCreateShader, which creates a new shader object of the type specified.

```
GLuint LoadShader(GLenum type, const char *shaderSrc)
{
    GLuint shader;
    GLint compiled;

    // Create the shader object
    shader = glCreateShader(type);

    if(shader == 0)
    return 0;
```

The shader source code itself is loaded to the shader object using glShaderSource. The shader is then compiled using the glCompileShader function.

```
    // Load the shader source
    glShaderSource(shader, 1, &shaderSrc, NULL);

    // Compile the shader
    glCompileShader(shader);
```

After compiling the shader, the status of the compile is determined and any errors that were generated are printed out.

```
    // Check the compile status
    glGetShaderiv(shader, GL_COMPILE_STATUS, &compiled);

    if(!compiled)
    {
        GLint infoLen = 0;

        glGetShaderiv(shader, GL_INFO_LOG_LENGTH, &infoLen);

        if(infoLen > 1)
```

```
      {
          char* infoLog = malloc(sizeof(char) * infoLen);

          glGetShaderInfoLog(shader, infoLen, NULL, infoLog);
          esLogMessage("Error compiling shader:\n%s\n", infoLog);

          free(infoLog);
      }

      glDeleteShader(shader);
      return 0;
   }

   return shader;

}
```

If the shader compiles successfully, a new shader object is returned that will be attached to the program later. The details of these shader object functions are covered in the first sections of Chapter 4.

Creating a Program Object and Linking the Shaders

Once the application has created a shader object for the vertex and fragment shader, it needs to create a program object. Conceptually, the program object can be thought of as the final linked program. Once each shader is compiled into a shader object, they must be attached to a program object and linked together before drawing.

The process of creating program objects and linking is fully described in Chapter 4. For now, we provide a brief overview of the process. The first step is to create the program object and attach the vertex shader and fragment shader to it.

```
// Create the program object
programObject = glCreateProgram();

if(programObject == 0)
   return 0;

glAttachShader(programObject, vertexShader);
glAttachShader(programObject, fragmentShader);
```

Once the two shaders have been attached, the next step the sample application does is to set the location for the vertex shader attribute vPosition:

```
// Bind vPosition to attribute 0
glBindAttribLocation(programObject, 0, "vPosition");
```

In Chapter 6, "Vertex Attributes, Vertex Arrays, and Buffer Objects," we go into more detail on binding attributes. For now, note that the call to glBindAttribLocation binds the vPosition attribute declared in the vertex shader to location 0. Later, when we specify the vertex data, this location is used to specify the position.

Finally, we are ready to link the program and check for errors:

```
// Link the program
glLinkProgram(programObject);

// Check the link status
glGetProgramiv(programObject, GL_LINK_STATUS, &linked);

if(!linked)
{
   GLint infoLen = 0;

   glGetProgramiv(programObject, GL_INFO_LOG_LENGTH, &infoLen);

   if(infoLen > 1)
   {
      char* infoLog = malloc(sizeof(char) * infoLen);

      glGetProgramInfoLog(programObject, infoLen, NULL, infoLog);
      esLogMessage("Error linking program:\n%s\n", infoLog);

      free(infoLog);
   }

   glDeleteProgram(programObject);
   return FALSE;
}

// Store the program object
userData->programObject = programObject;
```

After all of these steps, we have finally compiled the shaders, checked for compile errors, created the program object, attached the shaders, linked the program, and checked for link errors. After successful linking of the program object, we can now finally use the program object for rendering! To use the program object for rendering, we bind it using glUseProgram.

```
// Use the program object
glUseProgram(userData->programObject);
```

After calling `glUseProgram` with the program object handle, all subsequent rendering will occur using the vertex and fragment shaders attached to the program object.

Setting the Viewport and Clearing the Color Buffer

Now that we have created a rendering surface with EGL and initialized and loaded shaders, we are ready to actually draw something. The `Draw` callback function draws the frame. The first command that we execute in `Draw` is `glViewport`, which informs OpenGL ES of the origin, width, and height of the 2D rendering surface that will be drawn to. In OpenGL ES, the viewport defines the 2D rectangle in which all OpenGL ES rendering operations will ultimately be displayed.

```
// Set the viewport
glViewport(0, 0, esContext->width, esContext->height);
```

The viewport is defined by an origin (x, y) and a width and height. We cover `glViewport` in more detail in Chapter 7, "Primitive Assembly and Rasterization," when we discuss coordinate systems and clipping.

After setting the viewport, the next step is to clear the screen. In OpenGL ES, there are multiple types of buffers that are involved in drawing: color, depth, and stencil. We cover these buffers in more detail in Chapter 11, "Fragment Operations." In the Hello Triangle example, only the color buffer is drawn to. At the beginning of each frame, we clear the color buffer using the `glClear` function.

```
// Clear the color buffer
glClear(GL_COLOR_BUFFER_BIT);
```

The buffer will be cleared to the color specified with `glClearColor`. In the example program at the end of `Init`, the clear color was set to (0.0, 0.0, 0.0, 1.0) so the screen is cleared to black. The clear color should be set by the application prior to calling `glClear` on the color buffer.

Loading the Geometry and Drawing a Primitive

Now that we have the color buffer cleared, viewport set, and program object loaded, we need to specify the geometry for the triangle. The vertices for the triangle are specified with three (*x*, *y*, *z*) coordinates in the vVertices array.

```
GLfloat vVertices[] = {0.0f,  0.5f, 0.0f,
                      -0.5f, -0.5f, 0.0f,
                       0.5f, -0.5f, 0.0f};
...
// Load the vertex data
glVertexAttribPointer(0, 3, GL_FLOAT, GL_FALSE, 0, vVertices);
glEnableVertexAttribArray(0);

glDrawArrays(GL_TRIANGLES, 0, 3);
```

The vertex positions need to be loaded to the GL and connected to the vPosition attribute declared in the vertex shader. As you will remember, earlier we bound the vPosition variable to attribute location 0. Each attribute in the vertex shader has a location that is uniquely identified by an unsigned integer value. To load the data into vertex attribute 0, we call the glVertexAttribPointer function. In Chapter 6, we cover how to load vertex attributes and use vertex arrays in full.

The final step to drawing the triangle is to actually tell OpenGL ES to draw the primitive. That is done in this example using the function glDrawArrays. This function draws a primitive such as a triangle, line, or strip. We get into primitives in much more detail in Chapter 7.

Displaying the Back Buffer

We have finally gotten to the point where our triangle has been drawn into the framebuffer. There is one final detail we must address: how to actually display the framebuffer on the screen. Before we get into that, let's back up a little bit and discuss the concept of double buffering.

The framebuffer that is visible on the screen is represented by a two-dimensional array of pixel data. One possible way one could think about displaying images on the screen is to simply update the pixel data in the visible framebuffer as we draw. However, there is a significant issue with updating pixels directly on the displayable buffer. That is, in a typical display system, the physical screen is updated from framebuffer memory at a fixed rate. If one were to draw directly into the framebuffer, the user could see artifacts as partial updates to the framebuffer where displayed.

To address this problem, a system known as double buffering is used. In this scheme, there are two buffers: a front buffer and back buffer. All rendering occurs to the back buffer, which is located in an area of memory that is not visible to the screen. When all rendering is complete, this buffer is "swapped" with the front buffer (or visible buffer). The front buffer then becomes the back buffer for the next frame.

Using this technique, we do not display a visible surface until all rendering is complete for a frame. The way this is all controlled in an OpenGL ES application is through EGL. This is done using an EGL function called eglSwapBuffers:

```
eglSwapBuffers(esContext->eglDisplay, esContext->eglSurface);
```

This function informs EGL to swap the front buffer and back buffer. The parameters sent to eglSwapBuffers are the EGL display and surface. These two parameters represent the physical display and the rendering surface, respectively. In the next chapter, we explain eglSwapBuffers in more detail and further clarify the concepts of surface, context, and buffer management. For now, suffice to say that after swapping buffers we now finally have our triangle on screen!

Chapter 3

An Introduction to EGL

In Chapter 2, "Hello, Triangle: An OpenGL ES 2.0 Example," we drew a triangle into a window using OpenGL ES 2.0, but we used some custom functions of our own design to open and manage the window. Although that simplifies our examples, it obscures how you might need to work with OpenGL ES 2.0 on your own systems.

As part of the family of APIs provided by the Khronos Group for developing content, a (mostly) platform-independent API, EGL, is available for managing *drawing surfaces* (windows are just one type; we'll talk about others later). EGL provides the mechanisms for the following:

- Communicating with the native windowing system of your system.

- Querying the available types and configurations of drawing surfaces.

- Creating drawing surfaces.

- Synchronizing rendering between OpenGL ES 2.0 and other graphics-rendering APIs (like OpenVG, or the native drawing commands of your windowing system).

- Managing rendering resources such as texture maps.

We introduce the fundamentals required to open a window in this chapter. As we describe other operations, such as creating a texture map, we discuss the necessary EGL commands.

Communicating with the Windowing System

EGL provides a "glue" layer between OpenGL ES 2.0 (and other Khronos graphics APIs) and the native windowing system running on your computer, like the X Window System common on GNU/Linux systems, Microsoft Windows, or Mac OS X's Quartz. Before EGL can determine what types of drawing surfaces, or any other characteristics of the underlying system for that matter, it needs to open a communications channel with the windowing system.

Because every windowing system has different semantics, EGL provides a basic opaque type—the EGLDisplay—that encapsulates all of the system dependencies for interfacing with the native windowing system. The first operation that any application using EGL will need to do is create and initialize a connection with the local EGL display. This is done in a two-call sequence, as shown in Example 3-1.

Example 3-1   Initializing EGL

```
EGLint  majorVersion;
EGLint  minorVersion;
EGLDisplay  display;

display = eglGetDisplay(EGL_DEFAULT_DISPLAY);
if(display == EGL_NO_DISPLAY)
{
    // Unable to open connection to local windowing system
}
if(!eglInitialize(display, &majorVersion, &minorVersion))
{
    // Unable to initialize EGL. Handle and recover
}
```

To open a connection to the EGL display server, call

```
EGLDisplay eglGetDisplay(EGLNativeDisplayType display_id);
```

EGLNativeDisplayType is defined to match the native window system's display type. On Microsoft Windows, for example, an EGLNativeDisplayType would be defined to be an HDC—a handle to the Microsoft Windows device context. However, to make it easy to move your code to different operating systems and platforms, the token EGL_DEFAULT_DISPLAY is accepted and will return a connection to the default native display, as we did.

If a display connection isn't available, `eglGetDisplay` will return `EGL_NO_DISPLAY`. This error indicates that EGL isn't available, and you won't be able to use OpenGL ES 2.0.

Before we continue discussing more EGL operation, we need to briefly describe how EGL processes and reports errors to your application.

Checking for Errors

Most functions in EGL return `EGL_TRUE` when successful and `EGL_FALSE` otherwise. However, EGL will do more than just tell you if the call failed, it will record an error to indicate the reason for failure. However, that error code isn't returned to you directly; you need to query EGL explicitly for the error code, which you can do by calling

```
EGLint eglGetError();
```

You might wonder why this is a prudent approach, as compared to directly returning the error code when the call completes. Although we never encourage ignoring function return codes, allowing optional error code recovery reduces redundant code in applications verified to work properly. You should certainly check for errors during development and debugging, and all the time in critical applications, but once you're convinced your application is working as expected, you can likely reduce your error checking.

Initializing EGL

Once you've successfully opened a connection, EGL needs to be initialized, which is done by calling

```
EGLBoolean eglInitialize(EGLDisplay display, EGLint *majorVersion,
                         EGLint *minorVersion);
```

This initializes EGL's internal data structures and returns the major and minor version numbers of the EGL implementation. If EGL is unable to be initialized, this call will return `EGL_FALSE`, and set EGL's error code to:

- `EGL_BAD_DISPLAY` if `display` doesn't specify a valid `EGLDisplay`.
- `EGL_NOT_INITIALIZED` if the EGL cannot be initialized.

Determining the Available Surface Configurations

Once we've initialized EGL, we're able to determine what types and configurations of rendering surfaces are available to us. There are two ways to go
about this:

1. Query every surface configuration and find the best choice ourselves.

2. Specify a set of requirements and let EGL make a recommendation for the
   best match.

In many situations, the second option is simpler to implement, and most
likely yields what you would have found using the first option. In either
case, EGL will return an EGLConfig, which is an identifier to an EGL-
internal data structure that contains information about a particular surface
and its characteristics, such as number of bits for each color component, or
if there's a depth buffer associated with that EGLConfig. You can query any
of the attributes of an EGLConfig, using the eglGetConfigAttribute function, which we describe later.

To query all EGL surface configurations supported by the underlying windowing system, call

```
EGLBoolean eglGetConfigs(EGLDisplay display, EGLConfig *configs,
                         EGLint maxReturnConfigs,
                         EGLint *numConfigs);
```

which returns EGL_TRUE if the call succeeded.

There are two ways to call eglGetConfigs: First, if you specify NULL for the
value of configs, the system will return EGL_TRUE and set numConfigs to the
number of available EGLConfigs. No additional information about any of
the EGLConfigs in the system is returned, but knowing the number of available configurations allows you to allocate enough memory to get the entire
set of EGLConfigs, should you care to.

Alternatively, and perhaps more useful, is that you can allocate an array of
uninitialized EGLConfig values, and pass those into eglGetConfigs as the
configs parameter. Set maxReturnConfigs to the size of the array you allocated, which will also specify the maximum number of configs that will be
returned. When the call completes, numConfigs will be updated with the
number of entries in configs that were modified. You can then begin processing the list of returns, querying the characteristics of the configurations
to determine which one matches our needs the best.

Querying EGLConfig Attributes

We now describe the values that EGL associates with an EGLConfig, and how you can retrieve those values.

An EGLConfig contains all of the information about a surface made available by EGL. This includes information about the number of available colors, additional buffers associated with the configuration (like depth and stencil buffers, which we discuss later), the type of surfaces, and numerous other characteristics. What follows is a list of all of the attributes that can be queried from an EGLConfig. We only discuss a subset of these in this chapter, but we provide the entire list in Table 3-1 as a reference.

To query a particular attribute associated with an EGLConfig, use

```
EGLBoolean eglGetConfigAttrib(EGLDisplay display, EGLConfig config,
                              EGLint attribute, EGLint *value);
```

which will return the value for the specific attribute of the associated EGLConfig. This allows you total control over which configuration you choose for ultimately creating rendering surfaces. However, looking at Table 3.1, you might be somewhat intimidated given the number of options. EGL provides another routine, eglChooseConfig, that allows you to specify what's important for your application, and will return the best matching configuration to your requests.

Letting EGL Choose the Config

To have EGL make the choice of matching EGLConfigs, use

```
EGLBoolean eglChooseConfig(EGLDispay display, const EGLint *attribList,
                           EGLConfig *config, EGLint maxReturnConfigs,
                           EGLint *numConfigs );
```

You need to provide a list of the attributes, with associated preferred values for all the attributes that are important for the correct operation of your application. For example, if you need an EGLConfig that supports a rendering surface having five bits red and blue, six bits green (the common "RGB 565" format), a depth buffer, and supporting OpenGL ES 2.0, you might declare the array shown in Example 3-2.

Table 3-1 EGLConfig Attributes

Attribute	Description	Default Value
EGL_BUFFER_SIZE	Number of bits for all color components in the color buffer	0
EGL_RED_SIZE	Number of red bits in the color buffer	0
EGL_GREEN_SIZE	Number of green bits in the color buffer	0
EGL_BLUE_SIZE	Number of blue bits in the color buffer	0
EGL_LUMINANCE_SIZE	Number of luminance bits in the color buffer	0
EGL_ALPHA_SIZE	Number of alpha bits in the color buffer	0
EGL_ALPHA_MASK_SIZE	Number of alpha-mask bits in the mask buffer	0
EGL_BIND_TO_TEXTURE_RGB	True if bindable to RGB textures	EGL_DONT_CARE
EGL_BIND_TO_TEXTURE_RGBA	True if bindable to RGBA textures	EGL_DONT_CARE
EGL_COLOR_BUFFER_TYPE	Type of the color buffer: either EGL_RGB_BUFFER, or EGL_LUMINANCE_BUFFER	EGL_RGB_BUFFER
EGL_CONFIG_CAVEAT	Any caveats associated with the configuration	EGL_DONT_CARE
EGL_CONFIG_ID	The unique EGLConfig identifier value	EGL_DONT_CARE
EGL_CONFORMANT	True if contexts created with this EGLConfig are conformant	—
EGL_DEPTH_SIZE	Number of bits in the depth buffer	0
EGL_LEVEL	Frame buffer level	0
EGL_MAX_PBUFFER_WIDTH	Maximum width for a PBuffer created with this EGLConfig	—
EGL_MAX_PBUFFER_HEIGHT	Maximum height for a PBuffer created with this EGLConfig	—

Table 3-1   `EGLConfig` Attributes *(continued)*

Attribute	Description	Default Value
`EGL_MAX_PBUFFER_PIXELS`	Maximum size of a `PBuffer` created with this `EGLConfig`	—
`EGL_MAX_SWAP_INTERVAL`	Maximum buffer swap interval	`EGL_DONT_CARE`
`EGL_MIN_SWAP_INTERVAL`	Minimum buffer swap interval	`EGL_DONT_CARE`
`EGL_NATIVE_RENDERABLE`	True if native rendering libraries can render into a surface created with `EGLConfig`	`EGL_DONT_CARE`
`EGL_NATIVE_VISUAL_ID`	Handle of corresponding native window system visual ID	`EGL_DONT_CARE`
`EGL_NATIVE_VISUAL_TYPE`	Type of corresponding native window system visual	`EGL_DONT_CARE`
`EGL_RENDERABLE_TYPE`	A bitmask composed of the tokens `EGL_OPENGL_ES_BIT`, `EGL_OPENGL_ES2_BIT`, or `EGL_OPENVG_BIT` that represent the rendering interfaces supported with the config	`EGL_OPENGL_ES_BIT`
`EGL_SAMPLE_BUFFERS`	Number of available multisample buffers	0
`EGL_SAMPLES`	Number of samples per pixel	0
`EGL_STENCIL_SIZE`	Number of bits in the stencil buffer	0
`EGL_SURFACE_TYPE`	Type of EGL surfaces supported. Can be any of `EGL_WINDOW_BIT`, `EGL_PIXMAP_BIT`, or `EGL_PBUFFER_BIT`	`EGL_WINDOW_BIT`
`EGL_TRANSPARENT_TYPE`	Type of transparency supported	`EGL_NONE`
`EGL_TRANSPARENT_RED_VALUE`	Red color value interpreted as transparent	`EGL_DONT_CARE`
`EGL_TRANSPARENT_GREEN_VALUE`	Green color value interpreted as transparent	`EGL_DONT_CARE`
`EGL_TRANSPARENT_BLUE_VALUE`	Blue color value interpreted as transparent	`EGL_DONT_CARE`

Note: Various tokens do not have a default value mandated in the EGL specification, which are indicated by —for their default value.

Example 3-2   Specifying EGL Attributes

```
EGLint attribList[] =
{
    EGL_RENDERABLE_TYPE, EGL_OPENGL_ES2_BIT,
    EGL_RED_SIZE,   5,
    EGL_GREEN_SIZE, 6,
    EGL_BLUE_SIZE,  5,
    EGL_DEPTH_SIZE, 1,
    EGL_NONE
};
```

For values that aren't explicitly specified in the attribute list, EGL will use their default value as specified in Table 3-1. Additionally, when specifying a numeric value for an attribute, EGL will guarantee the returned configuration will have at least that value as a minimum if there's a matching EGLConfig available.

To use this set of attributes as a selection criteria, follow Example 3-3.

Example 3-3   Querying EGL Surface Configurations

```
const EGLint MaxConfigs = 10;
EGLConfig   configs[MaxConfigs];   // We'll only accept 10 configs

EGLint   numConfigs;
if(!eglChooseConfig(dpy, attribList, configs, MaxConfigs,
    &numConfigs))
{
    // Something didn't work … handle error situation
}
else
{
    // Everything's okay. Continue to create a rendering surface
}
```

If eglChooseConfig returns successfully, a set of EGLConfigs matching your criteria will be returned. If more than one EGLConfig matches (with at most the maximum number of configurations you specify), eglChooseConfig will sort the configurations using the following ordering:

1. By the value of EGL_CONFIG_CAVEAT. Precedence is given to configurations where there are no configuration caveats (when the value of EGL_CONFIG_CAVEAT is GL_NONE), then slow rendering configurations (EGL_SLOW_CONFIG), and finally nonconformant configurations (EGL_NON_CONFORMANT_CONFIG).

2. By the type of buffer as specified by `EGL_COLOR_BUFFER_TYPE`.

3. By the number of bits in the color buffer in descending sizes. The number of bits in a buffer depends on the `EGL_COLOR_BUFFER_TYPE`, and will be at least the value specified for a particular color channel. When the buffer type is `EGL_RGB_BUFFER`, the number of bits is computed as the total of `EGL_RED_SIZE`, `EGL_GREEN_SIZE`, and `EGL_BLUE_SIZE`. When the color buffer type is `EGL_LUMINANCE_BUFFER`, the number of bits is the sum of `EGL_LUMINANCE_SIZE` and `EGL_ALPHA_SIZE`.

4. By the `EGL_BUFFER_SIZE` in ascending order.

5. By the value of `EGL_SAMPLE_BUFFERS` in ascending order.

6. By the number of `EGL_SAMPLES` in ascending order.

7. By the value of `EGL_DEPTH_SIZE` in ascending order.

8. By the value of the `EGL_STENCIL_SIZE` in ascending order.

9. By the value of the `EGL_ALHPA_MASK_SIZE` (which is applicable only to OpenVG surfaces).

10. By the `EGL_NATIVE_VISUAL_TYPE` in an implementation-dependent manner.

11. By the value of the `EGL_CONFIG_ID` in ascending order.

Parameters not mentioned in this list are not used in the sorting process.

As mentioned in the example, if `eglChooseConfig` returns successfully, we have enough information to continue to create something to draw into. By default, if you don't specify what type of rendering surface type you would like (by specifying the `EGL_SURFACE_TYPE` attribute), EGL assumes you want an on-screen window.

Creating an On-Screen Rendering Area: The EGL Window

Once we have a suitable `EGLConfig` that meets our requirements for rendering, we're set to create our window. To create a window, call

```
EGLSurface eglCreateWindowSurface(EGLDisplay display,
                                  EGLConfig config,
                                  EGLNatvieWindowType window,
                                  const EGLint *attribList);
```

This function takes our connection to the native display manager, and the `EGLConfig` that we obtained in the previous step. Additionally, it requires a window from the native windowing system that was created previously. Because EGL is a software layer between many different windowing systems and OpenGL ES 2.0, demonstrating how to create a native window is outside the scope of this guide. Please reference the documentation for your native windowing system to determine what's required to create a window in that environment.

Finally, this call also takes a list of attributes; however this list differs from those shown in Table 3-1. Because EGL supports other rendering APIs (notably OpenVG), there are attributes accepted by `eglCreateWindowSurface` that don't apply when working with OpenGL ES 2.0 (see Table 3-2). For our purposes, there is a single attribute that's accepted by `eglCreateWindowSurface`, and it's used to specify which buffer of the front- or back-buffer we'd like to render into.

Table 3-2   Attributes for Window Creating Using `eglCreateWindowSurface`

Token	Description	Default Value
EGL_RENDER_BUFFER	Specifies which buffer should be used for rendering (using the EGL_SINGLE_BUFFER value), or back (EGL_BACK_BUFFER).	EGL_BACK_BUFFER

Note: For OpenGL ES 2.0 window rendering surfaces, only double-buffered windows are supported.

The attribute list might be empty (i.e., passing a NULL pointer as the value for `attribList`), or it might be a list populated with an `EGL_NONE` token as the first element. In such cases, all of the relevant attributes use their default values.

There are a number of ways that `eglCreateWindowSurface` could fail, and if any of them occur, `EGL_NO_SURFACE` is returned from the call, and the particular error is set. If this situation occurs, we can determine the reason for the failure by calling `eglGetError`, which will return one of the following reasons shown in Table 3-3.

Table 3-3   Possible Errors When `eglCreateWindowSurface` Fails

Error Code	Description
EGL_BAD_MATCH	This situation occurs when: • the attributes of the native window do not match those of the provided EGLConfig. • the provided EGLConfig doesn't support rendering into a window (i.e., the EGL_SURFACE_TYPE attribute doesn't have the EGL_WINDOW_BIT set.
EGL_BAD_CONFIG	This error is flagged if the provided EGLConfig is not supported by the system.
EGL_BAD_NATIVE_WINDOW	This error is specified if the provided native window handle is not valid.
EGL_BAD_ALLOC	This error occurs if eglCreateWindowSurface is unable to allocate the resources for the new EGL window, or if there is already an EGLConfig associated with the provided native window.

Putting this all together, our code for creating a window is shown in Example 3-4.

Example 3-4   Creating an EGL Window Surface

```
EGLRenderSurface  window;
EGLint attribList[] =
{
   EGL_RENDER_BUFFER, EGL_BACK_BUFFER,
   EGL_NONE
);

window = eglCreateWindowSurface(dpy, window, config, attribList);

if(window == EGL_NO_SURFACE)
{
   switch(eglGetError())
   {
      case EGL_BAD_MATCH:
         // Check window and EGLConfig attributes to determine
         // compatibility, or verify that the EGLConfig
         // supports rendering to a window,
         break;
```

```
        case EGL_BAD_CONFIG:
            // Verify that provided EGLConfig is valid
            break;

        case EGL_BAD_NATIVE_WINDOW:
            // Verify that provided EGLNativeWindow is valid
            break;

        case EGL_BAD_ALLOC:
            // Not enough resources available. Handle and recover
            break;
    }
}
```

This creates a place for us to draw into, but we still have two more steps before we'll be able to successfully use OpenGL ES 2.0 with our window. Windows, however, aren't the only rendering surfaces that you might find useful. We introduce another type of rendering surface next before completing our discussion.

Creating an Off-Screen Rendering Area: EGL Pbuffers

In addition to being able to render into an on-screen window using OpenGL ES 2.0, you can also render into nonvisible off-screen surfaces called pbuffers (short for *pixel buffer*). Pbuffers can take full advantage of any hardware acceleration available to OpenGL ES 2.0, just as a window does. Pbuffers are most often used for generating texture maps. If all you want to do is render to a texture, we recommend using framebuffer objects (covered in Chapter 12, "Framebuffer Objects") instead of pbuffers because they are more efficient. However, pbuffers can still be useful for some cases where framebuffer objects cannot be used, such as when rendering an off-screen surface with OpenGL ES and then using it as a texture in another API such as OpenVG.

Creating a pbuffer is very similar to creating an EGL window, with a few minor differences. To create a pbuffer, we need to find an EGLConfig just as we did for a window, with one modification: We need to augment the value of EGL_SURFACE_TYPE to include EGL_PBUFFER_BIT. Once we have a suitable EGLConfig, we can create a pbuffer using the function

```
EGLSurface eglCreatePbufferSurface(EGLDisplay display,
                                   EGLConfig config,
                                   const EGLint *attribList);
```

As with window creation, this function takes our connection to the native display manager, and the `EGLConfig` that we selected.

This call also takes a list of attributes described in Table 3-4.

Table 3-4   EGL Pixel Buffer Attributes

Token	Description	Default Value
EGL_WIDTH	Specifies the desired width (in pixels) of the pbuffer.	0
EGL_HEIGHT	Specifies the desired height (in pixels) of the pbuffer.	0
EGL_LARGEST_PBUFFER	Select the largest available pbuffer if one of the requested size isn't available. Values can be EGL_TRUE or EGL_FALSE.	EGL_FALSE
EGL_TEXTURE_FORMAT	Specifies the type of texture format (see Chapter 9) if the pbuffer is bound to a texture map. Valid values are EGL_TEXTURE_RGB, EGL_TEXTURE_RGBA, and EGL_NO_TEXTURE (which indicates that the pbuffer isn't going to be used directly as a texture).	EGL_NO_TEXTURE
EGL_TEXTURE_TARGET	Specifies the associated texture target that the pbuffer should be attached to if used as a texture map (see Chapter 9). Valid values are EGL_TEXTURE_2D or EGL_NO_TEXTURE.	EGL_NO_TEXTURE
EGL_MIPMAP_TEXTURE	Specifies whether storage for texture mipmap levels (see Chapter 9) should be additionally allocated. Valid values are EGL_TRUE and EGL_FALSE.	EGL_FALSE

There are a number of ways that `eglCreatePbufferSurface` could fail, and just as with window creation, if any of them occur, `EGL_NO_SURFACE` is returned from the call, and the particular error is set. In this situation, `eglGetError` will return one of the errors listed in Table 3-5.

Table 3-5   Possible Errors When `eglCreatePbufferSurface` Fails

Error Code	Description
EGL_BAD_ALLOC	This error occurs when the pbuffer is unable to be allocated due to a lack of resources.
EGL_BAD_CONFIG	This error is flagged if the provided EGLConfig is not a valid EGLConfig supported by the system.
EGL_BAD_PARAMETER	This error is generated if either the EGL_WIDTH or EGL_HEIGHT provided in the attribute list are negative values.
EGL_BAD_MATCH	This error is generated if any of the following situations occur: if the EGLConfig provided doesn't support pbuffer surfaces; or if the pbuffer is going to be used as a texture map (EGL_TEXTURE_FORMAT is not EGL_NO_TEXTURE), and the specified EGL_WIDTH and EGL_HEIGHT specify an invalid texture size; or if one of EGL_TEXTURE_FORMAT and EGL_TEXTURE_TARGET is EGL_NO_TEXTURE, and the other attributes is not EGL_NO_TEXTURE.
EGL_BAD_ATTRIBUTE	This error occurs if any of EGL_TEXTURE_FORMAT, EGL_TEXTURE_TARGET, or EGL_MIPMAP_TEXTURE are specified, but the provided EGLConfig doesn't support OpenGL ES rendering (e.g., only OpenVG rendering is supported).

Putting this all together, we would create a pbuffer as shown in Example 3-5.

Example 3-5   Creating an EGL Pixel Buffer

```
EGLint attribList[] =
{
   EGL_SURFACE_TYPE, EGL_PBUFFER_BIT,
   EGL_RENDERABLE_TYPE, EGL_OPENGL_ES2_BIT,
   EGL_RED_SIZE, 5,
   EGL_GREEN_SIZE, 6,
   EGL_BLUE_SIZE, 5,
   EGL_DEPTH_SIZE, 1,
   EGL_NONE
};

const EGLint MaxConfigs = 10;
EGLConfig  configs[MaxConfigs];   // We'll only accept 10 configs
```

```
EGLint  numConfigs;
if(!eglChooseConfig(dpy, attribList, configs, MaxConfigs,
    &numConfigs))
{
    // Something didn't work … handle error situation
}
else
{
    // We've found a pbuffer-capable EGLConfig
}

// Proceed to create a 512 x 512 pbuffer (or the largest available)
EGLRenderSurface  pbuffer;
EGLint attribList[] =
{
    EGL_WIDTH, 512,
    EGL_HEIGHT, 512,
    EGL_LARGEST_PBUFFER, EGL_TRUE,
    EGL_NONE
);

pbuffer = eglCreatePbufferSurface(dpy, config, attribList);

if(pbuffer == EGL_NO_SURFACE)
{
    switch(eglGetError())
    {
        case EGL_BAD_ALLOC:
            // Not enough resources available. Handle and recover
            break;

        case EGL_BAD_CONFIG:
            // Verify that provided EGLConfig is valid
            break;

        case EGL_BAD_PARAMETER:
            // Verify that the EGL_WIDTH and EGL_HEIGHT are
            // non-negative values
            break;

        case EGL_BAD_MATCH:
            // Check window and EGLConfig attributes to determine
            // compatibility and pbuffer-texture parameters
            break;

    }
}
```

```
// Check to see what size pbuffer we were allocated
EGLint  width;
EGLint  height;

if(!eglQuerySurface(dpy, pbuffer, EGL_WIDTH, &width) ||
   !eglQuerySurface(dpy, pbuffer, EGL_HEIGHT, &height))
{
    // Unable to query surface information.
}
```

Pbuffers support all OpenGL ES 2.0 rendering facilities just as windows do. The major difference—aside from you can't display a pbuffer on the screen—is that instead of swapping buffers when you're finished rendering as you do with a window, you will either copy the values from a pbuffer to your application, or modify the binding of the pbuffer as a texture.

Creating a Rendering Context

A rendering context is a data structure internal to OpenGL ES 2.0 that contains all of the state required for operation. For example, it contains references to the vertex and fragment shaders and the array of vertex data used in the example program in Chapter 2. Before OpenGL ES 2.0 can draw it needs to have a context available for its use.

To create a context, use

```
EGLContext eglCreateContext(EGLDisplay display, EGLConfig config,
                            EGLContext shareContext,
                            const EGLint* attribList);
```

Once again, you'll need the display connection as well as the EGLConfig best representing your application's requirements. The third parameter, shareContext, allows multiple EGLContexts to share specific types of data, like shader programs and texture maps. Sharing resources among contexts is an advanced concept that we discuss in Chapter 13, "Advanced Programming with OpenGL ES 2.0." For the time being, we pass EGL_NO_CONTEXT in as the value for shareContext, indicating that we're not sharing resources with any other contexts.

Finally, as with many EGL calls, a list of attributes specific to eglCreate-Context's operation is specified. In this case, there's a single attribute that's accepted, EGL_CONTEXT_CLIENT_VERSION, discussed in Table 3-6.

Table 3-6   Attributes for Context Creation Using `eglCreateContext`

Token	Description	Default Value
`EGL_CONTEXT_ CLIENT_VERSION`	Specifies the type of context associated with the version of OpenGL ES that you're using.	1 (which specifies an OpenGL ES 1.X context)

As we want to use OpenGL ES 2.0, we will always have to specify this attribute to obtain the right type of context.

When `eglCreateContext` succeeds, it returns a handle to the newly created context. If a context is not able to be created, then `eglCreateContext` returns `EGL_NO_CONTEXT`, and the reason for the failure is set, and can be obtained by calling `eglGetError`. With our current knowledge, the only reason that `eglCreateContext` would fail is if the `EGLConfig` we provide isn't valid, in which case the error returned by `eglGetError` is `EGL_BAD_CONFIG`.

Example 3-6 shows how to create a context after selecting an appropriate `EGLConfig`.

Example 3-6   Creating an EGL Context

```
const EGLint attribList[] = {
   EGL_CONTEXT_CLIENT_VERSION, 2,
   EGL_NONE
};

EGLContext  context;

context = eglCreateContext(dpy, config, EGL_NO_CONTEXT, attribList);

if(context == EGL_NO_CONTEXT)
{
   EGLError error = eglGetError();

   if(error == EGL_BAD_CONFIG)
   {
      // Handle error and recover
   }
}
```

Other errors may be generated by `eglCreateContext`, but for the moment, we'll only check for bad `EGLConfig` errors.

After successfully creating an EGLContext, we need to complete one final step before we can render.

Making an EGLContext Current

As an application might have created multiple EGLContexts for various purposes, we need a way to associate a particular EGLContext with our rendering surface—a process commonly called "make current."

To associate a particular EGLContext with an EGLSurface, use the call

```
EGLBoolean eglmakeCurrent(EGLDisplay display, EGLSurface draw,
                          EGLSurface read, EGLContext context);
```

You probably noticed that this call takes two EGLSurfaces. Although this allows flexibility that we exploit in our discussion of advanced EGL usage, we set both read and draw to the same value, the window that we created previously.

Putting All Our EGL Knowledge Together

We conclude this chapter with a complete example showing the entire process starting with the initialization of the EGL through binding an EGLContext to an EGLRenderSurface. We'll assume that a native window has already been created, and that if any errors occur, the application will terminate.

In fact, Example 3-7 is very similar to what is done in esCreateWindow as shown in Chapter 2, except those routines separate the creation of the window and the context (for reasons that we discuss later).

Example 3-7   A Complete Routine for Creating an EGL Window

```
EGLBoolean initializeWindow(EGLNativeWindow nativeWindow)
{
    const EGLint   configAttribs[] =
    {
        EGL_RENDER_TYPE, EGL_WINDOW_BIT,
        EGL_RED_SIZE, 8,
        EGL_GREEN_SIZE, 8,
        EGL_BLUE_SIZE, 8,
```

```
      EGL_DEPTH_SIZE, 24,
      EGL_NONE
};

const EGLint  contextAttribs[] =
{
      EGL_CONTEXT_CLIENT_VERSION, 2,
      EGL_NONE
};

EGLDisplay dpy;

dpy = eglGetNativeDispay(EGL_DEFAULT_DISPLAY);

if(dpy == EGL_NO_DISPLAY)
{
      return EGL_FALSE;
}

EGLint major, minor;

if(!eglInitialize(dpy, &major, &minor))
{
      return EGL_FALSE;
}

EGLConfig  config;
EGLint  numConfigs;
if(!eglChooseConfig(dpy, configAttribs, &config, 1,
      &numConfigs)) {
          return EGL_FALSE;
}

EGLSurface window;
window = eglCreateWindowSurface(dpy, config, nativeWindow, NULL);

if(window == EGL_NO_SURFACE)
{
      return EGL_FALSE;
}

EGLContext context;
context = eglCreateContext(dpy, config, EGL_NO_CONTEXT,
                            contextAttribs);

if(context == EGL_NO_CONTEXT)
{
      return EGL_FALSE;
}
```

```
    if(!eglMakeCurrent(dpy, window, window, context))
    {
        return EGL_FALSE;
    }

    return EGL_TRUE;
}
```

This code would be very similar if an application made the call in Example 3-8 to open a 512 × 512 window.

Example 3-8   Creating a Window Using the ESutil Library

```
ESContext   esContext;
const char* title = "OpenGL ES Application Window Title";

if(esCreateWindow(&esContext, title, 512, 512,
                  ES_WINDOW_RGB | ES_WINDOW_DEPTH))
{
    // Window creation failed
}
```

The last parameter to esCreateWindow specifies the characteristics we want in our window, and specified as a bitmask of the following values:

- ES_WINDOW_RGB—Specify an RGB-based color buffer.

- ES_WINDOW_ALPHA—Allocate a destination alpha buffer.

- ES_WINDOW_DEPTH—Allocate a depth buffer.

- ES_WINDOW_STENCIL—Allocate a stencil buffer.

- ES_WINDOW_MULTISAMPLE—Allocate a multisample buffer.

Specifying these values in the window configuration bitmask will add the appropriate tokens and values into the EGLConfig attribute list (i.e., configAttribs in the preceding example).

Synchronizing Rendering

You might find situations in which you need to coordinate the rendering of multiple graphics APIs into a single window. For example, you might find it easier to use OpenVG or the native windowing system's font rendering functions more suited for drawing characters into a window than OpenGL ES 2.0. In such cases, you'll need to have your application allow the various libraries to render into the shared window. EGL has a few functions to help with your synchronization tasks.

If your application is only rendering with OpenGL ES 2.0, then you can guarantee that all rendering has occurred by simply calling glFinish.

However, if you're using more than one Khronos API for rendering (such as OpenVG), and you might not know which API is used before switching to the window-system native rendering API, you can call the following.

EGLBoolean **eglWaitClient**()

Delays execution of the client until all rendering through a Khronos API (like OpenGL ES 2.0, or OpenVG) is completed. On success, it will return EGL_TRUE. On failure, EGL_FALSE is returned, and an EGL_BAD_CURRENT_ SURFACE error is posted.

Its operation is similar in operation to glFinish, but works regardless of which Khronos API is currently in operation.

Likewise, if you need to guarantee that the native windowing system rendering is completed, call eglWaitNative.

EGLBoolean **eglWaitNative**(EGLint *engine*)

---

engine   specifies the renderer to wait for rendering completion. EGL_CORE_NATIVE_ENGINE is always accepted, and represents the most common engine supported; other engines are implementation specific, and specified through EGL extensions. EGL_TRUE is returned on success. On failure, EGL_FALSE is returned, and an EGL_BAD_PARAMETER error is posted.

Chapter 4

Shaders and Programs

In Chapter 2, "Hello, Triangle: An OpenGL ES 2.0 Example," we introduced you to a simple program that draws a single triangle. In that example, we created two shader objects (one for the vertex shader and one for the fragment shader) and a single program object to render the triangle. Shader objects and program objects are fundamental concepts in working with shaders in OpenGL ES 2.0. In this chapter, we introduce you to the full details on how to create shaders, compile them, and link them together into a program object. The details of writing vertex and fragment shaders come later in the book. For now, we focus on:

- Shader and program object overview.

- Creating and compiling a shader.

- Creating and linking a program.

- Getting and setting uniforms.

- Getting and setting attributes.

- Shader compiler and shader binaries.

Shaders and Programs

There are two fundamental object types you need to create to render with shaders: *shader objects* and *program objects*. The best way to think of a shader object and a program object is by comparison to a C compiler and linker. A C compiler generates object code (e.g., .obj or .o files) for a piece of source code. After the object files have been created, the C linker then links the object files into a final program.

A similar paradigm is used in OpenGL ES for representing shaders. The shader object is an object that contains a single shader. The source code is given to the shader object and then the shader object is compiled into object form (like an .obj file). After compilation, the shader object can then be attached to a program object. A program object gets multiple shader objects attached to it. In OpenGL ES, each program object will need to have one vertex shader object and one fragment shader object attached to it (no more, and no less). The program object is then linked into a final "executable." The final program object can then be used to render.

The general process for getting to a linked shader object is to first create a vertex shader object and a fragment shader object, attach source code to each of them, and compile them. Then, you create a program object, attach the compiled shader objects to it, and link it. If there are no errors, you can then tell the GL to use the program for drawing any time you like. The next sections detail the API calls you need to use to execute this process.

Creating and Compiling a Shader

The first step to working with a shader object is to create it. This is done using glCreateShader.

GLuint	**glCreateShader**(GLenum *type*)
type	the type of the shader to create, either GL_VERTEX_SHADER or GL_FRAGMENT_SHADER

Calling glCreateShader causes a new vertex or fragment shader to be created, depending on the type passed in. The return value is a handle to the new shader object. When you are finished with a shader object, you can delete it using glDeleteShader.

void	**glDeleteShader**(GLuint *shader*)
shader	handle to the shader object to delete

Note that if a shader is attached to a program object (more on this later), calling glDeleteShader will not immediately delete the shader. Rather, the shader will be marked for deletion and its memory will be freed once the shader is no longer attached to any program objects.

Once you have a shader object created, typically the next thing you will do is provide the shader source code using glShaderSource.

void	**glShaderSource**(GLuint *shader*, GLsizei *count*, const char** *string*, const GLint* *length*)

shader	handle to the shader object
count	the number of shader source strings. A shader can be composed of a number of source strings, although each shader can have only one main function
string	pointer to an array of strings holding *count* number of shader source strings
length	pointer to an array of *count* integers that holds the size of each respective shader string. If *length* is NULL, the shader strings are assumed to be null terminated. If *length* is not NULL, then each element of *length* holds the number of characters in the corresponding shader in the *string* array. If the value of *length* for any element is less than zero, then that string is assumed to be null terminated

Once the shader source has been specified, the next step is to compile the shader. Before we get to that step, there is one big assumption we are making here of which we must make you aware. Not all implementations of OpenGL ES 2.0 provide the ability to compile a shader (some require shaders to be compiled offline). This is described later in the chapter in the section on shader binaries. For now, we proceed as if a shader can be compiled online and discuss shader binaries later.

Given an implementation of OpenGL ES supports online compilation and you have specified its source, you can then compile the shader using glCompileShader.

void	**glCompileShader**(GLuint *shader*)

shader	handle to the shader object to compile

Calling glCompileShader will cause the shader source code that has been stored in the shader object to be compiled. As with any normal language compiler, the first thing you want to know after compiling is whether there were any errors. This, along with other information about the shader object, can be queried for using glGetShaderiv.

void	**glGetShaderiv**(GLuint *shader,* GLenum *pname,* GLint **params*)

shader	handle to the shader object to get information about
pname	the parameter to get information about, can be: GL_COMPILE_STATUS GL_DELETE_STATUS GL_INFO_LOG_LENGTH GL_SHADER_SOURCE_LENGTH GL_SHADER_TYPE
params	pointer to integer storage location for the result of the query

To check whether a shader has compiled successfully, you can call glGet-Shaderiv on the shader object with the GL_COMPILE_STATUS argument for pname. If the shader compiled successfully, the result will be GL_TRUE. If the shader failed to compile, the result will be GL_FALSE. If the shader does fail to compile, the compile errors will be written into the *info log*. The info log is a log written by the compiler with any error messages or warnings. The info log can be written with information even if the compile is successful. To check the info log, the length of the info log can be queried using GL_INFO_LOG_LENGTH. The info log itself can be retrieved using glGet-ShaderInfoLog (described next). Querying for GL_SHADER_TYPE will return whether the shader is a GL_VERTEX_SHADER or GL_FRAGMENT_SHADER. Querying for GL_SHADER_SOURCE_LENGTH returns the length of the shader source code, including the null terminator. Finally, querying for GL_DELETE_STATUS returns whether the shader has been marked for deletion using glDeleteShader.

After compiling the shader and checking the info log length, you might want to retrieve the info log (especially if compilation failed to find out why). To do so, you first need to query for the GL_INFO_LOG_LENGTH and allocate a string with sufficient storage to store the info log. The info log can then be retrieved using glGetShaderInfoLog.

void	**glGetShaderInfoLog**(GLuint *shader*, GLsizei *maxLength*, GLsizei **length*, GLchar **infoLog*)
shader	handle to the shader object to get the info log for
maxLength	the size of the buffer to store the info log in
length	the length of the info log written (minus the null terminator). If the length does not need to be known, this parameter can be NULL
infoLog	pointer to the character buffer to store the info log in

The info log does not have any mandated format or required information. However, most OpenGL ES 2.0 implementations will return error messages that contain the line number of the source code line the compiler was working on when it detected the error. Some implementations will also provide warnings or additional information in the log.

We now have shown you all of the functions you need to create a shader, compile it, find out the compile status, and query the info log. For review, we show in Example 4-1 the code we had in Chapter 2 to load a shader that uses the functions we have just described.

Example 4-1   Loading a Shader

```
GLuint LoadShader(GLenum type, const char *shaderSrc)
{
   GLuint shader;
   GLint compiled;

   // Create the shader object
   shader = glCreateShader(type);

   if(shader == 0)
      return 0;

   // Load the shader source
   glShaderSource(shader, 1, &shaderSrc, NULL);
```

```
// Compile the shader
glCompileShader(shader);

// Check the compile status
glGetShaderiv(shader, GL_COMPILE_STATUS, &compiled);

if(!compiled)
{
   GLint infoLen = 0;

   glGetShaderiv(shader, GL_INFO_LOG_LENGTH, &infoLen);

   if(infoLen > 1)
   {
      char* infoLog = malloc(sizeof(char) * infoLen);

      glGetShaderInfoLog(shader, infoLen, NULL, infoLog);
      esLogMessage("Error compiling shader:\n%s\n", infoLog);

      free(infoLog);
   }

   glDeleteShader(shader);
   return 0;
}

return shader;
```

Creating and Linking a Program

Now that we have shown you how to create shader objects, the next step is to create a program object. As previously described, a program object is a container object to which you attach shaders and link a final executable program. The function calls to manipulate program objects are very similar to shader objects. A program object is created using glCreateProgram.

```
GLuint    glCreateProgram(void)
```

You might notice that glCreateProgram does not take any arguments; it simply returns a handle to a new program object. A program object can be deleted using glDeleteProgram.

void	**glDeleteProgram**(GLuint *program*)
program	handle to the program object to delete

Once you have a program object created, the next step is to attach shaders to it. In OpenGL ES 2.0, each program object will need to have one vertex shader and one fragment shader object attached to it. The function to attach shaders to a program is glAttachShader.

void	**glAttachShader**(GLuint *program*, GLuint *shader*)
program	handle to the program object
shader	handle to the shader object to attach to the program

This function will attach the shader to the given program. Note that a shader can be attached at any point. It does not necessarily need to be compiled or even have source code before being attached to a program. The only requirement is that every program object will have to have one and only one vertex shader and fragment shader object attached to it. In addition to attaching shaders, you can also detach shaders using glDetachShader.

void	**glDetachShader**(GLuint *program*, GLuint *shader*)
program	handle to the program object
shader	handle to the shader object to detach from the program

Once the shaders have been attached (and the shaders have been successfully compiled), we are finally ready to link the shaders together. Linking a program object is accomplished using glLinkProgram.

void	**glLinkProgram**(GLuint *program*)
program	handle to the program object to link

The link operation is responsible for generating the final executable program. There are a number of things the linker will check for to ensure successful linkage. We mention some of these conditions now, but until we describe vertex and fragment shaders in detail these conditions might be a bit confusing to you. The linker will make sure that any varying variables that are consumed by the fragment shader are written by the vertex shader (and declared with the same type). The linker will also make sure that any uniforms declared in both the vertex and fragment shader have matching types. The linker will also make sure that the final program fits within the limits of the implementation (e.g., the number of attributes, uniforms, varyings, or instructions consumed). Typically, the link phase is when the final hardware instructions are generated to run on the hardware.

After linking a program, you will need to check whether the link succeeded. The link status can be checked by using glGetProgramiv.

void	**glGetProgramiv**(GLuint *program*, GLenum *pname*, GLint **params*)

program	handle to the program object to get information about
pname	the parameter to get information about, can be:
	GL_ACTIVE_ATTRIBUTES
	GL_ACTIVE_ATTRIBUTE_MAX_LENGTH
	GL_ACTIVE_UNIFORMS
	GL_ACTIVE_UNIFORM_MAX_LENGTH
	GL_ATTACHED_SHADERS
	GL_DELETE_STATUS
	GL_INFO_LOG_LENGTH
	GL_LINK_STATUS
	GL_VALIDATE_STATUS
params	pointer to integer storage location for the result of the query

To check whether a link was successful, you can query for GL_LINK_STATUS. There are a large number of other queries available on program objects. Querying for GL_ACTIVE_ATTRIBUTES returns a count of the number of active attributes in the vertex shader. Querying for GL_ACTIVE_ATTRIBUTE_MAX_LENGTH returns the maximum length (in characters) of the largest attribute name. This can be used to determine how much memory to allocate to store attribute name strings. Likewise, GL_ACTIVE_UNIFORMS and GL_ACTIVE_UNIFORM_MAX_LENGTH return the number of active uniforms and the maximum length of the largest uniform name. The number of shaders attached to the program object can be queried using GL_ATTACHED_SHADERS. The GL_DELETE_STATUS query returns whether a program object has been marked for deletion. As with shader objects, program objects store an info log, the length of which can be queried for using GL_INFO_LOG_LENGTH. Finally, the status of the last validation operation can be queried for using GL_VALIDATE_STATUS. The validation of program objects is described later in this section.

After linking the program, we will now want to get information from the program info log (particularly if there was a link failure). Doing so is very similar to getting the info log for shader objects.

---

void   **glGetProgramInfoLog**(GLuint *program*,
                               GLsizei *maxLength*,
                               GLsizei **length*, GLchar **infoLog*)

---

program	handle to the program object to get information about
maxLength	the size of the buffer to store the info log in
length	the length of the info log written (minus the null terminator). If the length does not need to be known, this parameter can be NULL
infoLog	pointer to the character buffer to store the info log in

Once we have linked the program successfully, we are just about ready to render with it. One thing we might want to check is whether the program validates. That is, there are certain aspects of execution that a successful link cannot guarantee. For example, it might be the case that the application never binds valid texture units to samplers. This will not be known at link time, but instead at draw time. To check that your program will execute with the current state, you can call glValidateProgram.

---

void   **glValidateProgram**(GLuint *program*)

---

program	handle to the program object to validate

The result of the validation can be checked using GL_VALIDATE_STATUS described earlier. The info log will also be updated.

Note: You really only want to use glValidateProgram for debugging purposes. It is a slow operation and certainly not something you want to check before every render. Really, you can get away with never using it if you have an application that is successfully rendering. We want to make you aware that this function does exist though.

So we now have shown you the functions needed for creating a program object, attaching shaders to it, linking, and getting the info log. There is one more thing you need to do with a program object before rendering and that is to set it as the active program using glUseProgram.

---

void   **glUseProgram**(GLuint *program*)

---

program handle to the program object to make active

Now that we have our program active, we are set to render. Here again in Example 4-2 is the code from our sample in Chapter 2 that uses these functions.

Example 4-2   Create, Attach Shaders to, and Link a Program

```
// Create the program object
programObject = glCreateProgram();

if(programObject == 0)
   return 0;

glAttachShader(programObject, vertexShader);
glAttachShader(programObject, fragmentShader);

// Link the program
glLinkProgram(programObject);

// Check the link status
glGetProgramiv(programObject, GL_LINK_STATUS, &linked);

if(!linked)
{
   GLint infoLen = 0;
```

```
    glGetProgramiv(programObject, GL_INFO_LOG_LENGTH, &infoLen);

    if(infoLen > 1)
    {
        char* infoLog = malloc(sizeof(char) * infoLen);

        glGetProgramInfoLog(programObject, infoLen, NULL, infoLog);
        esLogMessage("Error linking program:\n%s\n", infoLog);

        free(infoLog);
    }

    glDeleteProgram(programObject);
    return FALSE;
}

// …

// Use the program object
glUseProgram(userData->programObject);
```

Uniforms and Attributes

Once you have a linked program object, there a number of queries that you
might want to do on it. The first is that you will likely need to find out about
the active uniforms in your program. Uniforms—as we detail more in the
next chapter on the shading language—are variables that store read-only
constant values that are passed in by the application through the OpenGL
ES 2.0 API to the shader. The set of uniforms is shared across a program
object. That is, there is one set of uniforms for a program object. If a uniform is declared in both a vertex and fragment shader, it must have the
same type and its value will be the same in both shaders. During the link
phase, the linker will assign uniform locations to each of the active uniforms in the program. These locations are the identifiers the application will
use to load the uniform with a value.

Getting and Setting Uniforms

To query for the list of active uniforms in a program, you first call glGet-
Programiv with the GL_ACTIVE_UNIFORMS parameter (as described in the
previous section). This will tell you the number of active uniforms in the
program. A uniform is considered "active" if it was used by the program. In

other words, if you declare a uniform in one of your shaders but never use it, the linker will likely optimize that away and not return it in the active uniform list. You can also find out the number of characters (including null terminator) that the largest uniform name has in the program. This can be done by calling glGetProgramiv with the GL_ACTIVE_UNIFORM_MAX_LENGTH parameter.

Once we know the number of active uniforms and the number of characters we need to store the uniform names, we can find out details on each uniform using glGetActiveUniform.

---

void	**glGetActiveUniform**(GLuint *program*, GLuint *index*, GLsizei *bufSize*, GLsizei* *length*, GLint* *size*, GLenum* *type*, char* *name*)

program	handle to the program object
index	the uniform index to be queried
bufSize	the number of characters in the name array
length	if not NULL, will be written with the number of characters written into the name array (less the null terminator)
size	if the uniform variable being queried is an array, this variable will be written with the maximum array element used in the program (plus 1). If the uniform variable being queried is not an array, this value will be 1
type	will be written with the uniform type, can be: GL_FLOAT, GL_FLOAT_VEC2, GL_FLOAT_VEC3, GL_FLOAT_VEC4, GL_INT, GL_INT_VEC2, GL_INT_VEC3, GL_INT_VEC4, GL_BOOL, GL_BOOL_VEC2, GL_BOOL_VEC3, GL_BOOL_VEC4, GL_FLOAT_MAT2, GL_FLOAT_MAT3, GL_FLOAT_MAT4, GL_SAMPLER_2D, GL_SAMPLER_CUBE
name	will be written with the name of the uniform up to bufSize number of characters. This will be a null terminated string

---

Using glGetActiveUniform you can determine nearly all of the properties of the uniform. You can determine the name of the uniform variable along with its type. In addition, you can find out if the variable is an array, and if so what the maximum element used in the array was. The name of the uniform is necessary to find the uniform's location, and type and size are also needed to figure out how to load it with data. Once we have the name of the uniform, we can find its location using glGetUniformLocation. The uniform location is an integer value used to identify the location of the uniform in the program. That location value is used by the subsequent calls for loading uniforms with values (e.g., glUniform1f).

GLint	**glGetUniformLocation**(GLuint *program*, const char* *name*)

program   handle to the program object

name   the name of the uniform to get the location of

This function will return the location of the uniform given by *name*. If the uniform is not an active uniform in the program, then the return value will be −1. Once we have the uniform location along with its type and array size, we can then load the uniform with values. There are a number of different functions for loading uniforms, with different functions for each uniform type.

```
void    glUniform1f(CLint location, GLfloat x)
void    glUniform1fv(GLint location, GLsizei count,
                     const GLfloat* v)
void    glUniform1i(GLint location, GLint x)
void    glUniform1iv(GLint location, GLsizei count,
                     const GLint* v)
void    glUniform2f(GLint location, GLfloat x, GLfloat y)
void    glUniform2fv(GLint location, GLsizei count,
                     const GLfloat* v)
void    glUniform2i(GLint location, GLint x, GLint y)
void    glUniform2iv(GLint location, GLsizei count,
                     const GLint* v)
void    glUniform3f(GLint location, GLfloat x, GLfloat y,
                     GLfloat z)
void    glUniform3fv(GLint location, GLsizei count,
                     const GLfloat* v)
void    glUniform3i(GLint location, GLint x, GLint y,
                     GLint z)
```

```
void    glUniform3iv(GLint location, GLsizei count,
                     const GLint* v)
void    glUniform4f(GLint location, GLfloat x, GLfloat y,
                    GLfloat z, GLfloat w);
void    glUniform4fv(GLint location, GLsizei count,
                     const GLfloat* v)
void    glUniform4i(GLint location, GLint x, GLint y,
                    GLint z, GLint w)
void    glUniform4iv(GLint location, GLsizei count,
                     const GLint* v)
void    glUniformMatrix2fv(GLint location, GLsizei count,
                           GLboolean transpose,
                           const GLfloat* value)
void    glUniformMatrix3fv(GLint location, GLsizei count,
                           GLboolean transpose,
                           const GLfloat* value)
void    glUniformMatrix4fv(GLint location, GLsizei count,
                           GLboolean transpose,
                           const GLfloat* value)
```

location	the location of the uniform to load with a value
count	for the functions that take a pointer value, there is also a *count*. The *count* specifies the number of array elements to load from the pointer. For single element uniforms, this value will always be 1. For arrays, it should be the size returned by glGetActiveUniform
transpose	the *transpose* argument for the matrix variants of these functions MUST BE FALSE in OpenGL ES 2.0. This argument was kept for function interface compatibility with desktop OpenGL, but does not function in OpenGL ES 2.0

The functions for loading uniforms are mostly self-explanatory. The determination of which function you need to use for loading the uniform is based on the type returned by the glGetActiveUniform function. For example, if the type is GL_FLOAT_VEC4 then either glUniform4f or glUniform4fv can be used. If the size returned by glGetActiveUniform is greater than one, then glUniform4fv would be used to load the entire array in one call. If the uniform is not an array, then either glUniform4f or glUniform4fv could be used.

One point worth noting here is that the glUniform* calls do not take a program object handle as a parameter. The reason for this is because the glUniform* calls always act on the current program that is bound with glUseProgram. The uniform values themselves will be kept with the program object. That is, once you set a uniform to a value in a program object, that value will remain with it even if you make another program active. In that sense, we can say that uniform values are *local to a program object*.

The block of code in Example 4-3 demonstrates how one would go about querying for uniform information on a program object using the functions we have described.

Example 4-3   Querying for Active Uniforms

```
GLint maxUniformLen;
GLint numUniforms;
char *uniformName;
GLint index;

glGetProgramiv(progObj, GL_ACTIVE_UNIFORMS, &numUniforms);
glGetProgramiv(progObj, GL_ACTIVE_UNIFORM_MAX_LENGTH,
               &maxUniformLen);
uniformName = malloc(sizeof(char) * maxUniformLen);

for(index = 0; index < numUniforms; index++)
{
   GLint size;
   GLenum type;
   GLint location;

   // Get the Uniform Info
   glGetActiveUniform(progObj, index, maxUniformLen, NULL,
                      &size, &type, uniformName);

   // Get the uniform location
   location = glGetUniformLocation(progObj, uniformName);


   switch(type)
   {
   case GL_FLOAT:
      // ...
      break;

   case GL_FLOAT_VEC2:
      // ...
      break;
```

```
case GL_FLOAT_VEC3:
   // ...
   break;

case GL_FLOAT_VEC4:
   // ...
   break;

case GL_INT:
   // ...
   break;

// ... Check for all the types ...

default:
   // Unknown type
   break;
}
}
```

Getting and Setting Attributes

In addition to querying for uniform information on the program object,
you will also need to use the program object to set up vertex attributes. The
queries for vertex attributes are very similar to the uniform queries. You can
find the list of active attributes using the GL_ACTIVE_ATTRIBUTES query.
You can find the properties of an attribute using glGetActiveAttrib.
There are then a set of routines for setting up vertex arrays to load the vertex
attributes with values.

However, setting up vertex attributes really requires a bit more understanding about primitives and the vertex shader than we are ready to explain yet.
As such, we have dedicated a whole chapter (Chapter 6, "Vertex Attributes,
Vertex Arrays, and Buffer Objects") to vertex attributes and vertex arrays. If
you want to jump ahead now to find out how to query for vertex attribute
info, jump to Chapter 6 and the section "Declaring Vertex Attribute Variables in a Vertex Shader."

Shader Compiler and Shader Binaries

As we mentioned earlier in this chapter, our examples thus far have
assumed that we are working with an OpenGL ES 2.0 implementation that
supports online compilation of shader source. That might not always be the

case. In the design of OpenGL ES 2.0, one of the goals was to try to enable implementations of the API on devices with very limited memory. As it turns out, writing a shader compiler (especially a good one) can take quite a bit of code and memory.

When you ask OpenGL ES to compile and link a shader, take a minute to think about what the implementation has to do. The shader code is typically parsed into some sort of intermediate representation as most compiled languages are (e.g., an Abstract Syntax Tree). There then must be a compiler that converts the abstract representation into machine instructions for the hardware. Ideally, this compiler should also do a great deal of optimization such as dead-code removal, constant propagation, and more. Doing all this work comes at a price, and the price is primarily CPU time and memory.

Instead of requiring that all implementations of OpenGL ES 2.0 provide such a compiler, the specification allows an implementation to instead support only binary shaders. The idea behind binary shaders is that the OpenGL ES 2.0 vendor provides an offline tool that can take shader source code and compile it to a binary format that can be consumed by the implementation. There is no standard binary format, so each vendor will have its own set of tools. This obviously means there is less portability, but it also means the vendor can create a less burdensome implementation of OpenGL ES 2.0. In Chapter 15, "OpenGL ES and EGL on Handheld Platforms," we discuss some of the issues with binary shaders and how they are typically generated. For now, we're going to introduce you to the API and how to use it.

First of all, you can determine whether an implementation supports online shader compilation by checking for the value of GL_SHADER_COMPILER using glGetBooleanv. If this value is GL_TRUE, then the implementation supports online shader source compilation. If this value is GL_FALSE, then only binary shaders are supported (more on that next). Given that an online compiler is supported, this means you can specify your shaders using glShaderSource as we have done so far in our examples. There is one thing you can do to try to mitigate the resource impact of shader compilation. Once you are finished compiling any shaders for your application, you can call glReleaseShaderCompiler. This function provides a hint to the implementation that you are done with the shader compiler and it can free its resources. Note that this function is only a hint, if you decide to compile more shaders using glCompileShader, the implementation will need to reallocate its resources for the compiler.

void	**glReleaseShaderCompiler**(void)

Provides a hint to the implementation that it can release resources used by the shader compiler. Because this function is only a hint, some implementation may ignore a call to this function.

Given we have an implementation that supports only binary shaders, the spec says that the implementation will need to support at least one binary format. That said, the OpenGL ES specification does not mandate any particular binary format. In fact, the binary format itself is left completely up to the vendor. The vendor will define its own extension that defines a binary shader format. The code in Example 4-4 demonstrates how you would query whether a shader compiler is available and which binary formats are supported.

Example 4-4   Querying for Whether a Shader Compiler is Available

```
GLboolean shaderCompiler;
GLint numBinaryFormats;
GLint *formats;


// Determine if a shader compiler available
glGetBooleanv(GL_SHADER_COMPILER, &shaderCompiler);

// Determine binary formats available
glGetIntegerv(GL_NUM_SHADER_BINARY_FORMATS, &numBinaryFormats);
formats = malloc(sizeof(GLint) * numBinaryFormats);

glGetIntegerv(GL_SHADER_BINARY_FORMATS, formats);

// "formats" now holds the list of supported binary formats
```

Note that some implementations will support both source and binary shaders. Every implementation must support at least one of the methods. Given that we are using binary shaders (and we have a vendor-defined binary shader token), we can load a binary shader using glShaderBinary.

```
void    glShaderBinary(GLint n, const GLuint* shaders,
                       GLenum binaryFormat,
                       const void* binary, GLint length)
```

n	the number of shader objects in the *shaders* array
shaders	an array of shader object handles. Depending on the specific binary format requirements, this will be either a vertex shader object, a fragment shader object, or both. This is defined by the vendor's shader binary format extension
binaryFormat	the vendor-specific binary format token
binary	pointer to the binary data generated by the offline compiler
length	the number of bytes in the binary data

Some vendors will require both a vertex shader and a fragment shader to be present in the shader binary. Some vendors will allow a binary vertex shader or binary fragment shader to be specified individually and then linked together online. This will be defined in the vendor-specific extension for its binary format. The reason that there are both options is that for some devices providing online linking is an expensive operation. For these implementations, they can require that shader pairs be linked together offline.

Once the shader binary is provided, the shader object can be used for linking in a program object. You can essentially think of a shader specified with binary data as being in the state of a compiled source shader object. The only real difference is that the source shader object will allow you to read back the shader source whereas the binary one will not. Otherwise, they are functionally equivalent. For the purposes of application development, this means you might want to have two code paths for loading shaders: source and binary. Depending on what is supported by the implementation, you will choose one or the other. If you know you will never be working with a platform that does not support online shader compilation, then this is not really necessary. However, for "industrial-strength" applications that will work with any implementation, developing code paths for both source and binary shaders is a good practice. After the shaders' objects are loaded with one or the other and in a compiled state, they can be used interchangeably and the rest of your application can remain the same.

Chapter 5

OpenGL ES Shading Language

As you have seen from Chapter 1, "Introduction to OpenGL ES 2.0," Chapter 2, "Hello, Triangle: An OpenGL ES 2.0 Example," and Chapter 4, "Shaders and Programs," shaders are a fundamental concept that is at the heart of the OpenGL ES 2.0 API. Every OpenGL ES 2.0 program requires both a vertex and fragment shader to render a meaningful picture. Given the centrality of the concept of shaders to the API, we want to make sure you are grounded in the fundamentals of writing shaders before diving into more details of the graphics API.

Our goal in this chapter is to make sure you understand the following concepts in the shading language:

- Variables and variable types
- Vector and matrix construction and selection
- Constants
- Structures and arrays
- Operators, control flow, and functions
- Attributes, uniforms, and varyings
- Preprocessor and directives
- Uniform and varying packing
- Precision qualifiers and invariance

You were introduced to some of these concepts in a small amount of detail with the Hello Triangle example in Chapter 2. Now we are going to fill in the concepts with a lot more detail to make sure you understand how to write and read shaders.

OpenGL ES Shading Language Basics

As you read through this book, you are going to be looking at a lot of shaders. If you ever start developing your own OpenGL ES 2.0 application, chances are you will be writing a lot of shaders. By now, you should understand the fundamental concepts of what a shader does and how it fits in the pipeline. If not, please go back and review Chapter 1, where we covered the pipeline and described where vertex and fragment shaders fit in.

What we want to look at now is what exactly makes up a shader. As you have probably already observed, the syntax bears great similarity to C. If you can understand C code, you likely will not have much difficulty understanding the syntax of shaders. However, there are certainly some major differences between the two languages, beginning with the native data types that are supported.

Variables and Variable Types

In computer graphics, there are two fundamental data types that form the basis of transformations: vectors and matrices. These two data types are central to the OpenGL ES Shading Language as well. Specifically, Table 5-1 describes the scalar-, vector-, and matrix-based data types that exist in the shading language.

Table 5-1   Data Types in the OpenGL ES Shading Language

Variable Class	Types	Description
Scalars	float, int, bool	Scalar-based data types for float-point, integer, and boolean values
Floating-point vectors	float, vec2, vec3, vec4	Floating-point-based vector types of one, two, three, or four components

Table 5-1   Data Types in the OpenGL ES Shading Language *(continued)*

Variable Class	Types	Description
Integer vector	`int, ivec2, ivec3, ivec4`	Integer-based vector types of one, two, three, or four components
Boolean vector	`bool, bvec2, bvec3, bvec4`	Boolean-based vector types of one, two, three, or four components
Matrices	`mat2, mat3, mat4`	Floating-point based matrices of size 2 × 2, 3 × 3, or 4 × 4

Variables in the shading language must be declared with a type. For example, the following declarations are examples of how to declare a scalar, vector, or matrix:

```
float specularAtten;    // A floating-point-based scalar
vec4  vPosition;        // A floating-point-based 4-tuple vector
mat4  mViewProjection;  // A 4 x 4 matrix variable declaration
ivec2 vOffset;          // An integer-based 2-tuple vector
```

Variables can be initialized either at declaration time or later. Initialization is done through the use of constructors, which are also used for doing type conversions.

Variable Constructors

The OpenGL ES Shading Language has very strict rules regarding type conversion. That is, variables can only be assigned to or operated on other variables of the same type. To cope with type conversions, there are a number of constructors available in the language. You can use constructors for initializing variables and as a way of type-casting between variables of different types. Variables can be initialized at declaration (or later in the shader) through the use of constructors. Each of the built-in variable types has a set of associated constructors.

Let's first take a look at how constructors can be used to initialize and type cast between scalar values.

```
float myFloat = 1.0;
bool  myBool = true;
int   myInt = 0;
myFloat = float(myBool); // Convert from bool -> float
```

```
myFloat = float(myInt);   // Convert from int -> float
myBool  = bool(myInt);    // Convert from int -> bool
```

Similarly, constructors can be used to convert to and initialize vector data types. The arguments to a vector constructor will be converted to the same basic type as the vector being constructed (`float`, `int`, or `bool`). There are two basic ways to pass arguments to vector constructors:

- If only one scalar argument is provided to a vector constructor, that value is used to set all values of the vector.

- If multiple scalar or vector arguments are provided, the values of the vector are set from left to right using those arguments. If multiple scalar arguments are provided, there must be at least as many components in the arguments as in the vector.

The following shows some examples of constructing vectors:

```
vec4 myVec4 = vec4(1.0);              // myVec4 = {1.0, 1.0, 1.0, 1.0}
vec3 myVec3 = vec3(1.0, 0.0, 0.5);    // myVec3 = {1.0, 0.0, 0.5}
vec3 temp   = vec3(myVec3);           // temp = myVec3
vec2 myVec2 = vec2(myVec3);           // myVec2 = {myVec3.x, myVec3.y}

myVec4 = vec4(myVec2, temp, 0.0);     // myVec4 = {myVec2.x, myVec2.y,
                                      //           temp, 0.0 }
```

For matrix construction, the language is very flexible. These basic rules describe how matrices can be constructed:

- If only one scalar argument is provided to a matrix constructor, that value is placed in the diagonal of the matrix. For example `mat4(1.0)` will create a 4 × 4 identity matrix.

- A matrix can be constructed out of multiple vector arguments, for example a `mat2` can be constructed from two `vec2`s.

- A matrix can be constructed out of multiple scalar arguments, one for each value in the matrix, consumed from left to right.

The matrix construction is even more flexible than the basic rules just stated in that a matrix can basically be constructed from any combination of scalars and vectors as long as enough components are provided to initialize the matrix. Matrices in OpenGL ES are stored in column major order. When using a matrix constructor, the arguments will be consumed to fill the matrix by column. The comments in the following example show how the matrix constructor arguments will map into columns.

```
mat3 myMat3 = mat3(1.0, 0.0, 0.0,   // First column
                   0.0, 1.0, 0.0,   // Second column
                   0.0, 1.0, 1.0);  // Third column
```

Vector and Matrix Components

The individual components of a vector can be accessed in two ways: either using the "." operator or through array subscripting. Depending on the number of components that make up a given vector, each of the components can be accessed through the use of the swizzles {x, y, z, w}, {r, g, b, a}, or {s, t, r, q}. The reason for the three different naming schemes is that vectors are used interchangeably to represent mathematical vectors, colors, and texture coordinates. The x, r, or s component will always refer to the first element of a vector. The different naming conventions are just provided as a convenience. That said, you cannot mix naming conventions when accessing a vector (in other words, you cannot do something like .xgr, as you can only use one naming convention at a time). When using the "." operator, it is also possible to reorder components of a vector in an operation. The following examples show how this can be done.

```
vec3 myVec3 = vec3(0.0, 1.0, 2.0); // myVec3 = {0.0, 1.0, 2.0}
vec3 temp;

temp = myVec3.xyz;              // temp = {0.0, 1.0, 2.0}
temp = myVec3.xxx;              // temp = {0.0, 0.0, 0.0}
temp = myVec3.zyx;              // temp = {2.0, 1.0, 0.0}
```

In addition to the "." operator, vectors can also be accessed using the array subscript "[]" operator. In array subscripting, element [0] corresponds to x, element [1] corresponds to y, and so forth. One thing you need to be careful of, though, is that if you access a vector with a non-constant integral expression (e.g., using an integer variable index), then this might not be supported in OpenGL ES 2.0. The reason is because doing dynamic indexing on a vector turns out to be a difficult operation for some hardware, so the OpenGL ES 2.0 spec does not mandate support for this behavior except for on a specific variable type (namely, uniform variables). We mention this to you now just to make you aware of the issue, but we cover the full details on this in Chapter 8, "Vertex Shaders," when we discuss the limitations of the shading language.

Matrices are treated as being composed of a number of vectors. For example, a mat2 can be thought of as two vec2s, a mat3 as three vec3s, and so forth. For matrices, the individual column is selected using the array subscript operator " [ ] ", and then each vector can be accessed using the vector access behavior. The following shows some examples of accessing matrices:

```
mat4 myMat4 = mat4(1.0);      // Initialize diagonal to 1.0 (identity)

vec4 col0 = myMat4[0];        // Get col0 vector out of the matrix
float m1_1 = myMat4[1][1];    // Get element at [1][1] in matrix
float m2_2 = myMat4[2].z;     // Get element at [2][2] in matrix
```

Constants

It is possible to declare any of the basic types as being constant variables. Constant variables are those whose values do not change within the shader. Constants are declared by adding the const qualifier to the declaration. Const variables must be initialized at declaration time. Some examples of const declarations follow.

```
const float zero = 0.0;
const float pi = 3.14159;
const vec4 red = vec4(1.0, 0.0, 0.0, 1.0);
const mat4 identity = mat4(1.0);
```

Just as in C or C++, a variable that is declared as const is read-only and cannot be modified within the source.

Structures

In addition to the basic types provided in the language, it is also possible to aggregate variables into structures much like in C. The declaration syntax for a structure in the OpenGL ES Shading Language is shown in the following example.

```
struct fogStruct
{
   vec4  color;
   float start;
   float end;
} fogVar;
```

The preceding definition will result in a new user type fogStruct and a new variable named fogVar. Structures can be initialized using constructors. After defining a new structure type, a new structure constructor is also defined with the same name of the type. There must be a one-to-one correspondence between types in the structure and those in the constructor. For example, the preceding structure could be initialized using the following construction syntax.

```
struct fogStruct
{
    vec4  color;
    float start;
    float end;
} fogVar;

fogVar = fogStruct(vec4(0.0, 1.0, 0.0, 0.0), // color
                   0.5,                       // start
                   2.0);                      // end
```

The constructor for the structure is based on the name of the type and it takes as arguments each of the components. Accessing the elements of a structure is done just as you would a structure in C as shown in the following example.

```
vec4  color = fogVar.color;
float start = fogVar.start;
float end   = fogVar.end;
```

Arrays

In addition to structures, the OpenGL ES Shading Language also supports arrays. The syntax is very similar to C, with the arrays being based on a 0 index. The following block of code shows some examples of creating arrays.

```
float floatArray[4];
vec4  vecArray[2];
```

There are two important things to note about the use of arrays in the OpenGL ES Shading Language. The first is that many OpenGL ES implementations will not allow an array to be indexed with a variable with an unknown value at compile time. That is, OpenGL ES only mandates that array indexing be supported by constant integral expressions (there is an exception to this, which is the indexing of uniform variables in vertex shaders that is discussed in Chapter 8).

The other note about arrays is that there is no syntax in the OpenGL ES Shading Language to initialize an array at creation time. The elements of the array need to be initialized one-by-one and also arrays cannot be const qualified because there is no syntax for initializing such an array.

These restrictions might at first sound odd to a programmer familiar with C, but the limitations are based on the underlying hardware support for array indexing. It turns out that many GPUs are only built with support for indexing constants (not registers) and this makes it difficult for arbitrary indexing on arrays to be supported.

Operators

Table 5-2 provides a list of the operators that are offered in the OpenGL ES Shading Language.

Table 5-2   OpenGL ES Shading Language Operators

Operator Type	Description
*	Multiply
/	Divide
+	Add
–	Subtract
++	Increment (prefix and postfix)
– –	Decrement (prefix and postfix)
=	Assignment
+=, –=, *=, /=	Arithmetic assignment
==, !=, <, >, <=, >=	Comparison operators
&&	Logical and
^^	Logical exclusive or
||	Logical inclusive or

Most of these operators behave just as you are used to in C. As mentioned in the constructor section, the OpenGL ES Shading Language has very strict type rules between operators. That is, the operators must occur between variables that have the same basic type. For the binary operators (*, /, +, –) the basic types of the variables must be floating point or integer. Furthermore, operators such as multiply can operate between combinations of floats, vectors, and matrices. Some examples are provided here.

```
float myFloat;
vec4   myVec4;
mat4   myMat4;

myVec4 = myVec4 * myFloat;   // Multiplies each component of myVec4
                             // by a scalar myFloat
myVec4 = myVec4 * myVec4;    // Multiplies each component of myVec4
                             // together (e.g., myVec4 ^ 2 )
myVec4 = myMat4 * myVec4;    // Does a matrix * vector multiply of
                             // myMat4 * myVec4
myMat4 = myMat4 * myMat4;    // Does a matrix * matrix multiply of
                             // myMat4 * myMat4
myMat4 = myMat4 * myFloat;   // Multiplies each matrix component by
                             // the scalar myFloat
```

The comparison operators (==, !=, <, etc.) can only be performed on scalar values. To compare vectors, there are special built-in functions that allow you to do comparisons (more on that later).

Functions

Functions are declared in much the same way as C. If a function is going to be used prior to its definition, then a prototype declaration must be provided. In general, functions work much as you are used to in C. The most significant difference is the way in which parameters are passed to functions. The OpenGL ES Shading Language provides special qualifiers to define whether a variable argument can be modified by the function. These qualifiers are shown in Table 5-3.

Table 5-3   OpenGL ES Shading Language Qualifiers

Qualifier	Description
in	(Default if none specified) This qualifier specifies that the parameter is passed by value and will not be modified by the function.
inout	This qualifier specifies that the variable is passed by reference into the function and if its value is modified it will be changed after function exit.
out	This qualifier says that the variable's value is not passed into the function, but it will be modified on return from the function.

An example function declaration is provided here. This example shows the use of parameter qualifiers.

```
vec4 myFunc(inout float myFloat,  // inout parameter
            out vec4 myVec4,      // out parameter
            mat4 myMat4);         // in parameter (default)
```

An example function definition is given here for a simple function that computes basic diffuse lighting.

```
vec4 diffuse(vec3 normal,
             vec3 light,
             vec4 baseColor)
{
    return baseColor * dot(normal, light);
}
```

One note about functions in the OpenGL ES Shading Language is that functions cannot be recursive. The reason for this limitation is that some implementations will implement function calls by actually making the function code inline in the final generated program for the GPU. The shading language was purposely structured to allow this sort of an inline implementation to enable GPUs that do not have a stack and flow control.

Built-In Functions

The preceding section described how a shader author creates a function. One of the most powerful features of the OpenGL ES Shading Language is the built-in functions that are provided in the language. As an example, here is some shader code for computing basic specular lighting in a fragment shader.

```
float nDotL = dot(normal , light);
float rDotV = dot(viewDir, (2.0 * normal) * nDotL - light);
float specular = specularColor * pow(rDotV, specularPower);
```

As you can see, this block of shader code use the dot built-in function to compute the dot product between two vectors and the pow built-in function to raise a scalar to a power. These are just two simple examples; there is a wide array of built-in functions in the OpenGL ES Shading Language for various computational tasks that one typically has to do in a shader. In Appendix B we provide a complete reference to the built-in functions provided in the OpenGL ES Shading Language. For now, we just want to make you aware that there are a lot of built-in functions in the language and to be proficient in writing shaders you are going to want to familiarize yourself with the most common ones.

Control Flow Statements

The syntax for control flow statements in the OpenGL ES Shading Language is similar to C. Simple if-then-else logical tests can be done using the same syntax as C. For example:

```
if(color.a < 0.25)
{
    color *= color.a;
}
else
{
    color = vec4(0.0);
}
```

The expression that is being tested in the conditional statement must evaluate to a boolean. That is, the test must either be based on a boolean value or some expression that evaluates to a boolean (e.g., a comparison operator). This is the basics of how conditionals can be expressed in the OpenGL ES Shading Language.

In addition to basic if-then-else statements, it is also possible to write simple for loops. There are a variety of restrictions placed on the types of loops supported in the OpenGL ES Shading Language. These restrictions have to do with the expected limitations of some of the OpenGL ES 2.0 hardware devices. To boil it down to its simplest form, for loops in OpenGL ES must have an iteration count that is known at compile time. An example of a for loop that would be supported in OpenGL ES is shown here.

```
for(int i = 0; i < 3; i++)
{
    sum += i;
}
```

You should generally tread with caution when using loops in OpenGL ES. The basic restrictions are as follows: there must be only one loop iteration variable and it must be incremented or decremented using a simple statement (i++, i--, i+=constant, i-=constant); the stop condition must be a comparison between the loop index and a constant expression; and you must not change the value of the iterator in the loop. Essentially, the OpenGL ES Shading Language does not require hardware to provide looping support.

Rather, it restricts the loops that can be expressed to those that can be unrolled by the compiler.

Some examples of loops that would not be supported in OpenGL ES are given here.

```
float myArr[4];
for(int i = 0; i < 3; i++)
{
    sum += myArr[i]; // NOT ALLOWED IN OPENGL ES, CANNOT DO
                     // INDEXING WITH NONCONSTANT EXPRESSION
}

...

uniform int loopIter;

// NOT ALLOWED IN OPENGL ES, loopIter ITERATION COUNT IS NONCONSTANT
for(int i = 0; i < loopIter; i++)
{
    sum += i;
}
```

These restrictions on loops might seem quite odd to a programmer used to the flexibility provided by CPUs. However, remember that OpenGL ES is an API for embedded systems and the specification authors intended to enable GPUs to use small area and power budgets. Flow control and looping tends to be a difficult operation for GPUs, so these restrictions on loops allow for simplified GPU implementations. These sorts of restrictions are also common on older generation desktop GPUs such as the ATI Radeon 9500, which did not support loops in the fragment shader.

Uniforms

One of the variable type modifiers in the OpenGL ES Shading Language is the uniform variable. Uniform variables are variables that store read-only values that are passed in by the application through the OpenGL ES 2.0 API to the shader. Uniforms are useful for storing all kinds of data that shaders need, such as transformation matrices, light parameters, or colors. Basically, any parameter to a shader that is constant across either all vertices or fragments (but that is not known at compile time) should be passed in as a uniform.

Uniform variables are declared at the global scope and simply require the uniform qualifier. Some examples of uniform variables are shown here.

```
uniform mat4 viewProjMatrix;
uniform mat4 viewMatrix;
uniform vec3 lightPosition;
```

In Chapter 4, we described how an application loads uniform variables to a shader. Note also that the namespace for uniform variables is shared across both a vertex and a fragment shader. That is, if a vertex and fragment shader are linked together into a program object, they share the same set of uniform variables. Therefore, if a uniform variable is declared in the vertex shader and also in the fragment shader, its declaration must match. When the application loads the uniform variable through the API, its value will be available in both the vertex and fragment shaders.

Another note about uniforms is that uniform variables generally are stored in hardware into what is known as the "constant store." This is a special space allocated in the hardware for the storage of constant values. Because this storage is typically of a fixed size, there is a limit on the number of uniforms that can be used in a program. This limitation can be determined by reading the value of the `gl_MaxVertexUniformVectors` and `gl_MaxFragmentUniformVectors` built-in variables (or by querying `GL_MAX_VERTEX_UNIFORM_VECTORS` or `GL_MAX_FRAGMENT_UNIFORM_VECTORS` using `glGetIntegerv`). An implementation of OpenGL ES 2.0 must provide at least 128 vertex uniform vectors and 16 fragment uniform vectors, although it is free to provide more. We cover the full set of limitations and queries available for the vertex and fragment shaders in Chapter 8, "Vertex Shaders," and Chapter 10, "Fragment Shaders."

Attributes

Another special variable type in the OpenGL ES Shading Language is the attribute variable. Attribute variables are available only in the vertex shader and are used to specify the per-vertex inputs to the vertex shader. Attributes typically store data such as positions, normals, texture coordinates, and colors. The key here to understand is that attributes are data that are specified for each vertex being drawn. It is really up to the user of the shader to determine what data belongs in the attributes. Example 5-1 is a sample vertex shader that has a position and texture coordinate attribute.

Example 5-1   Sample Vertex Shader

```
uniform mat4 u_matViewProjection;
attribute vec4 a_position;
attribute vec2 a_texCoord0;
varying vec2 v_texCoord;

void main(void)
{
    gl_Position = u_matViewProjection * a_position;
    v_texCoord = a_texCoord0;
}
```

The two vertex attributes in this shader a_position and a_texCoord0 will be loaded with data by the application. Essentially, the application will create a vertex array that contains a position and a texture coordinate for each vertex. We explain this process in full detail in Chapter 6, "Vertex Attributes, Vertex Arrays, and Buffer Objects." For now, just make sure you understand that attributes are the per-vertex inputs to the vertex shader.

As with uniform variables, the underlying hardware typically has limits on the number of attribute variables that can be input to a vertex shader. The maximum number of attributes that an implementation supports is given by the gl_MaxVertexAttribs built-in variable (or by querying for GL_MAX_VERTEX_ATTRIBS using glGetIntegerv). The minimum number of attributes that an OpenGL ES 2.0 implementation can support is eight. Implementations are free to support more, but if you want to write shaders that are guaranteed to run on any OpenGL ES 2.0 implementation you should restrict yourself to using no more than eight attributes. We cover attribute limitations in more detail in Chapter 8.

Varyings

The final variable type modifier in the OpenGL ES Shading Language that we describe is a varying. Varying variables are used to store the output of the vertex shader and also the input of a fragment shader. Basically, each vertex shader will output the data it needs to pass the fragment shader into one or more varying variables. These variables will then also be declared in the fragment shader (with matching types) and will be linearly interpolated across the primitive during rasterization (if you want more details on how this interpolation occurs during rasterization, jump to Chapter 6 on rasterization).

Some examples of varying declarations are as follows:

```
varying vec2 texCoord;
varying vec4 color;
```

The varying declarations will be put in both the vertex and fragment shader. As mentioned, the varyings are the output of the vertex shader and input to the fragment shader, so they must be declared identically. As with uniforms and attributes, the underlying hardware typically has a limit to the number of varyings (on the hardware, these are usually referred to as interpolators). The number of varyings supported by an implementation is given by the gl_MaxVaryingVectors built-in variable (or by querying for GL_MAX_VARYING_VECTORS using glGetIntegerv). The minimum number of varying vectors that an implementation of OpenGL ES 2.0 can support is eight.

Example 5-2 is a sample of a vertex shader and a fragment shader with matching varying declarations.

Example 5-2   Vertex and Fragment Shader with Matching Varying Declarations

```
// Vertex shader
uniform mat4 u_matViewProjection;
attribute vec4 a_position;
attribute vec2 a_texCoord0;
varying vec2 v_texCoord; // Varying in vertex shader

void main(void)
{
   gl_Position = u_matViewProjection * a_position;
   v_texCoord = a_texCoord0;
}

// Fragment shader
precision mediump float;
varying vec2 v_texCoord; // Varying in fragment shader

uniform sampler2D s_baseMap;
uniform sampler2D s_lightMap;
void main()
{
   vec4 baseColor;
   vec4 lightColor;

   baseColor = texture2D(s_baseMap, v_texCoord);
   lightColor = texture2D(s_lightMap, v_texCoord);
   gl_FragColor = baseColor * (lightColor + 0.25);
}
```

Preprocessor and Directives

One feature of the OpenGL ES Shading Language we have not mentioned yet is the preprocessor. The OpenGL ES Shading Language features a preprocessor that follows many of the conventions of a standard C++ preprocessor. Macros can be defined and conditional tests can be performed using the following directives:

```
#define
#undef
#if
#ifdef
#ifndef
#else
#elif
#endif
```

Note that macros cannot be defined with parameters (as they can be in C++ macros). The #if, #else, and #elif can use the defined test to see whether a macro is defined. The following macros are predefined and their description is given next:

```
__LINE__      // Replaced with the current line number in a shader
__FILE__      // Always 0 in OpenGL ES 2.0
__VERSION__   // The OpenGL ES shading language version (e.g., 100)
GL_ES         // This will be defined for ES shaders to a value of 1
```

The #error directive will cause a compilation error to occur during shader compilation with a message placed in the info log. The #pragma directive is used to specify implementation-specific directives to the compiler.

A new directive (not in C++) that was added to the preprocessor is #version. For OpenGL ES 2.0 shaders, this value should be set to 100. This directive sets the shader version with which the shader should be compiled. The purpose of this directive is that when future versions of the API add new features to the shading language, the version token can be used to make sure a shader is compiled to the language version it is written against. This token must occur at the beginning of the source code. The following shows the proper usage of the #version directive:

```
#version 100 // OpenGL ES Shading Language v1.00
```

Another important directive in the preprocessor is `#extension`, which is used to enable and set the behavior of extensions. When vendors (or groups of vendors) extend the OpenGL ES Shading Language, they will create a language extension specification (e.g., `GL_OES_texture_3D`). The shader must instruct the compiler whether or not to allow extensions to be used, and if not, what behavior should occur. This is done using the `#extension` directive. The general format of `#extension` usage is shown in the following code.

```
// Set behavior for an extension
#extension extension_name : behavior
// Set behavior for ALL extensions
#extension all : behavior
```

The first argument will be either the name of the extension (e.g., `GL_OES_texture_3D`) or `all`, which means that the behavior applies to all extensions. The behavior has four possible options, as shown in Table 5-4.

Table 5-4   Extension Behaviors

Extension Behavior	Description
require	The extension is required, so the preprocessor will throw an error if the extension is not supported. If `all` is specified, this will always throw an error.
enable	The extension is enabled, so the preprocessor will warn if the extension is not supported. The language will be processed as if the extension is enabled. If `all` is specified, this will always throw an error.
warn	Warn on any use of the extension, unless that use is required by another enabled extension. If `all` is specified, there will be a warning thrown whenever the extension is used. Also, a warning will be thrown if the extension is not supported.
disable	The extension is disabled, so errors will be thrown if the extension is used. If `all` is specified (this is specified by default), no extensions are enabled.

As an example, if you want the preprocessor to produce a warning if the 3D texture extension is not supported (and the shader to be processed as if it is supported), you would add the following at the top of your shader:

```
#extension GL_OES_texture_3D : enable
```

Uniform and Varying Packing

As noted in the preceding sections on uniforms and varyings, there is a fixed number of underlying hardware resources available for the storage of each variable. Uniforms are typically stored in what is known as the constant store, which can be thought of as a physical array of vectors. Varyings are typically stored in interpolators, which again are usually stored as an array of vectors. As you've probably noticed, shaders can declare uniforms and varyings of various types including scalars, various vector components, and matrices. The question arises of how these various variable declarations map to the physical space that's available on the hardware. In other words, if an OpenGL ES 2.0 implementation says it supports eight varying vectors, how does the physical storage actually get used?

The way that this is handled in OpenGL ES 2.0 is that there are packing rules that define how the varyings and uniforms will map to physical storage space. The rules for packing are based on the notion that the physical storage space is organized into a grid with four columns (one column for each vector component) and a row for each storage location. The packing rules seek to pack variables such that the complexity of the generated code will remain constant. In other words, the packing rules will not do reordering that will require the compiler to generate extra instructions to merge unpacked data. Rather, the packing rules seek to optimize the use of the physical address space without negatively impacting runtime performance.

Let's take a look at an example group of uniform declarations and how these would be packed.

```
uniform mat3 m;
uniform float f[6];
uniform vec3 v;
```

If no packing were done at all, you can see that a lot of constant storage space would be wasted. The matrix m would take up three rows, the array f would take up six rows, and the vector v would take up one row. This would use a total of 10 rows to store the variables. Figure 5-1 shows what the results would be without any packing.

With the packing rules, the variables will get organized such that they pack into the grid as shown in Figure 5-2.

With the packing rules, only six physical constant locations need to be used. You will notice that the array f needs to keep its elements spanning across row boundaries. The reason for this is because typically GPUs index the constant store by vector location index. The packing must keep the arrays spanning across row boundaries so that indexing will still work.

Location	X	Y	Z	W
0	M[0].x	m[0].y	m[0].z	-
1	M[1].x	m[1].y	m[1].z	-
2	M[2].x	m[2].y	m[2].z	-
3	f[0]	-	-	-
4	f[1]	-	-	-
5	f[2]	-	-	-
6	f[3]	-	-	-
7	f[4]	-	-	-
8	f[5]	-	-	-
9	v.x	v.y	v.z	-6

Figure 5-1   Uniform Storage without Packing

Location	X	Y	Z	W
0	M[0].x	m[0].y	m[0].z	f[0]
1	M[1].x	m[1].y	m[1].z	f[1]
2	M[2].x	m[2].y	m[2].z	f[2]
3	v.x	v.y	v.z	f[3]
4	-	-	-	f[4]
5	-	-	-	f[5]

Figure 5-2   Uniform Storage with Packing

All of the packing that is done is completely transparent to the user of the OpenGL ES Shading Language except for one detail: it impacts the way in which uniforms and varyings are counted. If you want to write shaders that are guaranteed to run on all implementations of OpenGL ES 2.0, you should not use more uniforms or varyings than would exceed the minimum allowed storage sizes after packing. For this reason, it's important to be aware of packing so that you can write portable shaders that will not exceed the minimum allowed storage on any implementation of OpenGL ES 2.0.

Precision Qualifiers

One notable new feature addition to OpenGL ES that differs from desktop OpenGL is the introduction of precision qualifiers to the shading language. Precision qualifiers enable the shader author to specify the precision with which computations for a shader variable are performed. Variables can be declared to have either low, medium, or high precision. These qualifiers are used as hints to the compiler to allow it to perform computations with variables at a potentially lower range and precision. It is possible that at lower precisions, some implementations of OpenGL ES might either be able to run the shaders faster or with better power efficiency. Of course, that efficiency savings comes at the cost of precision, which can result in artifacts if precision qualifiers are not used properly. Note that there is nothing in the OpenGL ES specification that says that multiple precisions must be supported in the underlying hardware, so it is perfectly valid for an implementation of OpenGL ES to do all calculations at the highest precision and simply ignore the qualifiers. However, on some implementations using a lower precision might be an advantage.

Precision qualifiers can be used to specify the precision of any float or integer-based variable. The keywords for specifying the precision are `lowp`, `mediump`, and `highp`. Some examples of declarations with precision qualifiers are shown here.

```
highp vec4 position;
varying lowp vec4 color;
mediump float specularExp;
```

In addition to precision qualifiers, there is also the notion of default precision. That is, if a variable is declared without having a precision qualifier, it will have the default precision for that type. The default precision qualifier is specified at the top of a vertex or fragment shader using the following syntax:

```
precision highp float;
precision mediump int;
```

The precision specified for `float` will be used as the default precision for all variables based on a floating-point value. Likewise, the precision specified for `int` will be used as the default precision for all integer-based variables.

In the vertex shader, if no default precision is specified, then the default precision for int and float is both highp. That is, all variables declared without a precision qualifier in a vertex shader will have the highest precision. The rules for the fragment shader are different. In the fragment shader, there is no default precision given for floats: Every shader must declare a default float precision or specify the precision for every float variable. In addition, OpenGL ES 2.0 does not require that an implementation support high precision in the fragment shader. The way to determine whether high precision is supported in the fragment shader is whether the GL_FRAGMENT_ PRECISION_HIGH preprocessor macro is defined (in addition, the implementation will export the OES_fragment_precision_high extension string).

In this book we often include the following code at the top of a fragment shader:

```
#ifdef GL_FRAGMENT_PRECISION_HIGH
    precision highp float;
#else
    precision mediump float;
#endif
```

This makes sure that whether the implementation supports medium or high precision, the shader will compile.

One final note is that the precision specified by a precision qualifier has an implementation-dependent range and precision. There is an associated API call for determining the range and precision for a given implementation, which is covered in Chapter 14, "State Queries."

Invariance

The final topic we'll discuss in the shading language is invariance. There is a keyword introduced in the OpenGL ES Shading Language invariant that can be applied to any varying output of a vertex shader. What do we mean by invariance and why is this necessary? The issue is that shaders are compiled and the compiler might perform optimizations that cause instructions to be reordered. This instruction reordering means that equivalent calculations between two shaders are not guaranteed to produce exactly identical results. This can be an issue in particular for multipass shader effects where the same object is being drawn on top of itself using alpha blending. If the precision of the values used to compute the output position are not exactly identical, then artifacts can exist due to the precision differences. This usually manifests itself as Z fighting, or when small Z precision differences per pixel cause the different passes to shimmer against each other.

The following example demonstrates visually why invariance is important to get right when doing multipass shading. The following torus object is drawn in two passes: The fragment shader computes specular lighting in the first pass and ambient and diffuse lighting in the second pass. The vertex shaders do not use invariance so small precision differences cause the Z fighting as shown in Figure 5-3.

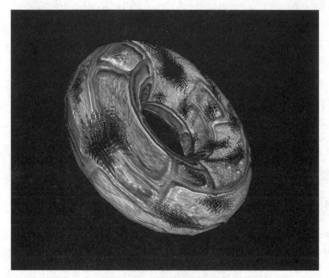

Figure 5-3   Z Fighting Artifacts Due to Not Using Invariance

The same multipass vertex shaders using invariance for position produce the correct image in Figure 5-4.

The introduction of invariance gives the shader writer a way to specify that if the same computations are used to compute an output, its value must be *exactly* the same (or invariant). The `invariant` keyword can be used either on varying declarations or for varyings that have already been declared. Some examples follow.

```
invariant gl_Position;
invariant varying texCoord;
```

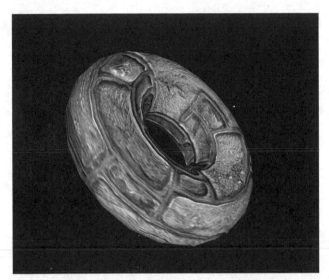

Figure 5-4   Z Fighting Avoided Using Invariance

Once invariance is declared for an output, the compiler guarantees that the results will be the same given the same computations and inputs into the shader. For example, given you have two vertex shaders that compute output position by multiplying the view projection matrix by the input position, you are guaranteed that those positions will be invariant.

```
uniform mat4 u_viewProjMatrix;
attribute vec4 a_vertex;
invariant gl_Position;
void main
{
   // …
   gl_Position = u_viewProjMatrix * a_vertex; // Will be the same
                                              // value in all
                                              // shaders with the
                                              // same viewProjMatrix
                                              // and vertex
}
```

It is also possible to make all variables globally invariant using a `#pragma` directive.

```
#pragma STDGL invariant(all)
```

One word of caution: Because the compiler needs to guarantee invariance, it might have to limit the optimizations it does. Therefore, the invariant qualifier should be used only when necessary; otherwise it might result in performance degradation. For this reason, the #pragma to globally enable invariance should only be used when invariance is really required for all variables. Note also that while invariance does imply that the calculation will have the same results on a given GPU, it does not mean that the computation would be invariant across any implementation of OpenGL ES.

Vertex Attributes, Vertex Arrays, and Buffer Objects

This chapter describes how vertex attributes and data are specified in OpenGL ES 2.0. We discuss what vertex attributes are, how to specify them and their supported data formats, and how to bind vertex attribute indices to the appropriate vertex attribute names used in a vertex shader. After reading this chapter, you should have a good grasp of what vertex attributes are and how to draw primitives with vertex attributes in OpenGL ES 2.0.

Vertex data, also referred to as vertex attributes, specify per-vertex data. This per-vertex data can be specified for each vertex or a constant value can be used for all vertices. For example, if you want to draw a triangle that has a solid color (for the sake of this example say the color is black as shown in Figure 6-1), you would specify a constant value that will be used by all three vertices of the triangle. However, the position of the three vertices that make up the triangle will not be the same and therefore we will need to specify a vertex array that stores three position values.

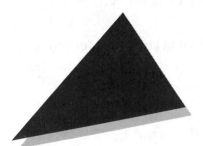

Figure 6-1   Triangle with a Constant Color Vertex and Per-Vertex Position Attributes

In OpenGL ES 1.1, vertex attributes had predefined names such as *position, normal, color,* and *texture coordinates*. This was acceptable because the fixed function pipeline implemented by OpenGL ES 1.1 only required these predefined vertex attributes. With a programmable pipeline, developers need to be able to specify their own vertex attribute names used in vertex shaders. Support for user-defined (i.e., generic) vertex attributes therefore became a requirement for OpenGL ES 2.0. If generic vertex attributes are supported by the API then there is no longer a need to support predefined vertex attribute names because they can be mapped by the application to one of the generic vertex attributes.

Specifying Vertex Attribute Data

As mentioned before, only generic vertex attributes are supported by OpenGL ES 2.0. The attribute data can be specified for each vertex using a vertex array or it can be a constant value that is used for all vertices of a primitive.

All OpenGL ES 2.0 implementations must support a minimum of eight vertex attributes. An application can query the exact number of vertex attributes that are supported by a particular implementation, which might be greater than eight. The following code describes how an application can query the number of vertex attributes an implementation actually supports.

```
GLint maxVertexAttribs;    // n will be >= 8
glGetIntegerv(GL_MAX_VERTEX_ATTRIBS, &maxVertexAttribs);
```

Constant Vertex Attribute

A constant vertex attribute is the same for all vertices of a primitive, and therefore only one value needs to be specified for all the vertices of a primitive.

A constant vertex attribute value is specified using any of the following functions:

```
void glVertexAttrib1f(GLuint index, GLfloat x);
void glVertexAttrib2f(GLuint index, GLfloat x, GLfloat y);
void glVertexAttrib3f(GLuint index, GLfloat x, GLfloat y, GLfloat z);
void glVertexAttrib4f(GLuint index, GLfloat x, GLfloat y, GLfloat z,
                      GLfloat w);
```

```
void glVertexAttrib1fv(GLuint index, const GLfloat *values);
void glVertexAttrib2fv(GLuint index, const GLfloat *values);
void glVertexAttrib3fv(GLuint index, const GLfloat *values);
void glVertexAttrib4fv(GLuint index, const GLfloat *values);
```

The glVertexAttrib* commands are used to load the generic vertex attribute specified by index. glVertexAttrib1f and glVertexAttrib1fv load (x, 0.0, 0.0, 1.0) into the generic vertex attribute. glVertexAttrib2f and glVertexAttrib2fv load (x, y, 0.0, 1.0) into the generic vertex attribute. glVertexAttrib3f and glVertexAttrib3fv load (x, y, z, 1.0) into the generic vertex attribute. glVertexAttrib4f and glVertexAttrib4fv load (x, y, z, w) into the generic vertex attribute.

A question arises: OpenGL version 2.0 and higher supports functions that specify the constant vertex attribute data as byte, unsigned byte, short, unsigned short, int, unsigned int, float, and double. Why does OpenGL ES 2.0 only support the float variant? The reason for this is that constant vertex attributes are not used that frequently. Because their use is infrequent, and because they will most likely be stored as single precision floating-point values internally, ES 2.0 only supports the float variant.

Vertex Arrays

Vertex arrays specify attribute data per vertex and are buffers stored in the application's address space (what OpenGL ES calls the *client* space). They provide an efficient and flexible way for specifying vertex attribute data. Vertex arrays are specified using the glVertexAttribPointer function.

void	**glVertexAttribPointer**(GLuint *index*, GLint *size*, GLenum *type*, GLboolean *normalized*, GLsizei *stride*, const void **ptr*)
index	specifies the generic vertex attribute index. This value is 0 to max vertex attributes supported – 1
size	number of components specified in the vertex array for the vertex attribute referenced by index. Valid values are 1–4

type	data format. Valid values are: GL_BYTE GL_UNSIGNED_BYTE GL_SHORT GL_UNSIGNED_SHORT GL_FLOAT GL_FIXED GL_HALF_FLOAT_OES*
normalized	is used to indicate whether the non-floating data format type should be normalized or not when converted to floating point
stride	the components of vertex attribute specified by size are stored sequentially for each vertex. *stride* specifies the delta between data for vertex index I and vertex (I + 1). If *stride* is 0, attribute data for all vertices are stored sequentially. If *stride* is > 0, then we use the stride value as the pitch to get vertex data for next index
ptr	Pointer to the buffer holding vertex attribute data

* GL_HALF_FLOAT_OES is an optional vertex data format supported by OpenGL ES 2.0. The extension string that implements this vertex data format is named GL_OES_vertex_half_float. To determine whether this feature is supported by an OpenGL ES 2.0 implementation, look for the string name GL_OES_vertex_half_float in the list of extensions returned by glGetString(GL_EXTENSIONS).

We present a few examples that illustrate how to specify vertex attributes with glVertexAttribPointer. The commonly used methods for allocating and storing vertex attribute data are:

- Store vertex attributes together in a single buffer. This method of storing vertex attributes is called an *array of structures*. The structure represents all attributes of a vertex and we have an array of these attributes per vertex.

- Store each vertex attribute in a separate buffer. This method of storing vertex attributes is called *structure of arrays*.

Let us say that each vertex has four vertex attributes—position, normal, and two texture coordinates—and that these attributes are stored together in one buffer that is allocated for all vertices. The vertex position attribute is specified as a vector of three floats (x, y, z), the vertex normal is also specified as a vector of three floats, and each texture coordinate is specified as a vector of two floats. Figure 6-2 gives the memory layout of this buffer.

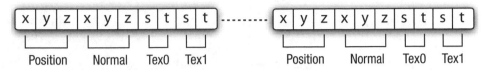

Figure 6-2   Position, Normal, and Two Texture Coordinates Stored As an Array

Example 6-1 describes how these four vertex attributes are specified with `glVertexAttribPointer`.

Example 6-1   Array of Structures

```
#define VERTEX_POS_SIZE          3   // x, y and z
#define VERTEX_NORMAL_SIZE       3   // x, y and z
#define VERTEX_TEXCOORD0_SIZE    2   // s and t
#define VERTEX_TEXCOORD1_SIZE    2   // s and t

#define VERTEX_POS_INDX          0
#define VERTEX_NORMAL_INDX       1
#define VERTEX_TEXCOORD0_INDX    2
#define VERTEX_TEXCOORD1_INDX    3

// the following 4 defines are used to determine location of various
// attributes if vertex data is are stored as an array of structures
#define VERTEX_POS_OFFSET        0
#define VERTEX_NORMAL_OFFSET     3
#define VERTEX_TEXCOORD0_OFFSET  6
#define VERTEX_TEXCOORD1_OFFSET  8

#define VERTEX_ATTRIB_SIZE     VERTEX_POS_SIZE + \
                               VERTEX_NORMAL_SIZE + \
                               VERTEX_TEXCOORD0_SIZE + \
                               VERTEX_TEXCOORD1_SIZE

float *p  = malloc(numVertices * VERTEX_ATTRIB_SIZE
                 * sizeof(float));

// position is vertex attribute 0
glVertexAttribPointer(VERTEX_POS_INDX, VERTEX_POS_SIZE,
                      GL_FLOAT, GL_FALSE,
                      VERTEX_ATTRIB_SIZE * sizeof(float),
                      p);
```

```
// normal is vertex attribute 1
glVertexAttribPointer(VERTEX_NORMAL_INDX, VERTEX_NORMAL_SIZE,
                      GL_FLOAT, GL_FALSE,
                      VERTEX_ATTRIB_SIZE * sizeof(float),
                      (p +  VERTEX_NORMAL_OFFSET));

// texture coordinate 0 is vertex attribute 2
glVertexAttribPointer(VERTEX_TEXCOORD0_INDX, VERTEX_TEXCOORD0_SIZE,
                      GL_FLOAT, GL_FALSE,
                      VERTEX_ATTRIB_SIZE * sizeof(float),
                      (p +  VERTEX_TEXCOORD0_OFFSET));

// texture coordinate 1 is vertex attribute 3
glVertexAttribPointer(VERTEX_TEXCOORD1_INDX, VERTEX_TEXCOORD1_SIZE,
                      GL_FLOAT, GL_FALSE,
                      VERTEX_ATTRIB_SIZE * sizeof(float),
                      (p + VERTEX_TEXCOORD1_OFFSET));
```

In Example 6-2 that follows, position, normal, and texture coordinate 0 and 1 are stored in separate buffers.

Example 6-2   Structure of Arrays

```
float *position  = malloc(numVertices * VERTEX_POS_SIZE *
                          sizeof(float));
float *normal     = malloc(numVertices * VERTEX_NORMAL_SIZE *
                          sizeof(float));
float *texcoord0 = malloc(numVertices * VERTEX_TEXCOORD0_SIZE *
                          sizeof(float));
float *texcoord1 = malloc(numVertices * VERTEX_TEXCOORD1_SIZE *
                          sizeof(float));

// position is vertex attribute 0
glVertexAttribPointer(VERTEX_POS_INDX, VERTEX_POS_SIZE,
                      GL_FLOAT, GL_FALSE,
                      VERTEX_POS_SIZE * sizeof(float), position);

// normal is vertex attribute 1
glVertexAttribPointer(VERTEX_NORMAL_INDX, VERTEX_NORMAL_SIZE,
                      GL_FLOAT, GL_FALSE,
                      VERTEX_NORMAL_SIZE * sizeof(float), normal);

// texture coordinate 0 is vertex attribute 2
glVertexAttribPointer(VERTEX_TEXCOORD0_INDX, VERTEX_TEXCOORD0_SIZE,
                      GL_FLOAT, GL_FALSE, VERTEX_TEXCOORD0_SIZE *
                      sizeof(float), texcoord0);
```

```
// texture coordinate 1 is vertex attribute 3
glVertexAttribPointer(VERTEX_TEXCOORD1_INDX, VERTEX_TEXCOORD1_SIZE,
                      GL_FLOAT, GL_FALSE,
                      VERTEX_TEXCOORD1_SIZE * sizeof(float),
                      texcoord1);
```

Performance Hints

How to store different attributes of a vertex

We described the two most common ways of storing vertex attributes—
array of structures and *structure of arrays*. The question to ask is which allocation method would be the most efficient for OpenGL ES 2.0 hardware
implementations. The answer is *array of structures*. The reason is that the
attribute data for each vertex can be read in sequential fashion and so will
most likely result in an efficient memory access pattern. A disadvantage of
using array of structures is when an application wants to modify specific
attributes. If a subset of vertex attribute data needs to be modified (e.g., texture coordinates), this will result in strided updates to the vertex buffer.
When vertex buffer is supplied as a buffer object, the entire vertex attribute
buffer will need to be reloaded. One can avoid this inefficiency by storing
vertex attributes that are dynamic in nature in a separate buffer.

Which data format to use for vertex attributes

The vertex attribute data format specified by the `type` argument in
`glVertexAttribPointer` cannot only impact the graphics memory
storage requirements for vertex attribute data, but can also impact the
overall performance, which is a function of memory bandwidth required to
render the frame(s). The smaller the data footprint, the lower the memory
bandwidth required. Our recommendation is that applications should use
`GL_HALF_FLOAT_OES` wherever possible. Texture coordinates, normals,
binormals, tangent vectors, and so on are good candidates to be stored
using `GL_HALF_FLOAT_OES` for each component. Color could be stored as
`GL_UNSIGNED_BYTE` with four components per vertex color. We also recommend `GL_HALF_FLOAT_OES` for vertex position, but recognize that this
might not be possible for quite a few cases. For such cases, the vertex position could be stored as `GL_FLOAT` or `GL_FIXED`.

How the Normalized Flag in glVertexAttribPointer Works

Vertex attributes are internally stored as a single precision floating-point number before they get used in a vertex shader. If the data *type* indicates that the vertex attribute is not a float, then the vertex attribute will be converted to a single precision floating-point number before it gets used in a vertex shader. The *normalized* flag controls the conversion of the nonfloat vertex attribute data to a single precision floating-point value. If the *normalized* flag is false, the vertex data is converted directly to a floating-point value. This would be similar to casting the variable that is not a float type to float. The following code gives an example.

```
GLfloat   f;
GLbyte    b;
f = (GLfloat)b;  // f represents values in the range [-128.0, 127.0]
```

If the *normalized* flag is true, the vertex data is mapped to the [–1.0, 1.0] range if the data *type* is GL_BYTE, GL_SHORT or GL_FIXED or to the [0.0, 1.0] range if the data *type* is GL_UNSIGNED_BYTE or GL_UNSIGNED_SHORT.

Table 6-1 describes conversion of non-floating-point data types with the normalized flag set.

Table 6-1   Data Conversions

Vertex Data Format	Conversion to Floating Point
GL_BYTE	$(2c + 1) / (2^8 - 1)$
GL_UNSIGNED_BYTE	$c / (2^8 - 1)$
GL_SHORT	$(2c + 1) / (2^{16} - 1)$
GL_UNSIGNED_SHORT	$c / (2^{16} - 1)$
GL_FIXED	$c / 2^{16}$
GL_FLOAT	c
GL_HALF_FLOAT_OES	c

Selecting Between a Constant Vertex Attribute or a Vertex Array

The application can enable whether it wants OpenGL ES to use the constant data or data from vertex array. Figure 6-3 describes how this works in OpenGL ES 2.0.

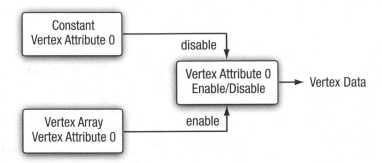

Figure 6-3   Selecting Constant or Vertex Array Vertex Attribute

The commands glEnableVertexAttribArray and glDisableVertex-AttribArray are used to enable and disable a generic vertex attribute array. If the vertex attribute array is disabled for a generic attribute index, the constant vertex attribute data specified for that index will be used.

```
void    glEnableVertexAttribArray(GLuint index);
void    glDisableVertexAttribArray(GLuint index);
```

index   specifies the generic vertex attribute index. This value is 0 to max vertex attributes supported – 1

Example 6-3 describes how to draw a triangle where one of the vertex attributes is constant and the other is specified using a vertex array.

Example 6-3   Using Constant and Vertex Array Attributes

```
GLbyte vertexShaderSrc[] =
     "attribute vec4 a_position;    \n"
     "attribute vec4 a_color;       \n"
     "varying vec4   v_color;       \n"
     "void main()                   \n"
     "{                             \n"
     "    v_color = a_color;        \n"
     "    gl_Position = a_position; \n"
     "}";

GLbyte fragmentShaderSrc[] =
     "varying vec4 v_color;         \n"
     "void main()                   \n"
```

```
"{                                   \n"
"    gl_FragColor = v_color;     \n"
"}";

GLfloat    color[4] = { 1.0f, 0.0f, 0.0f, 1.0f };
GLfloat    vertexPos[3 * 3];   // 3 vertices, with (x,y,z) per-vertex
GLuint     shaderObject[2];
GLuint     programObject;

shaderObject[0] = LoadShader(vertexShaderSrc, GL_VERTEX_SHADER);
shaderObject[1] = LoadShader(fragmentShaderSrc, GL_FRAGMENT_SHADER);

programObject = glCreateProgram();
glAttachShader(programObject, shaderObject[0]);
glAttachShader(programObject, shaderObject[1]);

glVertexAttrib4fv(0, color);
glVertexAttribPointer(1, 3, GL_FLOAT, GL_FALSE, 0, vertexPos);
glEnableVertexAttribArray(1);

glBindAttribLocation(programObject, 0, "a_color");
glBindAttribLocation(programObject, 1, "a_position");

glLinkProgram(programObject);
glUseProgram(programObject);

glDrawArrays(GL_TRIANGLES, 0, 3);
```

The vertex attribute color used in the code example is a constant value whereas the vertexPos attribute is specified using a vertex array. The value of color will be the same for all vertices of the triangle(s) drawn whereas the vertexPos attribute could vary for vertices of the triangle(s) drawn.

Declaring Vertex Attribute Variables in a Vertex Shader

We have looked at what a vertex attribute is, and how to specify vertex attributes in OpenGL ES. We now discuss how to declare vertex attribute variables in a vertex shader.

In a vertex shader, a variable is declared as a vertex attribute by using the attribute qualifier. The attribute qualifier can only be used in a vertex shader. If the attribute qualifier is used in a fragment shader, it should result in an error when the fragment shader is compiled.

A few example declarations of vertex attributes are given here.

```
attribute vec4    a_position;
attribute vec2    a_texcoord;
attribute vec3    a_normal;
```

The attribute qualifier can be used only with the data types float, vec2, vec3, vec4, mat2, mat3, and mat4. Attribute variables cannot be declared as arrays or structures. The following example declarations of vertex attributes are invalid and should result in a compilation error.

```
attribute foo_t  a_A;    // foo_t is a structure
attribute vec4    a_B[10];
```

An OpenGL ES 2.0 implementation supports GL_MAX_VERTEX_ATTRIBS vec4 vertex attributes. A vertex attribute that is declared as a float or vec2 or vec3 will count as one vec4 attribute. Vertex attributes declared as mat2, mat3, or mat4 will count as two, three, or four vec4 attributes, respectively. Unlike uniform and varying variables, which get packed automatically by the compiler, attributes do not get packed. Each component is stored internally by the implementation as a 32-bit single precision floating-point value. Please consider carefully when declaring vertex attributes with sizes less than vec4, as the maximum number of vertex attributes available is a limited resource. It might be better to pack them together into one vec4 attribute instead of declaring them as individual vertex attributes in the vertex shader.

Variables declared as vertex attributes in a vertex shader are *read-only* variables and cannot be modified. The following code should cause a compilation error.

```
attribute vec4    a_pos;
uniform   vec4    u_v;

void main()
{
    a_pos = u_v; <--- cannot assign to a_pos as it is read-only
}
```

An attribute can be declared inside a vertex shader but if it is not used then it is not considered active and does not count against the limit. If the number of attributes used in a vertex shader is greater than GL_MAX_VERTEX_ATTRIBS, the vertex shader will fail to link.

Once a program has been successfully linked, we need to find out the number of active vertex attributes used by the vertex shader attached to this program. The following line of code describes how to get the number of active vertex attributes.

```
glGetProgramiv(progam, GL_ACTIVE_ATTRIBUTES, &numActiveAttribs);
```

A detailed description of `glGetProgamiv` is given in Chapter 4, "Shaders and Programs."

The list of active vertex attributes used by a program and their data types can be queried using the `glGetActiveAttrib` command.

void	**glGetActiveAttrib**(GLuint *program*, GLuint *index*, GLsizei *bufsize*, GLsizei **length*, GLint **size*, GLenum **type*, GLchar **name*)

program	name of a program object that was successfully linked previously
index	specifies the vertex attribute to query and will be a value between 0 … GL_ACTIVE_ATTRIBUTES – 1. The value of GL_ACTIVE_ATTRIBUTES is determined with glGetProgramiv
bufsize	specifies the maximum number of characters that may be written into name, including the null terminator
length	returns the number of characters written into name excluding the null terminator, if length is not NULL
type	returns the type of the attribute. Valid values are: GL_FLOAT GL_FLOAT_VEC2 GL_FLOAT_VEC3 GL_FLOAT_VEC4 GL_FLOAT_MAT2 GL_FLOAT_MAT3 GL_FLOAT_MAT4
size	returns the size of the attribute. This is specified in units of the type returned by *type*. If the variable is not an array, *size* will always be 1. If the variable is an array, then *size* returns the size of the array
name	name of the attribute variable as declared in the vertex shader

The `glGetActiveAttrib` call provides information about the attribute selected by *index*. As described above, *index* must be a value between 0 and `GL_ACTIVE_ATTRIBUTES` - 1. The value of `GL_ACTIVE_ATTRIBUTES` is queried using `glGetProgramiv`. An *index* of 0 selects the first active attributes and an *index* of `GL_ACTIVE_ATTRIBUTES` - 1 selects the last vertex attribute.

Binding Vertex Attributes to Attribute Variables in a Vertex Shader

We discussed that in a vertex shader, vertex attribute variables are specified by the `attribute` qualifier, the number of active attributes can be queried using `glGetProgramiv` and the list of active attributes in a program can be queried using `glGetActiveAttrib`. We also described that generic attribute indices that range from 0 to (`GL_MAX_VERTEX_ATTRIBS` - 1) are used to enable a generic vertex attribute and specify a constant or per-vertex (i.e., vertex array) value using the `glVertexAttrib*` and `glVertexAttrib-Pointer` commands. Now we describe how to map this generic attribute index to the appropriate attribute variable declared in the vertex shader. This mapping will allow appropriate vertex data to be read into the correct vertex attribute variable in the vertex shader.

Figure 6-4 describes how generic vertex attributes are specified and bound to attribute names in a vertex shader.

There are two approaches that OpenGL ES 2.0 enables to map a generic vertex attribute index to an attribute variable name in the vertex shader. These approaches can be categorized as follows:

- OpenGL ES 2.0 will bind the generic vertex attribute index to the attribute name.

- The application can bind the vertex attribute index to an attribute name.

The `glBindAttribLocation` command can be used to bind a generic vertex attribute index to an attribute variable in a vertex shader. This binding takes effect when the program is linked the next time. It does not change the bindings used by the currently linked program.

```
void    glBindAttribLocation(GLuint program, GLuint index,
                             const GLchar *name)
```

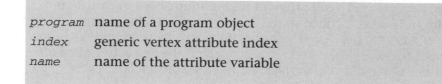

program	name of a program object
index	generic vertex attribute index
name	name of the attribute variable

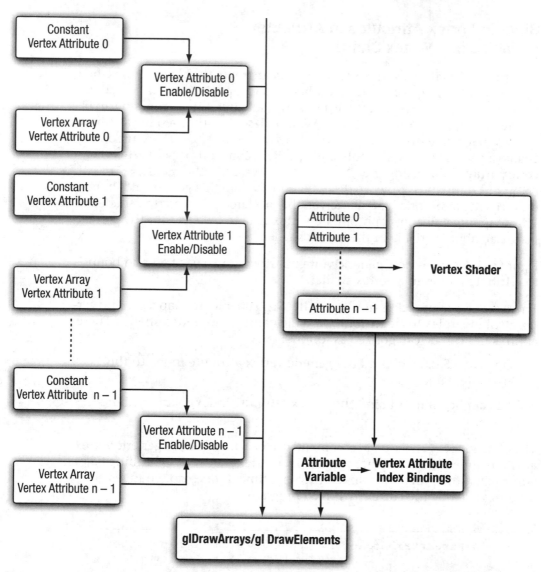

Figure 6-4   Specifying and Binding Vertex Attributes for Drawing a Primitive(s)

If name was bound previously, its assigned binding is replaced with an index. `glBindAttribLocation` can be called even before a vertex shader is attached to a program object. This means that this call can be used to bind any attribute name. Attribute names that do not exist or are not active in a vertex shader attached to the program object are ignored.

The other option is to let OpenGL ES 2.0 bind the attribute variable name to a generic vertex attribute index. This binding is performed when the program is linked. In the linking phase, the OpenGL ES 2.0 implementation performs the following operation for each attribute variable:

> For each attribute variable, check if a binding has been specified via `glBindAttribLocation`. If a binding is specified, the appropriate attribute index specified is used. If not, the implementation will assign a generic vertex attribute index.

This assignment is implementation specific and can vary from one OpenGL ES 2.0 implementation to another. An application can query the assigned binding by using the `glGetAttribLocation` command.

GLint **glGetAttribLocation**(GLuint *program*,
                             const GLchar **name*)

---

program program object

name name of attribute variable

`glGetAttribLocation` returns the generic attribute index bound to attribute variable *name* when the program object defined by *program* was last linked. If *name* is not an active attribute variable, or if *program* is not a valid program object or was not linked successfully, then –1 is returned, indicating an invalid attribute index.

Vertex Buffer Objects

The vertex data specified using vertex arrays is stored in client memory. This data has to be copied from client memory to graphics memory when a call to `glDrawArrays` or `glDrawElements` is made. These two commands are described in detail in Chapter 7, "Primitive Assembly and Rasterization." It would, however, be much better if we did not have to copy the vertex data on every draw call and instead cache the data in graphics memory. This can significantly improve the rendering performance and additionally reduce the memory bandwidth and power consumption requirements, both of which are quite important for handheld devices. This is where vertex buffer objects can help. Vertex buffer objects allow OpenGL ES 2.0 applications to allocate and cache vertex data in high-performance graphics memory and render from this memory, thus avoiding resending data every time a primitive is drawn. Not only the vertex data, but even the element indices that describe the vertex indices of the primitive and are passed as an argument to glDrawElements can also be cached.

There are two types of buffer objects supported by OpenGL ES: *array buffer objects* and *element array buffer objects*. The array buffer objects specified by the GL_ARRAY_BUFFER token are used to create buffer objects that will store vertex data. The element array buffer objects specified by the GL_ELEMENT_ARRAY_BUFFER token are used to create buffer objects that will store indices of a primitive.

Note: To get best performance, we recommend that OpenGL ES 2.0 applications use vertex buffer objects for vertex attribute data and element indices wherever possible.

Before we can render using buffer objects, we need to allocate the buffer objects and upload the vertex data and element indices into appropriate buffer objects. This is demonstrated by the sample code in Example 6-4.

Example 6-4   Creating and Binding Vertex Buffer Objects

```
void    initVertexBufferObjects(vertex_t *vertexBuffer,
                                GLushort *indices,
                                GLuint numVertices, GLuint numIndices,
                                GLuint *vboIds)
{
    glGenBuffers(2, vboIds);

    glBindBuffer(GL_ARRAY_BUFFER, vboIds[0]);
    glBufferData(GL_ARRAY_BUFFER, numVertices * sizeof(vertex_t),
            vertexBuffer, GL_STATIC_DRAW);

    // bind buffer object for element indices
    glBindBuffer(GL_ELEMENT_ARRAY_BUFFER, vboIds[1]);
    glBufferData(GL_ELEMENT_ARRAY_BUFFER,
            numIndices * sizeof(GLushort),indices,
            GL_STATIC_DRAW);
}
```

The code described in Example 6-4 creates two buffer objects: a buffer object to store the actual vertex attribute data, and a buffer object to store the element indices that make up the primitive. In this example, the `glGenBuffers` command is called to get two unused buffer object names in `vboIds`. The unused buffer object names returned in `vboIds` are then used to create an array buffer object and an element array buffer object. The array buffer object is used to store vertex attribute data for vertices of one or more primitives. The element array buffer object stores the indices of a primitive(s). The actual array or element data is specified using `glBufferData`. Note the `GL_STATIC_DRAW` that is passed as an argument to `glBufferData`. This is used to describe how the buffer is accessed by the application and will be described later in this section.

---

void   **glGenBuffers**(GLsizei *n*, GLuint **buffers*)

---

n   number of buffer objects names to return

buffers   pointer to an array of n entries, where allocated buffer objects are returned

---

`glGenBuffers` assigns *n* buffer object names and returns them in *buffers*. The buffer object names returned by `glGenBuffers` are unsigned integer numbers other than 0. The value 0 is reserved by OpenGL ES and does not refer to a buffer object. Applications trying to modify or query buffer object state for buffer object 0 will generate an appropriate error.

The `glBindBuffer` command is used to make a buffer object the current array buffer object or the current element array buffer object. The first time a buffer object name is bound by calling `glBindBuffer`, the buffer object is allocated with appropriate default state, and if the allocation is successful, this allocated object is bound as the current array buffer object or the current element array buffer object for the rendering context.

---

void   **glBindBuffer**(GLenum *target*, GLuint *buffer*)

---

target   can be set to GL_ARRAY_BUFFER or GL_ELEMENT_ARRAY_BUFFER

buffer   buffer object to be assigned as the current object to target

Note that `glGenBuffers` is not required to assign a buffer object name before it is bound using `glBindBuffer`. An application can specify an unused buffer object name to `glBindBuffer`. However, we do recommend that OpenGL ES applications call `glGenBuffers` and use buffer object names returned by `glGenBuffers` instead of specifying their own buffer object names.

The state associated with a buffer object can be categorized as follows:

- `GL_BUFFER_SIZE`. This refers to the size of the buffer object data that is specified by `glBufferData`. The initial value when the buffer object is first bound using `glBindBuffer` is zero.

- `GL_BUFFER_USAGE`. This is a hint as to how the application is going to use the data stored in the buffer object. This is described in detail in Table 6-2. The initial value is `GL_STATIC_DRAW`.

Table 6-2   Buffer Usage

Buffer Usage Enum	Description
GL_STATIC_DRAW	The buffer object data will be specified once by the application and used many times to draw primitives.
GL_DYNAMIC_DRAW	The buffer object data will be specified repeatedly by the application and used many times to draw primitives.
GL_STREAM_DRAW	The buffer object data will be specified once by the application and used a few times to draw primitives.

As mentioned earlier, `GL_BUFFER_USAGE` is a hint to OpenGL ES and not a guarantee. Therefore, an application could allocate a buffer object data store with `usage` set to `GL_STATIC_DRAW` and frequently modify it.

Missing OpenGL ES Buffer Usage Enums Supported by OpenGL

Note: The `GL_STATIC_READ`, `GL_STATIC_COPY`, `GL_DYNAMIC_READ`, `GL_DYNAMIC_COPY`, `GL_STREAM_READ`, and `GL_STREAM_COPY` enums supported by OpenGL are not defined by OpenGL ES. This is because these enums imply that the data store contents will be specified by reading data from the GL. OpenGL allows applications to read the contents of the vertex buffer storage but these API calls are missing from OpenGL ES. As there is no mechanism to read buffer data in OpenGL ES, these enums are no longer valid and are therefore not supported.

The vertex array data or element array data storage is created and initialized using the `glBufferData` command.

void	**glBufferData**(GLenum *target*, GLsizeiptr *size*, const void **data*, GLenum *usage*)
target	can be set to GL_ARRAY_BUFFER or GL_ELEMENT_ARRAY_BUFFER
size	size of buffer data store in bytes
data	pointer to the buffer data supplied by the application
usage	a hint on how the application is going to use the data stored in the buffer object. Refer to Table 6-2 for details

`glBufferData` will reserve appropriate data storage based on the value of *size*. The *data* argument can be a NULL value indicating that the reserved data store remains uninitialized. If *data* is a valid pointer, then contents of *data* are copied to the allocated data store. The contents of the buffer object data store can be initialized or updated using the `glBufferSubData` command.

void	**glBufferSubData**(GLenum *target*, GLintptr *offset*, GLsizeiptr *size*, const void **data*)
target	can be set to GL_ARRAY_BUFFER or GL_ELEMENT_ARRAY_BUFFER
offset	offset into the buffer data store and number of bytes of the
size	data store that is being modified
data	pointer to the client data that needs to be copied into the buffer object data storage

After the buffer object data store has been initialized or updated using `glBufferData` or `glBufferSubData`, the client data store is no longer needed and can be released. For static geometry, applications can free the client data store and reduce the overall system memory consumed by the application. This might not be possible for dynamic geometry.

We now look at drawing primitives with and without buffer objects. Example 6-5 describes drawing primitives with and without vertex buffer objects. Notice that the code to set up vertex attributes is very similar. In this example, we use the same buffer object for all attributes of a vertex. When a GL_ARRAY_BUFFER buffer object is used, the `pointer` argument in `glVertexAttribPointer` changes from being a pointer to the actual data to being an offset in bytes into the vertex buffer store allocated using `glBufferData`. Similarly if a valid GL_ELEMENT_ARRAY_BUFFER object is used, the `indices` argument in `glDrawElements` changes from being a pointer to the actual element indices to being an offset in bytes to the element index buffer store allocated using `glBufferData`.

Example 6-5   Drawing with and without Vertex Buffer Objects

```
#define VERTEX_POS_SIZE        3   // x, y and z
#define VERTEX_NORMAL_SIZE     3   // x, y and z
#define VERTEX_TEXCOORD0_SIZE  2   // s and t

#define VERTEX_POS_INDX        0
#define VERTEX_NORMAL_INDX     1
#define VERTEX_TEXCOORD0_INDX  2


//
// vertices    - pointer to a buffer that contains vertex attribute
//                 data
// vtxStride   - stride of attribute data / vertex in bytes
// numIndices  - number of indices that make up primitive
//                 drawn as triangles
// indices     - pointer to element index buffer.
//
void    drawPrimitiveWithoutVBOs(GLfloat *vertices, GLint vtxStride,
                                 GLint numIndices, GLushort *indices)
{
    GLfloat    *vtxBuf = vertices;

    glBindBuffer(GL_ARRAY_BUFFER, 0);
    glBindBuffer(GL_ELEMENT_ARRAY_BUFFER, 0);

    glEnableVertexAttribArray(VERTEX_POS_INDX);
    glEnableVertexAttribArray(VERTEX_NORMAL_INDX);
    glEnableVertexAttribArray{VERTEX_TEXCOORD0_INDX);

    glVertexAttribPointer(VERTEX_POS_INDX, VERTEX_POS_SIZE,
                          GL_FLOAT, GL_FALSE, vtxStride, vtxBuf);
    vtxBuf += VERTEX_POS_SIZE;
    glVertexAttribPointer(VERTEX_NORMAL_INDX, VERTEX_NORMAL_SIZE,
                          GL_FLOAT, GL_FALSE, vtxStride, vtxBuf);
    vtxBuf += VERTEX_NORMAL_SIZE;
```

```
    glVertexAttribPointer(VERTEX_TEXCOORD0_INDX,
                          VERTEX_TEXCOORD0_SIZE, GL_FLOAT,
                          GL_FALSE, vtxStride, vtxBuf);

    glBindAttribLocation(program, VERTEX_POS_INDX, "v_position");
    glBindAttribLocation(program, VERTEX_NORMAL_INDX, "v_normal");
    glBindAttribLocation(program, VERTEX_TEXCOORD0_INDX,
                         "v_texcoord");

    glDrawElements(GL_TRIANGLES, numIndices, GL_UNSIGNED_SHORT,
                   indices);
}

void   drawPrimitiveWithVBOs(GLint numVertices, GLfloat *vtxBuf,
                             GLint vtxStride, GLint numIndices,
                             GLushort *indices)
{
    GLuint   offset = 0;
    GLuint   vboIds[2];

    // vboIds[0] - used to store vertex attribute data
    // vboIds[1] - used to store element indices
    glGenBuffers(2, vboIds);

    glBindBuffer(GL_ARRAY_BUFFER, vboIds[0]);
    glBufferData(GL_ARRAY_BUFFER, vtxStride * numVertices,
                 vtxBuf, GL_STATIC_DRAW);
    glBindBuffer(GL_ELEMENT_ARRAY_BUFFER, vboIds[1]);
    glBufferData(GL_ELEMENT_ARRAY_BUFFER,
                 sizeof(GLushort) * numIndices,
                 indices, GL_STATIC_DRAW);

    glEnableVertexAttribArray(VERTEX_POS_INDX);
    glEnableVertexAttribArray(VERTEX_NORMAL_INDX);
    glEnableVertexAttribArray(VERTEX_TEXCOORD0_INDX);

    glVertexAttribPointer(VERTEX_POS_INDX, VERTEX_POS_SIZE,
                          GL_FLOAT, GL_FALSE, vtxStride,
                          (const void*)offset);

    offset += VERTEX_POS_SIZE * sizeof(GLfloat);
    glVertexAttribPointer(VERTEX_NORMAL_INDX, VERTEX_NORMAL_SIZE,
                          GL_FLOAT, GL_FALSE, vtxStride,
                          (const void*)offset);

    offset += VERTEX_NORMAL_SIZE * sizeof(GLfloat);
    glVertexAttribPointer(VERTEX_TEXCOORD0_INDX,
                          VERTEX_TEXCOORD0_SIZE,
                          GL_FLOAT, GL_FALSE, vtxStride,
                          (const void*)offset);
```

```
        glBindAttribLocation(program, VERTEX_POS_INDX, "v_position");
        glBindAttribLocation(program, VERTEX_NORMAL_INDX, "v_normal");
        glBindAttribLocation(program, VERTEX_TEXCOORD0_INDX,
                             "v_texcoord");

        glDrawElements(GL_TRIANGLES, numIndices, GL_UNSIGNED_SHORT, 0);

        glDeleteBuffers(2, vboIds);
}
```

In Example 6-5, we used one buffer object to store all the vertex data.
This represents the array of structures method of storing vertex attributes
described in Example 6-1. It is also possible to have a buffer object for each
vertex attribute. This would be the structure of arrays method of storing
vertex attributes described in Example 6-2. Example 6-6 describes how
drawPrimitiveWithVBOs would look with a separate buffer object for each
vertex attribute.

Example 6-6   Drawing with a Buffer Object per Attribute

```
#define VERTEX_POS_SIZE          3    // x, y and z
#define VERTEX_NORMAL_SIZE       3    // x, y and z
#define VERTEX_TEXCOORD0_SIZE    2    // s and t

#define VERTEX_POS_INDX          0
#define VERTEX_NORMAL_INDX       1
#define VERTEX_TEXCOORD0_INDX   ´2

//
// numVertices - number of vertices
// vtxBuf - an array of pointers describing attribute data
// vtxStrides - an array of stride values for each attribute
// numIndices - number of element indices of primitive
// indices - actual element index buffer
//
void    drawPrimitiveWithVBOs(GLint numVertices,
                              GLfloat **vtxBuf, GLint *vtxStrides,
                              GLint numIndices, GLushort *indices)
{
    GLuint    vboIds[4];

    // vboIds[0] - used to store vertex position
    // vboIds[1] - used to store vertex normal
    // vboIds[2] - used to store vertex texture coordinate 0
```

```
    // vboIds[3] - used to store element indices
    glGenBuffers(4, vboIds);

    glBindBuffer(GL_ARRAY_BUFFER, vboIds[0]);
    glBufferData(GL_ARRAY_BUFFER, vtxStrides[0] * numVertices,
                 vtxBuf[0], GL_STATIC_DRAW);
    glBindBuffer(GL_ARRAY_BUFFER, vboIds[1]);
    glBufferData(GL_ARRAY_BUFFER, vtxStrides[1] * numVertices,
                 vtxBuf[1], GL_STATIC_DRAW);
    glBindBuffer(GL_ARRAY_BUFFER, vboIds[2]);
    glBufferData(GL_ARRAY_BUFFER, vtxStrides[2] * numVertices,
                 vtxBuf[2], GL_STATIC_DRAW);

    glBindBuffer(GL_ELEMENT_ARRAY_BUFFER, vboIds[3]);
    glBufferData(GL_ELEMENT_ARRAY_BUFFER,
                 sizeof(GLushort) * numIndices,
                 indices, GL_STATIC_DRAW);

    glBindBuffer(GL_ARRAY_BUFFER, vboIds[0]);
    glEnableVertexAttribArray(VERTEX_POS_INDX);
    glBindBuffer(GL_ARRAY_BUFFER, vboIds[1]);
    glEnableVertexAttribArray(VERTEX_NORMAL_INDX);
    glBindBuffer(GL_ARRAY_BUFFER, vboIds[2]);
    glEnableVertexAttribArray(VERTEX_TEXCOORD0_INDX);

    glVertexAttribPointer(VERTEX_POS_INDX, VERTEX_POS_SIZE,
                          GL_FLOAT, GL_FALSE, vtxStrides[0], 0);
    glVertexAttribPointer(VERTEX_NORMAL_INDX, VERTEX_NORMAL_SIZE,
                          GL_FLOAT, GL_FALSE, vtxStrides[1], 0);
    glVertexAttribPointer(VERTEX_TEXCOORD0_INDX,
                          VERTEX_TEXCOORD0_SIZE,
                          GL_FLOAT, GL_FALSE, vtxStrides[2], 0);

    glBindAttribLocation(program, VERTEX_POS_INDX, "v_position");
    glBindAttribLocation(program, VERTEX_NORMAL_INDX, "v_normal");
    glBindAttribLocation(program, VERTEX_TEXCOORD0_INDX,
                         "v_texcoord");

    glDrawElements(GL_TRIANGLES, numIndices, GL_UNSIGNED_SHORT, 0);

    glDeleteBuffers(4, vboIds)
}
```

After the application is done using buffer objects, they can be deleted using the glDeleteBuffers command.

---

void   **glDeleteBuffers**(GLsizei *n*, const GLuint **buffers*)

---

n   number of buffer objects to be deleted

buffers array of n entries that contain the buffer objects to be deleted

---

glDeleteBuffers deletes the buffer objects specified in buffers. Once a buffer object has been deleted, it can be reused as a new buffer object that stores vertex attributes or element indices for a different primitive.

As you can see from these examples, using vertex buffer objects is very easy and requires very little extra work to implement over vertex arrays. This minimal extra work involved in supporting the vertex buffer is well worth it, considering the performance gain this feature provides. In the next chapter we discuss how to draw primitives using glDrawArrays and glDrawElements, and how the primitive assembly and rasterization pipeline stages in OpenGL ES 2.0 work.

Mapping Buffer Objects

The OES_map_buffer extension allows applications to map and unmap a vertex buffer object's data storage into the application's address space. The map command returns a pointer to this data storage. This pointer can be used by the application to update the contents of the buffer object. The unmap command is used to indicate that the updates have been completed and to release the mapped pointer. The following paragraphs provide an in-depth description of these commands and specific performance tips.

The glMapBufferOES command maps a vertex buffer object's data storage into the application's address space.

---

void   ****glMapBufferOES**(GLenum *target*, GLenum *access*)

---

target must be set to GL_ARRAY_BUFFER

access can only be set GL_WRITE_ONLY_OES

---

glMapBufferOES returns a pointer to this storage. The mapping operation provides write-only access to the vertex buffer object's data storage. A read of the memory region mapped by the returned pointer is undefined. Depending on the operating system's capabilities, the read operation may generate a fault or return bogus data. glMapBufferOES will return a valid pointer if the buffer could be mapped, or else returns zero.

The glUnmapBufferOES command unmaps a previously mapped buffer.

GLboolean   **glUnmapBufferOES**(GLenum *target*)

---

target   must be set to GL_ARRAY_BUFFER

---

glUnmapBufferOES returns GL_TRUE if the unmap operation is successful. The pointer returned by glMapBufferOES can no longer be used after a successful unmap has been performed. glUnmapBufferOES returns GL_FALSE if the data in the vertex buffer object's data storage have become corrupted after the buffer has been mapped. This can occur due to a change in the screen resolution, multiple screens being used by OpenGL ES context, or an out-of-memory event that causes the mapped memory to be discarded.[1]

Performance Tip

glMapBufferOES should only be used if the whole buffer is being updated. Using glMapBufferOES to update a subregion is not recommended, as there is no mechanism in glMapBufferOES to specify a subregion.

Even if glMapBufferOES is being used to update the entire buffer, the operation can still be expensive compared to glBufferData. With glMapBufferOES, the application gets a pointer to the buffer object data. However, this buffer might be in use by rendering commands previously queued by the application. If the buffer is currently in use, the GPU must wait for previous rendering commands that use this buffer to complete before

---

[1]   If the screen resolution changes to a larger width, height, and bits per pixel at runtime, the mapped memory may have to be released. Note that this is not a very common issue on handheld devices. A backing store is typically not implemented on most handheld and embedded devices. Therefore, an out-of-memory event will result in memory being freed up and reused for critical needs.

returning the pointer. However, if the entire region is being updated, there is no reason to wait. We already saw that there is no mechanism for the OpenGL ES implementation to know just from the `glMapBufferOES` command that the application is updating the entire region or just a few bytes. There is a way for an application to indicate that the entire region will be updated. This can be done by calling `glBufferData` with the `data` argument set to `NULL` followed by `glMapBufferOES`. Calling `glBufferData` with `data = NULL` tells the OpenGL ES implementation that the previous buffer data is invalidated and the succeeding call to `glMapBufferOES` can be correctly optimized by the implementation.

Chapter 7

Primitive Assembly and Rasterization

In this chapter, we describe the types of primitives and geometric objects that are supported by OpenGL ES, and how to draw them. We then describe the primitive assembly stage, which occurs after the vertices of a primitive are processed by the vertex shader. In the primitive assembly state, clipping, perspective divide, and viewport transformation operations are performed. These operations are discussed in detail. We then conclude with a description of the rasterization stage. Rasterization is the process that converts primitives into a set of two-dimensional fragments, which are processed by the fragment shader. These two-dimensional fragments represent pixels that may be drawn on the screen.

Refer to Chapter 8, "Vertex Shaders," for a detailed description of vertex shaders. Chapter 9, "Texturing," and Chapter 10, "Fragment Shaders," describe processing that is applied to fragments generated by the rasterization stage.

Primitives

A primitive is a geometric object that can be drawn using the `glDrawArrays` and `glDrawElements` commands in OpenGL ES. The primitive is described by a set of vertices that describe the vertex position, and other information such as color, texture coordinates, and normals.

The following are the primitives that can be drawn in OpenGL ES 2.0:

- Triangles.
- Lines.
- Point sprites.

Triangles

Triangles represent the most common method used to describe a geometry object rendered by a 3D application. The triangle primitives supported by OpenGL ES are GL_TRIANGLES, GL_TRIANGLE_STRIP, and GL_TRIANGLE_FAN. Figure 7-1 shows examples of supported triangle primitive types.

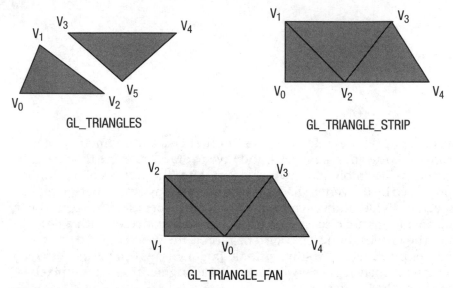

Figure 7-1   Triangle Primitive Types

GL_TRIANGLES draws a series of separate triangles. In Figure 7-1, two triangles given by vertices (V_0, V_1, V_2) and (V_3, V_4, V_5) are drawn. A total of $n/3$ triangles are drawn, where n is the number of indices specified as count in glDrawArrays or glDrawElements.

GL_TRIANGLE_STRIP draws a series of connected triangles. In the example shown in Figure 7-1, three triangles are drawn given by (V_0, V_1, V_2), (V_2, V_1, V_3) (note the order), and (V_2, V_3, V_4). A total of $(n - 2)$ triangles are drawn, where n is the number of indices specified as count in glDrawArrays or glDrawElements.

GL_TRIANGLE_FAN also draws a series of connected triangles. In the example shown in Figure 7-1, the triangles drawn are (V_0, V_1, V_2), (V_0, V_2, V_3), and (V_0, V_3, V_4). A total of $(n - 2)$ triangles are drawn, where n is the number of indices specified as count in glDrawArrays or glDrawElements.

Lines

The line primitives supported by OpenGL ES are GL_LINES, GL_LINE_STRIP, and GL_LINE_LOOP. Figure 7-2 shows examples of supported line primitive types.

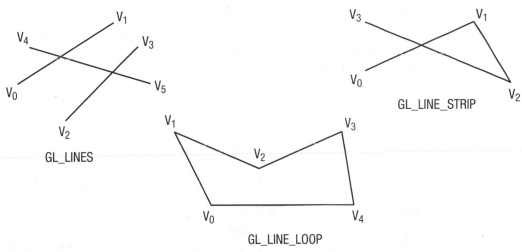

Figure 7-2   Line Primitive Types

GL_LINES draws a series of unconnected line segments. In the example shown in Figure 7-2, three individual lines are drawn given by (V_0, V_1), (V_2, V_3), and (V_4, V_5). A total of n/2 segments are drawn, where n is the number of indices specified as count in glDrawArrays or glDrawElements.

GL_LINE_STRIP draws a series of connected line segments. In the example shown in Figure 7-2, three line segments are drawn given by (V_0, V_1), (V_1, V_2), and (V_2, V_3). A total of $(n - 1)$ line segments are drawn, where n is the number of indices specified as count in glDrawArrays or glDraw-Elements.

GL_LINE_LOOP works similar to GL_LINE_STRIP, except that a final line segment is drawn from V_{n-1} to V_0. In the example shown in Figure 7-2, the line segments drawn are (V_0, V_1), (V_1, V_2), (V_2, V_3), (V_3, V_4), and (V_4, V_0). A total of n line segments are drawn, where n is the number of indices specified as count in glDrawArrays or glDrawElements.

The width of a line can be specified using the glLineWidth API call.

void	**glLineWidth**(GLfloat *width*)

width	specifies the width of the line in pixels. The default width is 1.0

The width specified by glLineWidth will be clamped to the line width range supported by the OpenGL ES 2.0 implementation. The supported line width range can be queried using the following command. There is no requirement for lines with widths greater than one to be supported.

```
GLfloat    lineWidthRange[2];
glGetFloatv(GL_ALIASED_LINE_WIDTH_RANGE, lineWidthRange);
```

Point Sprites

The point sprite primitive supported by OpenGL ES is GL_POINTS. A point sprite is drawn for each vertex specified. Point sprites are typically used for rendering particle effects efficiently by drawing them as points instead of quads. A point sprite is a screen-aligned quad specified as a *position* and a *radius*. The position describes the center of the square and the radius is then used to calculate the four coordinates of the quad that describes the point sprite.

gl_PointSize is the built-in variable that can be used to output the point radius (or point size) in the vertex shader. It is important that a vertex shader associated with the point primitive output gl_PointSize, otherwise the value of point size is considered undefined and will most likely result in drawing errors. The gl_PointSize value output by a vertex shader will be clamped to the aliased point size range supported by the OpenGL ES 2.0 implementation. This range can be queried using the following command.

```
GLfloat    pointSizeRange[2];
glGetFloatv(GL_ALIASED_POINT_SIZE_RANGE, pointSizeRange);
```

By default, OpenGL ES 2.0 describes the window origin (0, 0) to be the (left, bottom) region. However, for point sprites, the point coordinate origin is (left, top).

gl_PointCoord is a built-in variable available only inside a fragment shader when the primitive being rendered is a point sprite. gl_PointCoord is declared as a vec2 variable using the mediump precision qualifier. The values assigned to gl_PointCoord go from 0.0 to 1.0 as we move from left to right or from top to bottom, as illustrated by Figure 7-3.

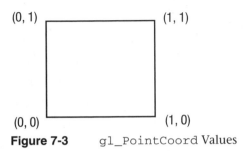

Figure 7-3   gl_PointCoord Values

The following fragment shader code illustrates how gl_PointCoord can be used as a texture coordinate to draw a textured point sprite.

```
uniform sampler2D s_texSprite;

void
main(void)
{
    gl_FragColor = texture2D(s_texSprite, gl_PointCoord);
}
```

Drawing Primitives

There are two API calls in OpenGL ES that can be used to draw primitives: glDrawArrays and glDrawElements.

void	**glDrawArrays**(GLenum *mode*, GLint *first*, GLsizei *count*)
mode	specifies the primitive to render. Valid values are: GL_POINTS GL_LINES GL_LINE_STRIP GL_LINE_LOOP GL_TRIANGLES GL_TRIANGLE_STRIP GL_TRIANGLE_FAN
first	specifies the starting vertex index in the enabled vertex arrays
count	specifies the number of indices to be drawn

| void | **glDrawElements**(GLenum *mode*, GLsizei *count*, |
| | GLenum *type*, const GLvoid **indices*) |

mode	specifies the primitive to render. Valid values are:
	GL_POINTS
	GL_LINES
	GL_LINE_STRIP
	GL_LINE_LOOP
	GL_TRIANGLES
	GL_TRIANGLE_STRIP
	GL_TRIANGLE_FAN
count	specifies the number of indices
type	specifies the type of element indices stored in indices. Valid values are:
	GL_UNSIGNED_BYTE
	GL_UNSIGNED_SHORT
	GL_UNSIGNED_INT—optional (can be used only if the OES_element_index_uint extension is implemented)
indices	specifies a pointer to location where element indices are stored

glDrawArrays draws primitives specified by mode using vertices given by element index first to first + count – 1. A call to glDrawArrays (GL_TRIANGLES, 0, 6) will draw two triangles, a triangle given by element indices (0, 1, 2) and another triangle given by element indices (3, 4, 5). Similarly, a call to glDrawArrays(GL_TRIANGLE_STRIP, 0, 5) will draw three triangles: a triangle given by element indices (0, 1, 2), the second triangle given by element indices (2, 1, 3), and the final triangle given by element indices (2, 3, 4).

glDrawArrays is great if you have a primitive described by a sequence of element indices and if vertices of geometry are not shared. However, typical objects used by games or other 3D applications are made up of multiple triangle meshes where element indices may not necessarily be in sequence and vertices will typically be shared between triangles of a mesh.

Consider the cube shown in Figure 7-4. If we were to draw this using glDrawArrays, the code would be as follows:

```
#define VERTEX_POS_INDX  0
#define NUM_FACES        6
GLfloat vertices[] = { … };  // (x, y, z) per vertex
```

```
glEnableVertexAttribArray(VERTEX_POS_INDX);
glVertexAttribPointer(VERTEX_POS_INDX, 3, GL_FLOAT, GL_FALSE,
                      0, vertices);
for (i=0; i<NUM_FACES; i++)
{
    glDrawArrays(GL_TRIANGLE_FAN, first, 4);
    first += 4;
}
```

or

```
glDrawArrays(GL_TRIANGLES, 0, 36);
```

To draw this cube with `glDrawArrays`, we would call `glDrawArrays` for each face of the cube. Vertices that are shared would need to be replicated, which means that instead of having eight vertices, we would now need to allocate 24 (if we draw each face as a `GL_TRIANGLE_FAN`) or 36 vertices (if we use `GL_TRIANGLES`). This is not a very efficient approach.

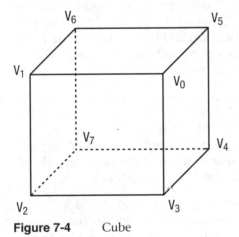

Figure 7-4   Cube

This is how the same cube would be drawn using `glDrawElements`.

```
#define VERTEX_POS_INDX 0
GLfloat vertices[] = { … };// (x, y, z) per vertex
GLubyte indices[36] = { 0, 1, 2, 0, 2, 3,
                        0, 3, 4, 0, 4, 5,
                        0, 5, 6, 0, 6, 1,
                        7, 6, 1, 7, 1, 2,
                        7, 4, 5, 7, 5, 6,
                        7, 2, 3, 7, 3, 4 };

glEnableVertexAttribArray(VERTEX_POS_INDX);
```

```
glVertexAttribPointer(VERTEX_POS_INDX, 3, GL_FLOAT, GL_FALSE,
                  0, vertices);
glDrawElements(GL_TRIANGLES, sizeof(indices)/sizeof(GLubyte),
            GL_UNSIGNED_BYTE, indices);
```

Even though we are drawing triangles with glDrawElements and a triangle fan with glDrawArrays, glDrawElements will run faster than glDrawArrays on a GPU for many reasons; for example, the size of vertex attribute data will be smaller with glDrawElements as vertices are reused. This also gives you a lower memory footprint and memory bandwidth requirement.

Performance Tips

Applications should make sure that glDrawElements should be called with as large a primitive size as possible. This is very easy to do if we are drawing GL_TRIANGLES. However, if we have meshes of triangle strips or fans, instead of making individual calls to glDrawElements for each triangle strip mesh, these meshes could be connected together by adding element indices that result in degenerate triangles. A degenerate triangle is a triangle where two or more vertices of the triangle are coincident. GPUs can detect and reject degenerate triangles very easily, so this is a good performance enhancement that allows us to queue a big primitive to be rendered by the GPU.

The number of element indices (or degenerate triangles) we need to add to connect distinct meshes will depend on whether each mesh is a triangle fan or a triangle strip and the number of indices defined in each strip. The number of indices in a mesh that is a triangle strip matters, as we need to preserve the winding order as we go from one triangle to the next triangle of the strip across distinct meshes that are now being connected.

When connecting separate triangle strips we need to check the order of the last triangle and the first triangle of the two strips being connected. As seen in Figure 7-2, the ordering of vertices that describe even-numbered triangles of a triangle strip is different from the ordering of vertices that describe odd-numbered triangles of the same strip.

Two cases need to be handled:

- Odd-numbered triangle of the first triangle strip is being connected to the first (and therefore even-numbered) triangle of the second triangle strip.

- Even-numbered triangle of the first triangle strip is being connected to the first (and therefore even-numbered) triangle of the second triangle strip.

Figure 7-5 shows two separate triangle strips that represent these two cases that need to be connected to allow us to draw both these strips using a single call to glDrawElements.

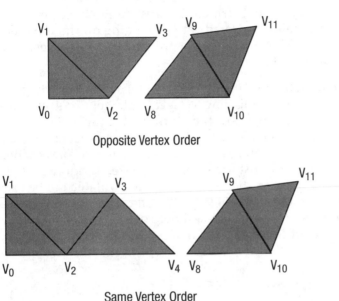

Opposite Vertex Order

Same Vertex Order

Figure 7-5   Connecting Triangle Strips

For triangle strips in Figure 7-5 with opposite vertex order for the last and first triangle of the two strips being connected, the element indices for each triangle strip are (0,1,2,3) and (8,9,10,11), respectively. The combined element index list if we were to draw both strips using one call to glDrawElements would be (0,1,2,3,**3**,**8**,8,9,10,11). This new element index results in the following triangles drawn: (0,1,2), (2,1,3), **(2, 3, 3)**, **(3, 3, 8)**, **(3, 8, 8)**, **(8, 8, 9)**, (8, 9, 10), (10,9,11). The triangles in boldface type are the degenerate triangles. The element indices in boldface type represent the additional indices added to the combined element index list.

For triangle strips in Figure 7-5 with the same vertex order for the last and first triangle of the two strips being connected, the element indices for each triangle strip are (0,1,2,3,4) and (8,9,10,11), respectively. The combined element index list if we were to draw both strips using one call to glDrawElements would be (0,1,2,3,4,**4**,**8**,8,9,10,11). This new element index results in the following triangles drawn: (0,1,2), (2,1,3), (2,3,4), **(4, 3, 4)**, **(4, 4, 8)**, **(8, 4, 9)**, (8,9,10), (10,9,11). The triangles in boldface type are the degenerate triangles. The element indices in boldface type represent the additional indices added to the combined element index list.

Note that the number of additional element indices required and the number of degenerate triangles generated vary depending on the number of vertices in the first strip. This is required to preserve the *winding order* of the next strip being connected.

It might also be worth investigating techniques that take the size of the *post-transform vertex cache* in determining how to arrange element indices of a primitive. Most GPUs implement a post-transform vertex cache. Before a vertex (given by its element index) is executed by the vertex shader, a check is performed to see if the vertex already exists in the post-transform cache. If the vertex exists in the post-transform cache, the vertex is not executed by the vertex shader. If it is not in the cache, the vertex will need to be executed by the vertex shader. Using the post-transform cache size to determine how element indices are created should help overall performance, as it will reduce the number of times a vertex that is reused gets executed by the vertex shader.

Primitive Assembly

Figure 7-6 shows the primitive assembly stage. Vertices that are supplied through `glDrawArrays` or `glDrawElements` get executed by the vertex shader. Each vertex transformed by the vertex shader includes the vertex position that describes the (x, y, z, w) value of the vertex. The primitive type and vertex indices determine the individual primitives that will be rendered. For each individual primitive (triangle, line, and point) and their corresponding vertices, the primitive assembly stage performs the operations as shown in Figure 7-6.

Before we discuss how primitives are rasterized in OpenGL ES, we need to understand the various coordinate systems used within OpenGL ES 2.0. This is needed to get a good understanding of what happens to vertex coordinates as they go through the various stages of the OpenGL ES 2.0 pipeline.

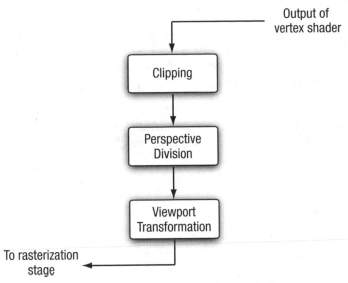

Figure 7-6   OpenGL ES Primitive Assembly Stage

Coordinate Systems

Figure 7-7 shows the coordinate systems as a vertex goes through the vertex shader and primitive assembly stages. Vertices are input to OpenGL ES in the object or local coordinate space. This is the coordinate space in which an object is most likely modeled and stored. After a vertex shader is executed, the vertex position is considered to be in the clip coordinate space. The transformation of the vertex position from the local coordinate system (i.e., object coordinates) to clip coordinates is done by loading the appropriate matrices that perform this conversion in appropriate uniforms defined in the vertex shader. Chapter 8 describes how to transform the vertex position from object to clip coordinates and how to load appropriate matrices in the vertex shader to perform this transformation.

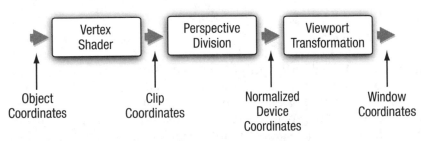

Figure 7-7   Coordinate Systems

Clipping

The vertex position after the vertex shader has been executed is in the clip coordinate space. The clip coordinate is a homogeneous coordinate given by (x_c, y_c, z_c, w_c). The vertex coordinates defined in clip space (x_c, y_c, z_c, w_c) get clipped against the viewing volume (also known as the clip volume).

The clip volume as shown in Figure 7-8 is defined by six clipping planes, referred to as the near, and far clip planes, the left and right clip planes, and the top and bottom clip planes. In clip coordinates, the clip volume is given as:

```
-wc <= xc <= wc
-wc <= yc <= wc
-wc <= zc <= wc
```

The preceding six checks help determine the list of planes against which the primitive needs to be clipped.

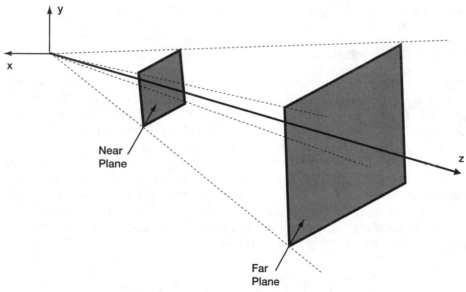

Figure 7-8   Viewing Volume

The clipping stage will clip each primitive to the clip volume shown in Figure 7-8. By a primitive here we imply each triangle of a list of separate triangles drawn using GL_TRIANGLES, or a triangle of a triangle strip or a fan, or a line from a list of separate lines drawn using GL_LINES, or a line of a line strip or line loop, or a specific point in a list of point sprites.

For each primitive type the following operations are performed:

- **Clipping triangles**—If the triangle is completely inside the viewing volume, no clipping is performed. If the triangle is completely outside the viewing volume, the triangle is discarded. If the triangle lies partially inside the viewing volume, then the triangle is clipped against the appropriate plans. The clipping operation will generate new vertices that are clipped to the plane that are arranged as a triangle fan.

- **Clipping lines**—If the line is completely inside the viewing volume, then no clipping is performed. If the line is completely outside the viewing volume, the line is discarded. If the line lies partially inside the viewing volume, then the line is clipped, and appropriate new vertices are generated.

- **Clipping point sprites**—The clipping stage will discard the point sprite if the point position lies outside the near or far clip plane or the quad that represents the point sprite is outside the clip volume. Otherwise it is passed unchanged and the point sprite will be scissored as it moves from inside the clip volume to the outside or vice versa.

After the primitives have been clipped against the six clipping planes, the vertex coordinates undergo perspective division to become normalized device coordinates. A normalized device coordinate is in the range –1.0 to +1.0.

Note: The clipping operation (especially for lines and triangles) can be quite expensive to perform in hardware. There are six clip planes of the viewing volume that a primitive must be clipped against, as shown in Figure 7-8. Primitives that are partially outside the near and far planes go through the clipping operations. However, primitives that are partially outside the x and y planes do not necessarily need to be clipped. By rendering into a viewport that is bigger than dimensions of viewport specified with glViewport, clipping in the x and y planes becomes a scissoring operation. Scissoring is implemented very efficiently by GPUs. This larger viewport region is called the *guard-band* region. Although OpenGL ES does not allow an application to specify a guard-band region, most if not all OpenGL ES implementations implement a guard-band.

Perspective Division

Perspective division takes the point given by clip coordinate (x_c, y_c, z_c, w_c) and projects it onto the screen or viewport. This projection is performed by dividing the (x_c, y_c, z_c) coordinates with w_c. After performing (x_c/w_c), (y_c/w_c), and (z_c/w_c) we get normalized device coordinates (x_d, y_d, z_d). These are called normalized device coordinates as they will be in the [–1.0 … 1.0] range. These normalized (x_d, y_d) coordinates will then be converted to actual screen (or window) coordinates depending on the dimensions of the viewport. The normalized (z_d) coordinate is converted to screen z value using the near and far depth values specified by glDepthRangef. These conversions are performed in the viewport transformation phase.

Viewport Transformation

The viewport transformation can be set by using the following API call:

void	**glViewport** (GLint x, GLint y, GLsizei w, GLsizei h)
x, y	specifies the screen coordinates of the viewport's lower left corner in pixels
w, h	specifies the width and height of viewport in pixels. These values must be > 0

The conversion from normalized device coordinates (x_d, y_d, z_d) to window coordinates (x_w, y_w, z_w) is given by the following transformation:

$$\begin{bmatrix} x_w \\ y_w \\ z_w \end{bmatrix} = \begin{bmatrix} (w/2)x_d + o_x \\ (h/2)y_d + o_y \\ ((f-n)/2)z_d + (n+f)/2 \end{bmatrix}$$

In the transformation $o_x = (x + w)/2$, and $o_y = (y + h)/2$, n and f represent the desired depth range.

The depth range values n and f can be set using the following API call:

void	**glDepthRangef** (GLclampf n, GLclampf f)
n, f	specify the desired depth range. Default values for n and f are 0.0 and 1.0. The values are clamped to lie within (0.0, 1.0)

The values specified by `glDepthRange` and `glViewport` are used to transform the vertex position from normalized device coordinates into window (screen) coordinates.

The initial (or default) viewport state is set to `w = width` and `h = height` of the window created by the app in which OpenGL ES is to do its rendering. The window is given by the `EGLNativeWindowType win` argument specified in `eglCreateWindowSurface`.

Rasterization

Figure 7-9 shows the rasterization pipeline. After the vertices have been transformed and primitives have been clipped, the rasterization pipelines take an individual primitive such as a triangle, a line segment, or a point sprite and generates appropriate fragments for this primitive. Each fragment is identified by its integer location (x, y) in screen space. A fragment represents a pixel location given by (x, y) in screen space and additional fragment data that will be processed by the fragment shader to produce a fragment color. This is described in detail in Chapter 9 and Chapter 10.

In this section we discuss the various options that an application can use to control rasterization of triangles, strips, and fans.

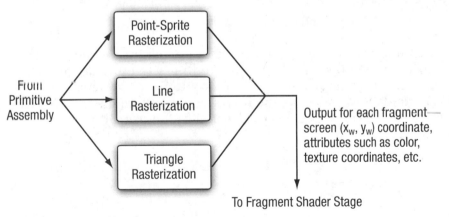

Figure 7-9   OpenGL ES Rasterization Stage

Culling

Before triangles are rasterized, we need to determine whether they are front-facing (i.e., facing the viewer) or back-facing (i.e., facing away from the viewer). The culling operation discards triangles that face away from the viewer. To determine if the triangle is front-facing or back-facing we first need to know the orientation of the triangle.

The orientation of a triangle specifies the winding order of a path that begins at the first vertex, goes through the second and third vertex and ends back at the first vertex. Figure 7-10 describes two examples of triangles with a clockwise and a counterclockwise winding order.

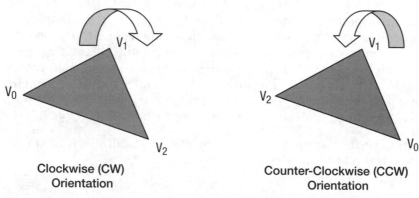

Clockwise (CW)
Orientation

Counter-Clockwise (CCW)
Orientation

Figure 7-10   Clockwise and Counterclockwise Triangles

The orientation of a triangle is computed by calculating the signed area of the triangle in window coordinates. We now need to translate the sign of the computed triangle area into a clockwise (CW) or counterclockwise (CCW) orientation. This mapping from the sign of triangle area to a CW or CCW orientation is specified by the application using the following API call:

void	**glFrontFace**(GLenum *dir*)
dir	specifies the orientation of front-facing triangles. Valid values are GL_CW or GL_CCW. The default value is GL_CCW

We have discussed how to calculate the orientation of a triangle. To determine whether the triangle needs to be culled, we need to know the facing of triangles that are to be culled. This is specified by the application using the following API call.

void	**glCullFace** (GLenum *mode*)

mode	specifies the facing of triangles that are to be culled. Valid values are GL_FRONT, GL_BACK, and GL_FRONT_AND_BACK. The default value is GL_BACK

Last but not least, we also need to know whether the culling operation should be performed or not. The culling operation will be performed if the GL_CULL_FACE state is enabled. The GL_CULL_FACE state can be enabled or disabled by the application using the following API calls.

void	**glEnable** (GLenum *cap*)
void	**glDisable** (GLenum *cap*)

where *cap* is set to GL_CULL_FACE. Initially, culling is disabled

To recap, to cull appropriate triangles, an OpenGL ES application must first enable culling using glEnable(GL_CULL_FACE), set the appropriate cull face using glCullFace, and the orientation of front-facing triangles using glFrontFace.

Note: Culling should always be enabled to avoid the GPU wasting time rasterizing triangles that are not visible. Enabling culling should help improve the overall performance of the OpenGL ES application.

Polygon Offset

Consider the case where we are drawing two polygons that overlap each other. You will most likely notice artifacts as shown in Figure 7-11. These artifacts, called *Z-fighting artifacts*, occur because of limited precision of triangle rasterization, which can impact the precision of the depth values generated per fragment, resulting in artifacts as shown in Figure 7-11. The limited precision of parameters used by triangle rasterization and generated depth values per fragment will get better and better but will never be completely resolved.

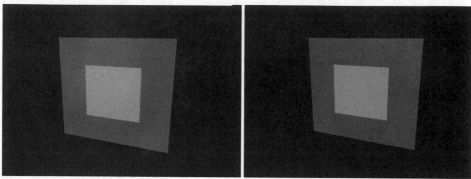

Polygon Offset Disabled   Polygon Offset Enabled

Figure 7-11   Polygon Offset

Figure 7-11 shows two coplanar polygons being drawn. The code to draw these two coplanar polygons without polygon offset is as follows:

```
glClear(GL_COLOR_BUFFER_BIT | GL_DEPTH_BUFFER_BIT);

// load vertex shader
// set the appropriate transformation matrices
// set the vertex attribute state

// draw the RED triangle
glDrawArrays(GL_TRIANGLE_FAN, 0, 4);

// set the depth func to <= as polygons are coplanar
glDepthFunc(GL_LEQUAL);

// set the vertex attribute state

// draw the GREEN triangle
glDrawArrays(GL_TRIANGLE_FAN, 0, 4);
```

To avoid the artifacts shown in Figure 7-11, we need to add a *delta* to the computed depth value before the depth test is performed and before the depth value is written to the depth buffer. If the depth test passes, the original depth value and not the original depth value + *delta* will be stored in the depth buffer.

The polygon offset is set using the following API call.

---

void **glPolygonOffset**(GLfloat *factor*, GLfloat *units*)

The depth offset is computed as:

$$\text{depth offset} = m * factor + r * units$$

m is maximum depth slope of the triangle and is calculated as:

$$m = \sqrt{(\partial z/\partial x^2 + \partial z/\partial y^2)}$$

m can also be calculated as max{$|\partial z/\partial x|$, $|\partial z/\partial y|$}.

The slope terms $\partial z/\partial x$ and $\partial z/\partial y$ are calculated by the OpenGL ES implementation during the triangle rasterization stage.

r is an implementation-defined constant and represents the smallest value that can produce a guaranteed difference in depth value.

Polygon offset can be enabled or disabled using glEnable(GL_POLYGON_OFFSET_FILL) and glDisable(GL_POLYGON_OFFSET_FILL).

With polygon offset enabled, the code for triangles rendered by Figure 7-11 is as follows.

```
const float polygonOffsetFactor = -1.0f;
const float polygonOffsetUnits  = -2.0f;

glClear(GL_COLOR_BUFFER_BIT | GL_DEPTH_BUFFER_BIT);

// load vertex shader
// set the appropriate transformation matrices
// set the vertex attribute state

// draw the RED triangle
glDrawArrays(GL_TRIANGLE_FAN, 0, 4);

// set the depth func to <= as polygons are coplanar
glDepthFunc(GL_LEQUAL);

glEnable(GL_POLYGON_OFFSET_FILL);
glPolygonOffset(polygonOffsetFactor, polygonOffsetUnits);
```

```
// set the vertex attribute state

// draw the GREEN triangle
glDrawArrays(GL_TRIANGLE_FAN, 0, 4);
```

Chapter 8

Vertex Shaders

This chapter describes the OpenGL ES 2.0 programmable vertex pipeline. Figure 8 1 illustrates the OpenGL ES 2.0 programmable pipeline. The shaded boxes in Figure 8-1 indicate the programmable stages in OpenGL ES 2.0. In this chapter we discuss the **vertex shader stage**. Vertex shaders can be used to do traditional vertex-based operations such as transforming the position by a matrix, computing the lighting equation to generate a per-vertex color, and generating or transforming texture coordinates.

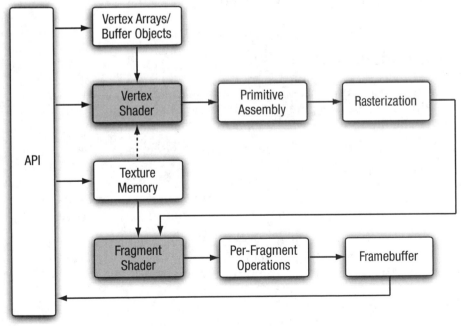

Figure 8-1   OpenGL ES 2.0 Programmable Pipeline

The previous chapters, specifically Chapter 5, "OpenGL ES Shading Language," and Chapter 6, "Vertex Attributes, Vertex Arrays, and Buffer Objects," discussed how to specify the vertex attribute and uniform inputs and also gave a good description of the OpenGL ES 2.0 shading language. In Chapter 7, "Primitive Assembly and Rasterization," we discussed how the output of the vertex shader, referred to as varying variables, is used by the rasterization stage to generate per-fragment values, which are then input to the fragment shader. In this chapter we begin with a high-level overview of a vertex shader including its inputs and outputs. We then discuss some of the limitations imposed by the OpenGL ES 2.0 shading language and describe points to keep in mind when writing shaders that need to be portable across multiple OpenGL ES 2.0 implementations. We then describe how to write vertex shaders by discussing a few examples. These examples describe common use cases such as transforming a vertex position with a model view and projection matrix, examples of vertex lighting that generate per-vertex diffuse and specular colors, texture coordinate generation, and vertex skinning. We hope that these examples help the reader get a good idea of how to write vertex shaders, rules to keep in mind to make vertex shaders portable as much as possible, and an upper limit on how big vertex shaders can be. Last but not least, we describe a vertex shader that implements the OpenGL ES 1.1 fixed function vertex pipeline. These two shaders should also give the reader a good understanding of the complexity of vertex shaders that will be supported by the first generation of handheld devices that implement OpenGL ES 2.0.

Vertex Shader Overview

The vertex shader provides a general-purpose programmable method for operating on vertices. Figure 8-2 shows the inputs and outputs of a vertex shader. The inputs to the vertex shader consist of the following:

- Attributes—Per-vertex data supplied using vertex arrays.

- Uniforms—Constant data used by the vertex shader.

- Shader program—Vertex shader program source code or executable that describes the operations that will be performed on the vertex.

The outputs of the vertex shader are called varying variables. In the primitive rasterization stage, these variables are computed for each generated fragment and are passed in as inputs to the fragment shader.

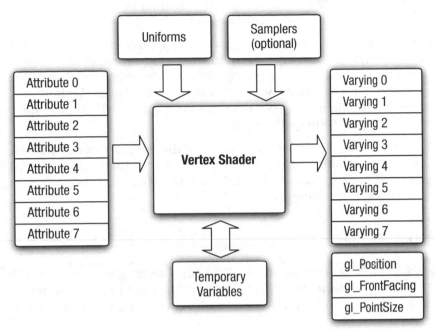

Figure 8-2   OpenGL ES 2.0 Vertex Shader

Vertex Shader Built-In Variables

The built-in variables of a vertex shader can be categorized into special variables that are output by the vertex shader, uniform state such as depth range, and constants that specify maximum values such as the number of attributes, number of varyings, and number of uniforms.

Built-In Special Variables

OpenGL ES 2.0 has built-in special variables that are either output by the vertex shader that then become input to the fragment shader, or are output by the fragment shader. The built-in special variables available to the vertex shader are as follows:

- **gl_Position**—gl_Position is used to output the vertex position in clip coordinates. The gl_Position values are used by the clipping and viewport stages to perform appropriate clipping of primitives and convert the vertex position from clip coordinates to screen coordinates. The value of gl_Position is undefined if the vertex shader does not write to `gl_Position`. `gl_Position` is a floating-point variable declared using the `highp` precision qualifier.

- **gl_PointSize**—`gl_PointSize` is used to write the size of the point sprite in pixels. `gl_PointSize` is used when point sprites are rendered. The `gl_PointSize` value output by a vertex shader is then clamped to the aliased point size range supported by the OpenGL ES 2.0 implementation. `gl_PointSize` is a floating-point variable declared using the `mediump` precision qualifier.

- **gl_FrontFacing**—This special variable, although not directly written by the vertex shader, is generated based on the position values generated by the vertex shader and primitive type being rendered. `gl_FrontFacing` is a boolean variable.

Built-In Uniform State

The only built-in uniform state available inside a vertex shader is the depth range in window coordinates. This is given by the built-in uniform name `gl_DepthRange`, which is declared as a uniform of type `gl_DepthRange-Parameters`.

```
struct gl_DepthRangeParameters {
   highp float near; // near Z
   highp float far;  // far Z
   highp float diff; // far - near
}

uniform gl_DepthRangeParameters gl_DepthRange;
```

Built-In Constants

The following built-in constants are also available inside the vertex shader.

```
const mediump int gl_MaxVertexAttribs         = 8;
const mediump int gl_MaxVertexUniformVectors  = 128;
const mediump int gl_MaxVaryingVectors        = 8;
const mediump int gl_MaxVertexTextureImageUnits  = 0;
const mediump int gl_MaxCombinedTextureImageUnits = 8;
```

The built-in constants describe the following maximum terms:

- **gl_MaxVertexAttribs**—This is the maximum number of vertex attributes that can be specified. The minimum value supported by all ES 2.0 implementations is eight.

- **gl_MaxVertexUniformVectors**—This is the maximum number of vec4 uniform entries that can be used inside a vertex shader. The minimum value supported by all ES 2.0 implementations is 128 vec4 entries. The number of vec4 uniform entries that can actually be used by a developer can vary from implementation to implementation and from one vertex shader to another. For example, some implementations might count user-specified literal values used in a vertex shader against the uniform limit. In other cases, implementation-specific uniforms (or constants) might need to be included depending on whether the vertex shader makes use of any built-in transcendental functions. There currently is no mechanism that an application can use to find the number of uniform entries that it can use in a particular vertex shader. The vertex shader compilation will fail and there might be information in the compile log that provides specific information with regards to number of uniform entries being used. However, the information returned by the compile log is implementation specific. We provide some guidelines in this chapter to help maximize the use of vertex uniform entries available in a vertex shader.

- **gl_MaxVaryingVectors**—This is the maximum number of varying vectors; that is, the number of vec4 entries that can be output by a vertex shader. The minimum value supported by all ES 2.0 implementations is eight vec4 entries.

- **gl_MaxVertexTextureImageUnits**—This is the maximum number of texture units available in a vertex shader. The minimum value is 0, which implies that the implementation does not support a vertex texture fetch.

- **gl_MaxCombinedTextureImageUnits**—This is the sum of the maximum number of texture units available in the vertex + fragment shaders. The minimum value is eight.

The values specified for each built-in constant are the minimum values that must be supported by all OpenGL ES 2.0 implementations. It is possible that implementations might support values greater than the minimum values described. The actual supported values can be queried using the following code.

```
GLint maxVertexAttribs, maxVertexUniforms, maxVaryings;
GLint maxVertexTextureUnits, maxCombinedTextureUnits;

glGetIntegerv(GL_MAX_VERTEX_ATTRIBS, &maxVertexAttribs);
glGetIntegerv(GL_MAX_VERTEX_UNIFORM_VECTORS, &maxVertexUniforms);
glGetIntegerv(GL_MAX_VARYING_VECTORS, &maxVaryings);
glGetIntegerv(GL_MAX_VERTEX_TEXTURE_IMAGE_UNITS,
              &maxVertexTextureUnits);
```

```
glGetIntegerv(GL_MAX_COMBINED_TEXTURE_IMAGE_UNITS,
              &maxCombinedTextureUnits);
```

Precision Qualifiers

We do a brief review of precision qualifiers. Precisions qualifiers are covered in Chapter 5. Precision qualifiers can be used to specify the precision of any float- or integer-based variable. The keywords for specifying the precision are `lowp`, `mediump`, and `highp`. Some examples of declarations with precision qualifiers are shown here.

```
highp vec4         position;
varying lowp vec4  color;
mediump float      specularExp;
```

In addition to precision qualifiers, there is also the notion of default precision. That is, if a variable is declared without having a precision qualifier, it will have the default precision for that type. The default precision qualifier is specified at the top of a vertex or fragment shader using the following syntax:

```
precision highp float;
precision mediump int;
```

The precision specified for float will be used as the default precision for all variables based on a floating-point value. Likewise, the precision specified for int will be used as the default precision for all integer-based variables. In the vertex shader, if no default precision is specified, the default precision for both int and float is `highp`.

For operations typically performed in a vertex shader, the precision qualifier that will most likely be needed is the `highp` precision qualifier. Operations that transform a position with a matrix, transform normals and texture coordinates, or generate texture coordinates will need to be done with `highp` precision. Color computations and lighting equations can most likely be done with `mediump` precision. Again, this will depend on the kind of color computations being performed and the range and precision required for operations that are being performed. We believe that `highp` will most likely be the default precision used for most operations in a vertex shader and therefore use `highp` as the default precision qualifier in the examples that follow.

ES 2.0 Vertex Shader Limitations

In this section we describe the limitations imposed by the OpenGL ES 2.0 shading language for vertex shaders. These limitations should help developers write a portable vertex shader that should compile and run on most OpenGL ES 2.0 implementations.

Length of Vertex Shader

There is no way to query the maximum number of instructions supported in a vertex shader across all OpenGL ES 2.0 implementations. It is therefore not possible to say with certainty whether a given vertex shader's instruction count is less than or equal to the number of instructions supported in a vertex shader by an implementation. If the instruction count exceeds the maximum number of instructions allowed in a vertex shader, the vertex shader source will fail to compile.

The OpenGL ES working group recognizes that not being able to query the maximum instruction count and the actual number of uniforms available in a vertex shader are serious issues that can make developers' lives somewhat difficult. The plan is to be able to provide a suite of vertex (and fragment) shaders that will help demonstrate the instruction complexity and uniform usage. In addition, this suite of shaders will be part of the OpenGL ES 2.0 conformance test, which means that all conformant OpenGL ES 2.0 implementations will be capable of running the shaders.

Temporary Variables

A temporary variable refers to a variable declared inside a function or a variable that stores an intermediate value. Because OpenGL ES shading language is a high-level language, there is no way to specify the minimum number of temporary variables that must be supported by all OpenGL ES 2.0 implementations. It is therefore possible that a vertex shader might run into this issue and not compile on all ES 2.0 implementations.

Flow Control

OpenGL ES 2.0 requires implementations to support `for` loops in a vertex shader without requiring that they must be unrolled. For example, you could have a `for` loop with a loop index that goes from 0 to 1023. This will typically not be unrolled by the shader compiler, as the code size of the unrolled shader will most likely be too big for most ES 2.0 implementations.

The following restrictions apply to `for` loops used in a vertex shader:

- Only one loop index can be used in a `for` loop.
- The loop index must be initialized to a constant integral expression.
- The condition expression declared in the `for` loop must be one of the following:

  loop_indx < constant_expression

  loop_indx <= constant_expression

  loop_indx > constant_expression

  loop_indx >= constant_expression

  loop_indx != constant_expression

  loop_indx == constant_expression

- The loop index can be modified in the `for` loop statement using one of the following expressions only:

  loop_index--

  loop_index++

  loop_index -= constant_expression

  loop_index += constant_expression

- The loop index can be passed as a read-only argument to functions inside the `for` loop (i.e., the loop index can be used with arguments declared using the `in` parameter qualifier).

Examples of valid `for` loop constructs are shown here.

```
const int numLights = 4;

int i, j;
for (i=0; i<numLights; i++)
{
    …
}

for (j=4; j>0; j--)
{
    …
    foo(j);   // argument to function foo that takes j
              // is declared with the in qualifier.
}
```

Examples of invalid `for` loop constructs are shown here.

```
uniform int numLights;

int i;
for (i=0; i<numLights; i++)   // conditional expression is
                              // not constant
{
    ...
}

for (i=0; i<8; i++)
{
    i = foo();    // return value of foo() cannot be
                  // assigned to loop index i
}

for (j=4; j>0;)
{
    ...
    j--;    // loop index j cannot be modified
            // inside for loop
}
```

`while` and `do-while` loops, though specified by the OpenGL ES 2.0 shading language specification, are not a requirement and therefore might not be supported by all OpenGL ES 2.0 implementations.

Conditional Statements

The following conditional statements are fully supported without any restrictions.

```
if(bool_expression)
{
    ...
}

if(bool_expression)
{
    ...
}
else
{
    ...
}
```

`bool_expression` must be a scalar boolean value.

GPUs typically execute a vertex shader with multiple vertices or a fragment shader with multiple fragments in parallel. The number of vertices or fragments that are executed in parallel will depend on the GPU's performance target. The `bool_expression` in the `if` and `if-else` conditional statements can have different values for the vertices or fragments being executed in parallel. This can impact performance as the number of vertices or fragments executed in parallel by the GPU is reduced. We recommend that for best performance, conditional statements should be used with `bool_expression` values that are the same for vertices or fragments being executed in parallel. This will be the case if a uniform expression is used.

Array Indexing

Array indexing of uniforms (excluding samplers) is fully supported. The array index can be a constant, uniform, or computed value. Samplers can only be indexed using a constant integral expression. A constant integral expression is a literal value (e.g., 4), a const integer variable (e.g., `const int sampler_indx = 3;`), or a constant expression (e.g., `3 + sampler_indx`).

Attribute matrices and vectors can be indexed using a constant integral expression. Indexing attribute matrices and vectors with a non-constant integral expression is not mandated. This, however, is a very useful feature. The following code shows a vertex shader that performs vertex skinning. `a_matrixweights` is a vertex attribute that stores the matrix weight, for up to four matrices.

```
attribute vec4  a_matrixweights;   // matrix weights
attribute vec4  a_matrixindices;   // matrix palette indices

int i;

for (i=0; i<=3; i++)
{
    float   m_wt = a_matrixweights[i];
    int     m_indx = int(a_matrixindices[i]) * 3;

    ...
}
```

The code `a_matrixweights[i]` and `a_matrixindices[i]` highlighted in bold is not required to be supported and can therefore fail to compile.

Note: The rules for indexing constant matrices and vectors, varyings and variables, or arrays of varyings and variables are the same as those for attributes already described.

Counting Number of Uniforms Used in a Vertex Shader

`gl_MaxVertexUniformVectors` describes the maximum number of uniforms that can be used in a vertex shader. The minimum value for `gl_MaxVertexUniformVectors` that must be supported by any compliant OpenGL ES 2.0 implementation is 128 `vec4` entries. The uniform storage is used to store the following variables:

- Variables declared with the uniform qualifier.

- Const variables.

- Literal values.

- Implementation-specific constants

The number of uniform variables used in a vertex shader along with the variables declared with the const qualifier, literal values, and implementation-specific constants must fit in `gl_MaxVertexUniformVectors` as per the packing rules described in Chapter 5. If these do not fit, then the vertex shader will fail to compile. It is possible for a developer to apply the packing rules and determine the amount of uniform storage needed to store uniform variables, const variables, and literal values. It is not possible to determine the number of implementation-specific constants as this value will not only vary from implementation to implementation but will also change depending on which built-in shading language functions are being used by the vertex shader. Typically, the implementation-specific constants are required when built-in transcendental functions are used.

As far as literal values are concerned, the OpenGL ES 2.0 shading language spec states that no constant propagation is assumed. This means that multiple instances of the same literal value(s) will be counted multiple times. Understandably it is easier to use literal values such as `0.0` or `1.0` in a vertex shader, but our recommendation is that this be avoided as much as possible. Instead of using literal values, appropriate const variables should be declared. This avoids having the same literal value count multiple times, which might cause the vertex shader to fail to compile if vertex uniform storage requirements exceed what the implementation supports.

Consider the following example that describes a snippet of vertex shader code that transforms two texture coordinates per vertex:

```
#define NUM_TEXTURES    2

uniform mat4   tex_matrix[NUM_TEXTURES];        // texture matrices
uniform bool   enable_tex[NUM_TEXTURES];        // texture enables
uniform bool   enable_tex_matrix[NUM_TEXTURES]; // texture matrix
                                                // enables

attribute vec4   a_texcoord0;   // available if enable_tex[0] is true
attribute vec4   a_texcoord1;   // available if enable_tex[1] is true

varying vec4     v_texcoord[NUM_TEXTURES];

v_texcoord[0] = vec4(0.0, 0.0, 0.0, 1.0);
// is texture 0 enabled
if (enable_tex[0])
{
   // is texture matrix 0 enabled
   if(enable_tex_matrix[0])
      v_texcoord[0] = tex_matrix[0] * a_texcoord0;
   else
      v_texcoord[0] = a_texcoord0;
}

v_texcoord[1] = vec4(0.0, 0.0, 0.0, 1.0);
// is texture 1 enabled
if (enable_tex[1])
{
   // is texture matrix 1 enabled
   if(enable_tex_matrix[1])
      v_texcoord[1] = tex_matrix[1] * a_texcoord1;
   else
      v_texcoord[1] = a_texcoord1;
}
```

The code just described might result in each reference to the literal values
0, 1, 0.0, 1.0 counting against the uniform storage. To guarantee that these
literal values count only once against the uniform storage, the vertex shader
code snippet should be written as follows:

```
#define NUM_TEXTURES    2

const int   c_zero = 0;
const int   c_one  = 1;

uniform mat4   tex_matrix[NUM_TEXTURES];        // texture matrices
uniform bool   enable_tex[NUM_TEXTURES];        // texture enables
uniform bool   enable_tex_matrix[NUM_TEXTURES]; // texture matrix
                                                // enables
```

```
attribute vec4  a_texcoord0;  // available if enable_tex[0] is true
attribute vec4  a_texcoord1;  // available if enable_tex[1] is true

varying vec4    v_texcoord[NUM_TEXTURES];

v_texcoord[c_zero] = vec4(float(c_zero), float(c_zero),
                          float(c_zero), float(c_one));
// is texture 0 enabled
if(enable_tex[c_zero])
{
   // is texture matrix 0 enabled
   if(enable_tex_matrix[c_zero])
      v_texcoord[c_zero] = tex_matrix[c_zero] * a_texcoord0;
   else
      v_texcoord[c_zero] = a_texcoord0;
}

v_texcoord[c_one] = vec4(float(c_zero), float(c_zero),
                         float(c_zero), float(c_one));
// is texture 1 enabled
if(enable_tex[c_one])
{
   // is texture matrix 1 enabled
   if(enable_tex_matrix[c_one])
      v_texcoord[c_one] = tex_matrix[c_one] * a_texcoord1;
   else
      v_texcoord[c_one] = a_texcoord1;
}
```

Hopefully this section has been helpful in providing a good understanding of the limitations of the OpenGL ES 2.0 shading language and how to write vertex shaders that should compile and run on most OpenGL ES 2.0 implementations.

Vertex Shader Examples

We now present a few examples that demonstrate how to implement the following features in a vertex shader:

- Transforming vertex position with a matrix.

- Lighting computations to generate per-vertex diffuse and specular color.

- Texture coordinate generation.

- Vertex skinning.

These features represent typical use cases that OpenGL ES 2.0 applications will want to perform in a vertex shader.

A Simple Vertex Shader

Example 8-1 describes a simple vertex shader written using the OpenGL ES shading language. The vertex shader takes a position and its associated color data as inputs or attributes, transforms the position by a 4 × 4 matrix and outputs the transformed position and color.

Example 8-1 A Simple Vertex Shader

```
// uniforms used by the vertex shader
uniform mat4    u_mvp_matrix; // matrix to convert P from
                              // model space to clip space.

// attributes input to the vertex shader
attribute vec4  a_position;   // input position value
attribute vec4  a_color;      // input vertex color

// varying variables - input to the fragment shader
varying vec4    v_color;      // output vertex color

void
main()
{
   v_color = a_color;
   gl_Position = u_mvp_matrix * a_position;
}
```

The transformed vertex positions and primitive type are then used by the setup and rasterization stages to rasterize the primitive into fragments. For each fragment, the interpolated v_color will be computed and passed as input to the fragment shader.

Lighting in a Vertex Shader

In this section, we look at examples that compute the lighting equation for directional lights and point, spot lights. The vertex shaders described in this section use the OpenGL ES 1.1 lighting equation model to compute the lighting equation for a directional or a spot (or point) light. In the lighting examples described here, the viewer is assumed to be at infinity.

A directional light is a light source that is at an infinite distance from the objects in the scene being lit. An example of a directional light is the sun. As the light is at infinite distance, the light rays from the light source are parallel. The light direction vector is a constant and does not need to be computed per vertex. Figure 8-3 describes the terms that are needed in computing the lighting equation for a directional light. P_{eye} is the position of the viewer, P_{light} is the position of the light ($P_{light}.w = 0$), N is the normal, and H is the half-plane vector. Because $P_{light}.w = 0$, the light direction vector will be $P_{light}.xyz$. The half-plane vector H is computed as $\| VP_{light} + VP_{eye} \|$. As both the light source and viewer are at infinity, the half-plane vector $H = \| P_{light}.xyz + (0, 0, 1) \|$.

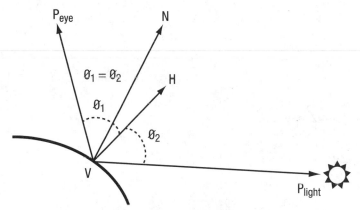

Figure 8-3   Geometric Factors in Computing Lighting Equation for a Directional Light

Example 8-2 describes the vertex shader code that computes the lighting equation for a directional light. The directional light properties are described by a `directional_light` `struct` that contains the following elements:

- **direction**—The normalized light direction in eye space.

- **halfplane**—The normalized half-plane vector H. This can be precomputed for a directional light, as it does not change.

- **ambient_color**—The ambient color of the light.

- **diffuse_color**—The diffuse color of the light.

- **specular_color**—The specular color of the light.

The material properties needed to compute the vertex diffuse and specular color are described by a `material_properties` `struct` that contains the following elements:

- **ambient_color**—The ambient color of the material.

- **diffuse_color**—The diffuse color of the material.

- **specular_color**—The specular color of the material.

- **specular_exponent**—The specular exponent that describes the shininess of the material and is used to control the shininess of the specular highlight.

Example 8-2   Directional Light

```
struct directional_light {
   vec3  direction;     // normalized light direction in eye space
   vec3  halfplane;     // normalized half-plane vector
   vec4  ambient_color;
   vec4  diffuse_color;
   vec4  specular_color;
};

struct material_properties {
   vec4   ambient_color;
   vec4   diffuse_color;
   vec4   specular_color;
   float  specular_exponent;
};

const float              c_zero = 0.0;
const float              c_one = 1.0;

uniform material_properties  material;
uniform directional_light    light;

// normal has been transformed into eye space and is a normalized
// value returns the computed color.
vec4
directional_light(vec3 normal)
{
   vec4   computed_color = vec4(c_zero, c_zero, c_zero, c_zero);
   float  ndotl;  // dot product of normal & light direction
   float  ndoth;  // dot product of normal & half-plane vector

   ndotl = max(c_zero, dot(normal, light.direction));
   ndoth = max(c_zero, dot(normal, light.halfplane));

   computed_color += (light.ambient_color * material.ambient_color);
   computed_color += (ndotl * light.diffuse_color
                      * material.diffuse_color);
```

```
if (ndoth > c_zero)
{
    computed_color += (pow(ndoth, material.specular_exponent) *
                      material.specular_color *
                      light.specular_color);
}

return computed_color;
}
```

The directional light vertex shader code described in Example 8-2 combines the per-vertex diffuse and specular color into a single color (given by computed_color). Another option would be to compute the per-vertex diffuse and specular colors and pass them as separate varying variables to the fragment shader.

Note: In Example 8-2 we multiply the material colors (ambient, diffuse, and specular) with the light colors. This is fine if we are computing the lighting equation for only one light. If we have to compute the lighting equation for multiple lights, we should compute the ambient, diffuse, and specular values for each light and then compute the final vertex color by multiplying the material ambient, diffuse, and specular colors to appropriate computed terms and then summing them all to generate a per-vertex color.

A point light is a light source that emanates light in all directions from a position in space. A point light is given by a position vector (x, y, z, w), where $w \neq 0$. The point light shines evenly in all directions but its intensity falls off (i.e., gets attenuated) based on the distance from the light to the object. This attenuation is computed using the following equation.

$$distance\ attenuation = 1\ /\ (K_0 + K_1 \times \|\ VP_{light}\ \| + K_2 \times \|\ VP_{light}\ \|^2)$$

K_0, K_1, and K_2 are the constant, linear, and quadratic attenuation factors.

A spotlight is a light source with both a position and a direction that simulates a cone of light emitted from a position (P_{light}) in a direction (given by $spot_{direction}$). Figure 8-4 describes the terms that are needed in computing the lighting equation for a spotlight.

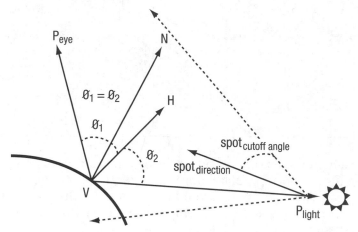

Figure 8-4   Geometric Factors in Computing Lighting Equation for a Spot Light

The intensity of the emitted light is attenuated by a spot cutoff factor based on the angle from the center of the cone. This angle from the center of the cone is computed as the dot product of VP_{light} and $spot_{direction}$. The spot cutoff factor is 1.0 in the spot light direction given by $spot_{direction}$ and falls off exponentially to 0.0 $spot_{cutoff\,angle}$ radians away.

Example 8-3 describes the vertex shader code that computes the lighting equation for a spot (and point) light. The spot light properties are described by a `spot_light struct` that contains the following elements:

- **direction**—The light direction in eye space.

- **ambient_color**—The ambient color of the light.

- **diffuse_color**—The diffuse color of the light.

- **specular_color**—The specular color of the light.

- **attenuation_factors**—The distance attenuation factors K_0, K_1, and K_2.

- **compute_distance_attenuation**—This boolean term determines if the distance attenuation must be computed.

- **spot_direction**—The normalized spot direction vector.

- **spot_exponent**—The spotlight exponent used to compute the spot cutoff factor.

- **spot_cutoff_angle**—The spotlight cutoff angle in degrees.

Example 8-3   Spot Light

```
struct spot_light {
    vec4    position;              // light position in eye space
    vec4    ambient_color;
    vec4    diffuse_color;
    vec4    specular_color;
    vec3    spot_direction;        // normalized spot direction
    vec3    attenuation_factors;   // attenuation factors K0, K1, K2
    bool    compute_distance_attenuation;
    float   spot_exponent;         // spotlight exponent term
    float   spot_cutoff_angle;     // spot cutoff angle in degrees
};

struct material_properties {
    vec4    ambient_color;
    vec4    diffuse_color;
    vec4    specular_color;
    float   specular_exponent;
};

const float                c_zero = 0.0;
const float                c_one = 1.0;

uniform material_properties  material;
uniform spot_light           light;

// normal and position are normal and position values in eye space.
// normal is a normalized vector.
// returns the computed color.

vec4
spot_light(vec3 normal, vec4 position)
{
    vec4    computed_color = vec4(c_zero, c_zero, c_zero, c_zero);
    vec3    lightdir;
    vec3    halfplane;
    float   ndotl, ndoth;
    float   att_factor;

    att_factor = c_one;

    // we assume "w" values for light position and
    // vertex position are the same
    lightdir = light.position.xyz - position.xyz;

    // compute distance attenuation
    if(light.compute_distance_attenuation)
    {
```

```
        vec3    att_dist;

    att_dist.x = c_one;
    att_dist.z = dot(lightdir, lightdir);
    att_dist.y = sqrt(att_dist.z);
    att_factor = c_one / dot(att_dist, light.attenuation_factors);
}

// normalize the light direction vector
lightdir = normalize(lightdir);

// compute spot cutoff factor
if(light.spot_cutoff_angle < 180.0)
{
    float   spot_factor = dot(-lightdir, light.spot_direction);

    if(spot_factor >= cos(radians(light.spot_cutoff_angle)))
        spot_factor = pow(spot_factor, light.spot_exponent);
    else
        spot_factor = c_zero;

    // compute combined distance & spot attenuation factor
    att_factor *= spot_factor;
}

if(att_factor > c_zero)
{
    // process lighting equation --> compute the light color
    computed_color += (light.ambient_color *
                        material.ambient_color);
    ndotl = max(c_zero, dot(normal, lightdir));
    computed_color += (ndotl * light.diffuse_color *
                        material.diffuse_color);
    halfplane = normalize(lightdir + vec3(c_zero, c_zero, c_one));
    ndoth = dot(normal, halfplane);
    if (ndoth > c_zero)
    {
        computed_color += (pow(ndoth, material.specular_exponent)*
                            material.specular_color *
                            light.specular_color);
    }

    // multiply color with computed attenuation
    computed_color *= att_factor;
}

return computed_color;
}
```

Generating Texture Coordinates

We look at two examples that generate texture coordinates in a vertex shader. The two examples are used when rendering shiny (i.e., reflective) objects in a scene by generating a reflection vector and then using this to compute a texture coordinate that indexes into a latitude longitude map (also called a sphere map) or a cube map (represents six views or faces that capture reflected environment assuming a single viewpoint in the middle of the shiny object). The OpenGL 2.0 specification describes the texture coordinate generation modes as GL_SPHERE_MAP and GL_REFLECTION_MAP, respectively. The GL_SPHERE_MAP mode generates a texture coordinate that uses a reflection vector to compute a 2D texture coordinate for lookup into a 2D texture map. The GL_REFLECTION_MAP mode generates a texture coordinate that is a reflection vector that can be used as a 3D texture coordinate for lookup into a cube map. Examples 8-4 and 8-5 describe the vertex shader code that generates texture coordinates that will be used by the appropriate fragment shader to calculate the reflected image on the shiny object.

Example 8-4   Sphere Map Texture Coordinate Generation

```
// position is the normalized position coordinate in eye space
// normal is the normalized normal coordinate in eye space
// returns a vec2 texture coordinate
vec2
sphere_map(vec3 position, vec3 normal)
{
    reflection = reflect(position, normal);
    m = 2.0 * sqrt(reflection.x * reflection.x +
                   reflection.y * reflection.y +
                   (reflection.z + 1.0) * (reflection.z + 1.0));
    return vec2((reflection.x / m + 0.5), (reflection.y / m + 0.5));
}
```

Example 8-5   Cube Map Texture Coordinate Generation

```
// position is the normalized position coordinate in eye space
// normal is the normalized normal coordinate in eye space
// returns the reflection vector as a vec3 texture coordinate
vec3
cube_map(vec3 position, vec3 normal)
{
    return reflect(position, normal);
}
```

The reflection vector will then be used inside a fragment shader as the texture coordinate to the appropriate cube map.

Vertex Skinning

Vertex skinning is a commonly used technique whereby the joins between polygons are smoothed. This is implemented by applying additional transform matrices with appropriate weights to each vertex. The multiple matrices used to skin vertices are stored in a matrix palette. Matrices indices per vertex are used to refer to appropriate matrices in the matrix palette that will be used to skin the vertex. Vertex skinning is commonly used for character models in 3D games to ensure that they appear smooth and realistic (as much as possible) without having to use additional geometry. The number of matrices used to skin a vertex is typically two to four.

The mathematics of vertex skinning is given by the following equations:

$$P' = \sum w_i \times M_i \times P$$
$$N' = \sum w_i \times M_i^{-1T} \times N$$
$$\sum w_i = 1, i = 1 \text{ to } n$$

where

n is the number of matrices that will be used to transform the vertex

P is the vertex position

P' is the transformed (skinned) position

N is the vertex normal

N' is the transformed (skinned) normal

M_i is the matrix associated with the ith matrix per vertex and is computed as

M_i = matrix_palette [matrix_index[i]]
with n matrix_index values specified per vertex

M_i^{-1T} is the inverse transpose of matrix M_i

w_i is the weight associated with the matrix

We discuss how to implement vertex skinning with a matrix palette of 32 matrices and up to four matrices per vertex to generate a skinned vertex. A matrix palette size of 32 matrices is quite common. The matrices in the matrix palette typically are 4 × 3 column major matrices (i.e., four `vec3` entries per matrix). If the matrices were to be stored in column-major order, this will take 128 uniform entries with three elements of each uniform entry used to store a row. The minimum value of `gl_MaxVertexUniformVectors` that is supported by all OpenGL ES 2.0 implementations is 128 `vec4` entries. This means we will only have the fourth row of these 128 `vec4` uniform entries available. This row of floats can only be used to store uniforms declared to be of type `float` (as per the uniform packing rule). There is no room therefore to store a `vec2`, `vec3`, or `vec4` uniform. It would be better to store the matrices in the palette in row-major order using three `vec4` entries per matrix. If we did this, then we use 96 `vec4`'s of uniform storage and the remaining 32 `vec4` entries can be used to store other uniforms. Note that we do not have enough uniform storage to store inverse transpose matrices needed to compute the skinned normal. This is typically not a problem as in most cases the matrices used are orthonormal and therefore can be used to transform the vertex position and the normal.

Example 8-6 describes the vertex shader code that computes the skinned normal and position. We assume 32 matrices in the matrix palette, and that the matrices are stored in row-major order. The matrices are also assumed to be orthonormal (i.e., the same matrix can be used to transform position and normal) and up to four matrices are used to transform each vertex.

Example 8-6   Vertex Skinning Shader with No Check to See if Matrix Weight = 0

```
#define NUM_MATRICES  32   // 32 matrices in matrix palette

const int      c_zero  = 0;
const int      c_one   = 1;
const int      c_two   = 2;
const int      c_three = 3;

// store 32 4 x 3 matrices as an array of floats representing
// each matrix in row-major order i.e. 3 vec4s
uniform vec4    matrix_palette[NUM_MATRICES * 3];

// vertex position and normal attributes
attribute vec4  a_position
attribute vec3  a_normal;

// matrix weights - 4 entries / vertex
attribute vec4  a_matrixweights;
```

```
// matrix palette indices
attribute vec4   a_matrixindices;

void
skin_position(in vec4 position, float m_wt, int m_indx,
                                out vec4 skinned_position)
{
    vec4    tmp;

    tmp.x = dot(position, matrix_palette[m_indx]);
    tmp.y = dot(position, matrix_palette[m_indx + c_one]);
    tmp.z = dot(position, matrix_palette[m_indx + c_two]);
    tmp.w = position.w;

    skinned_position += m_wt * tmp;
}

void
skin_normal(in vec3 normal, float m_wt, int m_indx,
                            out vec3 skinned_normal)
{
    vec3    tmp;

    tmp.x = dot(normal, matrix_palette[m_indx].xyz);
    tmp.y = dot(normal, matrix_palette[m_indx + c_one].xyz);
    tmp.z = dot(normal, matrix_palette[m_indx + c_two].xyz);

    skinned_position += m_wt * tmp;
}


void
do_skinning(in vec4 position, in vec3 normal,
            out vec4 skinned_position, out vec4 skinned_normal)
{
    skinned_position = vec4(float(c_zero));
    skinned_normal = vec3(float(c_zero));

    // transform position and normal to eye space using matrix
    // palette with four matrices used to transform a vertex

    m_wt = a_matrixweights[0];
    m_indx = int(a_matrixindices[0]) * c_three;
    skin_position(position, m_wt, m_indx, skinned_position);
    skin_normal(normal, m_wt, m_indx, skinned_normal);

    m_wt = a_matrixweights[1];
    m_indx = int(a_matrixindices[1]) * c_three;
    skin_position(position, m_wt, m_indx, skinned_position);
```

```
    skin_normal(normal, m_wt, m_indx, skinned_normal);

    m_wt = a_matrixweights[2];
    m_indx = int(a_matrixindices[2]) * c_three;
    skin_position(position, m_wt, m_indx, skinned_position);
    skin_normal(normal, m_wt, m_indx, skinned_normal);

    m_wt = a_matrixweights[3];
    m_indx = int(a_matrixindices[3]) * c_three;
    skin_position(position, m_wt, m_indx, skinned_position);
    skin_normal(normal, m_wt, m_indx, skinned_normal);

}
```

In Example 8-6, the vertex skinning shader generates a skinned vertex by transforming a vertex with four matrices and appropriate matrix weights. It is possible and quite common that some of these matrix weights may be zero. In Example 8-6, the vertex is transformed using all four matrices, irrespective of their weights. It might be better to use a conditional expression to check if matrix weight is zero before calling skin_position and skin_normal. Example 8-7 describes the vertex skinning shader that checks if the matrix weight is zero before applying the matrix transformation.

Example 8-7   Vertex Skinning Shader with Checks to See if Matrix Weight = 0

```
void
do_skinning(in vec4 position, in vec3 normal,
            out vec4 skinned_position, out vec4 skinned_normal)
{
    skinned_position = vec4(float(c_zero));
    skinned_normal = vec3(float(c_zero));

    // transform position and normal to eye space using matrix
    // palette with four matrices used to transform a vertex

    m_wt = a_matrixweights[0];
    if(m_wt > 0.0)
    {
        m_indx = int(a_matrixindices[0]) * c_three;
        skin_position(position, m_wt, m_indx, skinned_position);
        skin_normal(normal, m_wt, m_indx, skinned_normal);
    }

    m_wt = a_matrixweights[1];
    if(m_wt > 0.0)
    {
```

```
    m_indx = int(a_matrixindices[1]) * c_three;
    skin_position(position, m_wt, m_indx, skinned_position);
    skin_normal(normal, m_wt, m_indx, skinned_normal);
}

m_wt = a_matrixweights[2];
if(m_wt > 0.0)
{
    m_indx = int(a_matrixindices[2]) * c_three;
    skin_position(position, m_wt, m_indx, skinned_position);
    skin_normal(normal, m_wt, m_indx, skinned_normal);
}

m_wt = a_matrixweights[3];
if(m_wt > 0.0)
{
    m_indx = int(a_matrixindices[3]) * c_three;
    skin_position(position, m_wt, m_indx, skinned_position);
    skin_normal(normal, m_wt, m_indx, skinned_normal);
}
}
```

At first glance, we might conclude that the vertex skinning shader in Example 8-7 has better performance than the vertex skinning shader in Example 8-6. This is not necessarily true and the answer can vary across GPUs. This is because in the conditional expression if (m_wt > 0.0), m_wt is a dynamic value and can be different for vertices being executed in parallel by the GPU. We now run into divergent flow control where vertices being executed in parallel may have different values for m_wt and this can cause execution to serialize. If a GPU does not implement divergent flow control efficiently, the vertex shader in Example 8-7 might not be as efficient as the version in Example 8-6. Applications should, therefore, test performance of divergent flow control by executing a test shader on the GPU as part of the application initialization phase to determine which shaders to use.

We hope that the examples discussed so far have provided a good understanding of vertex shaders, how to write them, and how to use them for a wide-ranging array of effects.

OpenGL ES 1.1 Vertex Pipeline as an ES 2.0 Vertex Shader

We now discuss a vertex shader that implements the OpenGL ES 1.1 fixed function vertex pipeline without vertex skinning. This is also meant to be an interesting exercise in figuring out how big a vertex shader can be for it to run across all OpenGL ES 2.0 implementations.

This vertex shader implements the following fixed functions of the OpenGL ES 1.1 vertex pipeline:

- Transform the normal and position to eye space, if required (typically required for lighting). Rescale or normalization of normal is also performed.

- Computes the OpenGL ES 1.1 vertex lighting equation for up to eight directional, point, or spot lights with two-sided lighting and color material per vertex.

- Transform texture coordinates for up to two texture coordinates per vertex.

- Compute fog factor passed to fragment shader. The fragment shader uses the fog factor to interpolate between fog color and vertex color.

- Computes per-vertex user clip plane factor. Only one user clip plane is supported.

- Transform position to clip space.

Example 8-8 is the vertex shader that implements the OpenGL ES 1.1 fixed function vertex pipeline as already described.

Example 8-8   OpenGL ES 1.1 Fixed Function Vertex Pipeline

```
//*******************************************************************
//
// OpenGL ES 2.0 vertex shader that implements the following
// OpenGL ES 1.1 fixed function pipeline
//
// - compute lighting equation for up to eight directional/point/
// - spot lights
// - transform position to clip coordinates
// - texture coordinate transforms for up to two texture coordinates
// - compute fog factor
// - compute user clip plane dot product (stored as v_ucp_factor)
//
//*******************************************************************
```

```
#define NUM_TEXTURES              2
#define GLI_FOG_MODE_LINEAR       0
#define GLI_FOG_MODE_EXP          1
#define GLI_FOG_MODE_EXP2         2

struct light {
    vec4    position;  // light position for a point/spot light or
                       // normalized dir. for a directional light
    vec4    ambient_color;
    vec4    diffuse_color;
    vec4    specular_color;
    vec3    spot_direction;
    vec3    attenuation_factors;
    float   spot_exponent;
    float   spot_cutoff_angle;
    bool    compute_distance_attenuation;
};

struct material {
    vec4    ambient_color;
    vec4    diffuse_color;
    vec4    specular_color;
    vec4    emissive_color;
    float   specular_exponent;
};

const float     c_zero = 0.0;
const float     c_one = 1.0;
const int       indx_zero = 0;
const int       indx_one = 1;

uniform mat4    mvp_matrix;     // combined model-view +
                               // projection matrix

uniform mat4    modelview_matrix;      // model view matrix
uniform mat3    inv_modelview_matrix; // inverse model-view
                                      // matrix used
// to transform normal
uniform mat4    tex_matrix[NUM_TEXTURES]; // texture matrices
uniform bool    enable_tex[NUM_TEXTURES]; // texture enables
uniform bool    enable_tex_matrix[NUM_TEXTURES]; // texture matrix
                                                // enables

uniform material  material_state;
uniform vec4      ambient_scene_color;
uniform light     light_state[8];
uniform bool      light_enable_state[8];  // booleans to indicate
                                          // which of eight
                                          // lights are enabled
```

```
uniform int        num_lights;// number of lights enabled = sum of
                              // light_enable_state bools set to TRUE

uniform bool       enable_lighting;        // is lighting enabled
uniform bool       light_model_two_sided;  // is two-sided lighting
                                           // enabled
uniform bool       enable_color_material;  // is color material
                                           // enabled

uniform bool       enable_fog;             // is fog enabled
uniform float      fog_density;
uniform float      fog_start, fog_end;
uniform int        fog_mode;               // fog mode - linear, exp,
                                           // or exp2

uniform bool       xform_eye_p;   // xform_eye_p is set if we need
                                  // Peye for user clip plane,
                                  // lighting, or fog
uniform bool       rescale_normal;      // is rescale normal enabled
uniform bool       normalize_normal;    // is normalize normal enabled
uniform float      rescale_normal_factor; // rescale normal factor if
                                  // glEnable(GL_RESCALE_NORMAL)

uniform vec4       ucp_eqn;       // user clip plane equation -
                                  // - one user clip plane specified

uniform bool       enable_ucp;    // is user clip plane enabled

//*******************************************************
// vertex attributes - not all of them may be passed in
//*******************************************************
attribute vec4     a_position; // this attribute is always specified
attribute vec4     a_texcoord0;// available if enable_tex[0] is true
attribute vec4     a_texcoord1;// available if enable_tex[1] is true
attribute vec4     a_color;    // available if !enable_lighting or
                        // (enable_lighting && enable_color_material)
attribute vec3     a_normal;   // available if xform_normal is set
                                  // (required for lighting)


//*********************************************
// varying variables output by the vertex shader
//*********************************************
varying vec4       v_texcoord[NUM_TEXTURES];
varying vec4       v_front_color;
varying vec4       v_back_color;
varying float      v_fog_factor;
varying float      v_ucp_factor;
```

```
//****************************************************
// temporary variables used by the vertex shader
//****************************************************
vec4            p_eye;
vec3            n;
vec4            mat_ambient_color;
vec4            mat_diffuse_color;

vec4
lighting_equation(int i)
{
    vec4    computed_color = vec4(c_zero, c_zero, c_zero, c_zero);
    vec3    h_vec;
    float   ndotl, ndoth;
    float   att_factor;

    att_factor = c_one;
    if(light_state[i].position.w != c_zero)
    {
        float   spot_factor;
        vec3    att_dist;
        vec3    VPpli;

        // this is a point or spot light
        // we assume "w" values for PPli and V are the same
        VPpli = light_state[i].position.xyz - p_eye.xyz;
        if(light_state[i].compute_distance_attenuation)
        {
            // compute distance attenuation
            att_dist.x = c_one;
            att_dist.z = dot(VPpli, VPpli);
            att_dist.y = sqrt(att_dist.z);
            att_factor = c_one / dot(att_dist,
                light_state[i].attenuation_factors);
        }
        VPpli = normalize(VPpli);

        if(light_state[i].spot_cutoff_angle < 180.0)
        {
            // compute spot factor
            spot_factor = dot(-VPpli, light_state[i].spot_direction);
            if(spot_factor >= cos(radians(
                            light_state[i].spot_cutoff_angle)))
                spot_factor = pow(spot_factor,
                            light_state[i].spot_exponent);
            else
                spot_factor = c_zero;

            att_factor *= spot_factor;
```

```
      }
   }
   else
   {
      // directional light
      VPpli = light_state[i].position.xyz;
   }

   if(att_factor > c_zero)
   {
      // process lighting equation --> compute the light color
      computed_color += (light_state[i].ambient_color *
                         mat_ambient_color);
      ndotl = max(c_zero, dot(n, VPpli));
      computed_color += (ndotl * light_state[i].diffuse_color *
                         mat_diffuse_color);
      h_vec = normalize(VPpli + vec3(c_zero, c_zero, c_one));
      ndoth = dot(n, h_vec);
      if (ndoth > c_zero)
      {
         computed_color += (pow(ndoth,
                            material_state.specular_exponent) *
                            material_state.specular_color *
                            light_state[i].specular_color);
      }
      computed_color *= att_factor; // multiply color with
                                    // computed attenuation factor
                                    // * computed spot factor
   }
   return computed_color;
}

float
compute_fog()
{
   float   f;

   // use eye Z as approximation
   if(fog_mode == GLI_FOG_MODE_LINEAR)
   {
      f = (fog_end - p_eye.z) / (fog_end - fog_start);
   }
   else if(fog_mode == GLI_FOG_MODE_EXP)
   {
      f = exp(-(p_eye.z * fog_density));
   }
   else
   {
      f = (p_eye.z * fog_density);
```

```
        f = exp(-(f * f));
    }

    f = clamp(f, c_zero, c_one);
    return f;
}

vec4
do_lighting()
{
    vec4    vtx_color;
    int     i, j;

    vtx_color = material_state.emissive_color +
                (mat_ambient_color * ambient_scene_color);
    j = (int)c_zero;
    for (i=(int)c_zero; i<8; i++)
    {
        if(j >= num_lights)
            break;

        if (light_enable_state[i])
        {
            j++;
            vtx_color += lighting_equation(i);
        }
    }

    vtx_color.a = mat_diffuse_color.a;

    return vtx_color;
}


void
main(void)
{
    int     i, j;

    // do we need to transform P
    if(xform_eye_p)
        p_eye = modelview_matrix * a_position;

    if(enable_lighting)
    {
        n = inv_modelview_matrix * a_normal;
        if(rescale_normal)
            n = rescale_normal_factor * n;
        if (normalize_normal)
```

```
            n = normalize(n);
   mat_ambient_color = enable_color_material ? a_color
                                     : material_state.ambient_color;
   mat_diffuse_color = enable_color_material ? a_color
                                     : material_state.diffuse_color;
   v_front_color = do_lighting();
   v_back_color = v_front_color;

   // do 2-sided lighting
   if(light_model_two_sided)
   {
      n = -n;
      v_back_color = do_lighting();
   }
}
else
{
   // set the default output color to be the per-vertex /
   // per-primitive color
   v_front_color = a_color;
   v_back_color = a_color;
}

// do texture xforms
v_texcoord[indx_zero] = vec4(c_zero, c_zero, c_zero, c_one);
if(enable_tex[indx_zero])
{
   if(enable_tex_matrix[indx_zero])
      v_texcoord[indx_zero] = tex_matrix[indx_zero] *
                              a_texcoord0;
   else
      v_texcoord[indx_zero] = a_texcoord0;
}

v_texcoord[indx_one] = vec4(c_zero, c_zero, c_zero, c_one);
if(enable_tex[indx_one])
{
   if(enable_tex_matrix[indx_one])
      v_texcoord[indx_one] = tex_matrix[indx_one] * a_texcoord1;
   else
      v_texcoord[indx_one] = a_texcoord1;
}

 v_ucp_factor = enable_ucp ? dot(p_eye, ucp_eqn) : c_zero;
 v_fog_factor = enable_fog ? compute_fog() : c_one;

 gl_Position = mvp_matrix * a_position;
}
```

Chapter 9

Texturing

Now that we have covered vertex shaders in detail, you should be familiar with all of the gritty details in transforming vertices and preparing primitives for rendering. The next step in the pipeline is the fragment shader, where much of the visual magic of OpenGL ES 2.0 occurs. Programmable fragment shaders are fundamental in producing effects that include texturing, per-pixel lighting, and shadows. A fundamental aspect of fragment shaders is the application of textures to surfaces. This chapter covers all of the details of creating, loading, and applying textures:

- Texturing basics.

- Loading textures and mipmapping.

- Texture filtering and wrapping.

- Using textures in the fragment shader.

- Texture subimage specification.

- Copying texture data from the color buffer.

- Optional texturing extensions.

Texturing Basics

One of the most fundamental operations used in rendering 3D graphics is the application of textures to a surface. Textures allow for the representation of additional detail not available just from the geometry of a mesh. Textures in OpenGL ES 2.0 come in two forms: 2D textures and cube map textures.

Textures are typically applied to a surface by using texture coordinates that can be thought of as indices into texture array data. The following sections introduce the different texture types in OpenGL ES and how they are loaded and accessed.

2D Textures

A 2D texture is the most basic and common form of texture in OpenGL ES. A 2D texture is—as you might guess—a two-dimensional array of image data. The individual data elements of a texture are known as *texels*. A texel is a shortened way of describing a texture pixel. Texture image data in OpenGL ES can be represented in many different basic formats. The basic formats available for texture data are shown in Table 9-1.

Table 9-1   Texture Base Formats

Base Format	Texel Data Description
GL_RGB	(Red, Green, Blue)
GL_RGBA	(Red, Green, Blue, Alpha)
GL_LUMINANCE	(Luminance)
GL_LUMINANCE_ALPHA	(Luminance, Alpha)
GL_ALPHA	(Alpha)

Each texel in the image is specified according to its basic format and also its data type. Later, we describe in more detail the various data types that can represent a texel. For now, the important point to understand is that a 2D texture is a two-dimensional array of image data. When rendering with a 2D texture, a texture coordinate is used as an index into the texture image. Generally, a mesh will be authored in a 3D content authoring program with each vertex having a texture coordinate. Texture coordinates for 2D textures are given by a 2D pair of coordinates (s, t), sometimes also called (u, v) coordinates. These coordinates represent normalized coordinates used to look up into a texture map as shown in Figure 9-1.

The lower left corner of the texture image is specified by the *st*-coordinates (0.0, 0.0). The upper right corner of the texture image is specified by the *st*-coordinates (1.0, 1.0). Coordinates outside of the range [0.0, 1.0] are allowed, and the behavior of texture fetches outside of that range is defined by the texture wrapping mode (described in the section on texture filtering and wrapping).

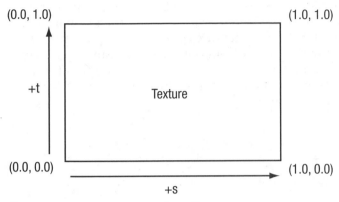

(0.0, 1.0)   (1.0, 1.0)

+t   Texture

(0.0, 0.0)   (1.0, 0.0)

+s

Figure 9-1   2D Texture Coordinates

Cubemap Textures

In addition to 2D textures, OpenGL ES 2.0 also supports cubemap textures. At its most basic, a cubemap is a texture made up of six individual 2D texture faces. Each face of the cubemap represents one of the six sides of a cube. Cubemaps have a variety of advanced uses in 3D rendering, but the most basic use is for an effect known as *environment mapping*. For this effect, the reflection of the environment onto the object is rendered by using a cubemap to represent the environment. The typical way that a cubemap is generated for environment mapping is that a camera is placed in the center of the scene and an image of the scene is captured from each of the six axis directions (+X, –X, +Y, –Y, +Z, –Z) and stored in each cube face.

The way that texels are fetched out of a cubemap is by using a 3D vector (s,t,r) as the texture coordinate to look up into a cubemap. The 3D vector is used to first select a face of the cubemap to fetch from, and then the coordinate is projected into a 2D (s,t) coordinate to fetch from the cubemap face. The actual math for computing the 2D (s,t) coordinate is outside our scope here, but suffice to say that a 3D vector is used to look up into a cubemap. You can visualize the way this works by picturing a 3D vector coming from the origin inside of a cube. The point at which that vector intersects the cube is the texel that would be fetched from the cubemap. This is shown in Figure 9-2, where a 3D vector intersects the cube face.

The faces of a cubemap are each specified in the same manner as one would specify a 2D texture. Each of the faces must be square (e.g., the width and height must be equal) and each of the faces must have the same width and height. The 3D vector that is used for the texture coordinate is not normally stored directly per-vertex on the mesh as it is for 2D texturing. Rather, the most common way cubemaps are fetched from is to use the normal vector as a basis for computing the cubemap texture coordinate. Typically the normal vector is used along with a vector from the eye to compute a reflection vector that is then used to look up into a cubemap. This computation is described in the environment mapping example in Chapter 13, "Advanced Programming with OpenGL ES 2.0."

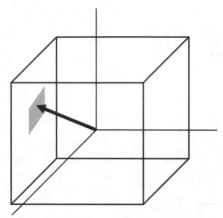

Figure 9-2   3D Texture Coordinate for Cubemap

Texture Objects and Loading Textures

The first step in the application of textures is to create a *texture object*. A texture object is a container object that holds the texture data that is needed for rendering such as image data, filtering modes, and wrap modes. In OpenGL ES, a texture object is represented by an unsigned integer that is a handle to the texture object. The function that is used for generating texture objects is glGenTextures.

void	**glGenTextures**(GLsizei *n*, GLuint **textures*)
n	specifies the number of texture objects to generate
textures	an array of unsigned integers that will hold *n* texture object IDs

Texture objects also need to be deleted when an application no longer needs them. This is typically either done at application shutdown or, for example, when changing levels in a game. This can be done using `glDeleteTextures`.

void **glDeleteTextures**(GLsizei *n*, GLuint **textures*)	
n	specifies the number of texture objects to delete
textures	an array of unsigned integers that hold *n* texture object IDs to delete

Once texture object IDs have been generated with `glGenTextures`, the application must bind the texture object to operate on it. Once texture objects are bound, subsequent operations such as `glTexImage2D` and `glTexParameter` affect the bound texture object. The function used to bind texture objects is `glBindTexture`.

void **glBindTexture**(GLenum *target*, GLuint *texture*)	
target	bind the texture object to target GL_TEXTURE_2D or GL_TEXTURE_CUBE_MAP
texture	the handle to the texture object to bind

Once a texture is bound to a particular texture target, that texture object will remain bound to that target until it is deleted. After generating a texture object and binding it, the next step to using a texture is to actually load the image data. The primary function that is used for loading textures is `glTexImage2D`.

void **glTexImage2D**(GLenum *target*, GLint *level*, GLenum *internalFormat*, GLsizei *width*, GLsizei *height*, GLint *border*, GLenum *format*, GLenum *type*, const void* *pixels*)

target	specifies the texture target, either `GL_TEXTURE_2D` or one of the cubemap face targets (e.g., `GL_TEXTURE_CUBE_MAP_POSITIVE_X`, `GL_TEXTURE_CUBE_MAP_NEGATIVE_X`, etc.)
level	specifies which mip level to load. The base level is specified by 0 followed by an increasing level for each successive mipmap
internalFormat	the internal format for the texture storage, can be: `GL_RGBA` `GL_RGB` `GL_LUMINANCE_ALPHA` `GL_LUMINANCE` `GL_ALPHA`
width	the width of the image in pixels
height	the height of the image in pixels
border	this parameter is ignored in OpenGL ES, but it was kept for compatibility with the desktop OpenGL interface; should be 0
format	the format of the incoming texture data. Note that in OpenGL ES the *format* and *internalFormat* arguments must have the same value. The supported formats are the same as the internal formats
type	the type of the incoming pixel data, can be: `GL_UNSIGNED_BYTE` `GL_UNSIGNED_SHORT_4_4_4_4` `GL_UNSIGNED_SHORT_5_5_5_1` `GL_UNSIGNED_SHORT_5_6_5`
pixels	contains the actual pixel data for the image. The data must contain (*width* * *height*) number of pixels with the appropriate number of bytes per pixel based on the format and *type* specification. The pixel rows must be aligned to the `GL_UNPACK_ALIGNMENT` set with `glPixelStorei` (defined next)

The code in Example 9-1 from the Simple_Texture2D example demonstrates generating a texture object, binding it, and then loading a 2 × 2 2D texture with RGB image data made from unsigned bytes.

Example 9-1   Generating a Texture Object, Binding It, and Loading Image Data

```
// Texture object handle
GLuint textureId;

// 2 x 2 Image, 3 bytes per pixel(R, G, B)
GLubyte pixels[4 * 3] =
{
   255,   0,   0, // Red
     0, 255,   0, // Green
     0,   0, 255, // Blue
   255, 255,   0  // Yellow
};

// Use tightly packed data
glPixelStorei(GL_UNPACK_ALIGNMENT, 1);

// Generate a texture object
glGenTextures(1, &textureId);

// Bind the texture object
glBindTexture(GL_TEXTURE_2D, textureId);

// Load the texture
glTexImage2D(GL_TEXTURE_2D, 0, GL_RGB, 2, 2, 0, GL_RGB,
             GL_UNSIGNED_BYTE, pixels);

// Set the filtering mode
glTexParameteri(GL_TEXTURE_2D, GL_TEXTURE_MIN_FILTER, GL_NEAREST);
glTexParameteri(GL_TEXTURE_2D, GL_TEXTURE_MAG_FILTER, GL_NEAREST);
```

In the first part of the code, the pixels array is initialized with simple 2 × 2 texture data. The data is composed of unsigned byte RGB triplets that are in the range [0, 255]. When data is fetched from an 8-bit unsigned byte texture component in the shader, the values are mapped from the range [0, 255] to the floating-point range [0.0, 1.0]. Typically, an application would not create texture data in this simple manner but rather load the data from an image file. This example is provided to demonstrate the use of the API.

Note that prior to calling glTexImage2D the application makes a call to glPixelStorei to set the unpack alignment. When texture data is uploaded via glTexImage2D, the rows of pixels are assumed to be aligned to the value set for GL_UNPACK_ALIGNMENT. By default, the value is 4, meaning that rows of pixels are assumed to begin on 4-byte boundaries. This application sets the unpack alignment to 1, meaning that each row of pixels begins on a byte boundary (in other words, the data is tightly packed). The full definition for glPixelStorei is given next.

void	**glPixelStorei**(GLenum *pname*, GLint *param*)
pname	specifies the pixel storage type to set, must be either GL_PACK_ALIGNMENT or GL_UNPACK_ALIGNMENT
param	specifies the integer value for the pack or unpack alignment

The GL_PACK_ALIGNMENT argument to glPixelStorei does not have any impact on texture image uploading. The pack alignment is used by glRead-Pixels, which is described in Chapter 11, "Fragment Operations." The pack and unpack alignments set by glPixelStorei are global state and are not stored or associated with a texture object.

Back to the example program, after defining the image data, a texture object is generated using glGenTextures and then that object is bound to the GL_TEXTURE_2D target using glBindTexture. Finally, the image data is loaded into the texture object using glTexImage2D. The format is set as GL_RGB, which signifies that the image data is composed of (R,G,B) triplets. The type is set as GL_UNSIGNED_BYTE, which signifies that each channel of the data is stored in an 8-bit unsigned byte. There are a number of other options for loading texture data, including different formats as described in Table 9-1. In addition, all of the components in a texel can be packed into 16 bits using GL_UNSIGNED_SHORT_4_4_4_4, GL_UNSIGNED_SHORT_5_5_5_1, or GL_UNSIGNED_SHORT_5_6_5.

The last part of the code uses glTexParameteri to set the minification and magnification filtering modes to GL_NEAREST. This code is required because we have not loaded a complete mipmap chain for the texture so we must select a nonmipmapped minification filter. The other option would have been to use minification and magnification modes of GL_LINEAR, which provides bilinear nonmipmapped filtering. The details of texture filtering and mipmapping are explained in the next section.

Texture Filtering and Mipmapping

So far, we have limited our explanation of 2D textures to describing a single 2D image. Although this allowed us to explain the concept of texturing, there is actually a bit more to how textures are specified and used in OpenGL ES. The reason has to do with the visual artifacts and performance issues that occur due to using a single texture map. As we have described texturing so far, the texture coordinate is used to generate a 2D index to fetch from the texture map. When the minification and magnification filters are set to GL_NEAREST, this is exactly what will happen: a single texel will be fetched at the texture coordinate location provided. This is known as point or nearest sampling.

However, nearest sampling might produce significant visual artifacts. The reason for the artifacts is that as a triangle becomes smaller in screen space, the texture coordinates take large jumps when being interpolated from pixel to pixel. As a result, a small number of samples are taken from a large texture map, resulting in aliasing artifacts. The solution that is used to resolve this type of artifact in OpenGL ES is known as *mipmapping*. The idea behind mipmapping is to build a chain of images known as a mipmap chain. The mipmap chain begins with the originally specified image and then continues with each subsequent image being half as large in each dimension as the one before it. This chain continues until we reach a single 1 × 1 texture at the bottom of the chain. The mip levels can be generated programmatically, typically by computing each pixel in a mip level as an average of the four pixels at the same location in the mip level above it (box filtering).

In the Chapter_9/MipMap2D sample program, we provide an example demonstrating how to generate a mipmap chain for a texture using a box filtering technique. The code to generate the mipmap chain is given by the GenMipMap2D function. This function takes an RGB8 image as input and generates the next mipmap level by performing a box filter on the preceding image. Please see the source code in the example for details on how the box filtering is done. The mipmap chain is then loaded using glTexImage2D as shown in Example 9-2.

Example 9-2 Loading a 2D Mipmap Chain

```
// Load mipmap level 0
glTexImage2D(GL_TEXTURE_2D, 0, GL_RGB, width, height,
             0, GL_RGB, GL_UNSIGNED_BYTE, pixels);

level = 1;
prevImage = &pixels[0];

while(width > 1 && height > 1)
{
    int newWidth,
        newHeight;
```

```
    // Generate the next mipmap level
    GenMipMap2D(prevImage, &newImage, width, height,
            &newWidth, &newHeight);

    // Load the mipmap level
    glTexImage2D(GL_TEXTURE_2D, level, GL_RGB,
            newWidth, newHeight, 0, GL_RGB,
            GL_UNSIGNED_BYTE, newImage);

    // Free the previous image
    free(prevImage);

    // Set the previous image for the next iteration
    prevImage = newImage;
    level++;

    // Half the width and height
    width = newWidth;
    height = newHeight;
}

free(newImage);
```

With a mipmap chain loaded, we can then set up the filtering mode to use mipmaps. The result is that we achieve a better ratio between screen pixels and texture pixels and thereby reduce aliasing artifacts. Aliasing is also reduced because each image in the mipmap chain is successively filtered so that high-frequency elements are attenuated further and further as we move down the chain.

There are two different types of filtering that occur when texturing: minification and magnification. Minification is what happens when the size of the projected polygon on the screen is smaller than the size of the texture. Magnification is what happens when the size of the projected polygon on screen is larger than the size of the texture. The determination of which filter type to use is all done automatically by the hardware, but the API provides control over what type of filtering to use in each case. For magnification, mipmapping is not relevant, because we will always be sampling from the largest level available. For minification, there are a variety of different sampling modes that can be used. The choice of which mode to use is based on the visual quality you need to achieve and how much performance you are willing to give up for texture filtering.

The way that the filtering modes are specified is with `glTexParameter[i |f][v]`.

void	**glTexParameteri**(GLenum *target*, GLenum *pname*, GLint *param*)
void	**glTexParameteriv**(GLenum *target*, GLenum *pname*, const GLint **params*)
void	**glTexParameterf**(GLenum *target*, GLenum *pname*, GLfloat *param*)
void	**glTexParameterfv**(GLenum *target*, GLenum *pname*, const GLfloat **params*)

target	bind the texture object to target GL_TEXTURE_2D or GL_TEXTURE_CUBE_MAP
pname	the parameter to set, one of: GL_TEXTURE_MAG_FILTER GL_TEXTURE_MIN_FILTER GL_TEXTURE_WRAP_S GL_TEXTURE_WRAP_T
params	the value (or array of values for the "v" entrypoints) to set the texture parameter to If *pname* is GL_TEXTURE_MAG_FILTER, then *param* can be: GL_NEAREST GL_LINEAR If *pname* is GL_TEXTURE_MIN_FILTER, then *param* can be: GL_NEAREST GL_LINEAR GL_NEAREST_MIPMAP_NEAREST GL_NEAREST_MIPMAP_LINEAR GL_LINEAR_MIPMAP_NEAREST GL_LINEAR_MIPMAP_LINEAR If *pname* is GL_TEXTURE_WRAP_S or GL_TEXTURE_WRAP_R, then *param* can be: GL_REPEAT GL_CLAMP_TO_EDGE GL_MIRRORED_REPEAT

The magnification filter can be either GL_NEAREST or GL_LINEAR. In GL_NEAREST magnification filtering, a single point sample will be taken from the texture nearest to the texture coordinate. In GL_LINEAR magnification filtering, a bilinear (average of four samples) will be taken from the texture about the texture coordinate.

The minification filter can be set to any of the following values:

- GL_NEAREST—A single point sample will be taken from the texture nearest to the texture coordinate.

- GL_LINEAR—A bilinear sample will be taken from the texture nearest to the texture coordinate.

- GL_NEAREST_MIPMAP_NEAREST—A single point sample will be taken from the closest mip level chosen.

- GL_NEAREST_MIPMAP_LINEAR—Will take a sample from the two closest mip levels and interpolate between those samples.

- GL_LINEAR_MIPMAP_NEAREST—Will take a bilinear fetch from the closest mip level chosen.

- GL_LINEAR_MIPMAP_LINEAR—Will take a bilinear fetch from each of the two closest mip levels and then interpolate between them. This last mode is typically referred to as trilinear filtering and produces the best quality of all modes.

Note: GL_NEAREST and GL_LINEAR are the only texture minification modes that do not require a complete mipmap chain to be specified for the texture. All of the other modes require that a complete mipmap chain exists for the texture.

The MipMap2D example in Figure 9-3 shows the difference between a polygon drawn with GL_NEAREST versus GL_LINEAR_MIPMAP_LINEAR filtering.

Figure 9-3   MipMap2D: Nearest Versus Trilinear Filtering

Color Plate 1 The OpenGL ES 2.0 Pinball Demo from AMD demonstrates the use of shaders for effects such as environment mapping and per-fragment lighting. (© 2008 Advanced Micro Devices, Inc. Reprinted with permission.)

Color Plate 2 Screenshot of RenderMonkey, a shader effect development tool from AMD. RenderMonkey is used in several examples throughout the book to demonstrate advanced shader effects. (© 2008 Advanced Micro Devices, Inc. Reprinted with permission.)

Color Plate 3 Screenshot from the Taiji scene in 3DMarkMobile ES 2.0 by Futuremark. The Taiji character is rendered using vertex skinning. Her shadow that is cast onto the ground by rendering to a depth texture bound to a framebuffer object and then using that depth texture as a shadow map.(Source: 3DMarkMobile ES 2.0 that is a trademark of Futuremark Corporation.)

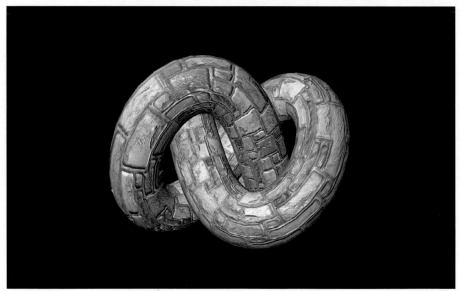

Color Plate 4 (see also Figure 13-1) Per-fragment Lighting example. This example uses a tangent-space normal map and evaluates the diffuse and specular lighting equations on a per-fragment basis.

Color Plate 5 (see also Figure 13-2) Environment Mapping example. This example uses a cubemap to perform environment mapping. The eye-space reflection vector is computed in the fragment shader based on the normal vector stored in the normal map.

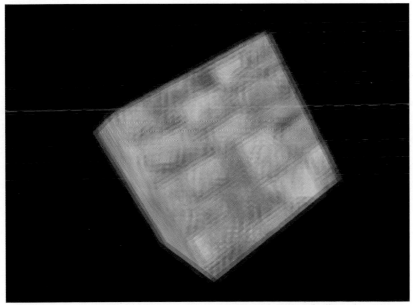

Color Plate 6 (see also Figure 13-4) Image post-processing example. This example renders a cube into a framebuffer object. The texture attachment to the framebuffer object is then bound to a full-screen quad. A fragment shader is run over the full-screen quad which performs a blur filter.

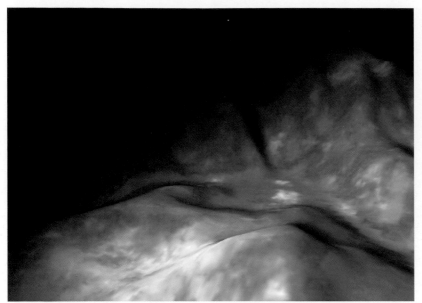

Color Plate 7   (see also Figure 13-7) Projective spotlight example. This example renders terrain and applies a projective spotlight texture. The 2D spotlight texture is used to emulate per-fragment spotlight fall-off. This technique produces good quality results yet requires very little per-fragment computation.

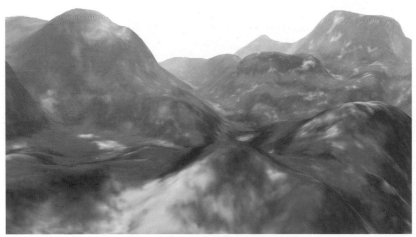

Color Plate 8   (see also Figure 13-9) Fog distorted by a 3D noise texture. This example renders terrain with a wispy animated fog effect. The effect is achieved by storing continuous 3D noise values in a 3D texture and scrolling the texture across the surface based on time.

It is worth mentioning some performance implications for the texture filtering mode that you choose. If minification occurs and performance is a concern, using a mipmap filtering mode is usually the best choice on most hardware. The reason is because you tend to get very poor texture cache utilization without mipmaps because fetches happen at sparse locations throughout a map. However, the higher the filtering mode you use, there usually is some performance cost in the hardware. For example, on most hardware it is the case that doing bilinear filtering is less costly than doing trilinear filtering. You should choose a mode that gives you the quality desired without unduly negatively impacting performance. On some hardware, you might get high-quality filtering virtually for free particularly if the cost of the texture filtering is not your bottleneck. This is something that needs to be tuned for the application and hardware on which you plan to run your application.

Automatic Mipmap Generation

In the `MipMap2D` example in the previous section, the application created an image for level zero of the mipmap chain. It then generated the rest of the mipmap chain by performing a box filter on each image and successively halving the width and height. This is one way to generate mipmaps, but OpenGL ES 2.0 also provides a mechanism for automatically generating mipmaps using `glGenerateMipmap`.

void	**glGenerateMipmap**(GLenum *target*)
target	the texture target to generate mipmaps for, can be GL_TEXTURE_2D or GL_TEXTURE_CUBE_MAP

When calling `glGenerateMipmap` on a bound texture object, this function will generate the entire mipmap chain from the contents of the image in level zero. For a 2D texture, this means that the contents of texture level zero will be successively filtered and used for each of the subsequent levels. For a cubemap, each of the cube faces will be generated from the level zero in each cube face. Note that to use this function with cubemaps you must have specified level zero for each cube face and each face must have a matching internal format, width, and height. An additional note is that OpenGL ES 2.0 does not mandate a particular filtering algorithm that will be used for generating mipmaps (although it recommends box filtering). If you require a particular filtering method, then you will still need to generate the mipmaps on your own.

Automatic mipmap generation becomes particularly important when you start to use framebuffer objects for rendering to a texture. When rendering to a texture, we don't want to have to read back the contents of the texture to the CPU to generate mipmaps. Instead, `glGenerateMipmap` can be used and the graphics hardware can then potentially generate the mipmaps without ever having to read the data back to the CPU. When we cover framebuffer objects in more detail in Chapter 12, "Framebuffer Objects," this point should become clear.

Texture Coordinate Wrapping

Texture wrap modes are used to set what the behavior is when a texture coordinate is outside of the range [0.0, 1.0]. The texture wrap modes are set using `glTexParameter[i|f][v]`. The texture wrap mode can be set independently for both the *s*-coordinate and *t*-coordinate. The `GL_TEXTURE_WRAP_S` mode defines what the behavior is when the *s*-coordinate is outside of the range [0.0, 1.0] and `GL_TEXTURE_WRAP_T` sets the behavior for the *t*-coordinate. In OpenGL ES, there are three wrap modes to choose from, as described in Table 9-2.

Table 9-2   Texture Wrap Modes

Texture Wrap Mode	Description
GL_REPEAT	Repeat the texture
GL_CLAMP_TO_EDGE	Clamp fetches to the edge of the texture
GL_MIRRORED_REPEAT	Repeat the texture and mirror

Note that the texture wrap modes also have an impact for the behavior of filtering. For example, when a texture coordinate is at the edge of a texture, the bilinear filter kernel might span beyond the edge of the texture. In this case, the wrap mode will determine which texels are fetched for the portion of the kernel that is outside the texture edge. `GL_CLAMP_TO_EDGE` should be used whenever you do not want any form of repeating.

In Chapter_9/TextureWrap there is an example that draws a quad with each of the three different texture wrap modes. The quads have a checkerboard image applied to them and are rendered with texture coordinates in the range from [−1.0, 2.0]. The results are shown in Figure 9-4.

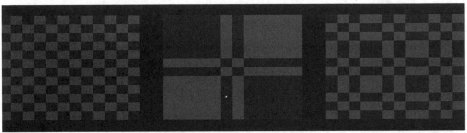

Figure 9-4 GL_REPEAT, GL_CLAMP_TO_EDGE, and GL_MIRRORED_REPEAT
Modes

The three quads are rendered using the following setup code for the texture
wrap modes.

```
// Draw left quad with repeat wrap mode
glTexParameteri(GL_TEXTURE_2D, GL_TEXTURE_WRAP_S, GL_REPEAT);
glTexParameteri(GL_TEXTURE_2D, GL_TEXTURE_WRAP_T, GL_REPEAT);
glUniform1f(userData->offsetLoc, -0.7f);
glDrawElements(GL_TRIANGLES, 6, GL_UNSIGNED_SHORT, indices);

// Draw middle quad with clamp to edge wrap mode
glTexParameteri(GL_TEXTURE_2D, GL_TEXTURE_WRAP_S, GL_CLAMP_TO_EDGE);
glTexParameteri(GL_TEXTURE_2D, GL_TEXTURE_WRAP_T, GL_CLAMP_TO_EDGE);
glUniform1f(userData->offsetLoc, 0.0f);
glDrawElements(GL_TRIANGLES, 6, GL_UNSIGNED_SHORT, indices);

// Draw right quad with mirrored repeat
glTexParameteri(GL_TEXTURE_2D, GL_TEXTURE_WRAP_S,
                GL_MIRRORED_REPEAT);
glTexParameteri(GL_TEXTURE_2D, GL_TEXTURE_WRAP_T,
                GL_MIRRORED_REPEAT);
glUniform1f(userData->offsetLoc, 0.7f);
glDrawElements GL_TRIANGLES, 6, GL_UNSIGNED_SHORT, indices);
```

In Figure 9-4, the quad on the far left is rendered using GL_REPEAT mode.
In this mode, the texture simply repeats outside of the range [0, 1] resulting in a tiling pattern of the image. The quad in the center is rendered
with GL_CLAMP_TO_EDGE mode. As you can see, when the texture coordinates go outside the range [0, 1], the texture coordinates get clamped to
sample from the edge of the texture. The quad on the right is rendered
with GL_MIRRORED_REPEAT, which mirrors and then repeats the image
when the texture coordinates are outside [0, 1].

Using Textures in the Fragment Shader

Now that we have covered the basics of setting up texturing, let's take a look at some sample shader code. The vertex–fragment shader pair in Example 9-3 from the Simple_Texture2D sample demonstrates the basics of how 2D texturing is done in a shader.

Example 9-3   Vertex and Fragment Shader for Performing 2D Texturing

```
GLbyte vShaderStr[] =
   "attribute vec4 a_position;    \n"
   "attribute vec2 a_texCoord;    \n"
   "varying vec2 v_texCoord;      \n"
   "void main()                   \n"
   "{                             \n"
   "   gl_Position = a_position;  \n"
   "   v_texCoord = a_texCoord;   \n"
   "}                             \n";

GLbyte fShaderStr[] =
   "precision mediump float;                              \n"
   "varying vec2 v_texCoord;                              \n"
   "uniform sampler2D s_texture;                          \n"
   "void main()                                           \n"
   "{                                                     \n"
   "  gl_FragColor = texture2D(s_texture, v_texCoord); \n"
   "}                                                     \n";
```

The vertex shader takes in a two-component texture coordinate as a vertex attribute and passes it through as a varying to the fragment shader. The fragment shader consumes that varying and will use it as a texture coordinate for the texture fetch. The fragment shader declares a uniform variable of type `sampler2D` called s_texture. A sampler is a special type of uniform variable that is used to fetch from a texture map. The sampler uniform will be loaded with a value specifying the texture unit to which the texture is bound; for example, specifying that a sampler with a value of 0 says to fetch from unit GL_TEXTURE0, and a value of 1 from GL_TEXTURE1, and so on. The way that textures get bound to texture units is using the glActiveTexture function.

void	**glActiveTexture**(GLenum *texture*)

texture	the texture unit to make active, GL_TEXTURE0, GL_TEXTURE1, ... , GL_TEXTURE31

The function `glActiveTexture` sets the current texture unit so that subsequent calls to `glBindTexture` will bind the texture to the currently active unit. The number of texture units available on an implementation of OpenGL ES can be queried for by using `glGetIntegeriv` with the parameter `GL_MAX_TEXTURE_IMAGE_UNITS`.

The following example code from the Simple_Texture2D example shows how the sampler and texture gets bound to the texture unit.

```
// Get the sampler locations
userData->samplerLoc = glGetUniformLocation(
                            userData->programObject,
                            "s_texture");

// ...
// Bind the texture
glActiveTexture(GL_TEXTURE0);
glBindTexture(GL_TEXTURE_2D, userData->textureId);

// Set the sampler texture unit to 0
glUniform1i(userData->samplerLoc, 0);
```

So finally, we have the texture loaded, the texture bound to texture unit 0, and the sampler set to use texture unit 0. Going back to the fragment shader in the Simple_Texture2D example, we see that the shader code then uses the built-in function `texture2D` to fetch from the texture map. The `texture2D` built-in function takes the form shown here.

vec4	**texture2D**(sampler2D *sampler*, vec2 *coord*[, float *bias*])
sampler	a sampler bound to a texture unit specifying the texture from which to fetch
coord	a 2D texture coordinate used to fetch from the texture map
bias	an optional parameter that provides a mipmap bias used for the texture fetch. This allows the shader to explicitly bias the computed LOD value used for mipmap selection

The `texture2D` returns a `vec4` representing the color fetched from the texture map. The way the texture data is mapped into the channels of this color is dependent on the base format of the texture. Table 9-3 shows the way in which texture formats are mapped to `vec4` colors.

Table 9-3   Mapping of Texture Formats to Colors

Base Format	Texel Data Description
GL_RGB	(R, G, B, 1.0)
GL_RGBA	(R, G, B, A)
GL_LUMINANCE	(L, L, L, 1.0)
GL_LUMINANCE_ALPHA	(L, L, L, A)
GL_ALPHA	(0.0, 0.0, 0.0, A)

In the case of the Simple_Texture2D example, the texture was loaded as GL_RGB so the result of the texture fetch will be a vec4 with values (R, G, B, 1.0).

Example of Using a Cubemap Texture

Using a cubemap texture is very similar to using a 2D texture. The example Simple_TextureCubemap demonstrates drawing a sphere with a simple cubemap. The cubemap contains six 1 × 1 faces, each with a different color. The code in Example 9-4 is used to load the cubemap texture.

Example 9-4   Loading a Cubemap Texture

```
GLuint CreateSimpleTextureCubemap()
{
   GLuint textureId;
   // Six 1 x 1 RGB faces
   GLubyte cubePixels[6][3] =
   {
      // Face 0 - Red
      255, 0, 0,
      // Face 1 - Green,
      0, 255, 0,
      // Face 3 - Blue
      0, 0, 255,
      // Face 4 - Yellow
      255, 255, 0,
      // Face 5 - Purple
      255, 0, 255,
      // Face 6 - White
      255, 255, 255
   };
```

```
    // Generate a texture object
    glGenTextures(1, &textureId);

    // Bind the texture object
    glBindTexture(GL_TEXTURE_CUBE_MAP, textureId);

    // Load the cube face - Positive X
    glTexImage2D(GL_TEXTURE_CUBE_MAP_POSITIVE_X, 0, GL_RGB, 1, 1,
                 0, GL_RGB, GL_UNSIGNED_BYTE, &cubePixels[0]);

    // Load the cube face - Negative X
    glTexImage2D(GL_TEXTURE_CUBE_MAP_NEGATIVE_X, 0, GL_RGB, 1, 1,
                 0, GL_RGB, GL_UNSIGNED_BYTE, &cubePixels[1]);

    // Load the cube face - Positive Y
    glTexImage2D(GL_TEXTURE_CUBE_MAP_POSITIVE_Y, 0, GL_RGB, 1, 1,
                 0, GL_RGB, GL_UNSIGNED_BYTE, &cubePixels[2]);

    // Load the cube face - Negative Y
    glTexImage2D(GL_TEXTURE_CUBE_MAP_NEGATIVE_Y, 0, GL_RGB, 1, 1,
                 0, GL_RGB, GL_UNSIGNED_BYTE, &cubePixels[3]);

    // Load the cube face - Positive Z
    glTexImage2D(GL_TEXTURE_CUBE_MAP_POSITIVE_Z, 0, GL_RGB, 1, 1,
                 0, GL_RGB, GL_UNSIGNED_BYTE, &cubePixels[4]);

    // Load the cube face - Negative Z
    glTexImage2D(GL_TEXTURE_CUBE_MAP_NEGATIVE_Z, 0, GL_RGB, 1, 1,
                 0, GL_RGB, GL_UNSIGNED_BYTE, &cubePixels[5]);

    // Set the filtering mode
    glTexParameteri(GL_TEXTURE_CUBE_MAP, GL_TEXTURE_MIN_FILTER,
                    GL_NEAREST);
    glTexParameteri(GL_TEXTURE_CUBE_MAP, GL_TEXTURE_MAG_FILTER,
                    GL_NEAREST);

    return textureId;

}
```

This code loads each individual cubemap face with 1 × 1 RGB pixel data by calling glTexImage2D for each cubemap face. The shader code to render the sphere with a cubemap is provided in Example 9-5.

Example 9-5   Vertex and Fragment Shader Pair for Cubemap Texturing

```
GLbyte vShaderStr[] =
    "attribute vec4 a_position;    \n"
    "attribute vec3 a_normal;      \n"
    "varying vec3 v_normal;        \n"
    "void main()                   \n"
    "{                             \n"
    "   gl_Position = a_position;  \n"
    "   v_normal = a_normal;       \n"
    "}                             \n";

GLbyte fShaderStr[] =
    "precision mediump float;                          \n"
    "varying vec3 v_normal;                            \n"
    "uniform samplerCube s_texture;                    \n"
    "void main()                                       \n"
    "{                                                 \n"
    "  gl_FragColor = textureCube(s_texture, v_normal); \n"
    "}                                                 \n";
```

The vertex shader takes in a position and normal as vertex attributes. A normal is stored at each vertex of the sphere that will be used as a texture coordinate. The normal is passed through to the fragment shader in a varying. The fragment shader then uses the built-in function textureCube to fetch from the cubemap using the normal as a texture coordinate. The texture-Cube built-in function takes the form shown here.

vec4	**textureCube**(samplerCube *sampler*, vec3 *coord*[, float *bias*])

sampler	the sampler is bound to a texture unit specifying the texture from which to fetch
coord	a 3D texture coordinate used to fetch from the cubemap
bias	an optional parameter that provides a mipmap bias used for the texture fetch. This allows the shader to explicitly bias the computed LOD value used for mipmap selection

The function for fetching a cubemap is very similar to a 2D texture. The only difference is that the texture coordinate is three components instead of two and the sampler type must be samplerCube. The same method is used to bind the cubemap texture and load the sampler as is used for the Simple_Texture2D example.

Compressed Textures

Thus far, we have been dealing with textures that were loaded with uncompressed texture image data using `glTexImage2D`. OpenGL ES 2.0 also supports the loading of compressed texture image data. There are several reasons why compressing textures is desirable. The first and obvious reason to compress textures is to reduce the memory footprint of the textures on the device. A second, less obvious reason to compress textures is that there is a memory bandwidth savings when fetching from compressed textures in a shader. Finally, compressed textures might allow you to reduce the download size of your application by reducing the amount of image data that must be stored.

The core OpenGL ES 2.0 specification does not define any compressed texture image formats. That is, OpenGL ES 2.0 core simply defines a mechanism whereby compressed texture image data can be loaded, but no compressed formats are defined. It is up to the vendor that implements OpenGL ES 2.0 to provide optional extension(s) that provide compressed image data types. One ratified compressed texture extension, Ericsson Texture Compression (ETC), is likely to be supported by a number of vendors. Vendors such as AMD, ARM, Imagination Technologies, and NVIDIA also provide hardware-specific extensions for formats that their hardware supports.

The function used to load compressed image data for 2D textures and cubemaps is `glCompressedTexImage2D`.

void	**glCompressedTexImage2D**(GLenum *target*, GLint *level*, GLenum *internalformat*, GLsizei *width*, GLsizei *height*, GLint *border*, GLsizei *imageSize*, const void **data*)
target	specifies the texture target, should be GL_TEXTURE_2D or one of the GL_TEXTURE_CUBE_MAP_* face targets
level	specifies which mip level to load. The base level is specified by 0 followed by an increasing level for each successive mipmap

internalFormat	the internal format for the texture storage. This is the compressed texture format to use. No compressed formats are defined by core OpenGL ES 2.0, so the format used here must come from an extension
width	the width of the image in pixels
height	the height of the image in pixels
border	this parameter is ignored in OpenGL ES, it was kept for compatibility with the desktop OpenGL interface. Should be 0
imageSize	the size of the image in bytes
data	contains the actual compressed pixel data for the image. These data must hold imageSize number of bytes

Once a texture has been loaded as a compressed texture, it can be used for texturing in exactly the same way as an uncompressed texture. Note that if you attempt to use a texture compression format on an OpenGL ES 2.0 implementation that does not support it, a GL_INVALID_ENUM error will be generated. It is important that you check that the OpenGL ES 2.0 implementation exports the extension string for the texture compression format you use. If it does not, you must fall back to using an uncompressed texture format.

In addition to checking extension strings, there is another method you can use to determine which texture compression formats are supported by an implementation. You can query for GL_NUM_COMPRESSED_TEXTURE_FORMATS using glGetIntegerv to determine the number of compressed image formats supported. You can then query for GL_COMPRESSED_TEXTURE_FORMATS using glGetIntegerv, which will return an array of GLenum values. Each GLenum value in the array will be a compressed texture format that is supported by the implementation.

Texture Subimage Specification

After uploading a texture image using glTexImage2D, it is possible to update portions of the image. This would be useful if you wanted to update just a subregion of an image. The function to load a portion of a 2D texture image is glTexSubImage2D.

```
void   glTexSubImage2D(GLenum target, GLint level,
                       GLint xoffset, GLint yoffset,
                       GLsizei width, GLsizei height,
                       GLenum format, GLenum type,
                       const void* pixels)
```

target	specifies the texture target, either GL_TEXTURE_2D or one of the cubemap face targets (e.g., GL_TEXTURE_CUBE_MAP_POSITIVE_X, GL_TEXTURE_CUBE_MAP_NEGATIVE_X, etc.)
level	specifies which mip level to update
xoffset	the x index of the texel to start updating from
yoffset	the y index of the texel to start updating from
width	the width of the subregion of the image to update
height	the height of the subregion of the image to update
format	the format of the incoming texture data, can be: GL_RGBA GL_RGB GL_LUMINANCE_ALPHA GL_LUMINANCE GL_ALPHA
type	the type of the incoming pixel data, can be: GL_UNSIGNED_BYTE GL_UNSIGNED_SHORT_4_4_4_4 GL_UNSIGNED_SHORT_5_5_5_1 GL_UNSIGNED_SHORT_5_6_5
pixels	contains the actual pixel data for the subregion of the image

This function will update the region of texels in the range (*xoffset*, *yoffset*) to (*xoffset* + *width* – 1, *yoffset* + *height* – 1). Note that to use this function, the texture must already be fully specified. The range of the subimage must be within the bounds of the previously specified texture image. The data in the pixels array must be aligned to the alignment that is specified by GL_UNPACK_ALIGNMENT with glPixelStorei.

There is also a function for updating a subregion of a compressed 2D texture image that is glCompressedTexSubImage2D. The definition for this function is more or less the same as glTexImage2D.

void	**glCompressedTexSubImage2D**(GLenum *target*, GLint *level*, GLint *xoffset*, GLint *yoffset*, GLsizei *width*, GLsizei *height*, GLenum *format*,GLenum *imageSize*, const void* *pixels*)

target	specifies the texture target, either GL_TEXTURE_2D or one of the cubemap face targets (e.g., GL_TEXTURE_CUBE_MAP_POSITIVE_X, GL_TEXTURE_CUBE_MAP_NEGATIVE_X, etc.)
level	specifies which mip level to update
xoffset	the *x* index of the texel to start updating from
yoffset	the *y* index of the texel to start updating from
width	the width of the subregion of the image to update
height	the height of the subregion of the image to update
format	the compressed texture format to use. No compressed formats are defined by core OpenGL ES 2.0, so the format used here must come from an extension and match the format with which the image was originally specified
pixels	contains the actual pixel data for the subregion of the image

Copying Texture Data from the Color Buffer

An additional texturing feature that is supported in OpenGL ES 2.0 is the ability to copy data from the color buffer to a texture. This can be useful if you want to use the results of rendering as an image in a texture. Please note that framebuffer objects (Chapter 12) provide a fast method for doing render-to-texture and are a faster method than copying image data. However, if performance is not a concern, the ability to copy image data out of the color buffer can be a useful feature.

Recall that OpenGL ES 2.0 only supports double-buffered EGL displayable surfaces. This means that all OpenGL ES 2.0 applications that draw to the display will have a color buffer for both the front and back buffer. The buffer that is currently front or back is determined by the most recent call to eglSwapBuffers (described in Chapter 3, "An Introduction to EGL"). When you copy image data out of the color buffer from a displayable EGL surface, you will always be copying the contents of the back buffer. If you are rendering to an EGL pbuffer, then copying will occur from the pbuffer surface. Finally, if you are rendering to a framebuffer object, then copying will occur out of the color buffer attached to the framebuffer object as the color attachment.

The functions to copy data from the color buffer to a texture are glCopyTexImage2D and glCopyTexSubImage2D.

void	**glCopyTexImage2D**(GLenum *target*, GLint *level*, GLenum *internalFormat*, GLint *x*, GLint *y*, GLsizei *width*, GLsizei *height*, GLint *border*)
target	specifies the texture target, either GL_TEXTURE_2D or one of the cubemap face targets (e.g., GL_TEXTURE_CUBE_MAP_POSITIVE_X, GL_TEXTURE_CUBE_MAP_NEGATIVE_X, etc.)
level	specifies which mip level to load
internalFormat	the internal format of the image, can be: GL_RGBA GL_RGB GL_LUMINANCE_ALPHA GL_LUMINANCE GL_ALPHA
x	the *x* window-coordinate of the lower left rectangle in the framebuffer to read from
y	the *y* window-coordinate of the lower left rectangle in the framebuffer to read from
width	the width in pixels of the region to read
height	the height in pixels of the region to read
border	borders are not supported in OpenGL ES 2.0, so this parameter must be 0

Calling this function will cause the texture image to be loaded with the pixels in the color buffer from region (x, y) to $(x + width - 1, y + height - 1)$. This width and height of the texture image will be the size of the region copied from the color buffer. You should be using this to fill the entire contents of the texture.

In addition, you can update just the subregion of an already specified image using glCopyTexSubImage2D.

---

void	**glCopyTexSubImage2D**(GLenum *target*, GLint *level*,
	GLint *level*, GLint *xoffset*,
	GLint *yoffset*, GLint *x*, GLint *y*,
	GLsizei *width*, GLsizei *height*)

---

target	specifies the texture target, either GL_TEXTURE_2D or one of the cubemap face targets (e.g., GL_TEXTURE_CUBE_MAP_POSITIVE_X, GL_TEXTURE_CUBE_MAP_NEGATIVE_X, etc.)
level	specifies which mip level to update
xoffset	the *x* index of the texel to start updating from
yoffset	the *y* index of the texel to start updating from
x	the *x* window-coordinate of the lower left rectangle in the framebuffer to read from
y	the *y* window-coordinate of the lower left rectangle in the framebuffer to read from
width	the width in pixels of the region to read
height	the height in pixels of the region to read

This function will update the subregion of the image starting at (*xoffset*, *yoffset*) to (*xoffset* + *width* – 1, *yoffset* + *height* – 1) with the pixels in the color buffer from (*x*, *y*) to (*x* + *width* – 1, *y* + *height* – 1).

One thing to keep in mind with both glCopyTexImage2D and glCopyTexSubImage2D is that the texture image format cannot have more components than the color buffer. In other words, when copying data out of the color buffer, it is possible to convert to a format with fewer components, but not with more. Table 9-4 shows the valid format conversions when doing a texture copy. For example, you can see from the table that it is possible to copy an RGBA image into any of the possible formats. However, it is not possible to copy an RGB into an RGBA image because no alpha component exists in the color buffer.

Table 9-4 Valid Format Conversions for `glCopyTex*Image2D`

Color Format	Texture Format				
	A	L	LA	RGB	RGBA
A	Y	N	N	N	N
L	N	Y	N	N	N
LA	Y	Y	Y	N	N
RGB	N	Y	N	Y	N
RGBA	Y	Y	Y	Y	Y

Optional Extensions

There are a number of Khronos-ratified extensions that provide additional texture functionality beyond what is available in core OpenGL ES 2.0. These extensions provide support for 3D textures, floating-point textures, Ericsson texture compression, and non-power-of-2 textures. The following sections contain descriptions of the Khronos-ratified texture extensions.

3D Textures

In addition to 2D textures and cubemaps, there is a ratified OpenGL ES 2.0 extension for 3D textures named `GL_OES_texture_3D`. This extension exposes methods for loading and rendering with 3D textures (or volume textures). 3D textures can be thought of as an array of multiple slices of 2D textures. A 3D texture is accessed with a three-tuple (s,t,r) coordinate much like a cubemap. For 3D textures, the r-coordinate selects which slice of the 3D texture to sample from and the (s,t) coordinate is used to fetch into the 2D map at each slice. Each mipmap level in a 3D texture contains half the number of slices in the texture above it.

The command to load 3D textures is `glTexImage3DOES`, which is very similar to `glTexImage2D`.

void	**glTexImage3DOES** (GLenum *target*, GLint *level*,
	GLenum *internalFormat*, GLsizei *width*,
	GLsizei *height*, GLsizei *depth*,
	GLint *border*, GLenum *format*,
	GLenum *type*, const void* *pixels*)

target   specifies the texture target, should be GL_TEXTURE_3D_OES

level   specifies which mip level to load. The base level is specified by 0 followed by an increasing level for each successive mipmap

internalFormat   the internal format for the texture storage, can be:
    GL_RGBA
    GL_RGB
    GL_LUMINANCE_ALPHA
    GL_LUMINANCE
    GL_ALPHA

width   the width of the image in pixels

height   the height of the image in pixels

depth   the number of slices of the 3D texture

border   this parameter is ignored in OpenGL ES. It was kept for compatibility with the desktop OpenGL interface. Should be 0

format   the format of the incoming texture data. Note that in OpenGL ES the *format* and *internalFormat* arguments must have the same value. The supported formats are the same as the internal formats

type   the type of the incoming pixel data, can be:
    GL_UNSIGNED_BYTE
    GL_UNSIGNED_SHORT_4_4_4_4
    GL_UNSIGNED_SHORT_5_5_5_1
    GL_UNSIGNED_SHORT_5_6_5

pixels   contains the actual pixel data for the image. The data must contain (*width* * *height* * *depth*) number of pixels with the appropriate number of bytes per pixel based on the format and type specification. The image data should be stored as a sequence of 2D texture slices

Once a 3D texture has been loaded using `glTexImage3DOES` the texture can be fetched in the shader using the `texture3D` built-in function. Before doing so, the shader must enable the 3D texture extension using the `#extension` mechanism.

```
#extension GL_OES_texture_3D : enable
```

Once the extension is enabled in the fragment shader, the shader can use the `texture3D` built-in function, which takes the following form:

---

vec4   **texture3D**(sampler3D *sampler*, vec3 *coord*[,
         float *bias*])

---

sampler	a sampler bound to a texture unit specifying the texture to fetch from
coord	a 3D texture coordinate used to fetch from the texture map
bias	an optional parameter that provides a mipmap bias use for the texture fetch. This allows the shader to explicitly bias the computed LOD value used for mipmap selection

Note that the *r*-coordinate is a floating point value. Depending on the filtering mode set, the texture fetch might span two slices of the volume. The 3D texture extension also adds support for GL_TEXTURE_WRAP_R_OES, which can be used to set the *r*-coordinate wrap mode (just like the *s*- and *t*-coordinate wrap modes for 2D textures). In addition, this extension adds support for loading compressed 3D texture data. Compressed 3D texture data can be loaded using the `glCompressedTexImage3DOES` function. As with compressed 2D textures, no specific compressed 3D texture formats are given by this extension.

---

void   **glCompressedTexImage3DOES**(GLenum *target*, GLint *level*,
                              GLenum *internalformat*,
                              GLsizei *width*, GLsizei *height*,
                              GLsizei *depth*, GLint *border*,
                              GLsizei *imageSize*,
                              const void **data*)

---

target	specifies the texture target, should be GL_TEXTURE_3D
level	specifies which mip level to load. The base level is specified by 0 followed by an increasing level for each successive mipmap
internalFormat	the internal format for the texture storage. This is the compressed texture format to use. No compressed formats are defined by OES_texture_3D, so the format used here must come from another extension
width	the width of the image in pixels
height	the height of the image in pixels
depth	the depth of the image in pixels
border	this parameter is ignored in OpenGL ES. It was kept for compatibility with the desktop OpenGL interface. Should be 0
imageSize	the size of the image in bytes
data	contains the actual compressed pixel data for the image. These data must hold imageSize number of bytes

In addition, just as with 2D textures, it is possible to update just a subregion of an existing 3D texture using glTexSubImage3DOES.

```
void   glTexSubImage3DOES (GLenum target, GLint level,
                           GLint xoffset, GLint yoffset,
                           GLint zoffset, GLsizei width,
                           GLsizei height, GLsizei depth,
                           GLenum format, GLenum type,
                           const void* pixels)
```

---

target	specifies the texture target, either GL_TEXTURE_2D or one of the cubemap face targets (e.g., GL_TEXTURE_CUBE_MAP_POSITIVE_X, GL_TEXTURE_CUBE_MAP_NEGATIVE_X, etc.)
level	specifies which mip level to update
xoffset	the x index of the texel to start updating from

yoffset	the *y* index of the texel to start updating from
zoffset	the *z* index of the texel to start updating from
width	the width of the subregion of the image to update
height	the height of the subregion of the image to update
depth	the depth of the subregion of the image to update
format	the format of the incoming texture data, can be: GL_RGBA GL_RGB GL_LUMINANCE_ALPHA GL_LUMINANCE GL_ALPHA
type	the type of the incoming pixel data, can be: GL_UNSIGNED_BYTE GL_UNSIGNED_SHORT_4_4_4_4 GL_UNSIGNED_SHORT_5_5_5_1 GL_UNSIGNED_SHORT_5_6_5
pixels	contains the actual pixel data for the subregion of the image

glTexSubImage3DOES behaves just like glTexSubImage2D, which was covered earlier in the chapter. The only difference is that the subregion contains a zoffset and a depth for specifying the subregion within the depth slices to update. For compressed 3D textures, it is also possible to update a subregion of the texture using glCompressedTexSubImage3DOES.

void	**glCompressedTexSubImage3DOES** (GLenum *target*, GLint *level*, GLint *xoffset*, GLint *yoffset*, GLint *zoffset*, GLsizei *width*, GLsizei *height*, GLsizei *depth*, GLenum *format*, GLenum *imageSize*, const void* *data*)
target	specifies the texture target, either GL_TEXTURE_2D or one of the cubemap face targets (e.g., GL_TEXTURE_CUBE_MAP_POSITIVE_X, GL_TEXTURE_CUBE_MAP_NEGATIVE_X, etc.)

level	specifies which mip level to update
xoffset	the *x* index of the texel to start updating from
yoffset	the *y* index of the texel to start updating from
zoffset	the *z* index of the texel to start updating from
width	the width of the subregion of the image to update
height	the height of the subregion of the image to update
depth	the depth of the subregion of the image to update
format	the compressed texture format to use. No compressed formats are defined by core OpenGL ES 2.0, so the format used here must come from an extension and match the format with which the image was originally specified
data	contains the actual pixel data for the subregion of the image

Finally, one can also copy the contents of the color buffer into a slice (or subregion of a slice) of a previously specified 3D texture using glCopyTexSubImage3DOES.

```
void    glCopyTexSubImage3DOES(GLenum target, GLint level,
                               GLint level, GLint xoffset,
                               GLint yoffset, GLint zoffset,
                               GLint x, GLint y,
                               GLsizei width, GLsizei height)
```

target	specifies the texture target, either GL_TEXTURE_2D or one of the cubemap face targets (e.g., GL_TEXTURE_CUBE_MAP_POSITIVE_X, GL_TEXTURE_CUBE_MAP_NEGATIVE_X, etc.)
level	specifies which mip level to update
xoffset	the *x* index of the texel to start updating from
yoffset	the *y* index of the texel to start updating from
zoffset	the *z* index of the texel to start updating from
x	the *x* window-coordinate of the lower left rectangle in the framebuffer to read from

This function takes exactly the same arguments as `glCopyTexSubImage2D` with the exception of the `zoffset` parameter. This parameter is used to select the slice into which to copy the color buffer contents. The rest of the arguments used are the same on the color buffer and within the 2D slice of the texture.

Ericsson Texture Compression (ETC)

The `GL_OES_compressed_ETC1_RGB8_texture` is a ratified OpenGL ES 2.0 extension for compressed textures. The texture compression technique described in this extension is the ETC format. The ETC format can be used to compress RGB textures into a block-based compression format. The ETC format stores data in 4 × 4 blocks of texels that are each 64 bits in size. This means that if an original source image is 24-bit RGB data the compression ratio that will be achieved by using ETC is 6:1. The details of the bit layout of this format are outside of our scope here. However, there are freely available tools such as The Compressonator from AMD that can be used to compress images using ETC. Once compressed texture image data has been generated, it can be loaded using the `glCompressedTexImage2D` function.

Floating-Point Textures

In core OpenGL ES 2.0, there is no way to store textures with 16-bit or 32-bit floating-point precision. There are a series of ratified extensions that allow for loading and fetching from 16-bit and 32-bit floating-point textures. The extensions `GL_OES_texture_half_float` and `GL_OES_texture_float` indicate support for 16-bit and 32-bit float textures, respectively. These textures can be loaded using the `GL_HALF_FLOAT_OES` and `GL_FLOAT_OES` token values. The extensions `GL_OES_texture_half_float_linear` and `GL_OES_texture_float_linear` indicate that floating-point textures can be filtered with more than nearest sampling (e.g., bilinear, trilinear). The format for a 16-bit floating point value is 1 bit of sign, a 5-bit exponent, and 10-bit mantissa. A full description of the format for 16-bit floating-point values is provided in Appendix A.

Non-Power-of-Two Textures

In OpenGL ES 2.0, textures can have non-power-of-two (npot) dimensions. In other words, the width and height do not need to be a power of two. However, OpenGL ES 2.0 does have a restriction on the wrap modes that can be used if the texture dimensions are not power of two. That is, for npot textures, the wrap mode can only be GL_CLAMP_TO_EDGE and the minification filter can only be GL_NEAREST or GL_LINEAR (in other words, not mipmapped). The extension GL_OES_texture_npot relaxes these restrictions and allows wrap modes of GL_REPEAT and GL_MIRRORED_REPEAT and also allows npot textures to be mipmapped with the full set of minification filters.

Chapter 10

Fragment Shaders

In Chapter 9, "Texturing," we introduced you to the basics of creating and applying textures in the fragment shader. In this chapter, we provide more details on the fragment shader and describe some of its uses. In particular, we focus on how to implement fixed function techniques using the fragment shader. The topics we cover in this chapter include:

- Fixed function fragment shaders.

- Fragment shader overview.

- Multitexturing.

- Fog.

- Alpha test.

- User clip planes.

Returning to our pipeline diagram in Figure 10-1, we have covered the vertex shader, primitive assembly, and rasterization stages of the pipeline. We have talked about using textures in the fragment shader. Now, we focus on the fragment shader portion of the pipeline and fill in the remaining details on writing fragment shaders.

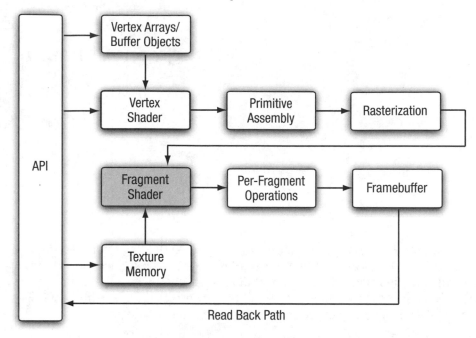

Figure 10-1   OpenGL ES 2.0 Programmable Pipeline

Fixed Function Fragment Shaders

For readers who are new to the programmable fragment pipeline but have worked with a previous version of OpenGL ES (or desktop OpenGL), you are probably familiar with the fixed function fragment pipeline. Before diving into details of the fragment shader, we think it is worthwhile to briefly review the old fixed function fragment pipeline. This will give you an understanding of how the old fixed function pipeline maps into fragment shaders. It's a good way to start before moving into more advanced fragment programming techniques.

In OpenGL ES 1.1 (and fixed function desktop OpenGL), you had a very limited set of equations that could be used to determine how to combine the various inputs to the fragment shader. In the fixed function pipeline, you essentially had three inputs you could use: the interpolated vertex color, the texture color, and the constant color. The vertex color would typically hold either a precomputed color or the result of the vertex lighting computation. The texture color came from fetching from whichever texture was bound using the primitive's texture coordinates and the constant color could be set for each texture unit.

The set of equations you could use to combine these inputs together was quite limited. For example, in OpenGL ES 1.1 the equations listed in Table 10-1 were available.

Table 10-1   OpenGL ES 1.1 RGB Combine Functions

RGB Combine Function	Equation
REPLACE	A
MODULATE	$A \times B$
ADD	$A + B$
ADD_SIGNED	$A + B - 0.5$
INTERPOLATE	$A \times C + B \times (1 - C)$
SUBTRACT	$A - B$
DOT3_RGB (and DOT3_RGBA)	$4 \times ((A.r - 0.5) \times (B.r - 0.5) + (A.g - 0.5) \times (B.g - 0.5) + (A.b - 0.5) \times (B.b - 0.5))$

The inputs A, B, and C to these equations could come from the vertex color, texture color, or constant color. There actually was a great number of interesting effects one could achieve, even with this limited set of equations. However, this was far from programmable, as the fragment pipeline could only be configured in a very fixed set of ways.

So why are we reviewing this here? It helps give an understanding of how traditional fixed function techniques can be achieved with shaders. For example, let's say we had configured the fixed function pipeline with a single base texture map that we wanted to modulate by the vertex color. In fixed function OpenGL ES (or OpenGL), we would enable a single texture unit, choose a combine equation of MODULATE, and set up the inputs to the equation to come from the vertex color and texture color. The code to do this in OpenGL ES 1.1 is provided here for reference.

```
glTexEnvi(GL_TEXTURE_ENV, GL_TEXTURE_ENV_MODE, GL_COMBINE);
glTexEnvi(GL_TEXTURE_ENV, GL_COMBINE_RGB, GL_MODULATE);
glTexEnvi(GL_TEXTURE_ENV, GL_SOURCE0_RGB, GL_PRIMARY_COLOR);
glTexEnvi(GL_TEXTURE_ENV, GL_SOURCE1_RGB, GL_TEXTURE);
glTexEnvi(GL_TEXTURE_ENV, GL_COMBINE_ALPHA, GL_MODULATE);
glTexEnvi(GL_TEXTURE_ENV, GL_SOURCE0_ALPHA, GL_PRIMARY_COLOR);
glTexEnvi(GL_TEXTURE_ENV, GL_SOURCE1_ALPHA, GL_TEXTURE);
```

This code configures the fixed function pipeline to perform a modulate
($A \times B$) between the primary color (the vertex color) and the texture color.
If this code doesn't make sense to you, don't worry, as none of this exists in
OpenGL ES 2.0. The point we are trying to make here is to show how this
would map to a fragment shader. In a fragment shader, this same computation could be accomplished as follows.

```
precision mediump float;
uniform sampler2D s_tex0;
varying vec2 v_texCoord;
varying vec4 v_primaryColor;
void main()
{
    gl_FragColor = texture2D(s_tex0, v_texCoord) * v_primaryColor;
}
```

The fragment shader performs the exact same operations that would be performed by the fixed function setup. The texture value is fetched from a sampler (that is bound to texture unit 0) and a 2D texture coordinate is used to
look up that value. Then, the result of that texture fetch is multiplied by
v_primaryColor, a varying value that is passed in from the vertex shader.
In this case, the vertex shader would have passed the color through to the
fragment shader.

It is possible to write a fragment shader that would perform the equivalent
computation as any possible fixed function texture combine setup. It is
also, of course, possible to write shaders with much more complex and var-
ied computations than just fixed function would allow. However, the point
of this section was just to drive home the point of how we have transitioned
from fixed function to programmable shaders. Now, we begin to look at
some specifics of fragment shaders.

Fragment Shader Overview

The fragment shader provides a general-purpose programmable method for
operating on fragments. The inputs to the fragment shader consist of the
following:

- Varyings—Interpolated data produced by the vertex shader.

- Uniforms—State used by the fragment shader.

- Textures—Texture images accessed through samplers.

- Code—Fragment shader source or binary that describes the operations
  that will be performed on the fragment.

The output of the fragment shader is the fragment color that gets passed on to the per-fragment operations portion of the pipeline. The inputs and outputs to the fragment shader are illustrated in Figure 10-2.

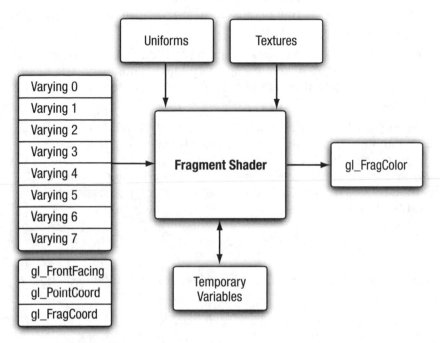

Figure 10-2   OpenGL ES 2.0 Fragment Shader

Built-In Special Variables

OpenGL ES 2.0 has built-in special variables that are output by the fragment shader or are input to the fragment shader. The built-in special variables available to the fragment shader are the following:

- **gl_FragColor**—gl_FragColor is used to output the fragment color from the shader. This color is then passed in to the per-fragment operations in the pipeline. If a fragment shader does not write to gl_FragColor its value is undefined. Note that it is potentially valid to not write to gl_FragColor in the shader. If, for example, you wish to render only to depth, you can turn off writes to the color buffer using glColorMask. Then it is perfectly valid to skip writing the fragment color in the shader.

- **gl_FragCoord**—gl_FragCoord is a read-only variable that is available in the fragment shader. This variable holds the window relative coordinates (x, y, z, $1/w$) of the fragment. There are a number of algorithms where it can be useful to know the window coordinates of the current fragment. For example, you can use the window coordinates as offsets into a texture fetch into a random noise map whose value is used to rotate a filter kernel on a shadow map. This is a technique that is used to reduce shadow map aliasing.

- **gl_FrontFacing**—gl_FrontFacing is a read-only variable that is available in the fragment shader. This variable is a boolean with a value of true if the fragment is part of a front-facing primitive and false otherwise.

- **gl_PointCoord**—gl_PointCoord is a read-only variable that can be used when rendering point sprites. It holds the texture coordinate for the point sprite that is automatically generated in the [0, 1] range during point rasterization. In Chapter 13, "Advanced Programming with OpenGL ES 2.0," there is an example of rendering point sprites that uses this variable.

Built-In Constants

The following built-in constants are also relevant to the fragment shader.

```
const mediump int gl_MaxTextureImageUnits = 8;
const mediump int gl_MaxFragmentUniformVectors = 16;
const mediump int gl_MaxDrawBuffers = 1;
```

The built-in constants describe the following maximum terms:

- **gl_MaxTextureImageUnits**—This is the maximum number of texture image units that are available. The minimum value supported by all ES 2.0 implementations is eight.

- **gl_MaxFragmentUniformVectors**—This is the maximum number of vec4 uniform entries that can be used inside a fragment shader. The minimum value supported by all ES 2.0 implementations is 16 vec4 entries. The number of vec4 uniform entries that can actually be used by a developer can vary from implementation to implementation and from one fragment shader to another. This issue is described in Chapter 8, "Vertex Shaders," and the same issue applies to fragment shaders.

- **gl_MaxDrawBuffers**—This is the maximum number of draw buffers available. The minimum value supported by all ES 2.0 implementations is 1. If more than 1 were supported, this would mean an implementation supported multiple-render targets (MRTs). As it turns out, support for MRTs is not provided in ES 2.0 and this variable was just left around for future expansion.

The values specified for each built-in constant are the minimum values that must be supported by all OpenGL ES 2.0 implementations. It is possible that implementations may support values greater than the minimum values described. The actual supported values can be queried using the following code.

```
GLint   maxTextureImageUnits, maxFragmentUniformVectors;

glGetIntegerv(GL_MAX_TEXTURE_IMAGE_UNITS, &maxTextureImageUnits);
glGetIntegerv(GL_MAX_FRAGMENT_UNIFORM_VECTORS,
              &maxFragmentUniformVectors);
```

Precision Qualifiers

Precision qualifiers were covered in detail in Chapter 8 on vertex shaders and also introduced in Chapter 5, "OpenGL ES Shading Language." Please review those sections for full details on precision qualifiers. We remind you here that there is no default precision for fragment shaders. This means that every fragment shader must declare a default precision (or provide precision qualifiers for all variable declarations).

OpenGL ES 2.0 mandates that implementations support at least medium precision in the fragment shader, but does not require support for high precision. The way to determine whether high precision is supported in the fragment shader is determining whether the GL_FRAGMENT_PRECISION_HIGH preprocessor macro is defined (in addition, the implementation will export the GL_OES_fragment_precision_high extension string).

ES 2.0 Fragment Shader Limitations

In Chapter 8, we provided a detailed review of the limitations on vertex shaders and how to write portable shaders. If you need a refresher, review that material, as almost all of the same limitations apply to fragment shaders. The only difference in limitations for fragment shaders is that uniform arrays can only be indexed with constant integral expressions. In the vertex shader, it is required that all implementations support indexing of uniform arrays using computed expressions. However, this is not the case for the fragment shader. Indexing of uniforms using anything other than constant integral expressions is not guaranteed to be supported by an ES 2.0 implementation.

Implementing Fixed Function Techniques Using Shaders

Now that we have given an overview of fragment shaders, we are going to show you how to implement several fixed function techniques using shaders. The fixed-function pipeline in OpenGL ES 1.x and desktop OpenGL provided APIs to perform multitexturing, fog, alpha test, and user clip planes. Although none of these techniques is provided explicitly in OpenGL ES 2.0, all of them are still possible to implement using shaders. This section reviews each of these fixed function processes and provides example fragment shaders that demonstrate each technique.

Multitexturing

We start with multitexturing, which is a very common operation in fragment shaders used for combining multiple texture maps. For example, a technique that has been used in many games such as Quake III is to store precomputed lighting from radiosity calculations in a texture map. That map is then combined with the base texture map in the fragment shader to represent static lighting. There are many other examples of using multiple textures, some of which we cover in Chapter 13. For example, often a texture map is used to store a specular exponent and mask to attenuate and mask specular lighting contributions. Many games also use normal maps, which are textures that store normal information at a higher level of detail than per-vertex normals so that lighting can be computed in the fragment shader.

The point of mentioning all this here is that you now have learned about all of the parts of the API that are needed to accomplish multitexturing techniques. In Chapter 9, you learned how to load textures on various texture units and fetch from them in the fragment shader. Combining the textures in various ways in the fragment shader is simply a matter of employing the many operators and built-in functions that exist in the shading language. Using these techniques, you can easily achieve all of the effects that were made possible with the fixed function fragment pipeline in previous versions of OpenGL ES.

An example of using multiple textures is provided in the Chapter_10/ MultiTexture example, which renders the image in Figure 10-3.

This example loads a base texture map and light map texture and combines them in the fragment shader on a single quad. The fragment shader for the sample program is provided in Example 10-1.

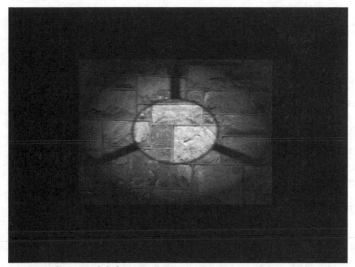

Figure 10-3　Multitextured Quad

Example 10-1　Multitexture Fragment Shader

```
precision mediump float;
varying vec2 v_texCoord;
uniform sampler2D s_baseMap;
uniform sampler2D s_lightMap;
void main()
{
    vec4 baseColor;
    vec4 lightColor;

    baseColor = texture2D(s_baseMap, v_texCoord);
    lightColor = texture2D(s_lightMap, v_texCoord);
    gl_FragColor = baseColor * (lightColor + 0.25);
}
```

The fragment shader has two samplers, one for each of the textures. The relevant code for setting up the texture units and samplers is next.

```
// Bind the base map
glActiveTexture(GL_TEXTURE0);
glBindTexture(GL_TEXTURE_2D, userData->baseMapTexId);

// Set the base map sampler to texture unit 0
glUniform1i(userData->baseMapLoc, 0);
```

```
// Bind the light map
glActiveTexture(GL_TEXTURE1);
glBindTexture(GL_TEXTURE_2D, userData->lightMapTexId);

// Set the light map sampler to texture unit 1
glUniform1i(userData->lightMapLoc, 1);
```

As you can see, this code binds each of the individual texture objects to textures units 0 and 1. The samplers are set with values to bind the samplers to the respective texture units. In this example, a single texture coordinate is used to fetch from both of the maps. In typical light mapping, there would be a separate set of texture coordinates for the base map and light map. The light maps are typically paged into a single large texture and the texture coordinates can be generated using offline tools.

Fog

A common technique that is used in rendering 3D scenes is the application of fog. In OpenGL ES 1.1 (and desktop OpenGL), fog was provided as a fixed function operation. One of the reasons fog is such a prevalent technique is that it can be used to reduce draw distances and remove "popping" of geometry as it comes in closer to the viewer.

There are a number of possible ways to compute fog and with programmable fragment shaders you are not limited to any particular equation. Here we show you how you would go about computing linear fog with a fragment shader. To compute any type of fog, there are two inputs we will need: the distance of the pixel to the eye and the color of the fog. To compute linear fog, we also need the minimum and maximum distance range that the fog should cover.

The equation for the linear fog factor

$$F = \frac{MaxDist - EyeDist}{MaxDist - MinDist}$$

computes a fog factor to multiply the fog color by. This color gets clamped in the [0.0, 1.0] range and then is linear interpolated with the overall color of a fragment to compute the final color. The distance to the eye is best computed in the vertex shader and interpolated across the primitive using a varying.

A RenderMonkey workspace is provided as an example in the Chapter_10/ RM_LinearFog folder that demonstrates the fog computation. A screenshot of the workspace is provided in Figure 10-4.

Figure 10-4   Linear Fog on Terrain in RenderMonkey

The code for the vertex shader that computes the distance to the eye is provided in Example 10-2.

Example 10-2   Vertex Shader for Computing Distance to Eye

```
uniform mat4 matViewProjection;
uniform mat4 matView;
uniform vec4 u_eyePos;

attribute vec4 rm_Vertex;
attribute vec2 rm_TexCoord0;

varying vec2 v_texCoord;
varying float v_eyeDist;

void main(void)
{
    // Transform vertex to view-space
    vec4 vViewPos = matView * rm_Vertex;

    // Compute the distance to eye
    v_eyeDist = sqrt((vViewPos.x - u_eyePos.x) *
                     (vViewPos.x - u_eyePos.x) +
                     (vViewPos.y - u_eyePos.y) *
                     (vViewPos.y - u_eyePos.y) +
```

```
                        (vViewPos.z - u_eyePos.z) *
                        (vViewPos.z - u_eyePos.z) );

    gl_Position = matViewProjection * rm_Vertex;
    v_texCoord  = rm_TexCoord0.xy;
}
```

The important part of this vertex shader is the computation of the v_eyeDist varying variable. First, the input vertex is transformed into view space using the view matrix and stored in vViewPos. Then, the distance from this point to the u_eyePos uniform variable is computed. This computation gives us the distance in eye space from the viewer to the transformed vertex. We can use this value in the fragment shader to compute the fog factor as provided in Example 10-3.

Example 10-3 Fragment Shader for Rendering Linear Fog

```
precision mediump float;

uniform vec4 u_fogColor;
uniform float u_fogMaxDist;
uniform float u_fogMinDist;
uniform sampler2D baseMap;

varying vec2 v_texCoord;
varying float v_eyeDist;

float computeLinearFogFactor()
{
    float factor;

    // Compute linear fog equation
    factor = (u_fogMaxDist - v_eyeDist) /
            (u_fogMaxDist - u_fogMinDist);

    // Clamp in the [0,1] range
    factor = clamp(factor, 0.0, 1.0);

    return factor;
}

void main(void)
{
    float fogFactor = computeLinearFogFactor();
    vec4  fogColor  = fogFactor * u_fogColor;
    vec4 baseColor = texture2D( baseMap, v_texCoord );
```

```
// Compute final color as a lerp with fog factor
gl_FragColor = baseColor * fogFactor +
               fogColor  * (1.0 - fogFactor);
}
```

In the fragment shader, the `computeLinearFogFactor()` function performs the computation for the linear fog equation. The minimum and maximum fog distances are stored in uniform variables and the interpolated eye distance that was computed in the vertex shader is used to compute the fog factor. The fog factor is then used to perform a linear interpolation between the base texture color and the fog color. The result is that we now have linear fog and can easily adjust the distances and colors by changing the uniform values.

Note that with the flexibility of programmable fragment shaders, it is very easy to implement other methods to compute fog. For example, one could easily compute exponential fog by simply changing the fog equation. Further, rather than computing fog based on distance to the eye, you could compute fog based on distance to the ground to have ground-based fog. There are a number of possible fog effects that can be easily achieved with small modifications to the fog computations provided here.

Alpha Test (Using Discard)

A very common effect used in 3D applications is to draw primitives that are fully transparent in certain fragments. This is very useful for rendering something like a chain-link fence. Representing a fence using geometry would require a significant amount of primitives. However, an alternative to using geometry is to store a mask value in a texture that specifies which texels should be transparent. For example, one could store the chain-link fence in a single RGBA texture where the RGB values represent the color of the fence and the A value represents the mask of whether the texture is transparent. Then one can easily render a fence using just one or two triangles and masking off pixels in the fragment shader.

In traditional fixed function rendering, this effect was achieved using the alpha test. The alpha test allowed you to specify a comparison test whereby if an alpha value of a fragment compared against a reference value failed, that fragment would be killed. That is, if a fragment failed the alpha test, the fragment would not be rendered. In OpenGL ES 2.0, there is no fixed function alpha test, but the same effect can be achieved in the fragment shader using the `discard` keyword.

The RenderMonkey example in Chapter_10/RM_AlphaTest shows a very simple example of doing the alpha test in the fragment shader as shown in Figure 10-5.

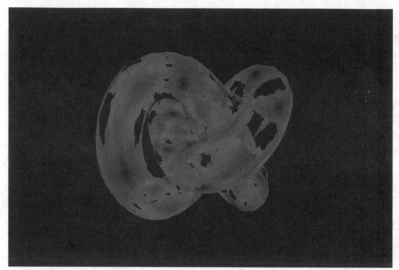

Figure 10-5   Alpha Test Using Discard

The fragment shader code for this example is provided in Example 10-4.

Example 10-4   Fragment Shader for Alpha Test Using Discard

```
precision mediump float;

uniform sampler2D baseMap;

varying vec2 v_texCoord;

void main(void)
{
    vec4 baseColor = texture2D(baseMap, v_texCoord);

    if(baseColor.a < 0.25)
    {
        discard;
    }
    else
    {
        gl_FragColor = baseColor;
    }
}
```

In this fragment shader, the texture is a four-channel RGBA texture. The alpha channel is used for the alpha test. The alpha color is compared against 0.25 and if it less than that, the fragment is killed using `discard`. Otherwise, the fragment is drawn using the texture color. This technique can be used for implementing the alpha test by simply changing the comparison or alpha reference value.

User Clip Planes

As described in Chapter 7, "Primitive Assembly and Rasterization," all primitives are clipped against the six planes that make up the view frustum. However, sometimes a user might want to clip against one or more additional user clip planes. There are a number of possible reasons you might want to clip against user clip planes. For example, when rendering reflections, you need to flip the geometry about the reflection plane and then render it into an off-screen texture. When rendering into the texture, you need to clip the geometry against the reflection plane, which requires a user clip plane.

In OpenGL ES 1.1, user clip planes could be provided to the API via a plane equation and the clipping would be handheld automatically. In OpenGL ES 2.0, you can still accomplish this same effect, but now you need to do it yourself in the shader. The key to implementing user clip planes is using the `discard` keyword that was introduced in the previous section.

Before showing you how to implement user clip planes, let's review the basics of the mathematics. A plane is specified by the equation

$$Ax + By + Cz + D = 0$$

The vector (A, B, C) represents the normal of the plane and the value D is the distance of the plane along that vector from the origin. To figure out whether a point should or should not be clipped against a plane, we need to evaluate the distance from a point P to a plane with the equation:

$$\text{Dist} = (A \times P.x) + (B \times P.y) + (C \times P.z) + D$$

If the distance is less than 0, we know the point is behind the plane and should be clipped and if the distance is greater than or equal to 0, it should not be clipped. Note that the plane equation and P must be in the same coordinate space. A RenderMonkey example is provided in Chapter_10/ RM_ClipPlane workspace as shown in Figure 10-6.

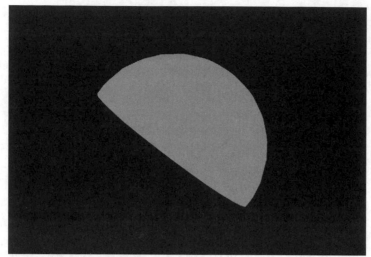

Figure 10-6   User Clip Plane Example

The first thing the shader needs to do is compute the distance to the plane as mentioned earlier. This could be done in either the vertex shader (and passed into a varying) or the fragment shader. It is cheaper to do this computation in the vertex shader rather than having to compute the distance in every fragment. The vertex shader listing in Example 10-5 shows the distance to plane computation.

Example 10-5   User Clip Plane Vertex Shader

```
uniform vec4 u_clipPlane;
uniform mat4 matViewProjection;
attribute vec4 rm_Vertex;

varying float u_clipDist;

void main(void)
{
   // Compute the distance between the vertex and the clip plane
   u_clipDist = dot(rm_Vertex.xyz, u_clipPlane.xyz) +
                u_clipPlane.w;
   gl_Position = matViewProjection * rm_Vertex;
}
```

The u_clipPlane uniform variable holds the plane equation for the clip plane. The u_clipDist varying variable then stores the computed clip distance. This value is passed into the fragment shader, which uses the interpolated distance to determine whether the fragment should be clipped as shown in Example 10-6.

Example 10-6   User Clip Plane Fragment Shader

```
precision mediump float;
varying float u_clipDist;
void main(void)
{
    // Reject fragments behind the clip plane
    if(u_clipDist < 0.0)
        discard;

    gl_FragColor = vec4(0.5, 0.5, 1.0, 0.0);
}
```

As you can see, if the u_clipDist varying variable is negative, this means the fragment is behind the clip plane and must be discarded. Otherwise, the fragment is processed as usual. This simple example just demonstrates the computations needed to implement user clip planes. You can easily implement multiple user clip planes by simply computing multiple clip distances and having multiple discard tests.

Chapter 11

Fragment Operations

This chapter discusses the operations that can be applied either to the entire framebuffer or to individual fragments after the execution of the fragment shader in the OpenGL ES 2.0 fragment pipeline. As you'll recall, the output of the fragment shader is the fragment's color and depth value. The operations that occur after fragment shader execution and can affect the visibility and final color of a pixel are:

- Scissor box testing.
- Stencil buffer testing.
- Depth buffer testing.
- Multisampling.
- Blending.
- Dithering.

The tests and operations that a fragment goes through on its way to the framebuffer are shown in Figure 11-1.

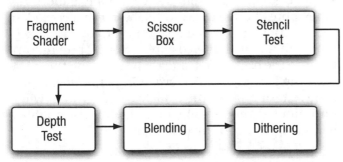

Figure 11-1   The Post-Shader Fragment Pipeline

As you might have noticed, there isn't a stage named "multisampling." Multisampling is an antialiasing technique that duplicates operations at a subfragment level. We describe more about how multisampling affects fragment processing later in the chapter.

The chapter concludes with a discussion of methods for reading pixels from and writing pixels to the framebuffer.

Buffers

OpenGL ES supports three types of buffers, each of which stores different data for every pixel in the framebuffer:

- Color buffer (composed of front and back color buffers).
- Depth buffer.
- Stencil buffer.

The size of a buffer—commonly referred to as the "depth of the buffer" (but not to be confused with the depth buffer)—is measured by the number of bits that are available for storing information for a single pixel. The color buffer, for example, will have three components for storing the red, green, and blue color components, and optional storage for the alpha component. The depth of the color buffer is the sum of the number of bits for all of its components. For the depth and stencil buffers, on the other hand, a single value represents the bit depth of a pixel in those buffers. For example, a depth buffer might have 16 bits per pixel. The overall size of the buffer is the sum of the bit depths of all of the components. Common framebuffer depths include 16-bit RGB buffers, with five bits for red and blue, and six bits for green (the human visual system is more sensitive to green than red or blue), and 32 bits divided equally for an RGBA buffer.

Additionally, the color buffer may be double buffered, where it will contain two buffers: one that is displayed on the output device (usually a monitor or LCD display) named the "front" buffer; and another buffer that is hidden from the viewer, but used for constructing the next image to be displayed, and called the "back" buffer. In double-buffered applications, animation is accomplished by drawing into the back buffer, and then swapping the front and back buffers to display the new image. This swapping of buffers is usually synchronized with the refresh cycle of the display device, which will give the illusion of a continuously smooth animation. Recall that double buffering was discussed in Chapter 3, "An Introduction to EGL."

Although every EGL configuration will have a color buffer, the depth and stencil buffers are optional. However, every EGL implementation must provide at least one configuration that contains all three of the buffers, with the depth buffer being at least 16 bits deep, and at least eight bits for the stencil buffer.

Requesting Additional Buffers

To include a depth or stencil buffer along with your color buffer, you need to request them when you specify the attributes for your EGL configuration. As you might recall from Chapter 3, you pass a set of attribute–value pairs into the EGL that specify the type of rendering surface your application needs. To include a depth buffer in addition to the color buffer, you would specify EGL_DEPTH_SIZE in the list of attributes with the desired bit depth you need. Likewise, you would add EGL_STENCIL_SIZE along with the number of required bits to obtain a stencil buffer.

Our convenience library, esUtil, simplifies those operations by merely allowing you to say that you'd like those buffers along with a color buffer, and it takes care of the rest of the work (requesting a maximally sized buffer). When using our library, you would add (by means of a bitwise-or operation) ES_WINDOW_DEPTH and ES_WINDOW_STENCIL in your call to esCreateWindow. For example,

```
esCreateWindow(&esContext, "Application Name",
            window_width, window_height,
            ES_WINDOW_RGB | ES_WINDOW_DEPTH | ES_WINDOW_STENCIL);
```

Clearing Buffers

OpenGL ES is an interactive rendering system, and assumes that at the start of each frame, you'll want to initialize all of the buffers to their default value. Buffers are cleared by calling the glClear function, which takes a bitmask representing the various buffers that should be cleared to their specified clear values.

void	**glClear**(GLbitfield *mask*);
mask	specifies the buffers to be cleared, and is composed of the union of the following bitmask representing the various OpenGL ES buffers: GL_COLOR_BUFFER_BIT, GL_DEPTH_BUFFER_BIT, GL_STENCIL_BUFFER_BIT

You're neither required to clear every buffer, nor clear them all at the same time, but you might obtain the best performance by only calling `glClear` once per frame with all the buffers you want simultaneously cleared.

Each buffer has a default value that's used when you request that buffer be cleared. For each buffer, you can specify your desired clear value using the functions shown here.

---

void   **glClearColor**(GLclampf *red*, GLclampf *green*,
                 GLclampf *blue*, GLclampf *alpha*);

---

red, *green*, *blue*, *alpha* — specifies the color value (in the range [0,1]) that all pixels in the color buffers should be initialized to when GL_COLOR_BUFFER_BIT is present in the bitmask passed to `glClear`

---

void   **glClearDepthf**(GLclampf *depth*);

---

depth — specifies the depth value (in the range [0,1]) that all pixels in the depth buffer should be initialized to when GL_DEPTH_BUFFER_BIT is present in the bitmask passed to `glClear`

---

void   **glClearStencil**(GLint *s*);

---

s — specifies the stencil value (in the range $[0,2^n - 1]$, where n is the number of bits available in the stencil buffer) that all pixels in the stencil buffer should be initialized to when GL_STENCIL_BUFFER_BIT is present in the bitmask passed to `glClear`

Using Masks to Control Writing to Framebuffers

You can also control which buffers, or components, in the case of the color buffer, are writable by specifying a buffer write mask. Before a pixel's value is written into a buffer, the buffer's mask is used to verify that the buffer is writable.

For the color buffer, the `glColorMask` routine specifies which components in the color buffer will be updated if a pixel is written. If the mask for a particular component is set to `GL_FALSE`, that component will not be updated if written to. By default, all color components are writable.

void	**glColorMask**(GLboolean *red*, GLboolean *green*, GLboolean *blue*, GLboolean *alpha*);
red, *green*, *blue*, *alpha*	specify whether the particular color component in the color buffer is modifiable while rendering

Likewise, the writing to the depth buffer is controlled by calling `glDepthMask` with `GL_TRUE` or `GL_FALSE` to specify if the depth buffer is writable.

Quite often, disabling writing to the depth buffer is used when rendering translucent objects. Initially, you would render all of the opaque objects in the scene with writing to the depth buffer enabled (i.e., set to `GL_TRUE`). This would make sure that all of the opaque objects are correctly depth sorted, and the depth buffer contains the appropriate depth information for the scene. Then, before rendering the translucent objects, you would disable writing to the depth buffer by calling `glDepthMask(GL_FALSE)`. While writing to the depth buffer is disabled, values can still be read from it and used for depth comparisons. This allows translucent objects that are obscured by opaque objects to be correctly depth buffered, but not modify the depth buffer such that opaque objects would be obscured by translucent ones.

void	**glDepthMask**(GLboolean *depth*);
depth	specifies whether the depth buffer is modifiable

Finally, you can also disable writing to the stencil buffer by calling `glStencilMask`, but as compared to `glColorMask` or `glDepthMask`, you specify which bits of the stencil buffer are writable by providing a mask.

void	**glStencilMask**(GLuint *mask*);
mask	specifies a bitmask (in the range $[0, 2^n - 1]$, where n is the number of bits in the stencil buffer) of which bits in a pixel in the stencil buffer are modifiable

The glStencilMaskSeparate routine allows you to set the stencil mask based on the face vertex order (sometimes called "facedness") of the primitive. This allows different stencil masks for front- and back-facing primitives. glStencilMaskSeparate(GL_FRONT_AND_BACK, mask) is identical to calling glStencilMask, which sets the same mask for the front and back polygon faces.

void	**glStencilMaskSeparate**(GLenum *face*, GLuint *mask*);
face	specifies the stencil mask to be applied based on the face vertex order of the rendered primitive. Valid values are GL_FRONT, GL_BACK, and GL_FRONT_AND_BACK
mask	specifies a bitmask (in the range $[0, 2^n]$, where n is the number of bits in the stencil buffer) of which bits in a pixel in the stencil buffer are specified by face

Fragment Tests and Operations

The following sections describe the various tests that can be applied to a fragment in OpenGL ES. By default, all fragment tests and operations are disabled, and fragments become pixels as they are written to the framebuffer in the order in which they're received. By enabling the various fragments, operational tests can be applied to choose which fragments become pixels and affect the final image.

Each fragment test is individually enabled by calling glEnable with the appropriate token listed in Table 11-1.

Table 11-1   Fragment Test Enable Tokens

glEnable Token	Description
GL_DEPTH_TEST	Control depth testing of fragments
GL_STENCIL_TEST	Control stencil testing of fragments
GL_BLEND	Control blending of fragments with colors stored in the color buffer
GL_DITHER	Control the dithering of fragment colors before being written in the color buffer
GL_SAMPLE_COVERAGE	Control the computation of sample coverage values
GL_SAMPLE_ALPHA_TO_COVERAGE	Control the use of a sample's alpha in the computation of a sample coverage value

Using the Scissor Test

The scissor test provides an additional level of clipping by specifying a rectangular region that further limits which pixels in the framebuffer are writable. Using the scissor box is a two-step process. First, you need to specify the rectangular region using the glScissor function.

```
void    glScissor(GLint x, GLint y, GLsizei width,
                  GLsizei height );
```

x, y   specify the lower left corner of the scissor rectangle in viewport coordinates

width   specifies the width of the scissor box (in pixels)

height   specifies the height of the scissor box (in pixels)

After specifying the scissor box, you'll need to enable it by calling glEnable(GL_SCISSOR_TEST) to employ the additional clipping. All rendering, including clearing the viewport, is restricted to the scissor box.

Generally, the scissor box is a subregion in the viewport, but there's no requirement that the two regions actually intersect.

Stencil Buffer Testing

The next operation that might be applied to a fragment is the stencil test. The stencil buffer is a per-pixel mask that holds values that can be used to determine whether a pixel should be updated or not. The stencil test is enabled or disabled by the application.

Using the stencil buffer can be considered a two-step operation. The first step is to initialize the stencil buffer with the per-pixel masks, which is done by rendering geometry and specifying how the stencil buffer should be updated. The second step is generally to use those values to control subsequent rendering into the color buffer. In both cases, you specify how the parameters are to be used in the stencil test.

The stencil test is essentially a bit test, as you might do in a C program where you use a mask to determine if a bit is set, for example. The stencil function, which controls the operator and values of the stencil test, is controlled by the `glStencilFunc` or `glStencilFuncSeparate` functions.

void	**glStencilFunc**(GLenum *func*, GLint *ref*, GLuint *mask*);
void	**glStencilFuncSeparate**(GLenum *face*, GLenum *func*, GLint *ref*, GLuint *mask*);

face	specifies the face associated with the provided stencil function. Valid values are GL_FRONT, GL_BACK, and GL_FRONT_AND_BACK
func	specifies the comparison function for the stencil test. Valid values are GL_EQUAL, GL_NOTEQUAL, GL_LESS, GL_GREATER, GL_LEQUAL, GL_GEQUAL, GL_ALWAYS, and GL_NEVER
ref	specifies the comparison value for the stencil test
mask	specifies the mask that is bitwise-anded with the bits in the stencil buffer before being compared against the reference value

To allow finer control of the stencil test, a masking parameter is used to select which bits of the stencil values should be considered for the test. After selecting those bits, their value is compared with a reference value using the operator provided. For example, to specify that the stencil test passes where the lowest three bits of the stencil buffer are equal to 2, you would call

```
glStencilFunc(GL_EQUAL, 2, 0x7);
```

and enable the stencil test.

With the stencil test configured, you generally also need to let OpenGL ES 2.0 know what to do with the values in the stencil buffer when the stencil test passes. In fact, modifying the values in the stencil buffer relies on more than just the stencil tests, but also incorporates the results of the depth test (discussed in the next section). There are three possible outcomes that can occur for a fragment with the combined stencil and depth tests:

1. The fragment fails the stencil tests. If this occurs, no further testing (i.e., the depth test) is applied to that fragment.

2. The fragment passes the stencil test, but fails the depth test.

3. The fragment passes both the stencil and depth tests.

Each of those possible outcomes can be used to affect the value in the stencil buffer for that pixel location. The glStencilOp and glStencilOpSeparate functions control the actions done on the stencil buffer's value for each of those test outcomes, and the possible operations on the stencil values are shown in Table 11-2.

Table 11-2   Stencil Operations

Stencil Function	Description
GL_ZERO	Set the stencil value to zero
GL_REPLACE	Replace the current stencil value with the reference value specified in glStencilFunc or glStencilFuncSeparate
GL_INCR, GL_DECR	Increment or decrement the stencil value; the stencil value is clamped to zero or 2^n, where n is the number of bits in the stencil buffer
GL_INCR_WRAP, GL_DECR_WRAP	Increment or decrement the stencil value, but "wrap" the value if the stencil value overflows (incrementing the maximum value will result in a new stencil value of zero) or underflows (decrementing zero will result in the maximum stencil value)
GL_KEEP	Keep the current stencil value, effectively not modifying the value for that pixel
GL_INVERT	Bitwise-invert the value in the stencil buffer

void	**glStencilOp** (GLenum sfail, GLenum zfail, GLenum zpass);
void	**glStencilOpSeparate** (GLenum face, GLenum sfail, GLenum zfail, GLenum zpass);

face	specifies the face associated with the provided stencil function. Valid values are GL_FRONT, GL_BACK, and GL_FRONT_AND_BACK
sfail	specifies the operation applied to the stencil bits if the fragment fails the stencil test. Valid values are GL_KEEP, GL_ZERO, GL_REPLACE, GL_INCR, GL_DECR, GL_INCR_WRAP, GL_DECR_WRAP, and GL_INVERT
zfail	specifies the operation applied when the fragment passes the stencil test, but fails the depth test
zpass	specifies the operation applied when the fragment passes both the stencil and depth tests

The following example illustrates using glStencilFunc and glStencilOp to control rendering in various parts of the viewport.

```
GLfloat vVertices[] =

{
    -0.75f,   0.25f,   0.50f, // Quad #0
    -0.25f,   0.25f,   0.50f,
    -0.25f,   0.75f,   0.50f,
    -0.75f,   0.75f,   0.50f,
     0.25f,   0.25f,   0.90f, // Quad #1
     0.75f,   0.25f,   0.90f,
     0.75f,   0.75f,   0.90f,
     0.25f,   0.75f,   0.90f,
    -0.75f,  -0.75f,   0.50f, // Quad #2
    -0.25f,  -0.75f,   0.50f,
    -0.25f,  -0.25f,   0.50f,
    -0.75f,  -0.25f,   0.50f,
     0.25f,  -0.75f,   0.50f, // Quad #3
     0.75f,  -0.75f,   0.50f,
     0.75f,  -0.25f,   0.50f,
     0.25f,  -0.25f,   0.50f,
    -1.00f,  -1.00f,   0.00f, // Big Quad
     1.00f,  -1.00f,   0.00f,
     1.00f,   1.00f,   0.00f,
    -1.00f,   1.00f,   0.00f
};
```

```
   GLubyte indices[][6] =
   {
       {  0,  1,  2,  0,  2,  3 }, // Quad #0
       {  4,  5,  6,  4,  6,  7 }, // Quad #1
       {  8,  9, 10,  8, 10, 11 }, // Quad #2
       { 12, 13, 14, 12, 14, 15 }, // Quad #3
       { 16, 17, 18, 16, 18, 19 }  // Big Quad
   };

#define NumTests  4
   GLfloat   colors[NumTests][4] =
   {
       { 1.0f, 0.0f, 0.0f, 1.0f },
       { 0.0f, 1.0f, 0.0f, 1.0f },
       { 0.0f, 0.0f, 1.0f, 1.0f },
       { 1.0f, 1.0f, 0.0f, 0.0f }
   };

   GLint   numStencilBits;
   GLuint  stencilValues[NumTests] =
   {
      0x7, // Result of test 0
      0x0, // Result of test 1
      0x2, // Result of test 2
      0xff // Result of test 3. We need to fill this
           // value in a run-time
   };

   // Set the viewport
   glViewport(0, 0, esContext->width, esContext->height);

   // Clear the color, depth, and stencil buffers. At this
   // point, the stencil buffer will be 0x1 for all pixels
   glClear(GL_COLOR_BUFFER_BIT | GL_DEPTH_BUFFER_BIT |
           GL_STENCIL_BUFFER_BIT);

   // Use the program object
   glUseProgram(userData->programObject);

   // Load the vertex position
   glVertexAttribPointer(userData->positionLoc, 3, GL_FLOAT,
                   GL_FALSE, 0, vVertices);

   glEnableVertexAttribArray(userData->positionLoc);

   // Test 0:
   //
   // Initialize upper-left region. In this case, the stencil-
   // buffer values will be replaced because the stencil test
```

```
// for the rendered pixels will fail the stencil test, which is
//
//         ref    mask     stencil  mask
//      ( 0x7 & 0x3 ) < ( 0x1 & 0x7 )
//
// The value in the stencil buffer for these pixels will
// be 0x7.
//
glStencilFunc(GL_LESS, 0x7, 0x3);
glStencilOp(GL_REPLACE, GL_DECR, GL_DECR);
glDrawElements(GL_TRIANGLES, 6, GL_UNSIGNED_BYTE, indices[0]);

// Test 1:
//
// Initialize the upper right region. Here, we'll decrement
// the stencil-buffer values where the stencil test passes
// but the depth test fails. The stencil test is
//
//         ref  mask     stencil  mask
//      ( 0x3 & 0x3 ) > ( 0x1 & 0x3 )
//
//    but where the geometry fails the depth test.  The
//    stencil values for these pixels will be 0x0.
//
glStencilFunc(GL_GREATER, 0x3, 0x3);
glStencilOp(GL_KEEP, GL_DECR, GL_KEEP);
glDrawElements(GL_TRIANGLES, 6, GL_UNSIGNED_BYTE, indices[1]);

// Test 2:
//
// Initialize the lower left region. Here we'll increment
// (with saturation) the stencil value where both the
// stencil and depth tests pass. The stencil test for
// these pixels will be
//
//         ref  mask     stencil  mask
//      ( 0x1 & 0x3 ) == ( 0x1 & 0x3 )
//
// The stencil values for these pixels will be 0x2.
//
glStencilFunc(GL_EQUAL, 0x1, 0x3);
glStencilOp(GL_KEEP, GL_INCR, GL_INCR);
glDrawElements(GL_TRIANGLES, 6, GL_UNSIGNED_BYTE, indices[2]);

// Test 3:
//
// Finally, initialize the lower right region. We'll invert
// the stencil value where the stencil tests fails. The
```

```
// stencil test for these pixels will be
//
//       ref    mask    stencil  mask
//      ( 0x2 & 0x1 ) == ( 0x1 & 0x1 )
//
// The stencil value here will be set to ~((2^s-1) & 0x1),
// (with the 0x1 being from the stencil clear value),
// where 's' is the number of bits in the stencil buffer
//
glStencilFunc(GL_EQUAL, 0x2, 0x1);
glStencilOp(GL_INVERT, GL_KEEP, GL_KEEP);
glDrawElements(GL_TRIANGLES, 6, GL_UNSIGNED_BYTE, indices[3]);

// As we don't know at compile time how many stencil bits are
// present, we'll query, and update the correct value in the
// stencilValues arrays for the fourth tests. We'll use this
// value later in rendering.
glGetIntegerv(GL_STENCIL_BITS, &numStencilBits);

stencilValues[3] = ~(((1 << numStencilBits) - 1) & 0x1) & 0xff;

// Use the stencil buffer for controlling where rendering will
// occur. We disable writing to the stencil buffer so we can
// test against them without modifying the values we generated.
glStencilMask(0x0);

for(i = 0; i < NumTests; ++i)
{
   glStencilFunc(GL_EQUAL, stencilValues[i], 0xff);
   glUniform4fv(userData->colorLoc, 1, colors[i]);
   glDrawElements(GL_TRIANGLES, 6, GL_UNSIGNED_BYTE, indices[4]);
}
```

Depth Buffer Testing

The depth buffer is usually used for hidden-surface removal. It traditionally keeps the distance value of the closest object to the viewpoint for each pixel in the rendering surface, and for every new incoming fragment, compares its distance from the viewpoint with the stored value. By default, if the incoming fragment's depth value is less than the value stored in the depth buffer (meaning it's closer to the viewer) the incoming fragment's depth value replaced the values stored in the depth buffer, and then its color value replaces the color value in the color buffer. This is the standard method for depth buffering, and if that's what you would like to do, all you need to do is request a depth buffer when you create a window, and then enable the depth test by calling glEnable with GL_DEPTH_TEST. If no depth buffer is associated with the color buffer, the depth test always passes.

Of course, that's only one way to use the depth buffer. You can modify the depth comparison operator by calling glDepthFunc.

void	**glDepthFunc** (GLenum *func*)
func	specifies the depth value comparison function, which can be one of GL_LESS, GL_GREATER, GL_LEQUAL, GL_GEQUAL, GL_EQUAL, GL_NOTEQUAL, GL_ALWAYS, or GL_NEVER

Blending

In this section, we discuss blending pixel colors. Once a fragment passes all of the enabled fragment tests, its color can be combined with the color that's already present in the fragment's pixel location. Before the two colors are combined, they're multiplied by a scaling factor and combined using the specified blending operator. The blending equation is

$$C_{final} = f_{source}\ C_{source}\ \text{op}\ f_{destination}\ C_{destination}$$

where f_{source} and C_{source} are the incoming fragment's scaling factor and color, respectively. Likewise, $f_{destination}$ and $C_{destination}$ are the pixel's scaling factor and color. op is the mathematical operator for combining the scaled values.

The scaling factors are specified by calling either glBlendFunc or glBlend-FuncSeparate.

void	**glBlendFunc** (GLenum *sfactor*, GLenum *dfactor*);
sfactor	specifies the blending coefficient for the incoming fragment
dfactor	specifies the blending coefficient for the destination pixel

void	**glBlendFuncSeparate** (GLenum *srcRGB*, GLenum *dstRGB*, GLenum *srcAlpha*, GLenum *dstAlpha*);
srcRGB	specifies the blending coefficient for the incoming fragment's red, green, and blue components

The possible values for the blending coefficients are shown in Table 11-3.

Table 11-3   Blending Functions

Blending Coefficient Enum	RGB Blending Factors	Alpha Blending Factor
GL_ZERO	$(0, 0, 0)$	0
GL_ONE	$(1, 1, 1)$	1
GL_SRC_COLOR	(R_s, G_s, B_s)	A_s
GL_ONE_MINUS_SRC_COLOR	$(1 - R_s, 1 - G_s, 1 - B_s)$	$1 - A_s$
GL_SRC_ALPHA	(A_s, A_s, A_s)	A_s
GL_ONE_MINUS_SRC_ALPHA	$(1 - A_s, 1 - A_s, 1 - A_s)$	$1 - A_s$
GL_DST_COLOR	(R_d, G_d, B_d)	A_d
GL_ONE_MINUS_DST_COLOR	$(1 - R_d, 1 - G_d, 1 - B_d)$	$1 - A_d$
GL_DST_ALPHA	(A_d, A_d, A_d)	A_d
GL_ONE_MINUS_DST_ALPHA	$(1 - A_d, 1 - A_d, 1 - A_d)$	$1 - A_d$
GL_CONSTANT_COLOR	(R_c, G_c, B_c)	A_c
GL_ONE_MINUS_CONSTANT_COLOR	$(1 - R_c, 1 - G_c, 1 - B_c)$	$1 - A_c$
GL_CONSTANT_ALPHA	(A_c, A_c, A_c)	A_c
GL_ONE_MINUS_CONSTANT_ALPHA	$(1 - A_c, 1 - A_c, 1 - A_c)$	$1 - A_c$
GL_SRC_ALPHA_SATURATE	$\min(A_s, 1 - A_d)$	1

In Table 11-3 (R_s, G_s, B_s, A_s) are the color components associated with the incoming fragment color, (R_d, G_d, B_d, A_d) are the components associated with the pixel color already in the color buffer, and (R_c, G_c, B_c, A_c) represent a constant color that you set by calling glBlendColor. In the case of GL_SRC_ALHPA_SATURATE, the minimum value that's computed is applied to the source color only.

---

void   **glBlendColor**(GLclampf *red*, GLclampf *green*,
                          GLclampf *blue*, GLclampf *alpha*);

---

red, *green*,   specify the component values for the constant
blue,   blending color
alpha

Once the incoming fragment and pixel color have been multiplied by their respective scaling factors, they're combined using the operator specified by glBlendEquation or glBlendEquationSeparate. By default, blended colors are accumulated using the GL_FUNC_ADD operator. The GL_FUNC_SUBTRACT operator subtracts the scaled color from the framebuffer from the incoming fragment's value. Likewise, the GL_FUNC_REVERSE_SUBTRACT reverses the blending equation such that the incoming fragment colors are subtracted from the current pixel value.

---

void   **glBlendEquation**(GLenum *mode*);

---

mode   specify the blending operator. Valid values are GL_FUNC_ADD,
          GL_FUNC_SUBTRACT, or GL_FUNC_REVERSE_SUBTRACT

---

void   **glBlendEquationSeparate**(GLenum *modeRGB*,
                                     GLenum *modeAlpha*);

---

modeRGB   specify the blending operator for the red, green, and blue
             components
modeAlpha specify the alpha component blending operator

Dithering

On a system where the number of colors available in the framebuffer is limited due to the number of bits per component in the framebuffer, we can simulate greater color depth using dithering. Dithering algorithms arrange colors in such ways that the image appears to have more available colors than are really present. OpenGL ES 2.0 doesn't specify which dithering algorithm is to be used in supporting its dithering stage; the technique is very implementation dependent.

The only control your application has over dithering is whether it is applied to the final pixels or not, which is entirely controlled by calling `glEnable` or `glDisable` to specify dithering's use in the pipeline.

Multisampled Antialiasing

Antialiasing is an important technique for improving the quality of generated images by trying to reduce the visual artifacts of rendering into discrete pixels. The geometric primitives that OpenGL ES 2.0 renders get rasterized onto a grid, and their edges may become deformed in that process. We've all seen that staircase effect that happens to lines drawn diagonally across a monitor.

There are various techniques for trying to reduce those aliasing effects, and OpenGL ES 2.0 supports a variant called *multisampling*. Multisampling divides every pixel into a set of samples, each of which is treated like a "mini-pixel" during rasterization. That is, when a geometric primitive is rendered, it's like rendering into a framebuffer that has many more pixels than the real display surface. Each sample has its own color, depth, and stencil value, and those values are preserved until the image is ready for display. When it's time to compose the final image, the samples are *resolved* into the final pixel color. What makes this process special is that in addition to using every sample's color information, OpenGL ES 2.0 also has additional information about how many samples for a particular pixel were occupied during rasterization. Each sample for a pixel is assigned a bit in the *sample coverage mask*. Using that coverage mask, we can control how the final pixels are resolved. Every rendering surface created for an OpenGL ES 2.0 application will be configured for multisampling, even if there's only a single sample per pixel.

Multisampling has multiple options that can be turned on and off (using `glEnable` and `glDisable`) to control the usage of sample coverage value.

First, you can specify that the sample's alpha value should be used to determine the coverage value by enabling GL_SAMPLE_ALPHA_TO_COVERAGE. In this mode, if the geometric primitive covers a sample, the alpha value of incoming fragment is used to determine an additional sample coverage mask computed that is bitwise AND'ed into the coverage mask that is computed using the samples of the fragment. This newly computed coverage value replaces the original one generated directly from the sample coverage calculation. These sample computations are implementation dependent.

Additionally you can specify GL_SAMPLE_COVERAGE, which uses the fragment's (potentially modified by previous operations listed earlier) coverage value, and computes the bitwise-and of that value with one specified using the glSampleCoverage function. The value specified with glSample-Coverage is used to generate an implementation-specific coverage mask, and includes an inversion flag, invert, that inverts the bits in the generated mask. Using this inversion flag, it is possible to create two transparency masks that don't use entirely distinct sets of samples.

---

void **glSampleCoverage**(GLfloat *value*, GLboolean *invert*);

---

value   specifies a value in the range [0, 1] that is converted into a sample mask. The resulting mask should have a proportional number of bits set corresponding to the value

invert   specifies that after determining the mask's value, all of the bits in the mask should be inverted

---

Although multisampling helps reduce aliasing in scenes, it is also prone to artifacts that may be visually displeasing. This usually occurs due to the sample locations with a pixel. This problem can be rectified by using centroid sampling, which is unfortunately not a feature that OpenGL ES 2.0 supports at the time of this writing.

Reading and Writing Pixels to the Framebuffer

If you would like to preserve your rendered image for posterity's sake, you can read the pixel values back from the color buffer, but not from the depth or stencil buffers. By calling glReadPixels, the pixels in the color buffer are returned to your application in an array that has been previously allocated.

```
void    glReadPixels(GLint x, GLint y, GLsizei width,
                     GLsizei height, GLenum format,
                     GLenum type, void *pixels);
```

x, y	specify the viewport coordinates of the lower left corner of the pixel rectangle read from the color buffer
width, height	specify the dimensions of the pixel rectangle read from the color buffer
format	specifies the pixel format that you would like returned. Two formats are available: GL_RGB, and the value returned by querying GL_IMPLEMENTATION_COLOR_READ_FORMAT, which is an implementation-specific pixel format
type	specifies the data type of the pixels returned. Two types are available: GL_UNSIGNED_BYTE, and the value returned from querying GL_IMPLEMENTATION_COLOR_READ_TYPE, which is an implementation-specific pixel type
pixels	is a contiguous array of bytes that contain the values read from the color buffer after glReadPixels returns

Aside from the fixed format (GL_RGB), and type (GL_UNSIGNED_BYTE), you'll notice there are implementation-dependent values that should return the best format and type combination for the implementation you're using. The implementation-specific values can be queried as follows:

```
GLenum    readType, readFormat;
GLubyte  *pixels;

glGetIntegerv(GL_IMPLEMENTATION_COLOR_READ_TYPE, &readType);
glGetIntegerv(GL_IMPLEMENTATION_COLOR_READ_FORMAT, &readFormat);

unsigned int  bytesPerPixel = 0;

switch(readType)
{
    case GL_UNSIGNED_BYTE:
        switch(readFormat)
        {
            case GL_RGBA:
                bytesPerPixel = 4;
                break;
```

```
            case GL_RGB:
                bytesPerPixel = 3;
                break;

            case GL_LUMINANCE_ALPHA:
                bytesPerPixel = 2;
                break;

            case GL_ALPHA:
            case GL_LUMINANCE:
                bytesPerPixel = 1;
                break;
        }
        break;

    case GL_UNSIGNED_SHORT_4444:    // GL_RGBA format
    case GL_UNSIGNED_SHORT_555_1:   // GL_RGBA format
    case GL_UNSIGNED_SHORT_565:     // GL_RGB  format
        bytesPerPixel = 2;
        break;
}

pixels = (GLubyte*) malloc(width * height * bytesPerPixel);

glReadPixels(0, 0, windowWidth, windowHeight, readFormat,
             readType, pixels );
```

You can read pixels from any currently bound framebuffer, whether it's one allocated by the windowing system, or from a framebuffer object. Because each buffer can have a different layout, you'll probably need to query the type and format for each buffer you want to read.

OpenGL ES 2.0 doesn't have a function to directly copy a block of pixels into the framebuffer. Instead, the available method is to create a texture map from the block of pixels, and use the texture-mapping technique described in Chapter 9, "Texturing," to initiate writing the pixels.

Chapter 12

Framebuffer Objects

In this chapter we describe what framebuffer objects are, how applications can create them, and how applications can use them for rendering to an off-screen buffer or rendering to a texture. We start by discussing why we need framebuffer objects. We then introduce framebuffer objects and discuss what they are, new object types they add to OpenGL ES, and how they differ from EGL surfaces that we read about in Chapter 3, "An Introduction to EGL." We go on to discuss how to create framebuffer objects; how to specify color, depth, and stencil attachments to a framebuffer object; and then provide examples that demonstrate rendering to a framebuffer object. Last but not least, we discuss performance tips and tricks applications that we should be aware of and use to ensure good performance when using framebuffer objects.

Why Framebuffer Objects?

A rendering context and a drawing surface need to be first created and made current before any OpenGL ES commands can be called by an application. The rendering context and the drawing surface are usually provided by the native windowing system through an API such as EGL. Chapter 3 describes how to create an EGL context and surface and how to attach them to a rendering thread. The rendering context contains appropriate state required for correct operation. The drawing surface provided by the native windowing system can be a surface that will be displayed on the screen, referred to as the window system provided framebuffer, or can be an off-screen surface, referred to as a pbuffer. The calls to create the EGL drawing surfaces let you specify the width and height of the surface in pixels, whether the surface uses color-, depth-, and stencil buffers, and bit depths of these buffers.

By default, OpenGL ES uses the window system provided framebuffer as the drawing surface. If the application is only drawing to an on-screen surface, the window system provided framebuffer is usually sufficient. However, many applications need to render to a texture, and for this using the window system provided framebuffer as your drawing surface is usually not an ideal option. Examples of where render to texture is useful are dynamic reflections and environment-mapping, multipass techniques for depth-of-field, motion blur effects, and post-processing effects.

There are two techniques that applications can use to render to a texture:

- Implement render to texture by drawing to the window system provided framebuffer and then copy the appropriate region of the framebuffer to the texture. This can be implemented using `glCopyTexImage2D` and `glCopyTexSubImage2D` APIs. As the name implies, these APIs perform a copy from the framebuffer to the texture buffer and this copy operation can often adversely impact performance. In addition, this only works if the dimensions of the texture are less than or equal to the dimensions of the framebuffer.

- Implement render to texture by using a pbuffer that is attached to a texture. We know that a window system provided surface must be attached to a rendering context. This can be inefficient on some implementations that require separate contexts for each pbuffer and window surface. Additionally, switching between window system provided drawables can sometimes require the implementation to completely finish all previous rendering prior to the switch. This can introduce expensive "bubbles" into the rendering pipeline. On such systems, our recommendation is to avoid using pbuffers to render to textures because of the overhead associated with context and window system provided drawable switching.

Neither of these two methods are ideal for rendering to a texture or other off-screen surface. What is needed are APIs that allow applications to directly render to a texture or the ability to create an off-screen surface within the OpenGL ES API and use it as a rendering target. Framebuffer objects and renderbuffer objects allow applications to do exactly this without requiring additional rendering contexts to be created. We no longer have to worry about the overhead of a context and drawable switch that can occur when using window system provided drawables. Framebuffer objects therefore provide a better and more efficient method for rendering to a texture or an off-screen surface.

The Framebuffer objects API supports the following operations:

- Creating framebuffer objects using OpenGL ES commands only.

- Creating and using multiple framebuffer objects within a single EGL context; that is, without requiring a rendering context per framebuffer.

- Creating off-screen color, depth, or stencil renderbuffers and textures, and attaching these to a framebuffer object.

- Sharing color, depth or stencil buffers across multiple framebuffers.

- Attaching textures directly to a framebuffer as color or depth and avoiding the need to do a copy operation.

Framebuffer and Renderbuffer Objects

We describe what a renderbuffer and a framebuffer object are, how they differ from window system provided drawables, and when to use a renderbuffer instead of a texture.

A *renderbuffer object* is a 2D image buffer allocated by the application. The renderbuffer can be used to allocate and store color, depth, or stencil values and can be used as a color, depth, or stencil attachment in a framebuffer object. A renderbuffer is similar to an off-screen window system provided drawable surface, such as a pbuffer. A renderbuffer, however, cannot be directly used as a GL texture.

A *framebuffer object* (often referred to as an FBO) is a collection of color, depth, and stencil buffer attachment points; state that describes properties such as the size and format of the color, depth, and stencil buffers attached to the FBO; and the names of the texture and renderbuffer objects attached to the FBO. Various 2D images can be attached to the color attachment point in the framebuffer object. These include a renderbuffer object that stores color values, a mip-level of a 2D texture or a cubemap face, or even a mip-level of a 2D slice in a 3D texture. Similarly, various 2D images containing depth values can be attached to the depth attachment point of an FBO. These can include a renderbuffer, a mip-level of a 2D texture or a cubemap face that stores depth values. The only 2D image that can be attached to the stencil attachment point of an FBO is a renderbuffer object that stores stencil values.

Figure 12-1 shows the relationship among framebuffer objects, renderbuffer objects, and textures. Note that there can only be one color, depth, and stencil attachment in a framebuffer object.

Note: The GL_OES_texture_3D optional extension allows a 2D slice of a 3D texture to be used as a framebuffer attachment.

The GL_OES_depth_texture optional extension allows for 2D and cubemap depth textures.

The GL_OES_packed_depth_stencil extension allows the application to use a packed depth stencil texture as a depth and stencil buffer attachment.

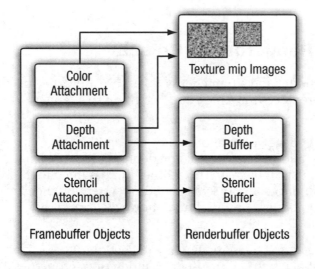

Figure 12-1   Framebuffer Objects, Renderbuffer Objects, and Textures

Choosing a Renderbuffer Versus a Texture as a Framebuffer Attachment

For render to texture use cases, attach a texture object to the framebuffer object. Examples include rendering to a color buffer that will be used as a color texture, or rendering into a depth buffer that will be used as a depth texture for shadows.

There are also several reasons to use renderbuffers instead of textures. These include the following:

- Certain image formats do not support texturing, such as stencil index values. A renderbuffer must be used instead.

- If the image will not be used as a texture, using a renderbuffer may have a performance advantage. This is because the implementation might be able to store the renderbuffer in a much more efficient format, better suited for rendering than for texturing. The implementation can only do so, however, if it knows in advance that the image will not be used as a texture.

Framebuffer Objects Versus EGL Surfaces

The differences between an FBO and the window system provided drawable surface are as follows:

- Pixel ownership test—This test determines if the pixel at location (x_w, y_w) in the framebuffer is currently owned by OpenGL ES. This test allows the window system to control which pixels in the framebuffer belong to the current OpenGL ES context. An example would be if a window that is being rendered into by OpenGL ES is obscured. For an application-created framebuffer object, the pixel ownership test always succeeds as the framebuffer object owns all the pixels.

- The window system might support only double-buffered surfaces. Framebuffer objects, on the other hand, only support single-buffered attachments.

- Sharing of stencil and depth buffers between framebuffers is possible using framebuffer objects but usually not with the window system provided framebuffer. Stencil and depth buffers and their corresponding state are usually allocated implicitly with the window system provided drawable surface and therefore cannot be shared between drawable surfaces. With application-created framebuffer objects, stencil and depth renderbuffers can be created independently and then associated with a framebuffer object by attaching these buffers to appropriate attachment points in multiple framebuffer objects, if desired.

- Window system provided framebuffers might support multisampling. Multisample buffers can be specified by using the window system surface creation API. In EGL, multisample buffers can be specified by setting the EGL_SAMPLE_BUFFERS value in EGLconfig used to create the window system provided framebuffer. Application-created framebuffer objects do not support multisample buffers as attachments.

Creating Framebuffer and Renderbuffer Objects

Creating framebuffer and renderbuffer objects is similar to how texture or vertex buffer objects are created in OpenGL ES 2.0.

The `glGenRenderbuffers` API call is used to allocate renderbuffer object names. This API is described next.

void	**glGenRenderbuffers**(GLsizei *n*, GLuint **renderbuffers*)

n	number of renderbuffer object names to return
renderbuffers	pointer to an array of *n* entries, where the allocated renderbuffer objects are returned

`glGenRenderbuffers` allocates *n* renderbuffer object names and returns them in `renderbuffers`. The renderbuffer object names returned by `glGenRenderbuffers` are unsigned integer numbers other than 0. The renderbuffer names returned are marked *in use* but do not have any state associated with them. The value 0 is reserved by OpenGL ES and does not refer to a renderbuffer object. Applications trying to modify or query buffer object state for renderbuffer object 0 will generate an appropriate error.

The `glGenFramebuffers` API call is used to allocate framebuffer object names. This API is described here.

void	**glGenFramebuffers**(GLsizei *n*, GLuint **ids*)

n	number of framebuffer object names to return
ids	pointer to an array of n entries, where allocated framebuffer objects are returned

`glGenFramebuffers` allocates *n* framebuffer object names and returns them in `ids`. The framebuffer object names returned by `glGenFramebuffers` are unsigned integer numbers other than 0. The framebuffer names returned are marked *in use* but do not have any state associated with them. The value 0 is reserved by OpenGL ES and refers to the window system provided framebuffer. Applications trying to modify or query buffer object state for framebuffer object 0 will generate an appropriate error.

Using Renderbuffer Objects

In this section, we describe how to specify the data storage, format, and dimensions of the renderbuffer image. To specify this information for a specific renderbuffer object, we need to make this object the current renderbuffer object. The `glBindRenderbuffer` command is used to set the current renderbuffer object.

void **glBindRenderbuffer**(GLenum *target*, GLuint *renderbuffer*)
target   must be set to GL_RENDERBUFFER
renderbuffer   renderbuffer object name

Note that `glGenRenderbuffers` is not required to assign a renderbuffer object name before it is bound using `glBindRenderbuffer`. Although it is a good practice to call `glGenRenderbuffers`, there are lots of applications that specify compile-time constants for their buffers. An application can specify an unused renderbuffer object name to `glBindRenderbuffer`. However, we do recommend that OpenGL ES applications call `glGenRenderbuffers` and use renderbuffer object names returned by `glGenRenderbuffers` instead of specifying their own buffer object names.

The first time the renderbuffer object name is bound by calling `glBindRenderbuffer`, the renderbuffer object is allocated with the appropriate default state and if the allocation is successful, this allocated object will become the newly bound renderbuffer object.

The following state and default values are associated with a renderbuffer object:

- Width and height in pixels—The default value is zero.

- Internal format—This describes the format of the pixels stored in the renderbuffer. It must be a color-, depth-, or stencil-renderable format.

- Color bit-depth—This is valid only if the internal format is a color-renderable format. The default value is zero.

- Depth bit-depth—This is valid only if the internal format is a depth-renderable format. The default value is zero.

- Stencil bit-depth—This is valid only if the internal format is a stencil-renderable format. The default value is zero.

`glBindRenderbuffer` can also be used to bind to an existing renderbuffer object (i.e., an object that has been assigned and used before and therefore has valid state associated with it). No changes to the state of the newly bound renderbuffer object are made by the bind command.

Once a renderbuffer object is bound, we can specify the dimensions and format of the image stored in the renderbuffer. The `glRenderbufferStorage` command can be used to specify this information.

void	**glRenderbufferStorage**(GLenum *target*, GLenum *internalformat*, GLsizei *width*, GLsizei *height*)

target   must be set to GL_RENDERBUFFER

internalformat   must be a format that can be used as a color buffer, depth buffer, or stencil buffer

The following formats must be supported:
GL_RGB565
GL_RGBA4
GL_RGB5_A1
GL_DEPTH_COMPONENT16
GL_STENCIL_INDEX8

The following formats are optional:
GL_RGB8_OES
GL_RGBA8_OES
GL_DEPTH_COMPONENT24_OES
GL_DEPTH_COMPONENT32_OES
GL_STENCIL_INDEX1_OES
GL_STENCIL_INDEX4_OES
GL_DEPTH24_STENCIL8_OES

width   width of the renderbuffer in pixels; must be <= GL_MAX_RENDERBUFFER_SIZE.

height   height of the renderbuffer in pixels; must be <= GL_MAX_RENDERBUFFER_SIZE.

`glRenderbufferStorage` looks very similar to `glTexImage2D` except that no image data is supplied. The width and height of the renderbuffer is specified in pixels and must be values that are smaller than the maximum renderbuffer size supported by the implementation. The minimum size value that must be supported by all OpenGL ES implementations is 1. The actual maximum size supported by the implementation can be queried using the following code example.

```
GLint maxRenderbufferSize;
glGetIntegerv(GL_MAX_RENDERBUFFER_SIZE, &maxRenderbufferSize);
```

The `internalformat` argument specifies the format that the application would like to use to store pixels in the renderbuffer object.

- If `internalformat` is `GL_RGB565`, `GL_RGBA4`, `GL_RGB5_A1`, `GL_RGB8_OES`, or `GL_RGBA8_OES`, the renderbuffer stores a color-renderable buffer.

- If `internalformat` is `GL_DEPTH_COMPONENT16`, `GL_DEPTH_COMPONENT24_OES`, or `GL_DEPTH_COMPONENT32_OES`, the renderbuffer stores a depth-renderable buffer.

- If `internalformat` is `GL_STENCIL_INDEX8`, `GL_STENCIL_INDEX4_OES`, or `GL_STENCIL_INDEX1_OES`, the renderbuffer stores a stencil-renderable buffer.

The renderbuffer object can be attached to the color, depth, or stencil attachment of the framebuffer object without the renderbuffer's storage format and dimensions specified. The renderbuffer's storage format and dimensions can be specified before or after the renderbuffer object has been attached to the framebuffer object. This information will, however, need to be correctly specified before the framebuffer object and renderbuffer attachment can be used for rendering.

Note: The `GL_RGB8_OES` and `GL_RGBA8_OES` formats can be used if the `GL_OES_rgb8_rgba8` extension is supported.

The `GL_DEPTH_COMPONENT24_OES` or `GL_DEPTH_COMPONENT32_OES` formats can be used if the `GL_OES_depth24` or `GL_OES_depth32` extensions are supported, respectively.

The `GL_STENCIL_INDEX1_OES` or `GL_STENCIL_INDEX4_OES` formats can be used if the `GL_OES_stencil1` or `GL_OES_stencil4` extensions are supported, respectively.

The `GL_DEPTH24_STENCIL8_OES` format can be used if the `GL_OES_packed_depth_stencil` extension is supported.

Using Framebuffer Objects

We describe how to use framebuffer objects to render to an off-screen buffer (i.e., renderbuffer) or to render to a texture. Before we can use a framebuffer object and specify its attachments, we need to make it the current framebuffer object. The `glBindFramebuffer` command is used to set the current framebuffer object.

void **glBindFramebuffer**(GLenum *target*, GLuint *framebuffer*)	
target	must be set to GL_FRAMEBUFFER
framebuffer	framebuffer object name

Note that `glGenFramebuffers` is not required to assign a framebuffer object name before it is bound using `glBindFramebuffer`. An application can specify an unused framebuffer object name to `glBindFramebuffer`. However, we do recommend that OpenGL ES applications call `glGenFramebuffers` and use framebuffer object names returned by `glGenFramebuffers` instead of specifying their own buffer object names.

The first time a framebuffer object name is bound by calling `glBindFramebuffer`, the framebuffer object is allocated with appropriate default state, and if the allocation is successful, this allocated object is bound as the current framebuffer object for the rendering context.

The following state is associated with a framebuffer object:

- Color attachment point—The attachment point for the color buffer.

- Depth attachment point—The attachment point for the depth buffer.

- Stencil attachment point—The attachment point for the stencil buffer.

- Framebuffer completeness status—Whether or not the framebuffer is in a complete state and can be rendered to.

For each attachment point, the following information is specified:

- Object type—Specifies the type of object that is associated with the attachment point. This can be GL_RENDERBUFFER if a renderbuffer object is attached or GL_TEXTURE if a texture object is attached. The default value is GL_NONE.

- Object name—Specifies the name of the object attached. This can be either the renderbuffer object name or the texture object name. The default value is 0.

- Texture level—If a texture object is attached, then this specifies the mip-level of the texture associated with the attachment point. The default value is 0.

- Texture cubemap face—If a texture object is attached and the texture is a cubemap, then this specifies which one of the six cubemap faces is to be used as the attachment point. The default value is GL_TEXTURE_CUBE_MAP_POSITIVE_X.

- Texture Z offset—This is an optional value only available if the GL_OES_texture_3D extension is supported by the OpenGL ES 2.0 implementation. It specifies the 2D slice of the 3D texture to be used as the attachment point. The default value is 0.

glBindFramebuffer can also be used to bind to an existing framebuffer object (i.e., an object that has been assigned and used before and therefore has valid state associated with it). No changes are made to the state of the newly bound framebuffer object.

Once a framebuffer object has been bound, the color, depth, and stencil attachments of the currently bound framebuffer object can be set to a renderbuffer object or a texture. As shown in Figure 12-1, the color attachment can be set to a renderbuffer that stores color values, or to a mip-level of a 2D texture or a cubemap face, or to a mip-level of a 2D slice in a 3D texture. The depth attachment can be set to a renderbuffer that stores depth values, to a mip-level of a 2D depth texture, or to a depth cubemap face. The stencil attachment must be set to a renderbuffer that stores stencil values.

Attaching a Renderbuffer as a Framebuffer Attachment

The glFramebufferRenderbuffer command is used to attach a renderbuffer object to a framebuffer attachment point.

```
void    glFramebufferRenderbuffer(GLenum target,
                                  GLenum attachment,
                                  GLenum renderbuffertarget,
                                  GLuint renderbuffer)
```

target	must be set to GL_FRAMEBUFFER
attachment	attachment must be one of the following enums: GL_COLOR_ATTACHMENT0 GL_DEPTH_ATTACHMENT GL_STENCIL_ATTACHMENT
renderbuffertarget	must be set to GL_RENDERBUFFER
renderbuffer	the renderbuffer object that should be used as attachment. renderbuffer must be either zero or the name of an existing renderbuffer object

If `glFramebufferRenderbuffer` is called with `renderbuffer` not equal to zero, this renderbuffer object will be used as the new color, depth, or stencil attachment point as specified by value of `attachment` argument.

The attachment point's state will be modified to:

* Object type = GL_RENDERBUFFER

* Object name = renderbuffer

* Texture level, texture cubemap face, and texture Z offset = 0

The newly attached renderbuffer object's state or contents of its buffer do not change.

If `glFramebufferRenderbuffer` is called with `renderbuffer` equal to zero, then the color, depth, or stencil buffer as specified by `attachment` is detached and reset to zero.

Attaching a 2D Texture as a Framebuffer Attachment

The `glFramebufferTexture2D` command is used to attach a mip-level of a 2D texture or a cubemap face to a framebuffer attachment point. It can be used to attach a texture as a color or depth attachment. A texture as a stencil attachment is not allowed.

```
void    glFramebufferTexture2D(GLenum target,
                               GLenum attachment,
                               GLenum textarget,
                               GLuint texture,
                               GLint  level)
```

target	must be set to GL_FRAMEBUFFER
attachment	attachment must be one of the following enums: GL_COLOR_ATTACHMENT0 GL_DEPTH_ATTACHMENT
textarget	specifies the texture target. This is the value specified in the *textarget* argument in **glTexImage2D**
texture	specifies the texture object
level	specifies the mip-level of texture image

If glFramebufferTexture2D is called with texture not equal to zero, then the color or depth attachment will be set to texture. If, on the other hand, glFramebufferTexture2D generates an error, no change is made to the state of framebuffer.

The attachment point's state will be modified to:

- Object type = GL_TEXTURE

- Object name = texture

- Texture level = level

- Texture cubemap face = valid if texture attachment is a cubemap and is one of the following values:
  GL_TEXTURE_CUBE_MAP_POSITIVE_X
  GL_TEXTURE_CUBE_MAP_POSITIVE_Y
  GL_TEXTURE_CUBE_MAP_POSITIVE_Z
  GL_TEXTURE_CUBE_MAP_NEGATIVE_X
  GL_TEXTURE_CUBE_MAP_NEGATIVE_Y
  GL_TEXTURE_CUBE_MAP_NEGATIVE_Z

- Texture Z offset = 0

The newly attached texture object's state or contents of its image are not modified by glFramebufferTexture2D. Note that the texture object's state and image can be modified after it has been attached to a framebuffer object.

If glFramebufferTexture2D is called with texture equal to zero, then the color or depth attachment is detached and reset to zero.

Attaching an Image of a 3D Texture as a Framebuffer Attachment

The `glFramebufferTexture3DOES` command is used to attach a 2D slice and a specific mip-level of a 3D texture to a framebuffer attachment point. It can only be used to attach a texture as a color attachment. A 3D texture as a depth or stencil attachment is not allowed. Refer to Chapter 9, "Texturing," for a detailed description of how 3D textures work.

```
void  glFramebufferTexture3DOES (GLenum  target,
                                 GLenum  attachment,
                                 GLenum  textarget,
                                 GLuint  texture,
                                 GLint   level,
                                 GLint   zoffset)
```

target	must be set to GL_FRAMEBUFFER
attachment	attachment must be the following enum: GL_COLOR_ATTACHMENT0
textarget	specifies the texture target. This is the value specified in the *textarget* argument in `glTexImage3DOES`
texture	specifies the texture object
level	specifies the mip-level of texture image
zoffset	specifies the z-offset, which identifies the 2D slice of 3D texture. Must be a value between 0 and (depth – 1), where depth is specified in `glTexImage3DOES`

If `glFramebufferTexture3DOES` is called with `texture` not equal to 0, then the color attachment will be set to `texture`. If, on the other hand, `glFramebufferTexture3DOES` generates an error, no change is made to the state of `framebuffer`.

The attachment point's state will be modified to:

- Object type = GL_TEXTURE
- Object name = `texture`
- Texture level = `level`

- Texture cubemap face = 0
- Texture Z offset = `zoffset`

The newly attached texture object's state or contents of its image are not modified by `glFramebufferTexture3DOES`. Note that the texture object's state and image can be modified after it has been attached to a framebuffer object.

If `glFramebufferTexture3DOES` is called with `texture` equal to zero, then the color attachment is detached and reset to zero.

One interesting question arises: What happens if we are rendering into a texture and at the same time use this texture object as a texture in a fragment shader? Will the OpenGL ES implementation generate an error when such a situation arises? In some cases, it is possible for the OpenGL ES implementation to determine if a texture object is being used as a texture input and a framebuffer attachment into which we are currently drawing. `glDrawArrays` and `glDrawElements` could then generate an error. To ensure that `glDrawArrays` and `glDrawElements` can be executed as fast as possible, however, these checks are not performed. Instead of generating an error, in this case, rendering results are undefined. It is the application's responsibility to make sure that this situation does not occur.

Checking for Framebuffer Completeness

A framebuffer object needs to be defined as *complete* before it can be used as rendering target. If the currently bound framebuffer object is not complete, OpenGL ES commands that draw primitives or read pixels will fail and generate an appropriate error that indicates the reason the framebuffer is incomplete.

The rules for a framebuffer object to be considered complete are as follows:

- Make sure that the color, depth, and stencil attachments are valid. A color attachment is valid if it is zero (i.e., there is no attachment) or if it is a color-renderable renderbuffer object or a texture object. The following formats are color-renderable: `GL_RGB565`, `GL_RGBA4`, `GL_RGB5_A1`, and optionally `GL_RGB8_OES` and `GL_RGBA8_OES` if the appropriate extensions are supported. A depth attachment is valid if it is zero or is a depth-renderable renderbuffer object or a depth texture. The following formats are depth-renderable: `GL_DEPTH_COMPONENT16` and optionally `GL_DEPTH_COMPONENT24_OES` and `GL_DEPTH_COMPONENT32_OES` if the appropriate extensions are supported. A stencil attachment is valid if it is zero or is a stencil-renderable renderbuffer object. The following formats are stencil-renderable: GL_STENCIL_INDEX8 and optionally GL_STENCIL_INDEX1_OES and GL_STENCIL_INDEX4_OES if the appropriate extensions are supported.

- There is a minimum of one valid attachment. A framebuffer is not complete if it has no attachments as there is nothing to draw into or read from.

- Valid attachments associated with a framebuffer object must have the same width and height.

- The combination of color, depth, and stencil internal formats results in a rendering target that can be used as a destination surface for a particular implementation. Even though there is a sufficient list of renderable formats for color, depth, and stencil buffers, not all combinations of formats might be supported by an implementation. For example, an implementation might not be able to support rendering into a surface that uses 16-bit depth and 8-bit stencil buffers. In such a case, a framebuffer object that uses a GL_DEPTH_COMPONENT16 attachment and a GL_STENCIL_INDEX8 stencil attachment will be considered unsupported.

The glCheckFramebufferStatus command can be used to verify if a framebuffer object is complete.

GLenum	**glCheckFramebufferStatus**(GLenum *target*)
target	must be set to GL_FRAMEBUFFER

glCheckFramebufferStatus returns 0 if target is not equal to GL_FRAMEBUFFER. If target is equal to GL_FRAMEBUFFER, one of the following enums is returned:

- **GL_FRAMEBUFFER_COMPLETE**—Framebuffer is complete.

- **GL_FRAMEBUFFER_INCOMPLETE_ATTACHMENT**—The framebuffer attachment points are not complete. This might be due to the fact that the required attachment is zero or is not a valid texture or renderbuffer object.

- **GL_FRAMEBUFFER_INCOMPLETE_MISSING_ATTACHMENT**—No valid attachments in the framebuffer.

- **GL_FRAMEBUFFER_INCOMPLETE_DIMENSIONS**—Attachments do not have the same width and height.

- **GL_FRAMEBUFFER_INCOMPLETE_FORMATS**—Internal format used by the attachments is not renderable.

- **GL_FRAMEBUFFER_UNSUPPORTED**—Combination of internal formats used by attachments in the framebuffer results in a nonrenderable target.

If the currently bound framebuffer object is not complete, attempts to use the framebuffer object for reading and writing pixels will fail. This means that calls to draw primitives such as glDrawArrays, glDrawElements, and commands that read the framebuffer such as glReadPixels and glCopyTexImage2D, glCopyTexSubImage2D, and glCopyTexSubImage3DOES will generate a GL_INVALID_FRAMEBUFFER_OPERATION error.

Deleting Framebuffer and Renderbuffer Objects

After the application is done using renderbuffer objects, they can be deleted. Deleting renderbuffer and framebuffer objects is very similar to deleting texture objects.

Renderbuffer objects are deleted using the glDeleteRenderbuffers API.

void	**glDeleteRenderbuffers**(GLsizei *n*, GLuint **renderbuffers*)
n	number of renderbuffer object names to delete
renderbuffers	pointer to an array of *n* renderbuffer object names to be deleted

glDeleteRenderbuffers deletes the renderbuffer objects specified in renderbuffers. Once a renderbuffer object is deleted, it has no state associated with it and is marked as unused and can later be reused as a new renderbuffer object. When deleting a renderbuffer object that is also the currently bound renderbuffer object, the renderbuffer object is deleted and the current renderbuffer binding is reset to zero. If renderbuffer object names specified in renderbuffers are invalid or zero, they are ignored (i.e., no error will be generated). Further if the renderbuffer is attached to the currently bound framebuffer object, it is first detached from the framebuffer and then deleted.

Framebuffer objects are deleted using the glDeleteFramebuffers API.

void	**glDeleteFramebuffers**(GLsizei *n*, GLuint **framebuffers*)
n	number of framebuffer object names to delete
framebuffers	pointer to an array of *n* framebuffer object names to be deleted

glDeleteFramebuffers deletes the framebuffer objects specified in framebuffers. Once a framebuffer object is deleted, it has no state associated with it and is marked as unused and can later be reused as a new framebuffer object. When deleting a framebuffer object that is also the currently bound framebuffer object, the framebuffer object is deleted and the current framebuffer binding is reset to zero. If framebuffer object names specified in framebuffers are invalid or zero, they are ignored and no error will be generated.

Deleting Renderbuffer Objects That Are Used as Framebuffer Attachments

What happens if a renderbuffer object being deleted is used as an attachment in a framebuffer object? If the renderbuffer object to be deleted is used as an attachment in the currently bound framebuffer object, glDeleteRenderbuffers will reset the attachment to zero. If the renderbuffer object to be deleted is used as an attachment in framebuffer objects that are not currently bound, then glDeleteRenderbuffers will not reset these attachments to zero. It is the responsibility of the application to detach these deleted renderbuffer objects from the appropriate framebuffer objects.

Reading Pixels and Framebuffer Objects

The glReadPixels command reads pixels from the color buffer and returns them in a user allocated buffer. The color buffer that will be read from is the color buffer allocated by the window system provided framebuffer or the color attachment of the currently bound framebuffer object. Two combinations of format and type arguments in glReadPixels are supported: a format and type of GL_RGB and GL_UNSIGNED_BYTE or implementation-specific format and type values returned by querying GL_IMPLEMENTATION_COLOR_READ_FORMAT and GL_IMPLEMENTATION_COLOR_READ_TYPE. The implementation-specific format and type returned will depend on the format and type of the currently attached color buffer. These values can change if the currently bound framebuffer changes. These must be queried anytime the currently bound framebuffer object changes to determine the correct implementation-specific format and type values that must be passed to `glReadPixels`.

Examples

Let's now look at some examples that demonstrate how to use framebuffer objects. Example 12-1 demonstrates how to render to texture using frame-buffer objects. In this example we draw to a texture using a framebuffer object. We then use this texture to draw a quad to the window system pro-vided framebuffer (i.e., the screen). Figure 12-2 shows the generated image.

Example 12-1   Render to Texture

```
GLuint    framebuffer;
GLuint    depthRenderbuffer;
GLuint    texture;
GLint     texWidth = 256, texHeight = 256;
GLint     maxRenderbufferSize;

glGetIntegerv(GL_MAX_RENDERBUFFER_SIZE, &maxRenderbufferSize);

// check if GL_MAX_RENDERBUFFER_SIZE is >= texWidth and texHeight
if((maxRenderbufferSize <= texWidth) ||
   (maxRenderbufferSize <= texHeight))
{
    // cannot use framebuffer objects as we need to create
    // a depth buffer as a renderbuffer object
    // return with appropriate error
}

// generate the framebuffer, renderbuffer, and texture object names
glGenFramebuffers(1, &framebuffer);
glGenRenderbuffers(1, &depthRenderbuffer);
glGenTextures(1, &texture);

// bind texture and load the texture mip-level 0
// texels are RGB565
// no texels need to be specified as we are going to draw into
// the texture
```

```
glBindTexture(GL_TEXTURE_2D, texture);
glTexImage2D(GL_TEXTURE_2D, 0, GL_RGB, texWidth, texHeight,
             0, GL_RGB, GL_UNSIGNED_SHORT_5_6_5, NULL);

glTexParameteri(GL_TEXTURE_2D, GL_TEXTURE_WRAP_S, GL_CLAMP_TO_EDGE);
glTexParameteri(GL_TEXTURE_2D, GL_TEXTURE_WRAP_T, GL_CLAMP_TO_EDGE);
glTexParameteri(GL_TEXTURE_2D, GL_TEXTURE_MAG_FILTER, GL_LINEAR);
glTexParameteri(GL_TEXTURE_2D, GL_TEXTURE_MIN_FILTER, GL_LINEAR);

// bind renderbuffer and create a 16-bit depth buffer
// width and height of renderbuffer = width and height of
// the texture
glBindRenderbuffer(GL_RENDERBUFFER, depthRenderbuffer);
glRenderbufferStorage(GL_RENDERBUFFER, GL_DEPTH_COMPONENT16,
                      texWidth, texHeight);

// bind the framebuffer
glBindFramebuffer(GL_FRAMEBUFFER, framebuffer);

// specify texture as color attachment
glFramebufferTexture2D(GL_FRAMEBUFFER, GL_COLOR_ATTACHMENT0,
                       GL_TEXTURE_2D, texture, 0);

// specify depth_renderbufer as depth attachment
glFramebufferRenderbuffer(GL_FRAMEBUFFER, GL_DEPTH_ATTACHMENT,
                          GL_RENDERBUFFER, depthRenderbuffer);

// check for framebuffer complete
status = glCheckFramebufferStatus(GL_FRAMEBUFFER);
if(status == GL_FRAMEBUFFER_COMPLETE)
{
    // render to texture using FBO
    // clear color and depth buffer
    glClearColor(0.0f, 0.0f, 0.0f, 1.0f);
    glClear(GL_COLOR_BUFFER_BIT | GL_DEPTH_BUFFER_BIT);

    // load uniforms for vertex and fragment shader
    // used to render to FBO. The vertex shader is the
    // ES 1.1 vertex shader described as Example 8-8 in
    // Chapter 8. The fragment shader outputs the color
    // computed by vertex shader as fragment color and
    // is described as Example 1-2 in Chapter 1.
    set_fbo_texture_shader_and_uniforms();

    // drawing commands to the framebuffer object
    draw_teapot();

    // render to window system provided framebuffer
    glBindFramebuffer(GL_FRAMEBUFFER, 0);
```

```
    // Use texture to draw to window system provided framebuffer
    // We draw a quad that is the size of the viewport.
    //
    // The vertex shader outputs the vertex position and texture
    // coordinates passed as inputs.
    //
    // The fragment shader uses the texture coordinate to sample
    // the texture and uses this as the per-fragment color value.
    set_screen_shader_and_uniforms();
    draw_screen_quad();
}

// cleanup
glDeleteRenderbuffers(1, &depthRenderbuffer);
glDeleteFramebuffers(1, &framebuffer);
glDeleteTextures(1, &texture);
```

Figure 12-2   Render to Color Texture

In Example 12-1 we create the `framebuffer`, `texture`, and `depthRender-buffer` objects using appropriate `glGen***` commands. `framebuffer` uses a color attachment that is a texture object (`texture`) and a depth attachment that is a renderbuffer object (`depthRenderbuffer`).

Before we create these objects, we query the maximum renderbuffer size (`GL_MAX_RENDERBUFFER_SIZE`) to make sure that the maximum renderbuffer size supported by the implementation is less than or equal to the width and height of texture that will be used as a color attachment. This is to ensure that we can create a depth renderbuffer successfully and use it as the depth attachment in `framebuffer`.

After the objects have been created, we call `glBindTexture(texture)` to make the texture the currently bound texture object. The texture mip-level is then specified using `glTexImage2D`. Note that the `pixels` argument is NULL. This is because we are rendering to the entire texture region and therefore there is no reason to specify any input data as it will get overwritten.

The `depthRenderbuffer` object is bound using `glBindRenderbuffer` and `glRenderbufferStorage` is called to allocate storage for a 16-bit depth buffer.

The framebuffer object is bound using `glBindFramebuffer`. `texture` is attached as a color attachment to `framebuffer` and `depthRenderbuffer` is attached as a depth attachment to `framebuffer`.

We now check if the framebuffer status is complete before we begin drawing into `framebuffer`. Once framebuffer rendering is complete, we reset the currently bound framebuffer to the window system provided framebuffer by calling `glBindFramebuffer(GL_FRAMEBUFFER, 0)`. We can now use `texture` that was used as a render target in `framebuffer` to draw to the window system provided framebuffer.

In Example 12-1, the depth buffer attachment to `framebuffer` was a renderbuffer object. In Example 12-2 we look at how to use a depth texture as a depth buffer attachment to `framebuffer`. This feature is available if the `OES_depth_texture` extension is supported by the implementation. Applications can render to the depth texture used as a framebuffer attachment from the light source. The rendered depth texture can then be used as a shadow map to calculate the percentage in shadow for each fragment. Figure 12-3 shows the generated image.

Example 12-2 Render to Depth Texture

```
#define COLOR_TEXTURE    0
#define DEPTH_TEXTURE    1

GLuint    framebuffer;
GLuint    textures[2];
GLint     texWidth = 256, texHeight = 256;

// generate the framebuffer, & texture object names
glGenFramebuffers(1, &framebuffer);
glGenTextures(2, textures);

// bind  color texture and load the texture mip-level 0
```

```
// texels are RGB565
// no texels need to specified as we are going to draw into
// the texture
glBindTexture(GL_TEXTURE_2D, textures[COLOR_TEXTURE]);
glTexImage2D(GL_TEXTURE_2D, 0, GL_RGB, texWidth, texHeight,
             0, GL_RGB, GL_UNSIGNED_SHORT_5_6_5, NULL);

glTexParameteri(GL_TEXTURE_2D, GL_TEXTURE_WRAP_S, GL_CLAMP_TO_EDGE);
glTexParameteri(GL_TEXTURE_2D, GL_TEXTURE_WRAP_T, GL_CLAMP_TO_EDGE);
glTexParameteri(GL_TEXTURE_2D, GL_TEXTURE_MAG_FILTER, GL_LINEAR);
glTexParameteri(GL_TEXTURE_2D, GL_TEXTURE_MIN_FILTER, GL_LINEAR);

// bind  depth texture and load the texture mip-level 0
// no texels need to specified as we are going to draw into
// the texture
glBindTexture(GL_TEXTURE_2D, textures[DEPTH_TEXTURE]);
glTexImage2D(GL_TEXTURE_2D, 0, GL_DEPTH_COMPONENT, texWidth,
             texHeight, 0, GL_DEPTH_COMPONENT, GL_UNSIGNED_SHORT,
             NULL);

glTexParameteri(GL_TEXTURE_2D, GL_TEXTURE_WRAP_S, GL_CLAMP_TO_EDGE);
glTexParameteri(GL_TEXTURE_2D, GL_TEXTURE_WRAP_T, GL_CLAMP_TO_EDGE);
glTexParameteri(GL_TEXTURE_2D, GL_TEXTURE_MAG_FILTER, GL_NEAREST);
glTexParameteri(GL_TEXTURE_2D, GL_TEXTURE_MIN_FILTER, GL_NEAREST);


// bind the framebuffer
glBindFramebuffer(GL_FRAMEBUFFER, framebuffer);

// specify texture as color attachment
glFramebufferTexture2D(GL_FRAMEBUFFER, GL_COLOR_ATTACHMENT0,
                       GL_TEXTURE_2D, textures[COLOR_TEXTURE], 0);

// specify texture as depth attachment
glFramebufferTexture2D(GL_FRAMEBUFFER, GL_DEPTH_ATTACHMENT,
                       GL_TEXTURE_2D, textures[DEPTH_TEXTURE], 0);

// check for framebuffer complete
status = glCheckFramebufferStatus(GL_FRAMEBUFFER);
if (status == GL_FRAMEBUFFER_COMPLETE)
{
   // render to color & depth textures using FBO
   // clear color & depth buffer
   glClearColor(0.0f, 0.0f, 0.0f, 1.0f);
   glClear(GL_COLOR_BUFFER_BIT | GL_DEPTH_BUFFER_BIT);

   // load uniforms for vertex and fragment shader
   // used to render to FBO. The vertex shader is the
   // ES 1.1 vertex shader described as Example 8-8 in
```

```
// Chapter 8. The fragment shader outputs the color
// computed by vertex shader as fragment color and
// is described as Example 1-2 in Chapter 1.
set_fbo_texture_shader_and_uniforms();

// drawing commands to the framebuffer object
draw_teapot();

// render to window system provided framebuffer
glBindFramebuffer(GL_FRAMEBUFFER, 0);

// Use depth texture to draw to window system framebuffer
// We draw a quad that is the size of the viewport.
//
// The vertex shader outputs the vertex position and texture
// coordinates passed as inputs.
//
// The fragment shader uses the texture coordinate to sample
// the texture and uses this as the per-fragment color value.
set_screen_shader_and_uniforms();
draw_screen_quad();
}

// cleanup
glDeleteRenderbuffers(1, &depthRenderbuffer);
glDeleteFramebuffers(1, &framebuffer);
glDeleteTextures(1, &texture);
```

Figure 12-3   Render to Depth Texture

Note: The width and height of the off-screen renderbuffers do not have to be a power of two. OpenGL ES supports non-power-of-two textures provided the texture only uses the base mip-level and the addressing mode is GL_CLAMP_TO_EDGE. These rules are relaxed by the OES_texture_npot extension.

Performance Tips and Tricks

Here we discuss some performance tips that developers should carefully consider when using framebuffer objects.

- Avoid switching between rendering to window system provided framebuffer and rendering to framebuffer objects frequently. This is an issue for handheld OpenGL ES 2.0 implementations as many of these implementations use a tile-based rendering architecture. With a tile-based rendering architecture, dedicated internal memory is used to store the color, depth, and stencil values for a tile (i.e., region) of the framebuffer. The internal memory is used as it is much more efficient in power, and has better memory latency and bandwidth compared with going to external memory. After rendering to a tile is completed, the tile is written out to device (or system) memory. Every time you switch from one rendering target to another, the appropriate texture and renderbuffer attachments will need to be rendered, saved, and restored. This can become quite expensive. The best method would be to render to the appropriate framebuffers in the scene first and then render to the window system provided framebuffer followed by the eglSwapBuffers command to swap the display buffer.

- Don't create and destroy framebuffer and renderbuffer objects (or any other large data objects for that matter) per frame.

- Try to avoid modifying textures (using glTexImage2D, glTexSubImage2D, glCopyTexImage2D, etc.) that are attachments to framebuffer objects used as rendering targets.

- Set pixels argument in glTexImage2D and glTexImage3DOES to NULL if the entire texture image will be rendered as the original data will not be used anyway. Make sure you do a glClear to clear the texture image before drawing to the texture if you are expecting the image to have any defined pixel values in it.

- Share depth and stencil renderbuffers as attachments used by framebuffer objects wherever possible to keep the memory footprint requirement to a minimum. We recognize that this has limited use as the width and height of these buffers have to be the same. In a future version of OpenGL ES, the rule that width and height of various attachments of a framebuffer object must be equal might be relaxed, making sharing easier.

Chapter 13

Advanced Programming with OpenGL ES 2.0

In this chapter, we put together many of the techniques you have learned throughout the book to discuss some advanced uses of OpenGL ES 2.0. There are a large number of advanced rendering techniques that can be accomplished with the programmable flexibility of OpenGL ES 2.0. In this chapter, we cover the following advanced rendering techniques:

- Per-fragment lighting.

- Environment mapping.

- Particle system with point sprites.

- Image postprocessing.

- Projective texturing.

- Noise using a 3D texture.

- Procedural textures.

Per-Fragment Lighting

In Chapter 8, "Vertex Shaders," we covered the lighting equations that can be used in the vertex shader to calculate per-vertex lighting. Commonly, to achieve higher quality lighting, we seek to evaluate the lighting equations on a per-fragment basis. In this section, we cover an example of evaluating ambient, diffuse, and specular lighting on a per-fragment basis. The example we cover is a RenderMonkey workspace that can be found in Chapter_13/ PerFragmentLighting/PerFragmentLighting.rfx as pictured in Figure 13-1.

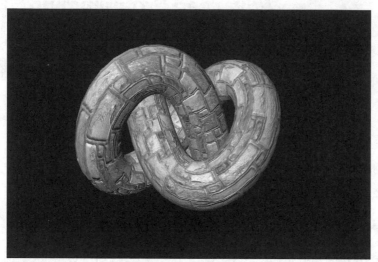

Figure 13-1   Per-Fragment Lighting Example (see Color Plate 4)

Lighting with a Normal Map

Before we get into the details of the shaders used in the RenderMonkey workspace, it's necessary to first discuss the general approach that is used in the example. The simplest way to do lighting per-fragment would be to use the interpolated vertex normal in the fragment shader and then move the lighting computations into the fragment shader. However, for the diffuse term, this would really not yield much better results than doing the lighting per-vertex. There would be the advantage that the normal vector could be renormalized, which would remove artifacts due to linear interpolation, but the overall quality would be only minimally better. To really take advantage of the ability to do computations on a per-fragment basis, using a normal map to store per-texel normals can provide significantly more detail.

A normal map is a 2D texture that stores at each texel a normal vector. The red channel represents the x component, the green channel the y component, and the blue channel the z component. For a normal map stored as GL_RGB8 with GL_UNSIGNED_BYTE data, the values will all be in the range [0, 1]. To represent a normal, these values need to be scaled and biased in the shader to remap to [-1, 1]. The following block of fragment shader code shows how you would go about fetching from a normal map.

```
// Fetch the tangent space normal from normal map
vec3 normal = texture2D(s_bumpMap, v_texcoord).xyz;

// Scale and bias from [0, 1] to [-1, 1] and normalize
normal = normalize(normal * 2.0 - 1.0);
```

As you can see, this small bit of shader code will fetch the color value from a texture map and then multiply the results by two and subtract one. The result is that the values are rescaled into the [–1, 1] range from the [0, 1] range. In addition, if the data in your normal map are not normalized, you will also need to normalize the results in the fragment shader. This step can be skipped if your normal map contains all unit vectors.

The other significant issue to tackle with per-fragment lighting has to do with in which space the normals in the texture are stored. To minimize computations in the fragment shader, we do not want to have to transform the result of the normal fetched from the normal map. One way to accomplish this would be to store world-space normals in your normal map. That is, the normal vectors in the normal map would each represent a world-space normal vector. Then, the light and direction vectors could be transformed into world space in the vertex shader and could be directly used with the value fetched from the normal map. However, there are significant issues with storing normal maps in world space. The most significant is that the object has to be assumed to be static because no transformation can happen on the object. Another significant issue is that the same surface oriented in different directions in space would not be able to share the same texels in the normal map, which can result in much larger maps.

A better solution than using world-space normal maps is to store normal maps in tangent space. The idea behind tangent space is that we define a space for each vertex by three coordinate axes: the normal, binormal, and tangent. The normals stored in the texture map are then all stored in this tangent space. Then, when we want to compute any lighting equations, we transform our incoming lighting vectors into the tangent space and those light vectors can then directly be used with the values in the normal map. The tangent space is typically computed as a preprocess and the binormal and tangent are added to the vertex attribute data. This work is done automatically by RenderMonkey, which computes a tangent space for any model that has a vertex normal and texture coordinates.

Lighting Shaders

Once we have tangent space normal maps and tangent space vectors set up, we can proceed with per-fragment lighting. First, let's take a look at the vertex shader in Example 13-1.

Example 13-1 Per-Fragment Lighting Vertex Shader

```
uniform mat4 u_matViewInverse;
uniform mat4 u_matViewProjection;
uniform vec3 u_lightPosition;
uniform vec3 u_eyePosition;

varying vec2 v_texcoord;
varying vec3 v_viewDirection;
varying vec3 v_lightDirection;

attribute vec4 a_vertex;
attribute vec2 a_texcoord0;
attribute vec3 a_normal;
attribute vec3 a_binormal;
attribute vec3 a_tangent;

void main(void)
{
   // Transform eye vector into world space
   vec3 eyePositionWorld =
            (u_matViewInverse * vec4(u_eyePosition, 1.0)).xyz;

   // Compute world space direction vector
   vec3 viewDirectionWorld = eyePositionWorld - a_vertex.xyz;

   // Transform light position into world space
   vec3 lightPositionWorld =
            (u_matViewInverse * vec4(u_lightPosition, 1.0)).xyz;

   // Compute world space light direction vector
   vec3 lightDirectionWorld = lightPositionWorld - a_vertex.xyz;

   // Create the tangent matrix
   mat3 tangentMat = mat3(a_tangent,
                          a_binormal,
                          a_normal);

   // Transform the view and light vectors into tangent space
   v_viewDirection = viewDirectionWorld * tangentMat;
   v_lightDirection = lightDirectionWorld * tangentMat;

   // Transform output position
   gl_Position = u_matViewProjection * a_vertex;

   // Pass through texture coordinate
   v_texcoord = a_texcoord0.xy;

}
```

We have two uniform matrices that we need as input to the vertex shader: u_matViewInverse and u_matViewProjection. The u_matViewInverse contains the inverse of the view matrix. This matrix is used to transform the light vector and eye vector (which are in view space) into world space. The first four statements in main are used to perform this transformation and compute the light vector and view vector in world space. The next step in the shader is to create a tangent matrix. The tangent space for the vertex is stored in three vertex attributes: a_normal, a_binormal, and a_tangent. These three vectors define the three coordinate axes of the tangent space for each vertex. We construct a 3 × 3 matrix out of these vectors to form the tangent matrix tangentMat.

The next step is to transform the view and direction vectors into tangent space by multiplying them by the tangentMat matrix. Remember, our purpose here is to get the view and direction vectors into the same space as the normals in the tangent-space normal map. By doing this transformation in the vertex shader, we avoid doing any transformations in the fragment shader. Finally, we compute the final output position and place it in gl_Position and pass the texture coordinate along to the fragment shader in v_texcoord.

Now we have the view and direction vector in view space and a texture coordinate passed in as varyings to the fragment shader. The next step is to actually light the fragments using the fragment shader as shown in Example 13-2.

Example 13-2 Per-Fragment Lighting Fragment Shader

```
precision mediump float;

uniform vec4 u_ambient;
uniform vec4 u_specular;
uniform vec4 u_diffuse;
uniform float u_specularPower;

uniform sampler2D s_baseMap;
uniform sampler2D s_bumpMap;

varying vec2 v_texcoord;
varying vec3 v_viewDirection;
varying vec3 v_lightDirection;

void main(void)
{
```

```
    // Fetch basemap color
    vec4 baseColor = texture2D(s_baseMap, v_texcoord);

    // Fetch the tangent-space normal from normal map
    vec3 normal = texture2D(s_bumpMap, v_texcoord).xyz;

    // Scale and bias from [0, 1] to [-1, 1] and normalize
    normal = normalize(normal * 2.0 - 1.0);

    // Normalize the light direction and view direction
    vec3 lightDirection = normalize(v_lightDirection);
    vec3 viewDirection = normalize(v_viewDirection);

    // Compute N.L
    float nDotL = dot(normal, lightDirection);

    // Compute reflection vector
    vec3 reflection = (2.0 * normal * nDotL) - lightDirection;

    // Compute R.V
    float rDotV = max(0.0, dot(reflection, viewDirection));

    // Compute Ambient term
    vec4 ambient = u_ambient * baseColor;

    // Compute Diffuse term
    vec4 diffuse = u_diffuse * nDotL * baseColor;

    // Compute Specular term
    vec4 specular = u_specular * pow(rDotV, u_specularPower);

    // Output final color
    gl_FragColor = ambient + diffuse + specular;
}
```

The first part of the fragment shader is a series of uniform declarations for the ambient, diffuse, and specular colors. These values are stored in the uniform variables u_ambient, u_diffuse, and u_specular. The shader is also configured with two samplers, s_baseMap and s_bumpMap, which are bound to a base color map and the normal map, respectively.

The first part of the fragment shader fetches the base color from the base map and the normal values from the normal map. As described earlier, the normal vector fetched from the texture map is scaled and biased and then normalized so that it is a unit vector with components in the [–1, 1] range. Next, the light vector and view vector are normalized and stored in light-

`Direction` and `viewDirection`. The reason that normalization is necessary is because of the way varying variables are interpolated across a primitive. The varying variables are linearly interpolated across the primitive. When linear interpolation is done between two vectors, the results can become denormalized during interpolation. To compensate for this artifact, the vectors must be normalized in the fragment shader.

Lighting Equations

At this point in the fragment shader, we now have a normal, light vector, and direction vector all normalized and in the same space. This gives us the inputs that are needed to compute the lighting equations. The lighting computations performed in this shader are as follows:

$$Ambient = k_{Ambient} \times C_{Base}$$

$$Diffuse = k_{Diffuse} \times N \bullet L \times C_{Base}$$

$$Specular = k_{Specular} \times \text{pow}(\max(R \bullet V, 0.0), k_{specular\ Power}$$

The k constants for ambient, diffuse, and specular colors come from the `u_ambient`, `u_diffuse`, and `u_specular` uniform variables. The C_{Base} is the base color fetched from the base texture map. The dot product between the light vector and normal vector $N \bullet L$ is computed and stored in the `nDotL` variable in the shader. This value is used to compute the diffuse lighting term. Finally, the specular computation requires R, which is the reflection vector computed from the equation

$$R = 2 \times N \times (N \bullet L) - L$$

Notice that the reflection vector also requires $N \bullet L$, so the computation used for the diffuse lighting term can be reused in the reflection vector computation. Finally, the lighting terms are stored in the `ambient`, `diffuse`, and `specular` variables in the shader. These results are summed and finally stored in the `gl_FragColor` output variable. The result is a per-fragment lit object with normal data coming from the normal map.

Many variations are possible on per-fragment lighting. One common technique is to store the specular exponent in a texture along with a specular mask value. This allows the specular lighting to vary across a surface. The main purpose of this example is to give you an idea of the types of computations that are typically done for per-fragment lighting. The use of tangent space along with the computation of the lighting equations in the fragment shader is typical of many modern games. Of course, it is also possible to add additional lights, more material information, and much more.

Environment Mapping

The next rendering technique we cover—related to the previous technique—is performing environment mapping using a cubemap. The example we cover is the RenderMonkey workspace Chapter_13/Environment Mapping/ EnvironmentMapping.rfx. The results are shown in Figure 13-2.

Figure 13-2   Environment Mapping Example (see Color Plate 5)

The concept behind environment mapping is to render the reflection of the environment on an object. In Chapter 9, "Texturing," we introduced you to cubemaps, which are commonly used to store environment maps. In the RenderMonkey example workspace, the environment of a mountain scene is stored in a cubemap. The way such cubemaps can be generated is by positioning a camera at the center of a scene and rendering along each of the positive and negative major axis directions using a 90-degree field of view. For reflections that change dynamically, one can render such a cubemap using a framebuffer object dynamically for each frame. For a static environment, this process can be done as a preprocess and the results stored in a static cubemap.

The vertex shader for the environment mapping example is provided in Example 13-3.

Example 13-3 Environment Mapping Vertex Shader

```
uniform mat4 u_matViewInverse;
uniform mat4 u_matViewProjection;
uniform vec3 u_lightPosition;
uniform vec3 u_eyePosition;

varying vec2 v_texcoord;
varying vec3 v_lightDirection;
varying vec3 v_normal;
varying vec3 v_binormal;
varying vec3 v_tangent;

attribute vec4 a_vertex;
attribute vec2 a_texcoord0;
attribute vec3 a_normal;
attribute vec3 a_binormal;
attribute vec3 a_tangent;

void main(void)
{
    // Transform light position into world space
    vec3 lightPositionWorld =
        (u_matViewInverse * vec4(u_lightPosition, 1.0)).xyz;

    // Compute world-space light direction vector
    vec3 lightDirectionWorld = lightPositionWorld - a_vertex.xyz;

    // Pass the world-space light vector to the fragment shader
    v_lightDirection = lightDirectionWorld;

    // Transform output position
    gl_Position = u_matViewProjection * a_vertex;

    // Pass through other attributes
    v_texcoord = a_texcoord0.xy;
    v_normal   = a_normal;
    v_binormal = a_binormal;
    v_tangent  = a_tangent;

}
```

The vertex shader in this example is very similar to the previous per-fragment lighting example. The primary difference is that rather than transforming the light direction vector into tangent space, we keep the light vector in world space. The reason we must do this is because we ultimately want to fetch from the cubemap using a world-space reflection vector. As such, rather than transforming the light vectors into tangent space, we are going to transform the normal vector from tangent into world space. To do so, the vertex shader passes the normal, binormal, and tangent as varyings into the fragment shader so that a tangent matrix can be constructed.

The fragment shader listing for the environment mapping sample is provided in Example 13-4.

Example 13-4   Environment Mapping Fragment Shader

```
precision mediump float;

uniform vec4 u_ambient;
uniform vec4 u_specular;
uniform vec4 u_diffuse;
uniform float u_specularPower;

uniform sampler2D s_baseMap;
uniform sampler2D s_bumpMap;
uniform samplerCube s_envMap;


varying vec2 v_texcoord;
varying vec3 v_lightDirection;
varying vec3 v_normal;
varying vec3 v_binormal;
varying vec3 v_tangent;

void main(void)
{
   // Fetch basemap color
   vec4 baseColor = texture2D(s_baseMap, v_texcoord);

   // Fetch the tangent-space normal from normal map
   vec3 normal = texture2D(s_bumpMap, v_texcoord).xyz;

   // Scale and bias from [0, 1] to [-1, 1]
   normal = normal * 2.0 - 1.0;

   // Construct a matrix to transform from tangent to world space
   mat3 tangentToWorldMat = mat3(v_tangent,
                                 v_binormal,
                                 v_normal);
```

```
    // Transform normal to world space and normalize
    normal = normalize(tangentToWorldMat * normal);

    // Normalize the light direction
    vec3 lightDirection = normalize(v_lightDirection);

    // Compute N.L
    float nDotL = dot(normal, lightDirection);

    // Compute reflection vector
    vec3 reflection = (2.0 * normal * nDotL) - lightDirection;

    // Use the reflection vector to fetch from the environment map
    vec4 envColor = textureCube(s_envMap, reflection);

    // Output final color
    gl_FragColor = 0.25 * baseColor + envColor;
}
```

In the fragment shader, you will notice that the normal vector is fetched from the normal map in the same way as in the per-fragment lighting example. The difference in this example is that rather than leaving the normal vector in tangent space, the fragment shader transforms the normal vector into world space. This is done by constructing the tangentToWorld matrix out of the v_tangent, v_binormal, and v_normal varying vectors and then multiplying that matrix by the fetched normal vector. The reflection vector is then calculated using the light direction vector and normal both in world space. The result of the computation is a reflection vector that is in world space, exactly what we need to fetch from the cubemap as an environment map. This vector is used to fetch into the environment map using the textureCube function with the reflection vector as a texture coordinate. Finally, the resultant gl_FragColor is written as a combination of the basemap color and the environment map color. The base color is attenuated by 0.25 for the purposes of this example so that the environment map is clearly visible.

This example shows the basics of environment mapping. This basic technique can be used to accomplish a large variety of effects. For example, one additional technique is attenuating the reflection using a fresnel term to more accurately model the reflection of light on a given material. As mentioned earlier, another common technique is to dynamically render a scene into a cubemap so that the environment reflection varies as an object moves through a scene and the scene itself changes. Using the basic technique we have shown you here, you can extend the technique to accomplish more advanced reflection effects.

Particle System with Point Sprites

The next example we cover is rendering a particle explosion using point sprites. The purpose of this example is to demonstrate how to animate a particle in a vertex shader and how to render particles using point sprites. The example we cover is the sample program in Chapter_13/ParticleSystem, the results of which are pictured in Figure 13-3.

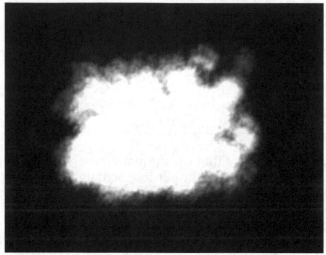

Figure 13-3   Particle System Sample

Particle System Setup

Before diving into the code for this example, it's helpful to cover at a high level the approach this sample uses. One of the goals of this sample was to show how to render a particle explosion without having any dynamic vertex data modified by the CPU. That is, with the exception of uniform variables, there are no changes to any of the vertex data as the explosion animates. To accomplish this goal, there are number of inputs that are fed into the shaders.

At initialization time, the program initializes the following values in a vertex array, one for each particle, based on a random value:

- Lifetime—The lifetime of a particle in seconds.

- Start position—The start position of a particle in the explosion.

- End position—The final position of a particle in the explosion (the particles are animated by linearly interpolating between the start and end position).

In addition, each explosion has several global settings that are passed in as uniforms:

- Center position—The center of the explosion (the per-vertex positions are offset from this center).

- Color—An overall color of the explosion.

- Time—The current time in seconds.

Particle System Vertex Shader

With this information, the vertex and fragment shaders are completely responsible for the motion, fading, and rendering of the particles. Let's begin by taking a look at the vertex shader code for the sample in Example 13-5.

Example 13-5 Particle System Vertex Shader

```
uniform float u_time;
uniform vec3 u_centerPosition;
attribute float a_lifetime;
attribute vec3 a_startPosition;
attribute vec3 a_endPosition;
varying float v_lifetime;
void main()
{
   if(u_time <= a_lifetime)
   {
      gl_Position.xyz = a_startPosition + (u_time * a_endPosition);
      gl_Position.xyz += u_centerPosition;
      gl_Position.w = 1.0;
   }
   else
      gl_Position = vec4(-1000, -1000, 0, 0);
   v_lifetime = 1.0 - (u_time / a_lifetime);
   v_lifetime = clamp(v_lifetime, 0.0, 1.0);
   gl_PointSize = (v_lifetime * v_lifetime) * 40.0;
}
```

The first input to the vertex shader is the uniform variable u_time. This variable is set to the current elapsed time in seconds by the application. The value is reset to 0.0 when the time exceeds the length of a single explosion. The next input to the vertex shader is the uniform variable u_centerPosition. This variable is set to the center location of the explosion at the start of a new explosion. The setup code for u_time and u_centerPosition is in the Update() function of the example program, which is provided in Example 13-6.

Example 13-6   Update Function for Particle System Sample

```
void Update (ESContext *esContext, float deltaTime)
{
    UserData *userData = esContext->userData;

    userData->time += deltaTime;

    if(userData->time >= 1.0f)
    {
        float centerPos[3];
        float color[4];

        userData->time = 0.0f;

        // Pick a new start location and color
        centerPos[0] = ((float)(rand() % 10000) / 10000.0f) - 0.5f;
        centerPos[1] = ((float)(rand() % 10000) / 10000.0f) - 0.5f;
        centerPos[2] = ((float)(rand() % 10000) / 10000.0f) - 0.5f;

        glUniform3fv(userData->centerPositionLoc, 1, &centerPos[0]);

        // Random color
        color[0] = ((float)(rand() % 10000) / 20000.0f) + 0.5f;
        color[1] = ((float)(rand() % 10000) / 20000.0f) + 0.5f;
        color[2] = ((float)(rand() % 10000) / 20000.0f) + 0.5f;
        color[3] = 0.5;

        glUniform4fv(userData->colorLoc, 1, &color[0]);
    }

    // Load uniform time variable
    glUniform1f(userData->timeLoc, userData->time);
}
```

As you can see, the Update() function resets the time after one second elapses and then sets up a new center location and time for another explosion. The function also keeps the u_time variable up-to-date each frame.

Returning to the vertex shader, the vertex attribute inputs to the vertex shader are the particle lifetime, particle start position, and end position. These are all initialized to randomly seeded values in the Init function in the program. The body of the vertex shader first checks to see whether a particle's lifetime has expired. If so, the gl_Position variable is set to the value (–1000, –1000), which is just a quick way of forcing the point to be off the screen. Because the point will be clipped, all of the subsequent processing for the expired point sprites can be skipped. If the particle is still alive, its position is set to be a linear interpolated value between the start and end positions. Next, the vertex shader passes the remaining lifetime of the particle down into the fragment shader in the varying variable v_lifetime. The lifetime will be used in the fragment shader to fade the particle as it ends its life. The final piece of the vertex shader sets the point size to be based on the remaining lifetime of the particle by setting the gl_PointSize built-in variable. This has the effect of scaling the particles down as they reach the end of their life.

Particle System Fragment Shader

The fragment shader code for the example program is provided in Example 13-7.

Example 13-7 Particle System Fragment Shader

```
precision mediump float;
uniform vec4 u_color;
varying float v_lifetime;
uniform sampler2D s_texture;
void main()
{
    vec4 texColor;
    texColor = texture2D(s_texture, gl_PointCoord);
    gl_FragColor = vec4(u_color) * texColor;
    gl_FragColor.a *= v_lifetime;
}
```

The first input to the fragment shader is the u_color uniform variable, which is set up at the beginning of each explosion by the Update function. Next, the v_lifetime varying variable set by the vertex shader is declared in the fragment shader. There is also a sampler declared to which a 2D texture image of smoke is bound.

The fragment shader itself is relatively simple. The texture fetch uses the gl_PointCoord variable as a texture coordinate. This is a special variable for point sprites that is set to fixed values for the corners of the point sprite (this was described in Chapter 7, "Primitive Assembly and Rasterization," on drawing primitives). One could also extend the fragment shader to rotate the point sprite coordinates if rotation of the sprite was required. This requires extra fragment shader instructions, but increases the flexibility of the point sprite.

The texture color is attenuated by the u_color variable and the alpha is attenuated by the particle lifetime. The application also enables alpha blending with the following blend function.

```
glEnable ( GL_BLEND );
glBlendFunc ( GL_SRC_ALPHA, GL_ONE );
```

The result of this is that the alpha produced in the fragment shader is modulated with the fragment color. This value is then added into whatever values are stored in the destination of the fragment. The result is to get an additive blend effect for the particle system. Note that various particle effects will use different alpha blending modes to accomplish the desired effect.

The code to actually draw the particles is given in Example 13-8.

Example 13-8 Draw Function for Particle System Sample

```
void Draw(ESContext *esContext)
{
   UserData *userData = esContext->userData;

   // Set the viewport
   glViewport(0, 0, esContext->width, esContext->height);

   // Clear the color buffer
   glClear(GL_COLOR_BUFFER_BIT);

   // Use the program object
   glUseProgram(userData->programObject);

   // Load the vertex attributes
   glVertexAttribPointer(userData->lifetimeLoc, 1, GL_FLOAT,
                         GL_FALSE, PARTICLE_SIZE * sizeof(GLfloat),
                         userData->particleData);
```

```
glVertexAttribPointer (userData->endPositionLoc, 3, GL_FLOAT,
                       GL_FALSE, PARTICLE_SIZE * sizeof(GLfloat),
                       &userData->particleData[1]);

glVertexAttribPointer (userData->startPositionLoc, 3, GL_FLOAT,
                       GL_FALSE, PARTICLE_SIZE * sizeof(GLfloat),
                       &userData->particleData[4]);


glEnableVertexAttribArray (userData->lifetimeLoc);
glEnableVertexAttribArray (userData->endPositionLoc);
glEnableVertexAttribArray (userData->startPositionLoc);

// Blend particles
glEnable (GL_BLEND);
glBlendFunc (GL_SRC_ALPHA, GL_ONE);

// Bind the texture
glActiveTexture (GL_TEXTURE0);
glBindTexture (GL_TEXTURE_2D, userData->textureId);
glEnable (GL_TEXTURE_2D);

// Set the sampler texture unit to 0
glUniform1i (userData->samplerLoc, 0);

glDrawArrays (GL_POINTS, 0, NUM_PARTICLES);

eglSwapBuffers (esContext->eglDisplay, esContext->eglSurface);
}
```

The Draw function begins by setting the viewport and clearing the screen.
It then selects the program object to use and loads the vertex data using
glVertexAttribPointer. Note that because the values of the vertex array
never change, this example could have used vertex buffer objects rather
than client-side vertex arrays. In general, this is recommended for any vertex data that does not change because it reduces the vertex bandwidth used.
Vertex buffer objects were not used in this example merely to keep the code
a bit simpler. After setting the vertex arrays, the function enables the blend
function, binds the smoke texture, and then uses glDrawArrays to draw
the particles.

Unlike triangles, there is no connectivity for point sprites, so using
glDrawElements does not really provide any advantage for rendering point
sprites in this example. However, often particle systems need to be sorted by
depth from back to front to get proper alpha blending results. In such cases,
one approach that can be used is to sort the element array to modify the

draw order. This is an efficient approach because it requires minimal bandwidth across the bus per-frame (only the index data need be changed, which is almost always smaller than the vertex data).

This example has shown you a number of techniques that can be useful in rendering particle systems using point sprites. The particles were animated entirely on the GPU using the vertex shader. The sizes of the particles were attenuated based on particle lifetime using the gl_PointSize variable. In addition, the point sprites were rendered with a texture using the gl_PointCoord built-in texture coordinate variable. These are the fundamental elements needed to implement a particle system using OpenGL ES 2.0.

Image Postprocessing

The next example we cover is image postprocessing. Using a combination of framebuffer objects and shaders, it is possible to perform a wide variety of image postprocessing techniques. The first example we cover is the Simple Bloom effect in the RenderMonkey workspace in Chapter_13/PostProcess, results of which are pictured in Figure 13-4.

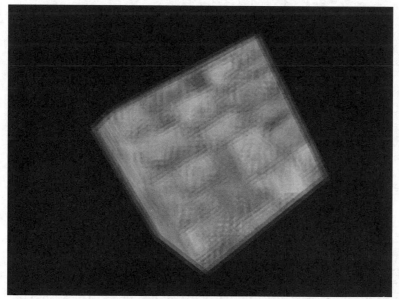

Figure 13-4   Image Postprocessing Example (see Color Plate 6)

Render-to-Texture Setup

This example renders a single textured cube into a framebuffer object and then uses the color attachment as a texture in a subsequent pass. A full-screen quad is drawn to the screen using the rendered texture as a source. A fragment shader is run over the full-screen quad, which performs a blur filter. In general, many types of postprocess techniques can be accomplished using this pattern:

1. Render the scene into an off-screen framebuffer object (FBO).

2. Bind the FBO texture as a source and render a full-screen quad to the screen.

3. Execute a fragment shader that performs filtering across the quad.

Some algorithms require performing multiple passes over an image and some require more complicated inputs. However, the general idea is to use a fragment shader over a full-screen quad that performs a postprocessing algorithm.

Blur Fragment Shader

The fragment shader used on the full-screen quad in the blurring example is provided in Example 13-9.

Example 13-9 Blur Fragment Shader

```
precision mediump float;
uniform sampler2D renderTexture;
varying vec2 v_texCoord;
uniform float u_blurStep;

void main(void)
{
   vec4 sample0,
        sample1,
        sample2,
        sample3;

   float step = u_blurStep / 100.0;

   sample0 = texture2D(renderTexture,
                    vec2(v_texCoord.x - step,
                         v_texCoord.y - step));
```

```
sample1 = texture2D(renderTexture,
                    vec2(v_texCoord.x + step,
                         v_texCoord.y + step));
sample2 = texture2D(renderTexture,
                    vec2(v_texCoord.x + step,
                         v_texCoord.y - step));
sample3 = texture2D(renderTexture,
                    vec2(v_texCoord.x - step,
                         v_texCoord.y + step));

gl_FragColor = (sample0 + sample1 + sample2 + sample3) / 4.0;
}
```

This shader begins by computing the step variable that is based on the u_blurStep uniform variable. The step is used to determine how much to offset the texture coordinate when fetching samples from the image. Overall, four different samples are taken from the image and they are averaged together at the end of the shader. The step is used to offset the texture coordinate in four directions such that four samples in each diagonal direction from the center are taken. The larger the step, the more the image is blurred. One possible optimization to this shader would be to compute the offset texture coordinates in the vertex shader and pass them into varyings in the fragment shader. This would reduce the amount of computation done per fragment.

Light Bloom

Now that we have looked at a simple image postprocessing technique, let's take a look at a slightly more complicated one. Using the blurring technique we introduced in the previous example, we can implement an effect known as *light bloom*. Light bloom is what happens when the eye views a bright light contrasted with a darker surface. The effect is that the light color bleeds into the darker surface. The example we cover is the Bloom effect in the RenderMonkey workspace in Chapter_13/PostProcess, the results of which are pictured in Figure 13-5.

As you can see from the screenshot, the background color bleeds over the car model. The algorithm works as follows:

1. Clear an off-screen render target (rt0) and draw the object in black.

2. Blur the off-screen render target (rt0) into another render target (rt1) using a blur step of 1.0.

3. Blur the off-screen render target (rt1) back into original render target (rt0) using a blur step of 2.0.

4. NOTE: For more blur, repeat steps 2 and 3 for the amount of blur, increasing the blur step each time

5. Render the object to the backbuffer.

6. Blend the final render target with the backbuffer.

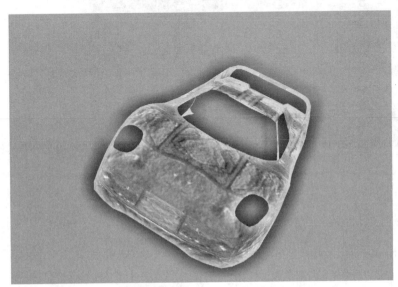

Figure 13-5   Light Bloom Effect

The process this algorithm uses is illustrated in Figure 13-6, which shows each of the steps that go into producing the final image.

As you can see from Figure 13-6, the object is first rendered in black to the render target. That render target is then blurred into a second render target in the next pass. The blurred render target is then blurred again with an expanded blur kernel back into the original render target. At the end, that blurred render target is blended with the original scene. The concept of using two render targets to do successive blurring is often referred to as *ping-ponging*. The amount of bloom can be increased by ping-ponging the blur targets over and over. The shader code for the blur steps is the same as from the previous example. The only difference is that the blur step is being increased for each pass.

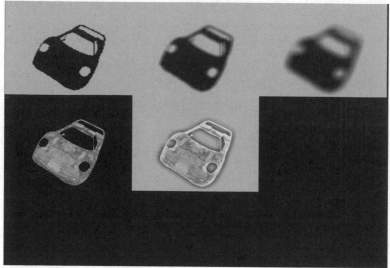

Figure 13-6   Light Bloom Stages

There are a large variety of other image postprocessing algorithms that can be performed using a combination of FBOs and shaders. Some other common techniques include tone mapping, selective blurring, distortion, screen transitions, and depth of field. Using the techniques we have shown you here, you can start to implement other postprocessing algorithms using shaders.

Projective Texturing

A common technique that is used in many effects such as shadow mapping and reflections is the use of projective texturing. To introduce you to the use of projective texturing, we cover an example of rendering a projective spotlight. Most of the complication in using projective texturing is in the mathematics that goes into calculating the projective texture coordinates. The method we show you here would also be the same method you would use in shadow mapping or reflections. The example we cover is the projective spotlight RenderMonkey workspace in Chapter_13/ProjectiveSpotlight, the results of which are pictured in Figure 13-7.

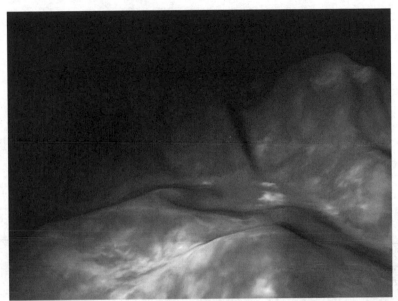

Figure 13-7   Projective Spotlight Example (see Color Plate 7)

Projective Texturing Basics

The example uses the 2D texture image pictured in Figure 13-8 and applies
it to the surface of terrain geometry using projective texturing. Projective
spotlights were a very common technique used to emulate per-pixel spotlight falloff before shaders were introduced to GPUs. Projective spotlights
can still provide an attractive solution because of the high level of efficiency. Applying the projective texture only takes a single texture fetch
instruction in the fragment shader and some setup in the vertex shader. In
addition, the 2D texture image that is projected can contain really any picture, so there are many possible effects that can be accomplished.

So what exactly do we mean by projective texturing? At its most basic, projective texturing is the use of a 3D texture coordinate to look up into a 2D
texture image. The (s, t) coordinates are divided by the (r) coordinate such
that a texel is fetched using $(s/r, t/r)$. There is a special built-in function in
the OpenGL ES Shading Language to do projective texturing called
`texture2DProj`.

vec4	**texture2DProj**(sampler2D *sampler*, vec3 *coord*[, float *bias*])

sampler	a sampler bound to a texture unit specifying the texture to fetch from
coord	a 3D texture coordinate used to fetch from the texture map. The (*x*, *y*) arguments are divided by (*z*) such that the fetch occurs at (*x/z*, *y/z*)
bias	an optional LOD bias to apply

Figure 13-8   2D Texture Projected onto Terrain

The idea behind projective lighting is to transform the position of an object into the projective view space of a light. The projective light space position, after application of a scale and bias, can then be used as a projective texture coordinate. The vertex shader in the RenderMonkey example workspace does the work of transforming the position into the projective view space of a light.

Matrices for Projective Texturing

There are three matrices that we need to transform the position into projective view space of the light and get a projective texture coordinate:

- *Light projection*—projection matrix of the light source using the field of view, aspect ratio, and near and far planes of the light.

- *Light view*—The view matrix of the light source. This would be constructed just as if the light were a camera.

- *Bias matrix*—A matrix that transforms the light-space projected position into a 3D projective texture coordinate.

The light projection matrix would be constructed just like any other projection matrix using the light's parameters for field of view (*FOV*), aspect ratio (*aspect*), and near (*zNear*) and far plane (*zFar*) distances.

$$\begin{bmatrix} \dfrac{\cot\left(\dfrac{FOV}{2}\right)}{aspect} & 0 & 0 & 0 \\ 0 & \cot\left(\dfrac{FOV}{2}\right) & 0 & 0 \\ 0 & 0 & \dfrac{zFar + zNear}{zNear - zFar} & \dfrac{2 \times zFar \times zNear}{zNear - zFar} \\ 0 & 0 & -1 & 0 \end{bmatrix}$$

The light view matrix is constructed by using the three primary axis directions that define the light's view axes and the light's position. We refer to the axes as the right, up, and look vectors.

$$\begin{bmatrix} right.x & up.x & look.x & 0 \\ right.y & up.y & look.y & 0 \\ right.z & up.z & look.z & 0 \\ dot(right, -lightPos) & dot(up, -lightPos) & dot(look, -lightPos) & 1 \end{bmatrix}$$

After transforming the object's position by the view and projection matrices, we must then turn the coordinates into projective texture coordinates. This is accomplished using a 3 × 3 bias matrix on the (x, y, z) components of the position in projective light space. The bias matrix does a linear transformation to go from the [–1, 1] range to the [0, 1] range. Having the coordinates in the [0, 1] range is necessary for the values to be used as texture coordinates.

$$\begin{bmatrix} 0.5 & 0.0 & 0.0 \\ 0.0 & -0.5 & 0.0 \\ 0.5 & 0.5 & 1.0 \end{bmatrix}$$

Typically, the matrix to transform the position into a projective texture coordinate would be computed on the CPU by concatenating the projection, view, and bias matrices together (using a 4 × 4 version of the bias matrix). This would then be loaded into a single uniform matrix that could transform the position in the vertex shader. However, in the example, we perform this computation in the vertex shader for illustrative purposes.

Projective Spotlight Shaders

Now that we have covered the basic mathematics, we can examine the vertex shader in Example 13-10.

Example 13-10 Projective Texturing Vertex Shader

```
uniform float u_time_0_X;
uniform mat4 u_matProjection;
uniform mat4 u_matViewProjection;
attribute vec4 a_vertex;
attribute vec2 a_texCoord0;
attribute vec3 a_normal;

varying vec2 v_texCoord;
varying vec3 v_projTexCoord;
varying vec3 v_normal;·
varying vec3 v_lightDir;

void main(void)
{
    gl_Position = u_matViewProjection * a_vertex;
    v_texCoord = a_texCoord0.xy;
```

```
// Compute a light position based on time
vec3 lightPos;
lightPos.x = cos(u_time_0_X);
lightPos.z = sin(u_time_0_X);
lightPos.xz = 100.0 * normalize(lightPos.xz);
lightPos.y = 100.0;

// Compute the light coordinate axes
vec3 look = -normalize(lightPos);
vec3 right = cross(vec3(0.0, 0.0, 1.0), look);
vec3 up = cross(look, right);

// Create a view matrix for the light
mat4 lightView = mat4(right, dot(right, -lightPos),
                      up,    dot(up, -lightPos),
                      look,  dot(look, -lightPos),
                      0.0, 0.0, 0.0, 1.0);

// Transform position into light view space

vec4 objPosLight = a_vertex * lightView;

// Transform position into projective light view space
objPosLight = u_matProjection * objPosLight;

// Create bias matrix
mat3 biasMatrix = mat3(0.5,  0.0, 0.5,
                       0.0, -0.5, 0.5,
                       0.0,  0.0, 1.0);

// Compute projective texture coordinates
v_projTexCoord = objPosLight.xyz * biasMatrix;

v_lightDir = normalize(a_vertex.xyz - lightPos);
v_normal = a_normal;
}
```

The first operation this shader does is to transform the position by the
u_matViewProjection matrix and output the texture coordinate for the
basemap to the v_texCoord varying. The next thing the shader does is to
compute a position for the light based on time. This bit of the code can really
be ignored, but it was added to animate the light in the vertex shader. In a
typical application, this would be done on the CPU and not in the shader.

Based on the position of the light, the vertex shader then computes the
three coordinate axis vectors for the light into the look, right, and up
variables. Those vectors are used to create a view matrix for the light in the

lightView variable using the equations previously described. The input position for the object is then transformed by the lightView matrix, which transforms the position into light space. The next step is to use the perspective matrix to transform the light space position into projected light space. Rather than creating a new perspective matrix for the light, this example uses the u_matProjection matrix for the camera. Typically, a real application would want to create its own projection matrix for the light based on how big the cone angle and falloff distance is.

Once the position is in projective light space, a biasMatrix is then created to transform the position into a projective texture coordinate. The final projective texture coordinate is stored in the vec3 varying variable v_projTexCoord. In addition, the vertex shader also passes the light direction and normal vectors into the fragment shader in the v_lightDir and v_normal varyings. These will be used to determine if a fragment is facing the light source or not in order to mask off the projective texture for fragments facing away from the light.

The fragment shader performs the actual projective texture fetch that applies the projective spotlight texture to the surface.

Example 13-11 Projective Texturing Fragment Shader

```
precision mediump float;

uniform sampler2D baseMap;
uniform sampler2D spotLight;
varying vec2 v_texCoord;
varying vec3 v_projTexCoord;
varying vec3 v_normal;
varying vec3 v_lightDir;

void main(void)
{
    // Projective fetch of spotlight
    vec4 spotLightColor = texture2DProj(spotLight, v_projTexCoord);

    // Basemap
    vec4 baseColor = texture2D(baseMap, v_texCoord);

    // Compute N.L
    float nDotL = max(0.0, -dot(v_normal, v_lightDir));

    gl_FragColor = spotLightColor * baseColor * 2.0 * nDotL;

}
```

The first operation the fragment shader performs is to do the projective texture fetch using `texture2DProj`. As you can see, the projective texture coordinate that was computed during the vertex shader and passed in the varying `v_projTexCoord` is used to perform the projective texture fetch. The wrap modes for the projective texture are set to `GL_CLAMP_TO_EDGE` and the min/mag filters are both set to `GL_LINEAR`. The fragment shader then fetches the color from the basemap using the `v_texCoord` varying. Next, the shader computes the dot product between the light direction and normal vector. This is used to attenuate the final color so that the projective spotlight is not applied to fragments that are facing away from the light. Finally, all of the components are multiplied together (and scaled by 2.0 to increase the brightness). This gives us our final image from Figure 13-7 of the terrain lit by the projective spotlight.

As mentioned at the beginning of this section, the important takeaway from this example is the set of computations that go into computing a projective texture coordinate. The computation shown here would be the exact same computation that you would use to produce a coordinate to fetch from a shadow map. Similarly, rendering reflections with projective texturing requires that you transform the position into the projective view space of the reflection camera. You would do the same thing we have done here, but substitute the light matrices for the reflection camera matrices. Projective texturing is a very powerful tool in advanced effects and you should now understand the basics of how to use it.

Noise Using a 3D Texture

The next rendering technique we cover is using a 3D texture for noise. In Chapter 9, we introduced you to the basics of 3D textures. As you will recall, a 3D texture is essentially a stack of 2D texture slices representing a 3D volume. There are many possible uses of 3D textures and one of them is the representation of noise. In this section, we show an example of using a 3D volume of noise to create a wispy fog effect. This example builds on the linear fog example from Chapter 10, "Fragment Shaders." The example we cover is the RenderMonkey workspace in Chapter_13/Noise3D, the results of which are pictured in Figure 13-9.

Figure 13-9 Fog Distorted by 3D Noise Texture (see Color Plate 8)

Generating Noise

The application of noise is a very common technique in a large variety of 3D effects. The OpenGL Shading Language (*not* OpenGL ES Shading Language) had functions for computing noise in one, two, three, or four dimensions. The functions return a pseudorandom continuous noise value that is repeatable based on the input value. However, the problem with these functions was that they were very expensive to implement. Most programmable GPUs did not implement noise functions natively in hardware, which meant the noise computations had to be implemented using shader instructions (or worse, in software on the CPU). It takes a lot of shader instructions to implement these noise functions, so the performance was too slow to be used in most real-time fragment shaders. This, by the way, is the reason that the OpenGL ES working group decided to drop noise from the OpenGL ES shading language (although vendors are still free to expose it through an extension).

Although computing noise in the fragment shader is prohibitively expensive, we can work around the problem using a 3D texture. It is possible to easily produce acceptable quality noise by precomputing the noise and placing the results in a 3D texture. There are a number of algorithms that can be used to generate noise. A list of references and links described at the end of this chapter can be used to read about the various noise algorithms. We discuss a specific algorithm that generates a lattice-based gradient noise. Ken Perlin's noise function (Perlin, 1985) is a lattice-based gradient noise. This is a very commonly used method for generating noise. For example, a lattice-based gradient noise is implemented by the *noise* function in the Renderman shading language.

The gradient noise algorithm takes a 3D coordinate as input and returns a floating-point noise value. To generate this noise value given an input (x, y, z), we map the x, y, and z values to appropriate integer locations in a lattice. The number of cells in a lattice is programmable and for our implementation is set to 256 cells. For each cell in the lattice, we need to generate and store a pseudorandom gradient vector. Example 13-12 describes how these gradient vectors are generated.

Example 13-12 Generating Gradient Vectors

```
// permTable describes a random permutation of
// 8-bit values from 0 to 255.
static unsigned char   permTable[256] = {
    0xE1, 0x9B, 0xD2, 0x6C, 0xAF, 0xC7, 0xDD, 0x90,
    0xCB, 0x74, 0x46, 0xD5, 0x45, 0x9E, 0x21, 0xFC,
    0x05, 0x52, 0xAD, 0x85, 0xDE, 0x8B, 0xAE, 0x1B,
    0x09, 0x47, 0x5A, 0xF6, 0x4B, 0x82, 0x5B, 0xBF,
    0xA9, 0x8A, 0x02, 0x97, 0xC2, 0xEB, 0x51, 0x07,
    0x19, 0x71, 0xE4, 0x9F, 0xCD, 0xFD, 0x86, 0x8E,
    0xF8, 0x41, 0xE0, 0xD9, 0x16, 0x79, 0xE5, 0x3F,
    0x59, 0x67, 0x60, 0x68, 0x9C, 0x11, 0xC9, 0x81,
    0x24, 0x08, 0xA5, 0x6E, 0xED, 0x75, 0xE7, 0x38,
    0x84, 0xD3, 0x98, 0x14, 0xB5, 0x6F, 0xEF, 0xDA,
    0xAA, 0xA3, 0x33, 0xAC, 0x9D, 0x2F, 0x50, 0xD4,
    0xB0, 0xFA, 0x57, 0x31, 0x63, 0xF2, 0x88, 0xBD,
    0xA2, 0x73, 0x2C, 0x2B, 0x7C, 0x5E, 0x96, 0x10,
    0x8D, 0xF7, 0x20, 0x0A, 0xC6, 0xDF, 0xFF, 0x48,
    0x35, 0x83, 0x54, 0x39, 0xDC, 0xC5, 0x3A, 0x32,
    0xD0, 0x0B, 0xF1, 0x1C, 0x03, 0xC0, 0x3E, 0xCA,
    0x12, 0xD7, 0x99, 0x18, 0x4C, 0x29, 0x0F, 0xB3,
    0x27, 0x2E, 0x37, 0x06, 0x80, 0xA7, 0x17, 0xBC,
    0x6A, 0x22, 0xBB, 0x8C, 0xA4, 0x49, 0x70, 0xB6,
    0xF4, 0xC3, 0xE3, 0x0D, 0x23, 0x4D, 0xC4, 0xB9,
    0x1A, 0xC8, 0xE2, 0x77, 0x1F, 0x7B, 0xA8, 0x7D,
    0xF9, 0x44, 0xB7, 0xE6, 0xB1, 0x87, 0xA0, 0xB4,
    0x0C, 0x01, 0xF3, 0x94, 0x66, 0xA6, 0x26, 0xEE,
    0xFB, 0x25, 0xF0, 0x7E, 0x40, 0x4A, 0xA1, 0x28,
    0xB8, 0x95, 0xAB, 0xB2, 0x65, 0x42, 0x1D, 0x3B,
```

```
        0x92, 0x3D, 0xFE, 0x6B, 0x2A, 0x56, 0x9A, 0x04,
        0xEC, 0xE8, 0x78, 0x15, 0xE9, 0xD1, 0x2D, 0x62,
        0xC1, 0x72, 0x4E, 0x13, 0xCE, 0x0E, 0x76, 0x7F,
        0x30, 0x4F, 0x93, 0x55, 0x1E, 0xCF, 0xDB, 0x36,
        0x58, 0xEA, 0xBE, 0x7A, 0x5F, 0x43, 0x8F, 0x6D,
        0x89, 0xD6, 0x91, 0x5D, 0x5C, 0x64, 0xF5, 0x00,
        0xD8, 0xBA, 0x3C, 0x53, 0x69, 0x61, 0xCC, 0x34,
};

#define NOISE_TABLE_MASK    255

// lattice gradients 3D noise
static float gradientTable[256*3];

#define FLOOR(x)        ((int)(x) - ((x) < 0 && (x) != (int)(x)))
#define smoothstep(t)   (t * t * (3.0f - 2.0f * t))
#define lerp(t, a, b)   (a + t * (b - a))

void
initNoiseTable()
{
    long        rnd;
    int         i;
    double      a;
    float       x, y, z, r, theta;
    float       gradients[256*3];
    unsigned int *p, *psrc;

    srandom(0);

    // build gradient table for 3D noise
    for(i=0; i<256; i++)
    {
        // calculate 1 - 2 * random number
        rnd = random();
        a = (random() & 0x7FFFFFFF) / (double) 0x7FFFFFFF;
        z = (float)(1.0 - 2.0 * a);

        r = (float)sqrt(1.0 - z * z);   // r is radius of circle

        rnd = random();
        a = (float)((random() & 0x7FFFFFFF) / (double) 0x7FFFFFFF);
        theta = (float)(2.0 * M_PI * a);
        x = (float)(r * (float)cos(a));
        y = (float)(r * (float)sin(a));

        gradients[i*3] = x;
        gradients[i*3+1] = y;
        gradients[i*3+2] = z;
    }
```

```
    // use the index in the permutation table to load the
    // gradient values from gradients to gradientTable
    p = (unsigned int *)gradientTable;
    psrc = (unsigned int *)gradients;
    for (i=0; i<256; i++)
    {
        int indx = permTable[i];
        p[i*3] = psrc[indx*3];
        p[i*3+1] = psrc[indx*3+1];
        p[i*3+2] = psrc[indx*3+2];
    }
}
```

Example 13-13 describes how the gradient noise is calculated using the pseudorandom gradient vectors and an input 3D coordinate.

Example 13-13   3D Noise

```
//
// generate the value of gradient noise for a given lattice point
//
// (ix, iy, iz) specifies the 3D lattice position
// (fx, fy, fz) specifies the fractional part
//
static float
glattice3D(int ix, int iy, int iz, float fx, float fy, float fz)
{
    float   *g;
    int     indx, y, z;

    z = permTable[iz & NOISE_TABLE_MASK];
    y = permTable[(iy + z) & NOISE_TABLE_MASK];
    indx = (ix + y) & NOISE_TABLE_MASK;
    g = &gradientTable[indx*3];

    return (g[0]*fx + g[1]*fy + g[2]*fz);
}

//
// generate the 3D noise value
// f describes input (x, y, z) position for which the noise value
//  needs to be computed. noise3D returns the scalar noise value
//
float
noise3D(float *f)
{
```

```
int    ix, iy, iz;
float    fx0, fx1, fy0, fy1, fz0, fz1;
float    wx, wy, wz;
float    vx0, vx1, vy0, vy1, vz0, vz1;

ix = FLOOR(f[0]);
fx0 = f[0] - ix;
fx1 = fx0 - 1;
wx = smoothstep(fx0);

iy = FLOOR(f[1]);
fy0 = f[1] - iy;
fy1 = fy0 - 1;
wy = smoothstep(fy0);

iz = FLOOR(f[2]);
fz0 = f[2] - iz;
fz1 = fz0 - 1;
wz = smoothstep(fz0);

vx0 = glattice3D(ix, iy, iz, fx0, fy0, fz0);
vx1 = glattice3D(ix+1, iy, iz, fx1, fy0, fz0);
vy0 = lerp(wx, vx0, vx1);
vx0 = glattice3D(ix, iy+1, iz, fx0, fy1, fz0);
vx1 = glattice3D(ix+1, iy+1, iz, fx1, fy1, fz0);
vy1 = lerp(wx, vx0, vx1);
vz0 = lerp(wy, vy0, vy1);

vx0 = glattice3D(ix, iy, iz+1, fx0, fy0, fz1);
vx1 = glattice3D(ix+1, iy, iz+1, fx1, fy0, fz1);
vy0 = lerp(wx, vx0, vx1);
vx0 = glattice3D(ix, iy+1, iz+1, fx0, fy1, fz1);
vx1 = glattice3D(ix+1, iy+1, iz+1, fx1, fy1, fz1);
vy1 = lerp(wx, vx0, vx1);
vz1 = lerp(wy, vy0, vy1);

return lerp(wz, vz0, vz1);;
}
```

The noise3D function returns a value between –1.0 and 1.0. The value of gradient noise is always 0 at the integer lattice points. For points in between, trilinear interpolation of gradient values across the eight integer lattice points that surround the point is used to generate the scalar noise value. Figure 13-10 shows a 2D slice of the gradient noise using the preceding algorithm.

Figure 13-10   2D Slice of Gradient Noise

Using Noise

Once we have created a 3D noise volume, it is very easy to use it for a variety of different effects. In the case of the wispy fog effect, the idea is simple: scroll the 3D noise texture in all three dimensions based on time and use the value from the texture to distort the fog factor. Let's take a look at the fragment shader in Example 13-14.

Example 13-14   Noise Distorted Fog Fragment Shader

```
#extension GL_OES_texture_3D : enable
precision mediump float;

uniform vec4 u_fogColor;
uniform float u_fogMaxDist;
uniform float u_fogMinDist;
uniform float u_time;
uniform sampler2D baseMap;
uniform sampler3D noiseVolume;

varying vec2 v_texCoord;
varying float v_eyeDist;
```

```
float computeLinearFogFactor()
{
   float factor;

   // Compute linear fog equation
   factor = (u_fogMaxDist - v_eyeDist) /
            (u_fogMaxDist - u_fogMinDist);

   return factor;
}

void main(void)
{
   float fogFactor = computeLinearFogFactor();
   vec4 baseColor = texture2D(baseMap, v_texCoord);

   // Distort fog factor by noise
   vec3 noiseCoord;
   noiseCoord.xy = v_texCoord.xy - (u_time * 0.1);
   noiseCoord.z = u_time * 0.1;

   fogFactor += texture3D(noiseVolume, noiseCoord).r;
   fogFactor = clamp(fogFactor, 0.0, 1.0);

   // Compute final color as a lerp with fog factor
   gl_FragColor = baseColor * fogFactor +
                  u_fogColor * (1.0 - fogFactor);
}
```

The first thing this shader does is to enable the 3D texture extension using the #extension mechanism. If an implementation does not support the GL_OES_texture_3D extension, then this shader will fail to compile. This shader is very similar to our linear fog example in Chapter 10. The primary difference is that the linear fog factor is distorted by the 3D noise texture. The shader computes a 3D texture coordinate based on time and places it in noiseCoord. The u_time uniform variable is tied to the current time and is updated each frame. The 3D texture is set up with wrap modes in *s*, *t*, and *r* of GL_REPEAT so that the noise volume scrolls smoothly on the surface. The (*s*, *t*) coordinates are based on the coordinates for the base texture and are scrolled in both directions. The (*r*) coordinate is based purely on time so that it is continuously scrolled.

The 3D texture is a single-channel (GL_LUMINANCE) texture so only the red component of the texture is used (the green and blue channels have the same value as the red channel). The value fetched from the volume is added to the computed fogFactor and then used to linearly interpolate between the fog color and base color. The result is a wispy fog appearing to roll in from the hilltops. The speed of the fog can be increased easily by applying a scale to the u_time variable when scrolling the 3D texture coordinates.

There are a number of different effects you can achieve by using a 3D texture to represent noise. Some other examples of using noise include representing dust in a light volume, adding a more natural appearance to a procedural texture, and simulating water waves. Using a 3D texture is a great way to save performance and still achieve high-quality visual effects. It is unlikely that you can expect handheld devices to compute noise functions in the fragment shader and have enough performance to run at a high frame rate. As such, having a precomputed noise volume will be a very valuable trick to have in your toolkit for creating effects.

Procedural Texturing

The next topic we cover is the generation of procedural textures. Textures are typically described as a 2D image, a cubemap, or a 3D image. These images store color or depth values. Built-in functions defined in the OpenGL ES shading language take a texture coordinate, a texture object referred to as a sampler, and return a color or depth value. Procedural texturing refers to textures that are described as a procedure instead of as an image. The procedure describes the algorithm that will generate a texture color or depth value given a set of inputs.

The following are some of the benefits of procedural textures:

- Much more compact representation versus a stored texture image. All you need to store is the code that describes the procedural texture. This will typically be much smaller in size over a stored image.

- Procedural textures, unlike stored images, have no fixed resolution. They can therefore be applied to the surface without loss of detail. This means that we will not see issues such as reduced detail as we zoom onto a surface that uses a procedural texture. We will, however, encounter these issues when using a stored texture image because of its fixed resolution.

The disadvantages of procedural textures are as follows:

- The procedural texture code could require quite a few instructions and could result in fragment shaders that might not compile because of fragment shader size restrictions. As OpenGL ES 2.0 primarily runs on handheld and embedded devices, this can be a serious problem limiting the algorithms developers can use for procedural effects. This problem should get better as handheld devices become more capable in their ability to do graphics.

- Although the procedural texture might have a smaller footprint than a stored texture, it might take a lot more cycles to execute the procedural texture versus doing a lookup in the stored texture. With procedural textures you are dealing with instruction bandwidth versus memory bandwidth for stored textures. Both the instruction and memory bandwidth are at a premium on handheld devices and a developer must carefully choose which approach to take.

- Repeatability might be hard to achieve. Differences in arithmetic precision and in the implementation of built-in functions across OpenGL ES 2.0 implementations can make this a difficult problem to deal with.

- Procedural textures can have serious aliasing artifacts. Most of these artifacts can be resolved but they result in additional instructions to the procedural texture code, which can impact the performance of a shader.

The decision whether to use a procedural or a stored texture will need to be made based on careful analysis of the performance and memory bandwidth requirements of each.

A Procedural Texture Example

We now look at a simple example that demonstrates procedural textures. We are very familiar with how we would use a checkerboard texture image to draw a checkerboard pattern on an object. We now look at a procedural texture implementation that renders a checkerboard pattern on an object. The example we cover is the Checker.rfx RenderMonkey workspace in Chapter_13/ProceduralTextures. Examples 13-15 and 13-16 describe the vertex and fragment shader that implements the checkerboard texture procedurally.

Example 13-15   Checker Vertex Shader

```
uniform mat4    mvp_matrix;    // combined modelview + projection
matrix

attribute vec4  a_position;    // input vertex position
attribute vec2  a_st;          // input texture coordinate
```

```
varying vec2    v_st;          // output texture coordinate

void
main()
{
    v_st = a_st;
    gl_Position = mvp_matrix * a_position;
}
```

The vertex shader code in Example 13-15 is really straightforward. It transforms the position using the combined model view and projection matrix and passes the texture coordinate (a_st) to the fragment shader as a varying variable (v_st).

Example 13-16 Checker Fragment Shader

```
#ifdef GL_ES
precision highp float;
#endif

// frequency of the checkerboard pattern
uniform int     u_frequency;

// alternate colors that make the checkerboard pattern
uniform vec4    u_color0;
uniform vec4    u_color1;

varying vec2    v_st;

void
main()
{
    vec2    tcmod = mod(v_st * float(u_frequency), 1.0);

    if(tcmod.s < 0.5)
    {
        if(tcmod.t < 0.5)
            gl_FragColor = u_color1;
        else
            gl_FragColor = u_color0;
    }
    else
    {
        if(tcmod.t < 0.5)
            gl_FragColor = u_color0;
```

```
        else
            gl_FragColor = u_color1;
    }

    gl_FragColor = mix(color1, color0, delta);
}
```

The fragment shader code in Example 13-16 uses the v_st texture coordinate to draw the texture pattern. Although easy to understand, the fragment shader might have poor performance because the multiple conditional checks are being done on values that can be different over fragments being executed in parallel. This can impact performance as the number of vertices or fragments executed in parallel by the GPU is reduced. Example 13-17 is a version of the fragment shader that no longer uses any conditional checks.

Example 13-17   Checker Fragment Shader

```
#ifdef GL_ES
precision highp float;
#endif

// frequency of the checkerboard pattern
uniform int     u_frequency;

// alternate colors that make the checkerboard pattern
uniform vec4    u_color0;
uniform vec4    u_color1;

varying vec2    v_st;

void
main()
{
    vec2    texcoord = mod(floor(v_st * float(u_frequency * 2)), 2.0);
    float   delta = abs(texcoord.x - texcoord.y);

    gl_FragColor = mix(u_color1, u_color0, delta);
}
```

Figure 13-11 shows the checkerboard image rendered using the fragment shader in Example 13-17 with u_frequency = 10, u_color0 set to black, and u_color1 set to white.

Figure 13-11 Checkerboard Procedural Texture

As you can see this was really easy to implement. We do see quite a bit of aliasing, which is never acceptable. With a texture checker image, aliasing issues are overcome using mipmapping and applying preferably a trilinear or bilinear filter. We now look at how to render an antialiased checkerboard pattern. To antialias a procedural texture, we need the built-in functions implemented by the GL_OES_standard_derivatives extension. Refer to Appendix B for a detailed description of the built-in functions implemented by this extension.

Antialiasing of Procedural Textures

In *Advanced RenderMan: Creating CGI for Motion Pictures*, Anthony Apodaca and Larry Gritz give a very thorough explanation on how to implement analytic antialiasing of procedural textures. We use the techniques described in this book to implement the antialiased checker fragment shader. Example 13-18 describes the antialiased checker fragment shader code from the CheckerAA.rfx RenderMonkey workspace in Chapter13/ ProceduralTextures.

Example 13-18 Antialiased Checker Fragment Shader

```
#ifdef GL_ES
precision highp float;
#extension GL_OES_standard_derivatives : enable
```

```
#endif

uniform int      u_frequency;
uniform vec4     u_color0;
uniform vec4     u_color1;

varying vec2     v_st;

void
main()
{
    vec4     color;
    vec2     st_width;
    vec2     fuzz;
    vec2     check_pos;
    float    fuzz_max;

    // calculate the filter width.
    st_width = fwidth(v_st);
    fuzz = st_width * float(u_frequency) * 2.0;
    fuzz_max = max(fuzz.s, fuzz.t);

    // get the place in the pattern where we are sampling
    check_pos = fract(v_st * float(u_frequency));

    if (fuzz_max <= 0.5)
    {
        // if the filter width is small enough, compute the pattern
        // color by performing a smooth interpolation between the
        // computed color and the average color.

        vec2   p = smoothstep(vec2(0.5), fuzz + vec2(0.5), check_pos)
             + (1.0 - smoothstep(vec2(0.0), fuzz, check_pos));

        color = mix(u_color0, u_color1,
                  p.x * p.y + (1.0 - p.x) * (1.0 - p.y));
        color = mix(color, (u_color0 + u_color1)/2.0,
                      smoothstep(0.125, 0.5, fuzz_max));
    }
    else
    {
        // filter is too wide. just use the average color.

        color = (u_color0 + u_color1)/2.0;
    }

    gl_FragColor = color;
}
```

Figure 13-12 shows the checkerboard image rendered using the antialiased checker fragment shader in Example 13-18 with u_frequency = 10, u_color0 set to black, and u_color1 set to white.

Figure 13-12   Antialiased Checkerboard Procedural Texture

To antialias the checkerboard procedural texture, we need to estimate the average value of the texture over an area covered by the pixel. Given a function g(v) that represents a procedural texture, we need to calculate the average value of g(v) of the region covered by this pixel. To determine this region, we need to know the rate of change of g(v). The GL_OES_standard_ derivatives extension allows us to compute the rate of change of q(v) in x and y using the functions dFdx and dFdy. The rate of change, called the gradient vector is given by [dFdx(g(v)), dFdy(g(v))]. The magnitude of the gradient vector is computed as sqrt((dFdx(g(v))2 + dFdx(g(v))2). This can also be approximated by abs(dFdx(g(v))) + abs(dFdy(g(v))). The function fwidth can be used to compute the magnitude of this gradient vector. This approach works fine if g(v) is a scalar expression. If g(v) is a point, we will need to compute the cross-product of dFdx(g(v)) and dFdy(g(v)). In the case of the checkerboard texture example, we need to compute the magnitude of the v_st.x and v_st.y scalar expressions and therefore the function fwidth can be used to compute the filter widths for v_st.x and v_st.y.

Let w be the filter width computed by fwidth. We need to know two additional things about the procedural texture:

- The smallest value of filter width `k` such that the procedural texture `g(v)` will not show any aliasing artifacts for filter widths < `k/2`.

- The average value of the procedural texture `g(v)` over very large widths.

If `w` < `k/2`, we should not see any aliasing artifacts. If `w` > `k/2` (i.e., the filter width is too large), aliasing will occur. We use the average value of `g(v)` in this case. For other values of `w`, we use a `smoothstep` to fade between the true function and average value.

This, hopefully, provided good insight into how to use procedural textures and how to resolve aliasing artifacts that become apparent when using procedural textures. The generation of procedural textures for many different applications is a very large subject. The following list of references provides some good places to start if you are interested in reading more on procedural texture generation.

Further Reading on Procedural Textures

1. Anthony A. Apodaca and Larry Gritz. *Advanced Renderman: Creating CGI for Motion Pictures* (Morgan Kaufmann, 1999).

2. David S. Ebert, F. Kenton Musgrave, Darwyn Peachey, Ken Perlin, and Steven Worley. *Texturing and Modeling: A Procedural Approach, 3rd ed.* (Morgan Kaufmann, 2002).

3. K. Perlin. An image synthesizer. *Computer Graphics* (SIGGRAPH 1985 Proceedings, pp. 287–296, July 1985).

4. K. Perlin. Improving noise. *Computer Graphics* (SIGGRAPH 2002 Proceedings, pp. 681–682).

5. K. Perlin. *Making Noise.* www.noisemachine.com/talk1/.

6. Pixar. The Renderman Interface Specification, Version 3.2. July 2000. renderman.pixar.com/products/rispec/index.htm.

7. Randi J. Rost. *OpenGL Shading Language, 2nd ed.* (Addison-Wesley Professional, 2006).

Chapter 14

State Queries

OpenGL ES 2.0 relies on a large collection of data and objects to render when you ask. You'll need to compile and link shader programs, initialize vertex arrays and attribute bindings, specify uniform values, and probably load and bind texture, and that only scratches the surface.

There is also a large quantity of values that are intrinsic to OpenGL ES 2.0's operation. You might need to determine how large of a viewport is supported, or the maximum number of texture units, for example. All of those values can be queried by your application.

This chapter describes the functions your applications can use to obtain values from OpenGL ES 2.0, and the parameters that you can query.

OpenGL ES 2.0 Implementation String Queries

One of the most fundamental queries that you will need to perform in your (well written) applications is information about the underlying OpenGL ES 2.0 implementation, like the version of OpenGL ES supported, whose implementation it is, and what extensions are available. These characteristics are all returned as ASCII strings from the `glGetString` function.

```
const GLubyte* glGetString(GLenum name)
```

name	specifies the parameter to be returned. Can be one of `GL_VENDOR`, `GL_RENDERER`, `GL_VERSION`, `GL_SHADING_LANGUAGE_VERSION`, or `GL_EXTENSIONS`

The GL_VENDOR and GL_RENDERER queries are formatted for human consumption, and have no set format; they're initialized with whatever the implementer felt were useful descriptions.

The GL_VERSION query will return a string starting with "OpenGL ES 2.0" for all OpenGL ES 2.0 implementations. The version string can additionally include vendor-specific information after those tokens, and will always have the format of:

```
OpenGL ES <version> <vendor-specific information>
```

with the <version> being the version number (e.g., 2.0), composed of a major release number, followed by a period and the minor release number, and optionally another period and a tertiary release value (often used by vendors to represent an OpenGL ES 2.0's driver revision number).

Likewise, the GL_SHADING_LANGUAGE_VERSION query will always return a string starting with OpenGL ES GLSL ES 1.00. This string can also have vendor-specific information appended to it, and will take the form:

```
OpenGL ES GLSL ES <version> <vendor-specific information>
```

with a similar formatting for the <version> value.

When OpenGL ES is updated to the next version, these version numbers will change accordingly.

Finally, the GL_EXTENSIONS query will return a space-separated list of all of the extensions supported by the implementation, or the NULL string if the implementation is not extended.

Querying Implementation-Dependent Limits

Many rendering parameters depend on the underlying capabilities of the OpenGL ES implementation; for example, how many texture units are available to a shader, or what is the maximum size for a texture map or aliased point. Values of those types are queried using one of the functions shown here.

```
void glGetBooleanv(GLenum pname, GLboolean* params)
void glGetFloatv(GLenum pname, GLfloat* params)
void glGetIntegerv(GLenum pname, GLint* params)
```

There are a number of implementation-dependent parameters that can be queried, as listed in Table 14-1.

Table 14-1   Implementation-Dependent State Queries

State Variable	Description	Minimum/ Initial Value	Get Function
GL_VIEWPORT	Current size of the viewport		glGetIntegerv
GL_DEPTII_RANGE	Current depth range values	(0, 1)	glGetFloatv
GL_LINE_WIDTH	Current line width	1.0	glGetFloatv
GL_CULL_FACE_MODE	Current face mode for polygon culling	GL_BACK	glGetIntegerv
GL_FRONT_FACE	Current vertex ordering for specifying a front-facing polygon	GL_CCW	glGetIntegerv
GL_POLYGON_OFFSET_FACTOR	Current polygon offset factor value	0	glGetFloatv
GL_POLYGON_OFFSET_UNITS	Current polygon offset units value	0	glGetFloatv
GL_SAMPLE_COVERAGE_VALUE	Current multisample coverage value	1	glGetFloatv
GL_SAMPLE_COVERAGE_INVERT	Current value of multisample inversion flag	GL_FALSE	glGetBooleanv
GL_COLOR_WRITEMASK	Current color buffer writemask value	GL_TRUE	glGetBooleanv
GL_DEPTH_WRITEMASK	Current depth buffer writemask value	GL_TRUE	glGetBooleanv
GL_STENCIL_WRITEMASK	Current stencil buffer writemask value	1s	glGetIntegerv

Table 14-1   Implementation-Dependent State Queries *(continued)*

State Variable	Description	Minimum/ Initial Value	Get Function
GL_STENCIL_BACK_WRITEMASK	Current back stencil buffer writemask value	1s	glGetIntegerv
GL_COLOR_CLEAR_VALUE	Current color buffer clear value	(0, 0, 0, 0)	glGetFloatv
GL_DEPTH_CLEAR_VALUE	Current depth buffer clear value	1	glGetIntegerv
GL_STENCIL_CLEAR_VALUE	Current stencil buffer clear value	0	glGetIntegerv
GL_SUBPIXEL_BITS	Number of subpixel bits supported	4	glGetIntegerv
GL_MAX_TEXTURE_SIZE	Maximum size of a texture	64	glGetIntegerv
GL_MAX_CUB_MAP_TEXTURE_SIZE	Maximum dimension of a cubemap texture	16	glGetIntegerv
GL_MAX_VIEWPORT_DIMS	Dimensions of the maximum supported viewport size		glGetIntegerv
GL_ALIASED_POINT_SIZE_RANGE	Range of aliased point sizes	1, 1	glGetFloatv
GL_ALIASED_LINE_WIDTH_RANGE	Range of aliased line width sizes	1, 1	glGetFloatv
GL_NUM_COMPRESSED_TEXTURE_ FORMATS	Number of compressed texture formats supported		glGetIntegerv
GL_COMPRESSED_TEXTURE_FORMATS	Compressed texture formats supported		glGetIntegerv
GL_RED_BITS	Number of red bits in current color buffer		glGetIntegerv
GL_GREEN_BITS	Number of green bits in current color buffer		glGetIntegerv
GL_BLUE_BITS	Number of blue bits in current color buffer		glGetIntegerv

Table 14-1 Implementation-Dependent State Queries *(continued)*

State Variable	Description	Minimum/ Initial Value	Get Function
GL_ALPHA_BITS	Number of alpha bits in current color buffer		glGetIntegerv
GL_DEPTH_BITS	Number of bits in the current depth buffer	16	glGetIntegerv
GL_STENCIL_BITS	Number of stencil bits in current stencil buffer	8	glGetIntegerv
GL_IMPLEMENTATION_READ_TYPE	Data type for pixel components for pixel read operations		glGetIntegerv
GL_IMPLEMENTATION_READ_FORMAT	Pixel format for pixel read operations		

Querying OpenGL ES State

There are many parameters that your application can modify to affect OpenGL ES 2.0's operation. Although it's usually more efficient for an application to track these values when it modifies them, you can retrieve any of the values listed in Table 14-2 from the currently bound context. For each token, the appropriate OpenGL ES 2.0 get function is provided.

Table 14-2 Application-Modifiable OpenGL ES State Queries

State Variable	Description	Minimum/ Initial Value	Get Function
GL_ARRAY_BUFFER_BINDING	Currently bound vertex attribute array binding	0	glGetIntegerv
GL_ELEMENT_ARRAY_BUFFER_BINDING	Currently bound element array binding	0	glGetIntegerv
GL_CULL_FACE_MODE	Current face culling mode	GL_BACK	glGetIntegerv
GL_FRONT_FACE	Current front-facing vertex winding mode	GL_CCW	glGetIntegerv

Table 14-2   Application-Modifiable OpenGL ES State Queries *(continued)*

State Variable	Description	Minimum/ Initial Value	Get Function
GL_SAMPLE_COVERAGE_VALUE	Current value specified for multisampling sample coverage value	1	glGetFloatv
GL_SAMPLE_COVERAGE_INVERT	Current multisampling coverage value inversion setting	GL_FALSE	glGetBooleanv
GL_TEXTURE_BINDING_2D	Current 2D texture binding	0	glGetIntegerv
GL_TEXTURE_BINDING_CUBE_MAP	Current cubemap texture binding	0	glGetIntegerv
GL_ACTIVE_TEXTURE	Current texture unit	0	glGetIntegerv
GL_COLOR_WRITEMASK	Color buffer writable	GL_TRUE	glGetBooleanv
GL_DEPTH_WRITEMASK	Depth buffer writable	GL_TRUE	glGetBooleanv
GL_STENCIL_WRITEMASK	Current write mask for front-facing polygons	1	glGetIntegerv
GL_STENCIL_BACK_WRITEMASK	Current write mask for back-facing polygons	1	glGetIntegerv
GL_COLOR_CLEAR_VALUE	Current color buffer clear value	0, 0, 0, 0	glGetFloatv
GL_DEPTH_CLEAR_VALUE	Current depth buffer clear value	1	glGetIntegerv
GL_STENCIL_CLEAR_VALUE	Current stencil buffer clear value	0	glGetIntegerv
GL_SCISSOR_BOX	Current offset and dimensions of the scissor box	0, 0, w, h	glGetIntegerv
GL_STENCIL_FUNC	Current stencil test operator function	GL_ALWAYS	glGetIntegerv
GL_STENCIL_VALUE_MASK	Current stencil test value mask	1s	glGetIntegerv

Table 14-2   Application-Modifiable OpenGL ES State Queries *(continued)*

State Variable	Description	Minimum/ Initial Value	Get Function
GL_STENCIL_REF	Current stencil test reference value	0	glGetIntegerv
GL_STENCIL_FAIL	Current operation for stencil test failure	GL_KEEP	glGetIntegerv
GL_STENCIL_PASS_DEPTH_FAIL	Current operation for when the stencil test passes, but the depth test fails	GL_KEEP	glGetIntegerv
GL_STENCIL_PASS_DEPTH_PASS	Current operation when both the stencil and depth tests pass	GL_KEEP	glGetIntegerv
GL_STENCIL_BACK_FUNC	Current back-facing stencil test operator function	GL_ALWAYS	glGetIntegerv
GL_STENCIL_BACK_VALUE_MASK	Current back-facing stencil test value mask	1s	glGetIntegerv
GL_STENCIL_BACK_REF	Current back-facing stencil test reference value	0	glGetIntegerv
GL_STENCIL_BACK_FAIL	Current operation for back-facing stencil test failure	GL_KEEP	glGetIntegerv
GL_STENCIL_BACK_PASS_DEPTH_FAIL	Current operation for when the back-facing stencil test passes, but the depth test fails	GL_KEEP	glGetIntegerv
GL_STENCIL_BACK_PASS_DEPTH_PASS	Current operation when both the back-facing stencil and depth tests pass	GL_KEEP	glGetIntegerv
GL_DEPTH_FUNC	Current depth test comparison function	GL_LESS	glGetIntegerv
GL_BLEND_SRC_RGB	Current source RGB blending coefficient	GL_ONE	glGetIntegerv
GL_BLEND_SRC_ALPHA	Current source alpha blending coefficient	GL_ONE	glGetIntegerv

Table 14-2   Application-Modifiable OpenGL ES State Queries *(continued)*

State Variable	Description	Minimum/ Initial Value	Get Function
GL_BLEND_DST_RGB	Current destination RGB blending coefficient	GL_ZERO	glGetIntegerv
GL_BLEND_DST_ALPHA	Current destination alpha blending coefficient	GL_ZERO	glGetIntegerv
GL_BLEND_EQUATION	Current blend equation operator	GL_FUNC_ADD	glGetIntegerv
GL_BLEND_EQUATION_RGB	Current RGB blend equation operator	GL_FUNC_ADD	glGetIntegerv
GL_BLEND_EQUATION_ALPHA	Current alpha blend equation operator	GL_FUNC_ADD	glGetIntegerv
GL_BLEND_COLOR	Current blend color	0, 0, 0, 0	glGetFloatv
GL_UNPACK_ALIGNMENT	Current byte-boundary alignment for pixel unpacking	4	glGetIntegerv
GL_PACK_ALIGNMENT	Current byte-boundary alignment for pixel packing	4	glGetIntegerv
GL_CURRENT_PROGRAM	Currently bound shader program	0	glGetIntegerv
GL_RENDERBUFFER_BINDING	Currently bound renderbuffer	0	glGetIntegerv
GL_FRAMEBUFFER_BINDING	Currently bound framebuffer	0	glGetIntegerv

Hints

OpenGL ES 2.0 uses hints to modify the operation of features, allowing a bias toward either performance or quality. You can specify a preference by calling the following.

```
void glHint (GLenum target, GLenum mode)
```

target	specifies the hint to be set, and must be either GL_GENERATE_MIPMAP_HINT or GL_FRAGMENT_SHADER_DERIVATIVE_HINT_OES
mode	specifies the operational mode the feature should use. Valid values are GL_FASTEST to specify performance, GL_NICEST to favor quality, or GL_DONT_CARE to reset any preferences to the implementation default

The current value of any hint can be retrieved by calling `glGetIntegerv` using the appropriate hint enumerated value.

Entity Name Queries

OpenGL ES 2.0 references numerous entities that you define—textures, shaders, programs, vertex buffers, framebuffers, and renderbuffers—by integer names. You can determine if a name is currently in use (and therefore a valid entity) by calling one of the following functions.

```
GLboolean glIsTexture (GLuint texture)
GLboolean glIsShader (GLuint shader)
GLboolean glIsProgram (GLuint program)
GLboolean glIsBuffer (GLuint buffer)
GLboolean glIsRenderbuffer (GLuint renderbuffer)
GLboolean glIsFramebuffer (GLunit framebuffer)
```

texture, shader, program, buffer, renderbuffer, framebuffer	specify the name of the respective entity to determine if the name is in use

Nonprogrammable Operations Control and Queries

Much of OpenGL ES 2.0's rasterization functionality, like blending or back-face culling, is controlled by turning on and off the features you need. The functions controlling the various operations are the following.

---

void **glEnable**(GLenum *capability*)

capability   specifies the feature that should be turned on and affects all rendering until the feature is turned off

---

void **glDisable**(GLenum *capability*)

capability   specifies the feature that should be turned off

Additionally, you can determine if a feature is in use by calling the following.

GLboolean **glIsEnabled**(GLenum *capability*)

capability   specifies which feature to determine if it's enabled

---

The capabilities controlled by glEnable and glDisable are listed in Table 14-3.

Table 14-3   OpenGL ES 2.0 Capabilities Controlled by glEnable and glDisable

Capability	Description
GL_CULL_FACE	Discard polygons whose vertex winding order is opposite of the specified front-facing mode (GL_CW or GL_CCW, as specified by glFrontFace)
GL_POLYGON_OFFSET_FILL	Offset the depth value of a fragment to aid in rendering coplanar geometry

Table 14-3 OpenGL ES 2.0 Capabilities Controlled by `glEnable` and `glDisable` (continued)

Capability	Description
GL_SCISSOR_TEST	Further restrict rendering to the scissor box
GL_SAMPLE_COVERAGE	Use a fragment's computed coverage value in multisampling operations
GL_SAMPLE_COVERAGE_TO_ALPHA	Use a fragment's alpha value as its coverage value in multisampling operations
GL_STENCIL_TEST	Enable the stencil test
GL_DEPTH_TEST	Enable the depth test
GL_BLEND	Enable blending
GL_DITHER	Enable dithering

Shader and Program State Queries

OpenGL ES 2.0 shaders and programs have a considerable amount of state that you can retrieve regarding their configuration, and attributes and uniform variables used by them. There are numerous functions provided for querying the state associated with shaders. To determine the shaders attached to a program, call the following.

void **glGetAttachedShaders**(GLuint *program*, GLsizei *maxcount*, GLsizei **count*, GLuint **shaders*)

program	Specifies the program to query to determine the attached shaders
maxcount	the maximum number of shader names to be returned
count	the actual number of shader names returned
shaders	an array of length maxcount used for storing the returned shader names

To retrieve the source code for a shader, call the following.

```
void glGetShaderSource(GLuint shader, GLsizei bufsize,
                       GLsizei *length, GLchar *source)
```

shader	specifies the shader to query
bufsize	the number of bytes available in the array source for returning the shader's source
length	the length of the returned shader string
source	specifies an array of GLchars to store the shader source to

To retrieve a value associated with a uniform variable at a particular uniform location associated with a shader program, call the following.

```
void glGetUniformfv(GLuint program, GLint location,
                    GLfloat *params)
void glGetUniformiv(GLuint program, GLint location,
                    GLint *params)
```

program	the program to query to retrieve the uniform's value
location	the uniform location associated with program to retrieve the values for
params	an array of the appropriate type for storing the uniform variable's values. The associated type of the uniform in the shader determines the number of values returned

Finally, to query the range and precision of OpenGL ES 2.0 shader language types, call the following.

```
void glGetShaderPrecisionFormat(GLenum shaderType,
                                GLenum precisionType,
                                GLint *range,
                                GLint *precision)
```

shaderType	specifies the type of shader, and must be either GL_VERTEX_SHADER or GL_FRAGMENT_SHADER
precisionType	specifies the precision qualifier type, and must be one of GL_LOW_FLOAT, GL_MEDIUM_FLOAT, GL_HIGH_FLOAT, GL_LOW_INT, GL_MEDIUM_INT, or GL_HIGH_INT
range	is a two-element array that returns the minimum and maximum value for *precisionType* as a log base-2 number
precision	returns the precision for *precisionType* as a log base-2 value

Vertex Attribute Queries

State about vertex attribute arrays can also be retrieved from the current OpenGL ES 2.0 context. To obtain the pointer to the current generic vertex attributes for a specific index, call the following.

```
void glGetVertexAttribPointerv (GLuint index, GLenum pname,
                                GLvoid** pointer)
```

index	specifies index of the generic vertex attribute array
pname	specifies the parameter to be retrieved, and must be GL_VERTEX_ATTRIB_ARRAY_POINTER
pointer	returns the address of the specified vertex attribute array

The associated state for accessing the data elements in the vertex attribute array such as value type, or stride can be obtained by calling the following.

```
void glGetVertexAttribfv (GLuint index, GLenum pname,
                          GLfloat* params)
void glGetVertexAttribiv (GLuint index, GLenum pname,
                          GLint* params)
```

index	specifies the index of generic vertex attribute array
pname	specifies the parameter to be retrieved, and must be one of GL_VERTEX_ATTRIB_ARRAY_BUFFER_BINDING, GL_VERTEX_ATTRIB_ARRAY_ENABLED, GL_VERTEX_ATTRIB_ARRAY_SIZE, GL_VERTEX_ATTRIB_ARRAY_STRIDE, GL_VERTEX_ATTRIB_ARRAY_TYPE, GL_VERTEX_ATTRIB_ARRAY_NORMALIZED, or GL_CURRENT_VERTEX_ATTRIB GL_CURRENT_VERTEX_ATTRIB returns the current vertex attribute as specified by glEnableVertexAttribeArray, and the other parameters are values specified when the vertex attribute pointer is specified by calling glVertexAttribPointer
params	specifies an array of the appropriate type for storing the returned parameter values

Texture State Queries

OpenGL ES 2.0 texture objects store a texture's image data, along with settings describing how the texels in the image should be sampled. The texture filter state, which includes the minification and magnification texture filters and texture-coordinate wrap modes are state that can be queried from the currently bound texture object. The following call retrieves the texture filter settings.

---

void **glGetTexParameterfv**(GLenum *target*, GLenum *pname*, GLfloat* *params*)

void **glGetTexParameteriv**(GLenum *target*, GLenum *pname*, GLint* *params*)

---

target	specifies the texture target, and can either be GL_TEXTURE_2D or GL_TEXTURE_CUBE_MAP
pname	specifies the texture filter parameter to be retrieved, and may be GL_TEXTURE_MINIFICATION_FILTER, GL_TEXTURE_MAGNIFICATION_FILTER, GL_TEXTURE_WRAP_S, or GL_TEXTURE_WRAP_T
params	specifies an array of the appropriate type for storing the returned parameter values

Vertex Buffer Queries

Vertex buffer objects have associated state describing the state and usage of the buffer. Those parameters can be retrieved by calling the following.

---

void **glGetBufferParameteriv**(GLenum *target*, GLenum *pname*, GLint* *params*)

---

target   specifies the buffer of the currently bound vertex buffer, and must be one of GL_ARRAY_BUFFER or GL_ELEMENT_ARRAY_BUFFER

pname   specifies the buffer parameter to be retrieved, and must be one of GL_BUFFER_SIZE, GL_BUFFER_USAGE, GL_BUFFER_ACCESS, or GL_BUFFER_MAPPED

params   specifies an integer array for storing the returned parameter values

---

Additionally, you can retrieve the current pointer address for a mapped buffer by calling the following.

---

void **glGetBufferPointervOES**(GLenum *target*, GLenum *pname*, void** *params*)

---

target   specifies the buffer of the currently bound vertex buffer, and must be one of GL_ARRAY_BUFFER or GL_ELEMENT_ARRAY_BUFFER

pname   specifies the parameter to retrieve, which must be GL_BUFFER_MAP_POINTER_OES

params   specifies a pointer for storing the returned address

---

Renderbuffer and Framebuffer State Queries

Characteristics of an allocated renderbuffer can be retrieved by calling the following.

```
void glGetRenderbufferParameteriv(GLenum target,
                                  GLenum pname,
                                  GLint* params)
```

target	specifies the target for the currently bound renderbuffer, and must be GL_RENDERBUFFER
pname	specifies the renderbuffer parameter to retrieve, and must be one of GL_RENDERBUFFER_WIDTH, GL_RENDERBUFFER_HEIGHT, GL_RENDERBUFFER_INTERNAL_FORMAT, GL_RENDERBUFFER_RED_SIZE, GL_RENDERBUFFER_GREEN_SIZE, GL_RENDERBUFFER_BLUE_SIZE, GL_RENDERBUFFER_ALPHA_SIZE, GL_RENDERBUFFER_DEPTH_SIZE, GL_RENDERBUFFER_STENCIL_SIZE
params	specifies an integer array for storing the returned parameter values

Likewise, the current attachments to a framebuffer can be queried by calling the following.

```
void glGetFramebufferAttachmentParameteriv(GLenum target,
        GLenum attachment, GLenum pname, GLint* params)
```

target	specifies the framebuffer target, and must be set to GL_FRAMEBUFFER
attachment	specifies which attachement point to query, and must be one of GL_COLOR_ATTACHMENT0, GL_DEPTH_ATTACHMENT or GL_STENCIL_ATTACHMENT.
pname	specifies GL_FRAMEBUFFER_ATTACHMENT_OBJECT_TYPE, GL_FRAMEBUFFER_ATTACHMENT_OBJECT_NAME, GL_FRAMEBUFFER_ATTACHMENT_TEXTURE_LEVEL, GL_FRAMEBUFFER_ATTACHMENT_TEXTURE_CUBE_MAP_FACE
params	specifies an integer array for storing the returned parameter values

Chapter 15

OpenGL ES and EGL on Handheld Platforms

By now, you should be familiar with the details of OpenGL ES 2.0 and EGL 1.3. In the final chapter, we divert ourselves a bit from the details of the APIs to talk about programming with OpenGL ES 2.0 and EGL in the real world. There are a diverse set of handheld platforms in the market that pose some interesting issues and challenges when developing applications for OpenGL ES 2.0. Here, we seek to cover some of those issues by discussing these handheld platform issues:

- C++ portability.
- OpenKODE.
- Platform-specific shader binaries.
- Targeting extensions.

Handheld Platforms Overview

Knowing OpenGL ES 2.0 and EGL 1.3 is a critical step to writing games and applications for handheld platforms. However, a big part of the challenge in targeting handheld devices is coping with the diversity of platforms. One of the biggest issues today in the handheld market is the fragmentation in development capabilities and environments available on handheld platforms. Let's start by taking a look at some of the biggest platforms out there today.

- Nokia—Series 60 on Symbian.
- Qualcomm—BREW.

- Microsoft—Windows Mobile.

- Embedded Linux.

- Sony Ericsson—UIQ on Symbian.

In addition to operating systems (OSs), a wide variety of CPUs are in use. Most of the architectures are based on the ARM processor family, which supports a wide variety of features. Some CPUs support floating-point natively, whereas others do not. Targeting ARM means you need to be cognizant of aligning data to 32-bit boundaries and potentially providing your own fast floating-point emulation library (or using fixed-point math).

Some of the OSs—Windows Mobile and Embedded Linux in particular—provide the most straightforward and familiar development environment for Windows/Linux developers. For example, Microsoft provides an embedded version of Visual C++ that contains much of the functionality of the desktop Windows version. In addition, a subset of the Win32 API is available, making portability easier.

Other of the OSs—Symbian and BREW in particular—are quite different than what PC and console developers are used to. One needs to be very careful about which C++ features are used, not having writeable static global variables, managing memory, and a host of other issues. The issue with writable static global variables is that some handheld OSs store applications as dynamic link libraries (DLLs) and the static data end up being in read-only memory (ROM) and therefore cannot be written to. In addition to code issues, Symbian, for example, provides an entirely new toolchain called Carbide based on the Eclipse IDE. This means learning to use a new debugger, new project files (called MMP files in Symbian), and a set of new OS APIs.

Online Resources

Given the wide array of handheld platforms, we thought it would be useful to give a quick guide to where to get information to start developing for each of the platforms. If you plan to target Nokia devices, you will want to visit http://forum.nokia.com, where you can freely download the Series 60 Software Development Kit (SDK) along with a wide array of documentation. As of this writing, Nokia already provides support in its SDK for OpenGL ES 1.1 so you can look at the existing OpenGL ES samples to get a feel for how you will develop OpenGL ES 2.0 applications. Developers targeting Symbian on Sony Ericsson devices using UIQ can find information at http://developer.sonyericsson.com.

Likewise, the Qualcomm BREW SDK is available from http://brew.qual-comm.com and supports OpenGL ES 1.0 plus extensions. As of this writing, OpenGL ES 2.0 is not yet supported. However, just as with the Series 60 SDK, you can begin developing applications for BREW and start learning about the platform portability issues. Qualcomm has already announced plans to support OpenGL ES 2.0 in its forthcoming MSM7850 with the LT graphics core.

For developers looking to get started with Windows Mobile, Microsoft hosts a Windows Mobile Developer Center at http://msdn2.microsoft.com/en-us/windowsmobile/default.aspx. If you already have Microsoft Visual Studio 2005, you can download the relevant Windows Mobile 6 SDK and develop directly in Visual Studio 2005. A large number of devices support Windows Mobile 6, such as the Moto Q, Palm Treo 750, Pantech Duo, HTC Touch, and many more. As of yet, there are no devices supporting OpenGL ES 2.0, but we can expect such devices in the future.

Finally, for developers looking to get started with Embedded Linux, check out www.linuxdevices.com. There were several Embedded Linux devices that entered the market in 2007, such as the Nokia N800 Internet tablet. For developers wanting to develop OpenGL ES 2.0 applications under regular Linux (not embedded), Imagination Technologies has released its OpenGL ES 2.0 wrapper for Linux. This can be downloaded from www.powervrin-sider.com.

C++ Portability

The first decision you need to make when developing your OpenGL ES 2.0 application is which language you will use. Many handheld developers choose to use plain vanilla C, and with good reason. C++ portability can be a significant issue because different platforms have varying levels of support for C++ features. The reason that many C++ features are not supported is because they can be burdensome for the implementation. Remember, we are working on handheld devices here, and conserving memory and power are significant goals of handheld OSs. However, this means the C++ features you might be accustomed to using are not available on handheld platforms.

For example, Symbian 8 does not support throwing C++ exceptions. This means that using exceptions in your C++ code would not be portable (Symbian does provide its own exception mechanism, but it is not the standard C++ way). This lack of exceptions also means that Symbian 8 does not support Standard Template Library (STL). To implement conformant STL, it is necessary to be able to throw exceptions. As a consequence, Symbian provides its own set of container classes that you can use. The long and short of this is that using STL might not be portable to certain platforms.

Another consequence of Symbian 8 not supporting C++ exceptions is that that the programmer must manually manage a cleanup stack. That is, to properly support the new operator failing in C++, one must be able to throw an exception. Instead, on Symbian, the programmer becomes responsible for managing the cleanup stack themselves and objects are created with two-phase construction. Having this sort of code in a portable engine is really not an option. As a consequence, some developers choose to write their own memory manager on Symbian. They allocate a block of memory at startup of a known size they will need and then manage all allocations themselves so that they do not have to litter their code with Symbian-specific cleanup code.

With all that said, a lot of the C++ portability issues were fixed in Symbian 9. However, the point here was to give you a flavor of the types of C++ limitations one finds on handheld platforms. There are a number of features you simply cannot be confident will be supported on all handheld devices. For example, features such as runtime type information, exceptions, multiple inheritance, and STL might not be present. To guarantee portability, you will want to restrict your use of C++. Or, like many developers, simply write your application in C.

If you choose to use C++, the following is a list of features that you should avoid to gain portability:

- Runtime type information—For example, the use of dynamic_cast, which requires an implementation to know the runtime type of a class.

- Exceptions—The standard C++ mechanism of try-catch is not supported on some handheld OSs.

- Standard Template Library—Although STL provides many useful classes, it also requires exceptions that are not supported on all handheld OSs.

- Multiple inheritance—Some handheld implementations of C++ do not allow classes that are derived from multiple classes.

- Global data—Some handheld OSs store applications in ROM, and thus having static writeable data is not possible.

This list is not comprehensive, but represents things we have run into as being issues on handheld platforms. You might ask yourself what good a language standard (e.g., C++) is if vendors choose to create nonstandard implementations. There is a valid argument to be made that one should not claim to be supporting C++ without supporting such basic features of the language. In time, it probably will be the case that full C++ will be supported on embedded devices. However, for now, we must live with the choices that platform vendors have made and adjust our code accordingly.

OpenKODE

Aside from C++ inconsistencies across platforms, another major barrier to portability is the lack of common OS APIs. For example, features like input/output, file access, time, math, and events are handled differently on various operating systems. Dealing with these sorts of differences is old hat for seasoned game developers. Most portable game engines are written with abstraction layers for each of the various platforms. The portable portions of the code will not make calls into any OS-specific functions but rather use the abstraction layers.

The issue on handheld platforms is that writing your own abstraction layers has been made orders of magnitude more difficult by the large number of handheld platforms. Also, finding a common set of features across different OSs is very difficult for someone new to handheld platforms. Fortunately, the Khronos group recognized this as a significant barrier to the handheld ecosystem and has invented a new API to deal with it called OpenKODE.

The OpenKODE 1.0 specification was released in February 2008. Open-KODE provides a standard set of APIs (including OpenGL ES and EGL) to which an application can write in order to access functionality on the system. OpenKODE Core provides APIs for events, memory allocation, file access, input/output, math, network sockets, and more. To introduce you to the concept of using OpenKODE, we ported our Hello Triangle example program to use OpenKODE. We removed any calls to OS-specific functions and removed any dependencies on our ES application framework.

A code listing for the example that can be found in Chapter_15/Hello_Triangle_KD is shown in Example 15-1.

Example 15-1 Hello Triangle Using OpenKODE

```
#include <KD/kd.h>
#include <EGL/egl.h>
#include <GLES2/gl2.h>
```

```
typedef struct
{
    // Handle to a program object
    GLuint programObject;

    // EGL handles
    EGLDisplay eglDisplay;
    EGLContext eglContext;
    EGLSurface eglSurface;

} UserData;

///
// Create a shader object, load the shader source, and
// compile the shader.
//
GLuint LoadShader(GLenum type, const char *shaderSrc) {
    GLuint shader;
    GLint compiled;

    // Create the shader object
    shader = glCreateShader(type);

    if(shader == 0)
        return 0;

    // Load the shader source
    glShaderSource(shader, 1, &shaderSrc, NULL);

    // Compile the shader
    glCompileShader(shader);

    // Check the compile status
    glGetShaderiv(shader, GL_COMPILE_STATUS, &compiled);

    if(!compiled)
    {
        GLint infoLen = 0;

        glGetShaderiv(shader, GL_INFO_LOG_LENGTH, &infoLen);

        if(infoLen > 1)
        {
            char* infoLog = kdMalloc(sizeof(char) * infoLen);

            glGetShaderInfoLog(shader, infoLen, NULL, infoLog);
            kdLogMessage(infoLog);

            kdFree(infoLog);
```

```
      }

      glDeleteShader(shader);
      return 0;
   }

   return shader;

}

///
// Initialize the shader and program object
//
int Init(UserData *userData) {
   GLbyte vShaderStr[] =
      "attribute vec4 vPosition;    \n"
      "void main()                  \n"
      "{                            \n"
      "   gl_Position = vPosition;  \n"
      "}                            \n";

   GLbyte fShaderStr[] =
      "precision mediump float;\n"\
      "void main()                                \n"
      "{                                          \n"
      "  gl_FragColor = vec4(1.0, 0.0, 0.0, 1.0); \n"
      "}                                          \n";

   GLuint vertexShader;
   GLuint fragmentShader;
   GLuint programObject;
   GLint linked;

   // Load the vertex/fragment shaders
   vertexShader = LoadShader(GL_VERTEX_SHADER, vShaderStr);
   fragmentShader = LoadShader(GL_FRAGMENT_SHADER, fShaderStr);

   // Create the program object
   programObject = glCreateProgram();

   if(programObject == 0)
      return 0;

   glAttachShader(programObject, vertexShader);
   glAttachShader(programObject, fragmentShader);

   // Bind vPosition to attribute 0
   glBindAttribLocation(programObject, 0, "vPosition");
```

```
   // Link the program
   glLinkProgram(programObject);

   // Check the link status
   glGetProgramiv(programObject, GL_LINK_STATUS, &linked);

   if(!linked)
   {
      GLint infoLen = 0;

      glGetProgramiv(programObject, GL_INFO_LOG_LENGTH, &infoLen);

      if(infoLen > 1)
      {
         char* infoLog = kdMalloc(sizeof(char) * infoLen);

         glGetProgramInfoLog(programObject, infoLen, NULL, infoLog);
         kdLogMessage(infoLog);

         kdFree(infoLog);
      }

      glDeleteProgram(programObject);
      return FALSE;
   }

   // Store the program object
   userData->programObject = programObject;

   glClearColor(0.0f, 0.0f, 0.0f, 0.0f);
   return TRUE;
}

///
// Draw a triangle using the shader pair created in Init()
//
void Draw(UserData *userData) {
   GLfloat vVertices[] = {  0.0f,  0.5f, 0.0f,
                           -0.5f, -0.5f, 0.0f,
                            0.5f, -0.5f, 0.0f };

   // Set the viewport
   glViewport(0, 0, 320, 240);

   // Clear the color buffer
   glClear(GL_COLOR_BUFFER_BIT);

   // Use the program object
   glUseProgram(userData->programObject);
```

```
    // Load the vertex data
    glVertexAttribPointer(0, 3, GL_FLOAT, GL_FALSE, 0, vVertices);
    glEnableVertexAttribArray(0);

    glDrawArrays(GL_TRIANGLES, 0, 3);

    eglSwapBuffers(userData->eglDisplay, userData->eglSurface); }


///
// InitEGLContext()
//
// Initialize an EGL rendering context and all associated elements
//
EGLBoolean InitEGLContext(UserData *userData,
                          KDWindow *window,
                          EGLConfig config) {
    EGLContext context;
    EGLSurface surface;
    EGLint contextAttribs[] = { EGL_CONTEXT_CLIENT_VERSION, 2,
                                EGL_NONE, EGL_NONE };

    // Get native window handle
    EGLNativeWindowType hWnd;
    if(kdRealizeWindow(window, &hWnd) != 0)
    {
        return EGL_FALSE;
    }
    surface = eglCreateWindowSurface(userData->eglDisplay, config,
                                     hWnd, NULL);
    if(surface == EGL_NO_SURFACE)
    {
        return EGL_FALSE;
    }

    // Create a GL context
    context = eglCreateContext(userData->eglDisplay, config,
                               EGL_NO_CONTEXT, contextAttribs );
    if(context == EGL_NO_CONTEXT)
    {
        return EGL_FALSE;
    }

    // Make the context current
    if(!eglMakeCurrent(userData->eglDisplay, surface, surface,
                       context))
    {
        return EGL_FALSE;
    }
```

```
        userData->eglContext = context;
        userData->eglSurface = surface;

        return EGL_TRUE;
}

///
// kdMain()
//
// Main function for OpenKODE application
//
KDint kdMain(KDint argc, const KDchar *const *argv) {
    EGLint attribList[] =
    {
        EGL_RED_SIZE,        8,
        EGL_GREEN_SIZE,      8,
        EGL_BLUE_SIZE,       8,
        EGL_ALPHA_SIZE,      EGL_DONT_CARE,
        EGL_DEPTH_SIZE,      EGL_DONT_CARE,
        EGL_STENCIL_SIZE,    EGL_DONT_CARE,
        EGL_NONE
    };
    EGLint majorVersion,
        minorVersion;
    UserData userData;
    EGLint numConfigs;
    EGLConfig config;
    KDWindow *window = KD_NULL;

    userData.eglDisplay = eglGetDisplay(EGL_DEFAULT_DISPLAY);

    // Initialize EGL
    if(!eglInitialize(userData.eglDisplay, &majorVersion,
                      &minorVersion) )
    {
        return EGL_FALSE;
    }

    // Get configs
    if(!eglGetConfigs(userData.eglDisplay, NULL, 0, &numConfigs))
    {
        return EGL_FALSE;
    }

    // Choose config
    if(!eglChooseConfig(userData.eglDisplay, attribList, &config,
        1, &numConfigs))
    {
```

```
        return EGL_FALSE;
    }


    // Use OpenKODE to create a Window
    window = kdCreateWindow(userData.eglDisplay, config, KD_NULL);
    if(!window)
        kdExit(0);

    if(!InitEGLContext(&userData, window, config))
        kdExit(0);

    if(!Init(&userData))
        kdExit(0);

    // Main Loop
    while(1)
    {
        // Wait for an event
        const KDEvent *evt = kdWaitEvent(0);
        if ( evt )
        {
            // Exit app
            if(evt->type == KD_EVENT_WINDOW_CLOSE)
                break;
        }

        // Draw frame
        Draw(&userData);
    }

    // EGL clean up
    eglMakeCurrent(0, 0, 0, 0);
    eglDestroySurface(userData.eglDisplay, userData.eglSurface);
    eglDestroyContext(userData.eglDisplay, userData.eglContext);

    // Destroy the window
    kdDestroyWindow(window);

    return 0;
}
```

The functions that are part of OpenKODE Core are preceded by the `kd` prefix. The main function of an OpenKODE application is named `kdMain()`. You will notice that this example uses OpenKODE functions for all of the window creation and setup. EGL is used for creating and initializing the OpenGL ES rendering surface in the window. In addition, the example uses

OpenKODE functions for memory allocation (`kdMalloc()` and `kdFree()`) and logging of messages (`kdLogMessage()`).

This example was purposefully simple just to show that by using Open-KODE we were able to remove any OS-specific calls from our sample application. There are many more functions available in OpenKODE. Had we chosen to do so, the entire application framework we wrote could have been layered on OpenKODE to provide more portability. A full treatment of the OpenKODE core API would warrant a book unto itself so we are just barely scratching the surface here. If you are interested in using OpenKODE in your application, you can go to www.khronos.org/ to download the specification.

Platform-Specific Shader Binaries

In addition to code portability, one of the other issues OpenGL ES 2.0 developers are going to have to tackle is the building and distribution of shader binaries. As you will recall, OpenGL ES 2.0 provides a mechanism whereby an application can provide its shaders in a precompiled binary format. This will be desirable on some platforms for a number of reasons. First, it will very likely reduce load times for your application because the driver will not need to do compilation of shaders. Second, offline shader compilers might be able to do a better job of optimization because they do not have to run under the same memory and time constraints as an online compiler. Third, some implementations of OpenGL ES 2.0 will support only shader binaries, which will mean that you will have to compile your shaders offline.

There are a few issues as a developer of an OpenGL ES 2.0 application you need to consider for targeting multiple platforms with shader binaries. First, it must be understood that shader binaries are inherently non-portable. The binaries may be tied to the device, GPU, or even the driver or OS revision on which your application will run. The binary shader format is defined to be opaque. That is, device vendors are free to store binary shaders in any non-portable format they wish. In general, it is likely that vendors will store the shaders in their final hardware binary.

The second issue is that generation of binary shaders does not have any defined mechanism in the API standard. Each device or GPU vendor is free to build its own tool suite for generating binary shaders and it will be incumbent on you to make sure your engine can support each vendor's toolchain. For example, AMD provides a Windows executable called MakeBinaryShader.exe, which compiles text shaders into binary. AMD also provides a library-based interface, BinaryShader.lib, which provides functions that you can call into to compile your shaders directly from within an application. Imagination Technologies also provides its own binary shader compilation tool called PVRUniSCo along with an editor called PVRUniSCo Editor. You can be sure that other vendors will come along with their own binary compilation tools as well.

A third issue with binary shaders is that the vendor extension that defines the shader binaries might put restrictions on how those binaries can be used. For instance, the shader compiler binaries might only be optimal (or possibly only even functional) when used with a specific OpenGL ES state vector. As an example, it's possible that a vendor can define that the shader compilation process accepts input defining that the binary will be used only with fragment blending or multisampling, and the binary might not be valid if these features are not enabled. These restrictions are left to the vendor to define, so application developers are encouraged to consult the vendor-specific extensions defining a given shader binary format.

Your engine will need to support a preprocessing path whereby you can choose one of the device vendors' tools and store a binary shader package to go along with the app. There is one alternative that AMD (and likely other vendors) will offer in its OpenGL ES 2.0 implementation. AMD will provide an extension whereby an application can call into the driver to retrieve a compiled program binary. In other words, an application will load and compile shaders online in the driver and then it can request the final compiled binary back from the driver and store it out to a file. This binary is in the same format as the binary provided by the offline compilation tool. The advantage to this approach is that an application can compile its shaders on first run (or at install time) using the driver and then read back the shader binaries and store them directly on the device. You should be prepared to handle this type of binary shader compilation path in your engine as well.

Targeting Extensions

Throughout the book, we have introduced you to a number of extensions for features such as 3D textures, ETC, depth textures, and derivatives. The extensions we covered in the book were all Khronos-ratified extensions that will be supported by multiple vendors. That said, not all vendors will support these extensions, which is why they are not part of the standard. You will also encounter extensions that are specific to a single vendor. For example, both AMD and Imagination Technologies provide their own extensions for texture compression formats supported by their hardware. To fully take advantage of the underlying hardware, it will often be useful to use such extensions in your engine.

To maintain portability across OpenGL ES devices, you must have proper fallback paths in your engine. For any extension you use, you must check that the extension string is present in the GL_EXTENSIONS string. For extensions that modify the shading language, you must use the #extension mechanism to explicitly enable them. If an extension is not present, you will need to write fallback paths. For example, if you use some extension for a compressed texture format, you will need to retain the ability to load an uncompressed version of the texture if the extension does not exit. If you use the 3D texture extension, you will need to provide a fallback texture and shader path to substitute for the effect.

If you want to guarantee portability across platforms and are unable to write fallback paths for specific extensions, you should avoid using them. Given the level of platform fragmentation that already exists in terms of OS and device capabilities, you do not want to make the problem worse by making your engine use OpenGL ES 2.0 in a non-portable way. The good news here is that the rules for writing portable OpenGL ES 2.0 applications are really no different than for desktop OpenGL. Checking for extensions and writing fallback paths is a fact of life you need to live with if you want to harness the latest features offered by OpenGL ES 2.0 implementations.

GL_HALF_FLOAT_OES

GL_HALF_FLOAT_OES is an optional vertex data format supported by OpenGL ES 2.0. The extension string that implements this vertex data format is named GL_OES_vertex_half_float. To determine whether this feature is supported by an OpenGL ES 2.0 implementation, look for the string name GL_OES_vertex_half_float in the list of extensions returned by glGetString(GL_EXTENSIONS).

The GL_HALF_FLOAT_OES vertex data type is used to specify 16-bit floating-point vertex data attributes. This can be very useful in specifying vertex attributes such as texture coordinates, normal, binormal, and tangent vectors. Using GL_HALF_FLOAT_OES over GL_FLOAT provides a two times reduction in memory footprint. In addition, memory bandwidth required to read vertex attributes by the GPU is also reduced by approximately two times.

One can argue that we can use GL_SHORT or GL_UNSIGNED_SHORT instead of a 16-bit floating-point data type and get the same memory footprint and bandwidth savings. However you will now need to scale the data or matrices appropriately and apply a transform in the vertex shader. For example, consider the case where a texture pattern is to be repeated four times horizontally and vertically over a quad. GL_SHORT can be used to store the texture coordinates. The texture coordinates could be stored as a 4.12 or 8.8 value. The texture coordinate values stored as GL_SHORT are scaled by $(1 << 12)$ or $(1 << 8)$ to give us a fixed-point representation that uses 4 bits or 8 bits of integer and 12 bits or 8 bits of fraction. Because OpenGL ES does not understand such a format, the vertex shader will then need to apply a matrix to unscale these values, which impacts the vertex shading performance. These additional transforms are not required if a 16-bit floating-point format is used.

Note: Note that if `GL_SHORT` is used to describe the texture coordinates, the texture coordinates will probably be generated using fixed-point. This implies a different error metric as the absolute error in a floating-point number is proportional to the magnitude of the value, whereas absolute error in a fixed-point format is constant. Developers need to be aware of these precision issues when choosing which data type to use when generating coordinates for a particular format.

16-Bit Floating-Point Number

Figure A-1 describes the representation of a half-float number. A half-float is a 16-bit floating-point number with 10 bits of mantissa **m**, 5 bits of exponent **e**, and a sign bit **s**.

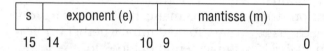

s	exponent (e)	mantissa (m)
15	14 10	9 0

Figure A-1   16-Bit Floating-Point Number

The following rules should be used when interpreting a 16-bit floating-point number:

- If exponent e is between 1 and 30, the half-float value is computed as $(-1)^s * 2^{e-15} * (1 + m/1{,}024)$.

- If exponent e and mantissa m are both 0, the half-float value is 0.0. The sign bit is used to represent a –ve 0.0 or a +ve 0.0.

- If exponent e is 0 and mantissa m is not 0, the half-float value is a denormalized number.

- If exponent e is 31, the half-float value is either infinity (+ve or –ve) or a NaN depending on whether the mantissa m is zero or not.

A few examples follow.

```
0   00000   0000000000   = 0.0
0   00000   0000001111   = a denorm value
0   11111   0000000000   = positive infinity
1   11111   0000000000   = negative infinity
0   11111   0000011000   = NaN
1   11111   1111111111   = NaN
0   01111   0000000000   = 1.0
1   01110   0000000000   = -0.5
0   10100   1010101010   = 54.375
```

OpenGL ES 2.0 implementations must be able to accept input half-float data values that are infinity, NaN or denormalized numbers. They do not have to support 16-bit floating-point arithmetic operations with these values. Typically most implementations will convert denorms and NaN values to zero.

Converting Float to Half-Float

The following routines describe how to convert a single precision floating-point number to a half-float value and vice versa. The conversion routines are useful when vertex attributes are generated using single precision floating-point calculations but then get converted to half-floats before they are used as vertex attributes.

```
// -15 stored using a single precision bias of 127
const unsigned int  HALF_FLOAT_MIN_BIASED_EXP_AS_SINGLE_FP_EXP = 0x38000000;
// max exponent value in single precision that will be converted
// to Inf or Nan when stored as a half-float
const unsigned int  HALF_FLOAT_MAX_BIASED_EXP_AS_SINGLE_FP_EXP = 0x47800000;

// 255 is the max exponent biased value
const unsigned int  FLOAT_MAX_BIASED_EXP = (0xFF << 23);

const unsigned int  HALF_FLOAT_MAX_BIASED_EXP = (0x1F << 10);

typedef unsigned short    hfloat;

hfloat
convertFloatToHFloat(float *f)
{
    unsigned int    x = *(unsigned int *)f;
    unsigned int    sign = (unsigned short)(x >> 31);
    unsigned int    mantissa;
    unsigned int    exp;
    hfloat          hf;

    // get mantissa
    mantissa = x & ((1 << 23) - 1);
    // get exponent bits
    exp = x & FLOAT_MAX_BIASED_EXP;
    if (exp >= HALF_FLOAT_MAX_BIASED_EXP_AS_SINGLE_FP_EXP)
    {
        // check if the original single precision float number is a NaN
        if (mantissa && (exp == FLOAT_MAX_BIASED_EXP))
        {
            // we have a single precision NaN
            mantissa = (1 << 23) - 1;
        }
        else
        {
            // 16-bit half-float representation stores number as Inf
            mantissa = 0;
        }
        hf = (((hfloat)sign) << 15) | (hfloat)(HALF_FLOAT_MAX_BIASED_EXP) |
            (hfloat)(mantissa >> 13);
    }
    // check if exponent is <= -15
    else if (exp <= HALF_FLOAT_MIN_BIASED_EXP_AS_SINGLE_FP_EXP)
    {
```

```
            // store a denorm half-float value or zero
            exp = (HALF_FLOAT_MIN_BIASED_EXP_AS_SINGLE_FP_EXP - exp) >> 23;
            mantissa >>= (14 + exp);

            hf = (((hfloat)sign) << 15) | (hfloat)(mantissa);
        }
        else
        {
            hf = (((hfloat)sign) << 15) |
                 (hfloat)((exp - HALF_FLOAT_MIN_BIASED_EXP_AS_SINGLE_FP_EXP) >> 13) |
                 (hfloat)(mantissa >> 13);
        }

    return hf;
}

float
convertHFloatToFloat(hfloat hf)
{
    unsigned int    sign = (unsigned int)(hf >> 15);
    unsigned int    mantissa = (unsigned int)(hf & ((1 << 10) - 1));
    unsigned int    exp = (unsigned int)(hf & HALF_FLOAT_MAX_BIASED_EXP);
    unsigned int    f;

    if (exp == HALF_FLOAT_MAX_BIASED_EXP)
    {
        // we have a half-float NaN or Inf
        // half-float NaNs will be converted to a single precision NaN
        // half-float Infs will be converted to a single precision Inf
        exp = FLOAT_MAX_BIASED_EXP;
        if (mantissa)
            mantissa = (1 << 23) - 1;    // set all bits to indicate a NaN
    }
    else if (exp == 0x0)
    {
        // convert half-float zero/denorm to single precision value
        if (mantissa)
        {
            mantissa <<= 1;
            exp = HALF_FLOAT_MIN_BIASED_EXP_AS_SINGLE_FP_EXP;
            // check for leading 1 in denorm mantissa
            while ((mantissa & (1 << 10)) == 0)
            {
                // for every leading 0, decrement single precision exponent by 1
                // and shift half-float mantissa value to the left
                mantissa <<= 1;
                exp -= (1 << 23);
            }
            // clamp the mantissa to 10-bits
            mantissa &= ((1 << 10) - 1);
            // shift left to generate single-precision mantissa of 23-bits
            mantissa <<= 13;
        }
    }
    else
    {
        // shift left to generate single-precision mantissa of 23-bits
        mantissa <<= 13;
        // generate single precision biased exponent value
        exp = (exp << 13) + HALF_FLOAT_MIN_BIASED_EXP_AS_SINGLE_FP_EXP;
    }

    f = (sign << 31) | exp | mantissa;
    return *((float *)&f);
}
```

Built-In Functions

The OpenGL ES shading language built-in functions described in this appendix are copyrighted by Khronos and are reprinted with permission. The latest OpenGL ES 2.0 specification can be downloaded from www.khronos.org/opengles/2_X/.

The OpenGL ES shading language defines an assortment of built-in convenience functions for scalar and vector operations. Many of these built-in functions can be used in more than one type of shader, but some are intended to provide a direct mapping to hardware and so are available only for a specific type of shader.

The built-in functions basically fall into three categories:

- They expose some necessary hardware functionality in a convenient way such as accessing a texture map. There is no way in the language for these functions to be emulated by a shader.

- They represent a trivial operation (clamp, mix, etc.) that is very simple for the user to write, but they are very common and might have direct hardware support. It is a very hard problem for the compiler to map expressions to complex assembler instructions.

- They represent an operation graphics hardware that is likely to accelerate at some point. The trigonometry functions fall into this category.

Many of the functions are similar to the same named ones in common C libraries, but they support vector input as well as the more traditional scalar input.

Applications should be encouraged to use the built-in functions rather than do the equivalent computations in their own shader code because the built-in functions are assumed to be optimal (e.g., perhaps supported directly in hardware).

User code can overload the built-in functions but cannot redefine them. When the built-in functions are specified here, where the input arguments (and corresponding output) can be `float`, `vec2`, `vec3`, or `vec4`, `genType` is used as the argument. For any specific use of a function, the actual type has to be the same for all arguments and for the return type. Similarly for `mat`, which can be a `mat2`, `mat3`, or `mat4`. Precision qualifiers for parameters and return values are not shown. For the texture functions, the precision of the return type matches the precision of the sampler type.

```
uniform lowp sampler2D sampler;

highp vec2 coord;

...

lowp vec4 col = texture2D(sampler, coord); // texture2D returns lowp
```

The precision qualification of other built-in function formal parameters is irrelevant. A call to these built-in functions will return a precision qualification matching the highest precision qualification of the call's input arguments.

Angle and Trigonometry Functions

Table B-1 describes the built-in angle and trigonometry functions. These functions can be used within vertex and fragment shaders. The function parameters specified as *angle* are assumed to be in units of radians. In no case will any of these functions result in a divide by zero error. If the divisor of a ratio is 0, then results will be undefined. These all operate component-wise.

Table B-1   Angle and Trigonometry Functions

Syntax	Description
float **radians** (float *degrees*) vec2 **radians** (vec2 *degrees*) vec3 **radians** (vec3 *degrees*) vec4 **radians** (vec4 *degrees*)	Converts *degrees* to radians, i.e., π / 180 * *degrees*.

Table B-1   Angle and Trigonometry Functions *(continued)*

Syntax	Description
float **degrees** (float *radians*) vec2 **degrees** (vec2 *radians*) vec3 **degrees** (vec3 *radians*) vec4 **degrees** (vec4 *radians*)	Converts *radians* to degrees, i.e., 180 / π * *radians*.
float **sin** (float *angle*) vec2 **sin** (vec2 *angle*) vec3 **sin** (vec3 *angle*) vec4 **sin** (vec4 *angle*)	The standard trigonometric sine function. Returns values are in the range [–1, 1].
float **cos** (float *angle*) vec2 **cos** (vec2 *angle*) vec3 **cos** (vec3 *angle*) vec4 **cos** (vec4 *angle*)	The standard trigonometric cosine function. Returns values are in the range [–1, 1].
float **tan** (float *angle*) vec2 **tan** (vec2 *angle*) vec3 **tan** (vec3 *angle*) vcc4 **tan** (vec4 *angle*)	The standard trigonometric tangent function.
float **asin** (float *x*) vec2 **asin** (vec2 *x*) vec3 **asin** (vec3 *x*) vec4 **asin** (vec4 *x*)	Arc sine. Returns an angle whose sine is *x*. The range of values returned by this function is [–π/2, π/2] . Results are undefined if |*x*| > 1.
float **acos** (float *x*) vec2 **acos** (vec2 *x*) vec3 **acos** (vec3 *x*) vec4 **acos** (vec4 *x*)	Arc cosine. Returns an angle with cosine *x*. The range of values returned by this function is [0, π]. Results are undefined if |*x*|>1.
float **atan** (float *y*, float *x*) vec2 **atan** (vec2 *y*, vec2 *x*) vec3 **atan** (vec3 *y*, vec3 *x*) vec4 **atan** (vec4 *y*, vec4 *x*)	Arc tangent. Returns an angle with tangent *y/x*. The signs of *x* and *y* are used to determine what quadrant the angle is in. The range of values returned by this function is [–π, π]. Results are undefined if *x* and *y* are both 0.
float **atan** (float *y_over_x*) vec2 **atan** (vec2 *y_over_x*) vec3 **atan** (vec3 *y_over_x*) vec4 **atan** (vec4 *y_over_x*)	Arc tangent. Returns an angle with tangent *y_over_x*. The range of values returned by this function is [–π/2, π/2].

Exponential Functions

Table B-2 describes the built-in exponential functions. These functions can be used within vertex and fragment shaders. These functions operate component-wise.

Table B-2   Exponential Functions

Syntax	Description
float **pow** (float x, float y) vec2 **pow** (vec2 x, vec2 y) vec3 **pow** (vec3 x, vec3 y) vec4 **pow** (vec4 x, vec4 y)	Returns x raised to the y power, i.e., x^y. Results are undefined if $x < 0$. Results are undefined if $x = 0$ and $y <= 0$.
float **exp** (float x) vec2 **exp** (vec2 x) vec3 **exp** (vec3 x) vec4 **exp** (vec4 x)	Returns the natural exponentiation of x, i.e., e^x.
float **log** (float *angle*) vec2 **log** (vec2 *angle*) vec3 **log** (vec3 *angle*) vec4 **log** (vec4 *angle*)	Returns the natural logarithm of x, i.e., returns the value y, which satisfies the equation $x = e^y$. Results are undefined if $x <= 0$.
float **exp2** (float *angle*) vec2 **exp2** (vec2 *angle*) vec3 **exp2** (vec3 *angle*) vec4 **exp2** (vec4 *angle*)	Returns 2 raised to the x power, i.e., 2^x.
float **log2** (float *angle*) vec2 **log2** (vec2 *angle*) vec3 **log2** (vec3 *angle*) vec4 **log2** (vec4 *angle*)	Returns the base 2 logarithm of x, i.e., returns the value y, which satisfies the equation $x = 2^y$. Results are undefined if $x <= 0$.
float **sqrt** (float x) vec2 **sqrt** (vec2 x) vec3 **sqrt** (vec3 x) vec4 **sqrt** (vec4 x)	Returns the positive square root of x. Results are undefined if $x < 0$.
float **inversesqrt** (float x) vec2 **inversesqrt** (vec2 x) vec3 **inversesqrt** (vec3 x) vec4 **inversesqrt** (vec4 x)	Returns the reciprocal of the positive square root of x. Results are undefined if x <= 0.

Common Functions

Table B-3 describes the built-in common functions. These functions can be used within vertex and fragment shaders. These functions operate component-wise.

Table B-3   Common Functions

Syntax	Description
float **abs** (float x) vec2 **abs** (vec2 x) vec3 **abs** (vec3 x) vec4 **abs** (vec4 x)	Returns x if $x >= 0$, otherwise it returns $-x$.
float **sign** (float x) vec2 **sign** (vec2 x) vec3 **sign** (vec3 x) vec4 **sign** (vec4 x)	Returns 1.0 if $x > 0$, 0.0 if $x = 0$, or -1.0 if $x < 0$.
float **floor** (float x) vec2 **floor** (vec2 x) vec3 **floor** (vec3 x) vec4 **floor** (vec4 x)	Returns a value equal to the nearest integer that is less than or equal to x.
float **ceil** (float x) vec2 **ceil** (vec2 x) vec3 **ceil** (vec3 x) vec4 **ceil** (vec4 x)	Returns a value equal to the nearest integer that is greater than or equal to x.
float **fract** (float x) vec2 **fract** (vec2 x) vec3 **fract** (vec3 x) vec4 **fract** (vec4 x)	Returns $x -$ **floor** (x).
float **mod** (float x, float y) vec2 **mod** (vec2 x, vec2 y) vec3 **mod** (vec3 x, vec3 y) vec4 **mod** (vec4 x, vec4 y)	Modulus (modulo). Returns $x - y *$ **floor** (x/y).

Table B-3   Common Functions *(continued)*

Syntax	Description
float **mod** (float *x*, float *y*) vec2 **mod** (vec2 *x*, float *y*) vec3 **mod** (vec3 *x*, float *y*) vec4 **mod** (vec4 *x*, float *y*)	Modulus (modulo). Returns $x - y$ * **floor** (x/y).
float **min** (float *x*, float *y*) vec2 **min** (vec2 *x*, vec2 *y*) vec3 **min** (vec3 *x*, vec3 *y*) vec4 **min** (vec4 *x*, vec4 *y*)	Returns *y* if $y < x$, otherwise it returns *x*.
float **min** (float *x*, float *y*) vec2 **min** (vec2 *x*, float *y*) vec3 **min** (vec3 *x*, float *y*) vec4 **min** (vec4 *x*, float *y*)	Returns *y* if $y < x$, otherwise it returns *x*.
float **max** (float *x*, float *y*) vec2 **max** (vec2 *x*, vec2 *y*) vec3 **max** (vec3 *x*, vec3 *y*) vec4 **max** (vec4 *x*, vec4 *y*)	Returns *y* if $x < y$, otherwise it returns *x*.
float **max** (float *x*, float *y*) vec2 **max** (vec2 *x*, float *y*) vec3 **max** (vec3 *x*, float *y*) vec4 **max** (vec4 *x*, float *y*)	Returns *y* if $x < y$, otherwise it returns *x*.
float **clamp** (float *x*, float *y*) vec2 **clamp** (vec2 *x*, vec2 *y*) vec3 **clamp** (vec3 *x*, vec3 *y*) vec4 **clamp** (vec4 *x*, vec4 *y*)	Returns **min** (**max** (*x*, *minVal*), *maxVal*) Results are undefined if *minVal* > *maxVal*.
float **clamp** (float *x*, float *y*) vec2 **clamp** (vec2 *x*, float *y*) vec3 **clamp** (vec3 *x*, float *y*) vec4 **clamp** (vec4 *x*, float *y*)	Returns **min** (**max** (*x*, *minVal*), *maxVal*) Results are undefined if *minVal* > *maxVal*.

Table B-3   Common Functions *(continued)*

Syntax	Description
float **mix** (float *x*, float *y*) vec2 **mix** (vec2 *x*, vec2 *y*) vec3 **mix** (vec3 *x*, vec3 *y*) vec4 **mix** (vec4 *x*, vec4 *y*)	Returns the linear blend of *x* and *y*, i.e., $x * (1 - a) + y * a$.
float **mix** (float *x*, float *y*) vec2 **mix** (vec2 *x*, float *y*) vec3 **mix** (vec3 *x*, float *y*) vec4 **mix** (vec4 *x*, float *y*)	Returns the linear blend of *x* and *y*, i.e., $x * (1 - a) + y * a$.
float **step** (float *edge*, float *x*) vec2 **step** (vec2 *edge*, vec2 *x*) vec3 **step** (vec3 *edge*, vec3 *x*) vec4 **step** (vec4 *edge*, vec4 *x*)	Returns 0.0 if $x < edge$, otherwise it returns 1.0.
float **step** (float *edge*, float *x*) vec2 **step** (float *edge*, vec2 *x*) vec3 **step** (float *edge*, vec3 *x*) vec4 **step** (float *edge*, vec4 *x*)	Returns 0.0 if $x < edge$, otherwise it returns 1.0.

float **smoothstep** (float *edge0*,
             float *edge1*,
             float *x*)
vec2 **smoothstep** (vec2 *edge0*,
             vec2 *edge1*,
             vec2 *x*)
vec3 **smoothstep** (vec3 *edge0*,
             vec3 *edge1*,
             vec3 *x*)
vec4 **smoothstep** (vec4 *edge0*,
             vec4 *edge1*,
             vec4 *x*)
	Returns 0.0 if $x <= edge0$ and 1.0 if $x >= edge1$ and performs smooth Hermite interpolation between 0 and 1 when $edge0 < x < edge1$. This is useful in cases where you would want a threshold function with a smooth transition. This is equivalent to:
	
	```\n// genType is float, vec2, vec3,\n// or vec4\ngenType t;\nt = clamp((x - edge0)/\n (edge1 - edge0), 0, 1);\nreturn t * t * (3 - 2 * t);\n```
	Results are undefined if $edge0 >= edge1$.

Table B-3   Common Functions *(continued)*

Syntax	Description
float **smoothstep** (float *edge0*, float *edge1*, float *x*) vec2 **smoothstep** (float *edge0*, float *edge1*, vec2 *x*) vec3 **smoothstep** (float *edge0*, float *edge1*, vec3 *x*) vec4 **smoothstep** (float *edge0*, float *edge1*, vec4 *x*)	Returns 0.0 if *x* <= *edge0* and 1.0 if *x* >= *edge1* and performs smooth Hermite interpolation between 0 and 1 when *edge0* < *x* < *edge1*. This is useful in cases where you would want a threshold function with a smooth transition. This is equivalent to: ```// genType is float, vec2, vec3,\n// or vec4\ngenType t;\nt = clamp((x - edge0)/\n (edge1 - edge0), 0, 1);\nreturn t * t * (3 - 2 * t);``` Results are undefined if *edge0* >= *edge1*.

Geometric Functions

Table B-4 describes the built-in geometric functions. These functions can be used within vertex and fragment shaders. These functions operate on vectors as vectors, not component-wise.

Table B-4   Geometric Functions

Syntax	Description
float **length** (float *x*) float **length** (vec2 *x*) float **length** (vec3 *x*) float **length** (vec4 *x*)	Returns the length of vector *x*, $$\sqrt{x[0]^2 + x[1]^2 + \ldots}$$
float **distance** (float *p0*, float *p1*) float **distance** (vec2 *p0*, vec2 *p1*) float **distance** (vec3 *p0*, vec3 *p1*) float **distance** (vec4 *p0*, vec4 *p1*)	Returns the distance between *p0* and *p1*, i.e., **length** (*p0* – *p1*).
float **dot** (float *x*, float *y*) float **dot** (vec2 *x*, vec2 *y*) float **dot** (vec3 *x*, vec3 *y*) float **dot** (vec4 *x*, vec4 *y*)	Returns the dot product of *x* and *y*, i.e., *x*[0] * *y*[0] + *x*[1] * *y*[1] + ...

Table B-4   Geometric Functions *(continued)*

Syntax	Description
vec3 **cross** (vec3 *x*, vec3 *y*)	Returns the cross product of *x* and *y*, i.e., $result[0] = x[1] * y[2] - y[1] * x[2]$ $result[1] = x[2] * y[0] - y[2] * x[0]$ $result[2] = x[0] * y[1] - y[0] * x[1]$
float **normalize** (float *x*) vec2 **normalize** (vec2 *x*) vec3 **normalize** (vec3 *x*) vec4 **normalize** (vec4 *x*)	Returns a vector in the same direction as *x* but with a length of 1. Returns *x* / **length** (*x*).

float **faceforward** (float *N*,
       float *I*, float N_{ref})
 vec2 **faceforward** (vec2 *N*,
       vec2 *I*, vec2 N_{ref})
 vec3 **faceforward** (vec3 *N*,
       vec3 *I*, vec3 N_{ref})
 vec4 **faceforward** (vec4 *N*,
       vec4 *I*, vec4 N_{ref})
	If **dot**(N_{ref}, *I*) < 0 return *N*, otherwise return –*N*.

float **reflect** (float *I*, float *N*) vec2 **reflect** (vec2 *I*, vec2 *N*) vec3 **reflect** (vec3 *I*, vec3 *N*) vec4 **reflect** (vec4 *I*, vec4 *N*)	For the incident vector *I* and surface orientation *N*, returns the reflection direction: $I - 2 * \textbf{dot}(N, I) * N$ *N* must already be normalized to achieve the desired result.

float **refract** (float *I*, float *N*, float *eta*)
 vec2 **refract** (vec2 *I*, vec2 *N*, float *eta*)
 vec3 **refract** (vec3 *I*, vec3 *N*, float *eta*)
 vec4 **refract** (vec4 *I*, vec4 *N*, float *eta*)
	For the incident vector *I* and surface normal *N*, and the ratio of indices of refraction *eta*, return the refraction vector. The result is computed by
	
	 ```k = 1.0 - eta * eta *```
	``` (1.0 - dot(N, I) * dot(N, I))```
	```if (k < 0.0)```
	``` // genType is float, vec2,```
	``` // vec3, or vec4```
	``` return genType(0.0)```
	```else```
	``` return eta * I - (eta *```
	``` dot(N, I) + sqrt(k)) * N```
	
	 Input parameters for the incident vector *I* and the surface normal *N* must already be normalized to get the desired results.

Note: The float version of **length**, **distance**, and **normalize** functions are not very useful but are defined by the shading language for completeness. **length**(float x) returns $|x|$, **distance**(float $p0$, float $p1$) returns $|p0 - p1|$ and **normalize**(float x) returns 1.

The **faceforward** function makes sure that the normal vector is pointing in the right direction. The corrected normal will typically be used for lighting.

The **reflect** function computes a reflection vector R given an incident vector I and the normal N. The reflection vector is computed using the following equation:

$$R = I - 2 * (N . I) * N$$

where . is the dot operator

If the vectors I and N are normalized, the computed reflection vector R will also be a normalized vector.

$R.R = (I - 2 * (N . I) * N) . (I - 2 * (N . I) * N)$

$\quad = (I . I) - (2 * (I . N) * (N . I)) - (2 * (I . N) * (N . I) + (4 * (N . I) * (N . I) * (N . N))$

$\quad = 1 - 4 * (N . I)^2 + 4 * (N . I)^2 \text{ // } (I . I) \text{ and } (N . N) = 1$

$\quad = 1$

Matrix Functions

Table B-5 describes the built-in matrix functions. These functions can be used within vertex and fragment shaders. These functions operate on vectors as vectors, not component-wise.

Table B-5   Matrix Functions

Syntax	Description
mat2 **matrixCompMult** (mat2 x, mat2 y) mat3 **matrixCompMult** (mat3 x, mat3 y) mat4 **matrixCompMult** (mat4 x, mat4 y)	Multiply matrix x by matrix y component-wise, i.e., *result*[i][j] is the scalar product of x[i][j] and y[i][j]. Note: To get linear algebraic matrix multiplication, use the multiply operator (*).

matrixCompMult performs a component-wise multiplication. For example, let **m_a** and **m_b** be two `mat3` matrices described as follows:

$$m\_a = \begin{bmatrix} a_{00} & a_{01} & a_{02} \\ a_{10} & a_{11} & a_{12} \\ a_{20} & a_{21} & a_{22} \end{bmatrix} \qquad m\_b = \begin{bmatrix} b_{00} & b_{01} & b_{02} \\ b_{10} & b_{11} & b_{12} \\ b_{20} & b_{21} & b_{22} \end{bmatrix}$$

matrixCompMult will return a `mat3` matrix with the following components:

$$m\_r = \begin{bmatrix} a_{00}*b_{00} & a_{01}*b_{01} & a_{02}*b_{02} \\ a_{10}*b_{10} & a_{11}*b_{11} & a_{12}*b_{12} \\ a_{20}*b_{20} & a_{21}*b_{21} & a_{22}*b_{22} \end{bmatrix}$$

This is quite different from a matrix multiplication. To multiply the two matrices **m_a** and **m_b** we use the expression **m_r = m_a * m_b**.

$$\text{If} \qquad m\_a = \begin{bmatrix} a_{00} & a_{01} & a_{02} \\ a_{10} & a_{11} & a_{12} \\ a_{20} & a_{21} & a_{22} \end{bmatrix} \qquad m\_b = \begin{bmatrix} b_{00} & b_{01} & b_{02} \\ b_{10} & b_{11} & b_{12} \\ b_{20} & b_{21} & b_{22} \end{bmatrix}$$

then **m_r = m_a * m_b** is given as:

$$\begin{bmatrix} a_{00}*b_{00}+a_{01}*b_{10}+a_{02}*b_{20} & a_{00}*b_{01}+a_{01}*b_{11}+a_{02}*b_{21} & a_{00}*b_{02}+a_{01}*b_{12}+a_{02}*b_{22} \\ a_{10}*b_{00}+a_{11}*b_{10}+a_{12}*b_{20} & a_{10}*b_{01}+a_{11}*b_{11}+a_{12}*b_{21} & a_{10}*b_{02}+a_{11}*b_{12}+a_{12}*b_{22} \\ a_{20}*b_{00}+a_{21}*b_{10}+a_{22}*b_{20} & a_{20}*b_{01}+a_{21}*b_{11}+a_{22}*b_{21} & a_{20}*b_{02}+a_{21}*b_{12}+a_{22}*b_{22} \end{bmatrix}$$

Vector Relational Functions

Table B-6 describes the built-in vector relational functions. These functions can be used within vertex and fragment shaders. Relational and equality operators (<, <=, >, >=, ==, !=) are defined (or reserved) to produce scalar boolean results. For vector results, use the built-in functions given in Table B-6.

Table B-6   Vector Relational Functions

Syntax	Description
bvec2 **lessThan** (vec2 x, vec2 y) bvec3 **lessThan** (vec3 x, vec3 y) bvec4 **lessThan** (vec4 x, vec4 y) bvec2 **lessThan** (ivec2 x, ivec2 y) bvec3 **lessThan** (ivec3 x, ivec3 y) bvec4 **lessThan** (ivec4 x, ivec4 y)	Returns the component-wise compare of $x < y$.
bvec2 **lessThanEqual** (vec2 x, vec2 y) bvec3 **lessThanEqual** (vec3 x, vec3 y) bvec4 **lessThanEqual** (vec4 x, vec4 y) bvec2 **lessThanEqual** (ivec2 x, ivec2 y) bvec3 **lessThanEqual** (ivec3 x, ivec3 y) bvec4 **lessThanEqual** (ivec4 x, ivec4 y)	Returns the component-wise compare of $x <= y$.
bvec2 **greaterThan** (vec2 x, vec2 y) bvec3 **greaterThan** (vec3 x, vec3 y) bvec4 **greaterThan** (vec4 x, vec4 y) bvec2 **greaterThan** (ivec2 x, ivec2 y) bvec3 **greaterThan** (ivec3 x, ivec3 y) bvec4 **greaterThan** (ivec4 x, ivec4 y)	Returns the component-wise compare of $x > y$.
bvec2 **greaterThanEqual** (vec2 x, vec2 y) bvec3 **greaterThanEqual** (vec3 x, vec3 y) bvec4 **greaterThanEqual** (vec4 x, vec4 y) bvec2 **greaterThanEqual** (ivec2 x, ivec2 y) bvec3 **greaterThanEqual** (ivec3 x, ivec3 y) bvec4 **greaterThanEqual** (ivec4 x, ivec4 y)	Returns the component-wise compare of $x >= y$.
bvec2 **equal** (vec2 x, vec2 y) bvec3 **equal** (vec3 x, vec3 y) bvec4 **equal** (vec4 x, vec4 y) bvec2 **equal** (ivec2 x, ivec2 y) bvec3 **equal** (ivec3 x, ivec3 y) bvec4 **equal** (ivec4 x, ivec4 y)	Returns the component-wise compare of $x == y$.

Table B-6 Vector Relational Functions *(continued)*

Syntax	Description
bvec2 **notEqual** (vec2 *x*, vec2 *y*) bvec3 **notEqual** (vec3 *x*, vec3 *y*) bvec4 **notEqual** (vec4 *x*, vec4 *y*) bvec2 **notEqual** (ivec2 *x*, ivec2 *y*) bvec3 **notEqual** (ivec3 *x*, ivec3 *y*) bvec4 **notEqual** (ivec4 *x*, ivec4 *y*)	Returns the component-wise compare of *x* != *y*.
bool **any** (bvec2 x) bool **any** (bvec3 x) bool **any** (bvec4 x)	Returns true if any component of *x* is **true**.
bool **all** (bvec2 x) bool **all** (bvec3 x) bool **all** (bvec4 x)	Returns true only if all components of *x* are **true**.
bvec2 **not** (bvec2 *x*) bvec3 **not** (bvec3 *x*) bvec4 **not** (bvec4 *x*)	Returns the component-wise logical complement of *x*.

Texture Lookup Functions

Table B-7 describes the built-in texture lookup functions. Texture lookup functions are available to both vertex and fragment shaders. However, the level of detail is not computed by fixed functionality for vertex shaders, so there are some differences in operation between vertex and fragment texture lookups. The functions in Table B-7 provide access to textures through samplers, as set up through the OpenGL ES API. Texture properties such as size, pixel format, number of dimensions, filtering method, number of mipmap levels, depth comparison, and so on, are also defined by OpenGL ES API calls. Such properties are taken into account as the texture is accessed via the built-in functions defined in Table B-7.

Functions containing the *bias* parameter are available only in the fragment shader. If *bias* is present, it is added to the calculated level of detail prior to performing the texture access operation. If the *bias* parameter is not provided, then the implementation automatically selects level of detail: For a texture that is not mipmapped, the texture is used directly. If it is mipmapped and running in a fragment shader, the LOD computed by the implementation is used to do the texture lookup. If it is mipmapped and running on the vertex shader, then the base texture is used.

The built-ins suffixed with "**Lod**" are allowed only in a vertex shader. For the "**Lod**" functions, *lod* is directly used as the level of detail.

Table B-7   Texture Lookup Functions

Syntax	Description

vec4 **texture2D** (sampler2D *sampler*, vec2 *coord*)
 	
vec4 **texture2D** (sampler2D *sampler*,
              vec2 *coord*, float *bias*)
 	
vec4 **texture2DProj** (sampler2D *sampler*, vec3 *coord*)
 	
vec4 **texture2DProj** (sampler2D *sampler*,
              vec3 *coord*, float *bias*)
 	
vec4 **texture2DProj** (sampler2D *sampler*, vec4 *coord*)
 	
vec4 **texture2DProj** (sampler2D *sampler*,
              vec4 *coord*, float *bias*)
 	
vec4 **texture2DLod** (sampler2D *sampler*,
              vec2 *coord*, float *lod*)
 	
vec4 **texture2DProjLod** (sampler2D *sampler*,
              vec3 *coord*, float *lod*)
 	
vec4 **texture2DProjLod** (sampler2D *sampler*,
              vec4 *coord*, float *lod*)
	Use the texture coordinate *coord* to do a texture lookup in the 2D texture currently bound to *sampler*. For the projective ("**Proj**") versions, the texture coordinate (*coord.s*, *coord.t*) is divided by the last component of *coord*. The third component of *coord* is ignored for the vec4 coord variant.

vec4 **textureCube** (samplerCube *sampler*, vec3 *coord*)
 	
vec4 **textureCube** (samplerCube *sampler*,
              vec3 *coord*, float *bias*)
 	
vec4 **textureCubeLod** (samplerCube *sampler*,
              vec3 *coord*, float *lod*)
	Use the texture coordinate *coord* to do a texture lookup in the cubemap texture currently bound to *sampler*. The direction of *coord* is used to select which face to do a 2D texture lookup in, as described in section 3.8.6 in version 2.0 of the OpenGL specification.

Table B-7   Texture Lookup Functions *(continued)*

Syntax	Description

vec4 **texture3D** (sampler3D *sampler*, vec3 *coord*)
 	
vec4 **texture3D** (sampler2D *sampler*,
                vec3 *coord*, float *bias*)
 	
vec4 **texture3DProj** (sampler2D *sampler*, vec4 *coord*)
 	
vec4 **texture3DProj** (sampler2D *sampler*,
                vec4 *coord*, float *bias*)
 	
vec4 **texture3DLod** (sampler3D *sampler*,
                vec3 *coord*, float *lod*)
 	
vec4 **texture3DProjLod** (sampler3D *sampler*,
                vec4 *coord*, float *lod*)
	Use the texture coordinate *coord* to do a texture lookup in the 3D texture currently bound to *sampler*. For the projective (**Proj**) versions, the texture coordinate (*coord.s, coord.t, coord.r*) is divided by the last component of *coord*.

The **texture3D**, **texture3DProj**, **texture3DLod**, and **texture3DProjLod** functions defined in Table B-7 are only available if the #extension GL_OES_texture_3d directive is set to enable and the OpenGL ES implementation supports this extension.

Derivative Functions

Table B-8 describes the built-in derivative functions. The derivative functions can only be used inside fragment shaders. These functions are available if the #extension GL_OES_standard_derivatives directive is set to enable and the OpenGL ES implementation supports this extension.

Derivatives might be computationally expensive and numerically unstable. Therefore, an OpenGL ES implementation can approximate the true derivatives by using a fast but not entirely accurate derivative computation.

The expected behavior of a derivative is specified using forward–backward differencing.

Forward differencing:

$$F(x + dx) - F(x) \sim dFdx(x) * dx$$

$$dFdx \sim (F(x + dx) - F(x)) / dx$$

Backward differencing:

$$F(x - dx) - F(x) \sim -dFdx(x) * dx$$

$$dFdx \sim (F(x) - F(x - dx)) / dx$$

With single-sample rasterization, $dx <= 1.0$ in the preceding equations. For multisample rasterization, $dx < 2.0$ in the preceding equations.

dFdy is approximated similarly, with y replacing x.

An OpenGL ES implementation can use the preceding or other methods to perform the calculation, subject to the following conditions:

- The method can use piecewise linear approximations. Such linear approximations imply that higher order derivatives, **dFdx(dFdx(**x**))** and above, are undefined.

- The method can assume that the function evaluated is continuous. Therefore derivatives within the body of a nonuniform conditional are undefined.

- The method can differ per fragment, subject to the constraint that the method can vary by window coordinates, not screen coordinates. The invariance requirement is relaxed for derivative calculations, because the method can be a function of fragment location.

Other properties that are desirable, but not required, are:

- Functions should be evaluated within the interior of a primitive (interpolated, not extrapolated).

- Functions for **dFdx** should be evaluated while holding y constant. Functions for **dFdy** should be evaluated while holding x constant. However, mixed higher order derivatives, like **dFdx(dFdy(**y**))** and **dFdy(dFdx(**x**))** are undefined.

- Derivatives of constant arguments should be 0.

In some implementations, varying degrees of derivative accuracy can be obtained by providing hints using `glHint(GL_FRAGMENT_SHADER_DERIVATIVE_HINT)`, allowing a user to make an image quality versus speed trade-off.

Table B-8   Derivative Functions

Syntax	Description
float **dFdx** (float *p*) vec2 **dFdx** (vec2 *p*) vec3 **dFdx** (vec3 *p*) vec4 **dFdx** (vec4 p)	Returns the derivative in *x* using local differencing for the input argument *p*.
float **dFdy** (float *p*) vec2 **dFdy** (vec2 *p*) vec3 **dFdy** (vec3 *p*) vec4 **dFdy** (vec4 p)	Returns the derivative in *y* using local differencing for the input argument *p*.
float **fwidth** (float *p*) vec2 **fwidth** (vec2 *p*) vec3 **fwidth** (vec3 *p*) vec4 **fwidth** (vec4 p)	Returns the sum of the absolute derivative in *x* and *y* using local differencing for the input argument *p*, i.e., *result* = **abs** (**dFdx** (*p*)) + **abs** (**dFdy** (*p*));

dFdx and **dFdy** are commonly used to estimate the filter width used to anti-alias procedural textures. We are assuming that the expression is being evaluated in parallel on an SIMD array so that at any given point in time the value of the function is known at the grid points represented by the SIMD array. Local differencing between SIMD array elements can therefore be used to calculate these derivatives.

Shading Language Grammar

This appendix describes the shading language grammar. The shading language grammar is copyrighted by Khronos and is reprinted with permission. The latest OpenGL ES 2.0 specification can be downloaded at www.khronos.org/opengles/2_X/.

The grammar is fed from the output of lexical analysis. The tokens returned from lexical analysis are

```
ATTRIBUTE CONST BOOL FLOAT INT
BREAK CONTINUE DO ELSE FOR IF DISCARD RETURN
BVEC2 BVEC3 BVEC4 IVEC2 IVEC3 IVEC4 VEC2 VEC3 VEC4
MAT2 MAT3 MAT4 IN OUT INOUT UNIFORM VARYING
SAMPLER2D SAMPLERCUBE
STRUCT VOID WHILE

IDENTIFIER TYPE_NAME FLOATCONSTANT INTCONSTANT BOOLCONSTANT
FIELD_SELECTION
LEFT_OP RIGHT_OP
INC_OP DEC_OP LE_OP GE_OP EQ_OP NE_OP
AND_OP OR_OP XOR_OP MUL_ASSIGN DIV_ASSIGN ADD_ASSIGN
MOD_ASSIGN LEFT_ASSIGN RIGHT_ASSIGN AND_ASSIGN XOR_ASSIGN OR_ASSIGN
SUB_ASSIGN

LEFT_PAREN RIGHT_PAREN LEFT_BRACKET RIGHT_BRACKET LEFT_BRACE
RIGHT_BRACE DOT
COMMA COLON EQUAL SEMICOLON BANG DASH TILDE PLUS STAR SLASH PERCENT
LEFT_ANGLE RIGHT_ANGLE VERTICAL_BAR CARET AMPERSAND QUESTION

INVARIANT
HIGH_PRECISION MEDIUM_PRECISION LOW_PRECISION PRECISION
```

The following describes the grammar for the OpenGL ES Shading Language in terms of the above tokens.

```
variable_identifier:
        IDENTIFIER

primary_expression:
        variable_identifier
        INTCONSTANT
        FLOATCONSTANT
        BOOLCONSTANT
        LEFT_PAREN expression RIGHT_PAREN

postfix_expression:
        primary_expression
        postfix_expression LEFT_BRACKET integer_expression
RIGHT_BRACKET
        function_call
        postfix_expression DOT FIELD_SELECTION
        postfix_expression INC_OP
        postfix_expression DEC_OP

integer_expression:
        expression

function_call:
        function_call_generic

function_call_generic:
        function_call_header_with_parameters RIGHT_PAREN
        function_call_header_no_parameters RIGHT_PAREN

function_call_header_no_parameters:
        function_call_header VOID
        function_call_header

function_call_header_with_parameters:
        function_call_header assignment_expression
        function_call_header_with_parameters COMMA
assignment_expression

function_call_header:
        function_identifier LEFT_PAREN

function_identifier:
        constructor_identifier
        IDENTIFIER
```

```
// Grammar Note: Constructors look like functions, but lexical
// analysis recognized most of them as keywords

constructor_identifier:
        FLOAT
        INT
        BOOL
        VEC2
        VEC3
        VEC4
        BVEC2
        BVEC3
        BVEC4
        IVEC2
        IVEC3
        IVEC4
        MAT2
        MAT3
        MAT4
        TYPE_NAME

unary_expression:
        postfix_expression
        INC_OP unary_expression
        DEC_OP unary_expression
        unary_operator unary_expression

// Grammar Note: No traditional style type casts.

unary_operator:
        PLUS
        DASH
        BANG
        TILDE // reserved

// Grammar Note: No '*' or '&' unary ops. Pointers are not
// supported.

multiplicative_expression:
        unary_expression
        multiplicative_expression STAR unary_expression
        multiplicative_expression SLASH unary_expression
        // reserved
        multiplicative_expression PERCENT unary_expression

additive_expression:
        multiplicative_expression
        additive_expression PLUS multiplicative_expression
        additive_expression DASH multiplicative_expression
```

```
shift_expression:
        additive_expression
        shift_expression LEFT_OP additive_expression // reserved
        shift_expression RIGHT_OP additive_expression // reserved

relational_expression:
        shift_expression
        relational_expression LEFT_ANGLE shift_expression
        relational_expression RIGHT_ANGLE shift_expression
        relational_expression LE_OP shift_expression
        relational_expression GE_OP shift_expression

equality_expression:
        relational_expression
        equality_expression EQ_OP relational_expression
        equality_expression NE_OP relational_expression

and_expression:
        equality_expression
        and_expression AMPERSAND equality_expression // reserved

exclusive_or_expression:
        and_expression
        exclusive_or_expression CARET and_expression // reserved

inclusive_or_expression:
        exclusive_or_expression
        // reserved
       inclusive_or_expression VERTICAL_BAR exclusive_or_expression

logical_and_expression:
        inclusive_or_expression
        logical_and_expression AND_OP inclusive_or_expression

logical_xor_expression:
        logical_and_expression
        logical_xor_expression XOR_OP logical_and_expression

logical_or_expression:
        logical_xor_expression
        logical_or_expression OR_OP logical_xor_expression

conditional_expression:
        logical_or_expression
        logical_or_expression QUESTION expression COLON
            assignment_expression
```

```
assignment_expression:
        conditional_expression
        unary_expression assignment_operator assignment_expression

assignment_operator:
        EQUAL
        MUL_ASSIGN
        DIV_ASSIGN
        MOD_ASSIGN // reserved
        ADD_ASSIGN
        SUB_ASSIGN
        LEFT_ASSIGN // reserved
        RIGHT_ASSIGN // reserved
        AND_ASSIGN // reserved
        XOR_ASSIGN // reserved
        OR_ASSIGN // reserved

expression:
        assignment_expression
        expression COMMA assignment_expression

constant_expression:
        conditional_expression

declaration:
        function_prototype SEMICOLON
        init_declarator_list SEMICOLON
        PRECISION precision_qualifier
           type_specifier_no_prec SEMICOLON

function_prototype:
        function_declarator RIGHT_PAREN

function_declarator:
        function_header
        function_header_with_parameters

function_header_with_parameters:
        function_header parameter_declaration
        function_header_with_parameters COMMA parameter_declaration

function_header:
        fully_specified_type IDENTIFIER LEFT_PAREN

parameter_declarator:
        type_specifier IDENTIFIER
        type_specifier IDENTIFIER LEFT_BRACKET constant_expression
           RIGHT_BRACKET
```

```
parameter_declaration:
        type_qualifier parameter_qualifier parameter_declarator
        parameter_qualifier parameter_declarator
        type_qualifier parameter_qualifier parameter_type_specifier
        parameter_qualifier parameter_type_specifier

parameter_qualifier:
        /* empty */
        IN
        OUT
        INOUT

parameter_type_specifier:
        type_specifier
        type_specifier LEFT_BRACKET constant_expression
            RIGHT_BRACKET

init_declarator_list:
        single_declaration
        init_declarator_list COMMA IDENTIFIER
        init_declarator_list COMMA IDENTIFIER LEFT_BRACKET
            constant_expression  RIGHT_BRACKET
        init_declarator_list COMMA IDENTIFIER EQUAL initializer

single_declaration:
        fully_specified_type
        fully_specified_type IDENTIFIER
        fully_specified_type IDENTIFIER LEFT_BRACKET
            constant_expression RIGHT_BRACKET
        fully_specified_type IDENTIFIER EQUAL initializer
        INVARIANT IDENTIFIER // Vertex only.

// Grammar Note: No 'enum' or 'typedef'.

fully_specified_type:
        type_specifier
        type_qualifier type_specifier

type_qualifier:
        CONST
        ATTRIBUTE // Vertex only.
        VARYING
        INVARIANT VARYING
        UNIFORM

type_specifier:
        type_specifier_no_prec
        precision_qualifier type_specifier_no_prec
```

```
type_specifier_no_prec:
        VOID
        FLOAT
        INT
        BOOL
        VEC2
        VEC3
        VEC4
        BVEC2
        BVEC3
        BVEC4
        IVEC2
        IVEC3
        IVEC4
        MAT2
        MAT3
        MAT4

        SAMPLER2D

        SAMPLERCUBE

struct_specifier
        TYPE_NAME

precision_qualifier:
        HIGH_PRECISION
        MEDIUM_PRECISION
        LOW_PRECISION

struct_specifier:
        STRUCT IDENTIFIER LEFT_BRACE struct_declaration_list
            RIGHT_BRACE
        STRUCT LEFT_BRACE struct_declaration_list RIGHT_BRACE

struct_declaration_list:
        struct_declaration
        struct_declaration_list struct_declaration

struct_declaration:
        type_specifier struct_declarator_list SEMICOLON

struct_declarator_list:
        struct_declarator
        struct_declarator_list COMMA struct_declarator

struct_declarator:
        IDENTIFIER
        IDENTIFIER LEFT_BRACKET constant_expression RIGHT_BRACKET
```

```
initializer:
        assignment_expression

declaration_statement:
        declaration

statement_no_new_scope:
        compound_statement_with_scope
        simple_statement

// Grammar Note: No labeled statements; 'goto' is not supported.

simple_statement:
        declaration_statement
        expression_statement
        selection_statement
        iteration_statement
        jump_statement

compound_statement_with_scope:
        LEFT_BRACE RIGHT_BRACE
        LEFT_BRACE statement_list RIGHT_BRACE

statement_no_new_scope:
        compound_statement_no_new_scope
        simple_statement

compound_statement_no_new_scope:
        LEFT_BRACE RIGHT_BRACE
        LEFT_BRACE statement_list RIGHT_BRACE

statement_list:
        statement_no_new_scope
        statement_list statement_no_new_scope

expression_statement:
        SEMICOLON
        expression SEMICOLON

selection_statement:
        IF LEFT_PAREN expression RIGHT_PAREN selection_rest_statement


selection_rest_statement:
        statement_with_scope ELSE statement_with_scope
        statement_with_scope
        statement_with_scope
        compound_statement_no_new_scope
        simple_statement
```

```
condition:
        expression
        fully_specified_type IDENTIFIER EQUAL initializer

iteration_statement:
        WHILE LEFT_PAREN condition RIGHT_PAREN
            statement_no_new_scope
        DO statement_no_new_scope WHILE LEFT_PAREN
            expression RIGHT_PAREN SEMICOLON
        FOR LEFT_PAREN for_init_statement for_rest_statement
            RIGHT_PAREN statement_no_new_scope

for_init_statement:
        expression_statement
        declaration_statement

conditionopt:
        condition
        /* empty */

for_rest_statement:
        conditionopt SEMICOLON
        conditionopt SEMICOLON expression

jump_statement:
        CONTINUE SEMICOLON
        BREAK SEMICOLON
        RETURN SEMICOLON
        RETURN expression SEMICOLON
        DISCARD SEMICOLON // Fragment shader only.

translation_unit:
        external_declaration
        translation_unit external_declaration

external_declaration:
        function_definition
        declaration

function_definition:
        function_prototype compound_statement_no_new_scope
```

ES Framework API

The example programs throughout the book use a framework of utility functions for performing common OpenGL ES 2.0 functions. The API provides routines for tasks such as creating a window, setting up callback functions, loading a shader, loading a program, and creating geometry. The purpose of this appendix is to provide documentation for the ES Framework API functions used throughout the book.

Framework Core Functions

This section provides documentation on the core functions in the ES Framework API.

```
void ESUTIL_API esInitContext(ESContext * esContext)
```

Initialize ES framework context. This must be called before calling any other functions.

Parameters:

esContext application context

```
GLboolean ESUTIL_API esCreateWindow(ESContext * esContext,
                                    const char * title,
                                    GLint width,
                                    GLint height,
                                    GLuint flags)
```

Create a window with the specified parameters.

Parameters:

esContext	application context
title	name for title bar of window
width	width in pixels of window to create
height	height in pixels of window to create
flags	bitfield for the window creation flags

ES_WINDOW_RGB—specifies that the color buffer should have R,G,B channels

ES_WINDOW_ALPHA—specifies that the color buffer should have alpha

ES_WINDOW_DEPTH—specifies that a depth buffer should be created

ES_WINDOW_STENCIL—specifies that a stencil buffer should be created

ES_WINDOW_MULTISAMPLE—specifies that a multisample buffer should be created

Returns:

GL_TRUE if window creation is successful, GL_FALSE otherwise

```
void ESUTIL_API esMainLoop(ESContext * esContext)
```

Start the main loop for the OpenGL ES application.

Parameters:

esContext	application context

```
void ESUTIL_API esRegisterDrawFunc(ESContext * esContext,
                    void(ESCALLBACK *drawFunc)(ESContext *))
```

Register a draw callback function to be used to render each frame.

Parameters:

esContext   application context

drawFunc   draw callback function that will be used to render the scene

```
void ESUTIL_API esRegisterUpdateFunc(ESContext * esContext,
                    void(ESCALLBACK *updateFunc)
                    (ESContext *, float))
```

Register an update callback function to be used to update on each time step.

Parameters:

esContext   application context

updateFunc   update callback function that will be used to render the scene

```
void ESUTIL_API esRegisterKeyFunc(ESContext * esContext,
                    void(ESCALLBACK *keyFunc)
                    (ESContext *, unsigned char, int, int))
```

Register a keyboard input processing callback function.

Parameters:

esContext   application context

keyFunc   key callback function for application processing of keyboard input

```
GLuint ESUTIL_API esLoadShader(GLenum type,
                                const char * shaderSrc)
```

Load a shader, check for compile errors, print error messages to output log.

Parameters:

type   type of shader (GL_VERTEX_SHADER or GL_FRAGMENT_SHADER)

shaderSrc   shader source string

Returns:

A new shader object on success, 0 on failure

```
GLuint ESUTIL_API esLoadProgram(const char * vertShaderSrc,
                                 const char * fragShaderSrc)
```

Load a vertex and fragment shader, create a program object, link program. Errors output to log.

Parameters:

vertShaderSrc   vertex shader source code

fragShaderSrc   fragment shader source code

Returns:

A new program object linked with the vertex/fragment shader pair, 0 on failure

```
char* ESUTIL_API esLoadTGA(char * fileName, int * width,
                            int * height)
```

Loads a 24-bit TGA image from a file.

Parameters:

fileName   name of the file on disk

width   width of loaded image in pixels

height   height of loaded image in pixels

Returns:

Pointer to loaded image. NULL on failure.

```
int ESUTIL_API esGenSphere(int numSlices, float radius,
                GLfloat ** vertices, GLfloat ** normals,
                GLfloat ** texCoords, GLuint ** indices)
```

Generates geometry for a sphere. Allocates memory for the vertex data and stores the results in the arrays. Generate index list for a `GL_TRIANGLE_STRIP`.

Parameters:

numSlices   the number of vertical and horizontal slices in the sphere

vertices   if not NULL, will contain array of float3 positions

normals   if not NULL, will contain array of float3 normals

texCoords   if not NULL, will contain array of float2 texCoords

indices   if not NULL, will contain the array of indices for the triangle strip

Returns:

The number of indices required for rendering the buffers (the number of indices stored in the indices array if it is not NULL) as a `GL_TRIANGLE_STRIP`

```
int ESUTIL_API esGenCube(float scale, GLfloat ** vertices,
                GLfloat ** normals,GLfloat ** texCoords,
                GLuint ** indices)
```

Generates geometry for a cube. Allocates memory for the vertex data and stores the results in the arrays. Generate index list for `GL_TRIANGLES`.

Parameters:

scale   the size of the cube, use 1.0 for a unit cube

vertices   if not NULL, will contain array of float3 positions

normals   if not NULL, will contain array of float3 normals

texCoords   if not NULL, will contain array of float2 texCoords

indices   if not NULL, will contain the array of indices for the triangle list

Returns:

The number of indices required for rendering the buffers (the number of indices stored in the indices array if it is not NULL) as `GL_TRIANGLES`

```
void ESUTIL_API esLogMessage (const char * formatStr, ...)
```

Log a message to the debug output for the platform.

Parameters:

formatStr   format string for error log

Transformation Functions

We now describe utility functions that perform commonly used transformations such as scale, rotate, translate, and matrix multiplication. Most vertex shaders will use one or more matrices to transform the vertex position from local coordinate space to clip coordinate space (refer to Chapter 7, "Primitive Assembly and Rasterization," for a description of various coordinate systems). Matrices are also used to transform other vertex attributes such as normals, and texture coordinates. The transformed matrices can then be used as values for appropriate matrix uniforms used in a vertex or fragment shader. You will notice similarities between these functions and appropriate functions defined in OpenGL and OpenGL ES 1.x. For example, esScale should be quite similar to glScale, esFrustum should be similar to glFrustum, and so on.

A new type ESMatrix is defined in the framework. This is used to represent a 4 × 4 floating-point matrix and is declared as follows:

```
typdedef struct {
   GLfloat   m[4][4];
}ESMatrix;
```

```
void ESUTIL_API esFrustum(ESMatrix *result,
                          GLfloat left, GLfloat right,
                          GLfloat bottom, GLfloat top,
                          GLfloat nearZ, GLfloat farZ)
```

Multiply matrix specified by result with a perspective projection matrix and return new matrix in result.

Parameters:

result   the input matrix

left, *right*	specifies the coordinates for the left and right clipping planes
bottom, *top*	specifies the coordinates for the bottom and top clipping planes
nearZ, *farZ*	specifies the distances to the near and far depth clipping planes. Both distances must be positive

Returns:

The new matrix after the perspective projection matrix has been multiplied is returned in result.

```
void ESUTIL_API esPerspective(ESMatrix *result,
                              GLfloat fovy, GLfloat aspect
                              GLfloat nearZ, GLfloat farZ)
```

Multiply matrix specified by result with a perspective projection matrix and return new matrix in result. This function is provided as a convenience to more easily create a perspective matrix than directly using esFrustum.

Parameters:

result	the input matrix
fovy	specifies the field of view in degrees, should be between (0, 180)
aspect	the aspect ratio of the rendering window (e.g., width/height)
nearZ, *farZ*	specifies the distances to the near and far depth clipping planes. Both distances must be positive

Returns:

The new matrix after the perspective projection matrix has been multiplied is returned in result.

```
void ESUTIL_API esOrtho(ESMatrix *result,
                        GLfloat left, GLfloat right,
                        GLfloat bottom, GLfloat top,
                        GLfloat nearZ, GLfloat farZ)
```

Multiply matrix specified by result with an orthographic projection matrix and return new matrix in result.

Parameters:

result   the input matrix

left, *right* specifies the coordinates for the left and right clipping planes

bottom, *top* specifies the coordinates for the bottom and top clipping planes

nearZ, *farZ* specifies the distances to the near and far depth clipping planes. Both nearZ and farZ can be positive or negative

Returns:

The new matrix after the orthographic projection matrix has been multiplied is returned in result.

```
void ESUTIL_API esScale(ESMatrix *result, GLfloat sx,
                        GLfloat sy, GLfloat sz)
```

Multiply matrix specified by result with a scaling matrix and return new matrix in result.

Parameters:

result   the input matrix

sx, *sy*, *sz* specifies the scale factors along the *x*-, *y*-, and *z*-axes, respectively

Returns:

The new matrix after the scaling operation has been performed is returned in result.

```
void ESUTIL_API esTranslate(ESMatrix *result, GLfloat tx,
                            GLfloat ty, GLfloat tz)
```

Multiply matrix specified by result with a translation matrix and return new matrix in result.

Parameters:

result   the input matrix

tx, ty, tz specifies the translate factors along the x-, y-, and z-axes, respectively.

Returns:

The new matrix after the translation operation has been performed is returned in result.

```
void ESUTIL_API esRotate(ESMatrix *result, GLfloat angle,
                         GLfloat x, GLfloat y, GLfloat z)
```

Multiply matrix specified by result with a rotation matrix and return new matrix in result.

Parameters:

result   the input matrix

angle   specifies the angle of rotation, in degrees

x, y, z specifies the x-, y-, and z-coordinates of a vector

Returns:

The new matrix after the rotation operation has been performed is returned in result.

```
void ESUTIL_API esMatrixMultiply(ESMatrix *result,
                                 ESMatrix *srcA,
                                 ESMatrix *srcB)
```

This function multiplies the matrices srcA and srcB and returns the multiplied matrix in result.

```
result = srcA × srcB
```

Parameters:

result   pointer to memory where the multiplied matrix will be returned

srcA, srcB input matrices to be multiplied

Returns:

This function returns a multiplied matrix.

```
void ESUTIL_API esMatrixLoadIdentity(ESMatrix *result)
```

Parameters:

result   pointer to memory where the identity matrix will be returned

Returns:

This function returns an identity matrix.

OpenGL ES 2.0 on the iPhone 3GS

On June 8, 2009, at the Apple Worldwide Developer Conference (WWDC), the new iPhone 3GS was announced, which Apple confirmed would support OpenGL ES 2.0. At the same time, Apple made available to developers a seed version of the iPhone SDK 3.0 that included support for OpenGL ES 2.0. The new iPhone SDK allows developers to write applications for the iPhone 3GS that use OpenGL ES 2.0 for rendering 3D graphics.

The introduction of the iPhone 3GS to the market marks a major milestone in the adoption of OpenGL ES 2.0. This new iPhone will put the power of programmable 3D graphics in the hands of millions of consumers. With this capability comes the challenge to developers of getting the most out of the programmable hardware by developing high-performance shader-based 3D applications. *The OpenGL ES 2.0 Programming Guide* was written with exactly this goal in mind. The book covers every aspect of the API along with various advanced 3D rendering techniques to help you get the most out of OpenGL ES 2.0.

Upon first publication of *The OpenGL ES 2.0 Programming Guide*, the only implementations of OpenGL ES 2.0 that were available were PC-based emulators. While these emulators were very useful in developing the relevant OpenGL ES code for an application, many of the platform details that developers encounter when working with real-world devices are missed. With the release of the iPhone SDK 3.0, you can now develop OpenGL ES 2.0 applications for one of the world's most popular handheld devices.

The purpose of this appendix is to help you get started developing OpenGL ES 2.0 on the iPhone 3GS. Throughout the book we provided sample code to demonstrate various techniques and rendering functionality in OpenGL

ES 2.0. We ported all of that sample code to run on the iPhone 3GS; this appendix details what was involved in that process and what information you need to know to develop OpenGL ES 2.0 applications for the iPhone 3GS.

Getting Started with the iPhone SDK 3.0

The iPhone 3.0 SDK is available from the Apple developer Web site at http://developer.apple.com/ (it requires registering as an iPhone developer). As of this writing, the iPhone SDK 3.0 requires that you have an Intel-based Mac running Mac OS X 10.5.7 or later and iTunes v8.2. The iPhone SDK 3.0 includes everything you will need to get started developing OpenGL ES 2.0 applications, including Apple's Xcode integrated development environment (IDE) as well as the iPhone Simulator. The iPhone Simulator allows you to run, test, and debug your iPhone applications directly on the Mac and provides support for running both OpenGL ES 1.1- and OpenGL ES 2.0-based applications. In addition, the iPhone SDK 3.0 includes *Instruments*, a performance profiling tool that can be used to tune OpenGL ES applications. *Instruments* works with code that runs both on the iPhone Simulator and on the device, and it can be a very helpful tool in learning OpenGL ES.

Getting the Sample Code for the iPhone

In order to aid you in using the content of *The OpenGL ES 2.0 Programming Guide* on the iPhone platform, we have ported all of the C-based sample code to the iPhone SDK 3.0. The updated code can be downloaded from the book's Web site at www.opengles-book.com/. The package on the Web site includes all of the sample code along with Xcode projects for building each of the samples.

Throughout the book we developed an ES Utility Framework that provided the basic functionality needed by most OpenGL ES 2.0 applications. This framework includes functions for generating simple geometry, compiling and linking shaders, computing model-view and projection transformation matrices, and creating rendering surfaces.

The ES Utility Framework developed for the original book has been adapted to run on the iPhone. Given the rich application framework available on the iPhone 3GS, many of the functions in the ES Utility Framework became unnecessary. These generally include the functions that use EGL (e.g., esCreateWindow) and the callback functions associated with the framework (e.g., `esRegisterDrawFunc`, `esRegisterUpdateFunc`, etc.). However, all of the other routines relevant to creating 3D geometry, transformations, and loading shaders and objects were ported without modification. These functions will be especially helpful to developers migrating from the OpenGL ES 1.1 fixed-function pipeline (as found on previous generations of the iPhone and iPod Touch) to the shader-based transformation pipeline that requires you to generate the equivalent transformation matrices.

Building the Sample Code Using Xcode

Similar to the Windows-based version of the sample code, each example and the ES Utility Framework are provided in their own project files. The ES Utility Framework is built as a static library that each of the individual sample programs links with. All of the other sample projects contain only the relevant rendering and setup code and reference the ES Utility Framework. The project is organized in the following directory structure:

- /Common—holds the source code and an Xcode project for building the ES Framework library (called *libCommon.a*)
- /Chapter_*X*—holds each of the individual sample code examples for Chapter *X* along with the Xcode projects

In order to build any of the sample programs, the first thing you will need to do is build the ES Utility Framework located in the *Common* folder. Assuming you have installed the iPhone SDK 3.0, the only thing you need to do is open the *Common.xcodeproj* project and do a build (using the "Build" menu bar or associated keyboard shortcut; there isn't an executable associated with this project, so the *Build and Go* button on the workspace will be inactive). This will generate the *libCommon.a* file that contains the ES Utility Framework. All of the other sample code is set up to link to this library.

The next step is to simply open any of the individual sample projects in Xcode. For example, to build the MipMap2D texture sample from Chapter 9, simply open *Chapter_9/MipMap2D/MipMap2D.xcodeproj* and then click *Build and Go*. The sample will come up in the iPhone Simulator as pictured in Figure E.1.

Figure E-1   MipMap2D sample on iPhone Simulator

That's all there is to getting the samples to run on the iPhone. The iPhone SDK 3.0 simplifies application development, which allows you to focus on the relevant graphics code of each sample.

Porting the Sample Code to the iPhone

The process of porting the sample code from the book to the iPhone highlights some of the unique features of the iPhone. In particular, some of the unique features of the development environment include

- The use of Objective C

- The process of creating an EGL rendering context using `EAGLContext`

- Detection of device capabilities and creating an OpenGL ES 2.0 context

- The use of a framebuffer object as the primary rendering surface

Once you have created a rendering context, programming with OpenGL ES 2.0 on the iPhone is identical to programming on any other platform. However, there are some unique aspects of the platform that are worth understanding before jumping into the code.

Objective C

Apple uses the Objective C language within its development framework. Objective C is an object-oriented language that is a superset of C. Objective C files have a *.m* file extension. There are a number of great tutorials available online that will help you understand the fundamental differences between C/C++ and Objective C. As Objective C is the primary language used on the iPhone, you will definitely want to have a firm understanding of it before moving too far in your development.

One of the great things about Objective C is that because it is a strict superset of C, any code written in C will compile with the Objective C compiler. All of the sample code in our book was written in C, so it ported quite easily. The main changes to the code were around the event system and EGL initialization. By and large, the core of each sample ported to the platform without modification. In addition to Objective C, developers on the iPhone can also use Objective C++, which allows incorporating regular C++ in your iPhone applications. Objective C++ files have a *.mm* file extension. This flexible language support means that it is relatively easy to port C or C++ code to run on the iPhone and interoperate with Objective C or Objective C++.

Creating an OpenGL ES 2.0 Rendering Surface

In Chapter 3 we cover in detail how to create a rendering surface and context using EGL. We developed the esCreateWindow function that used EGL to initialize a rendering surface and create a context. On the iPhone, Apple provides its own framework for initializing with EGL, so the developer doesn't have to do this. This framework is documented in the iPhone SDK.

In Xcode there is a project template for creating an iPhone *OpenGL ES Application*. This template creates an object named *EAGLView*, implemented in the files *EAGLView.m* and *EAGLView.h*, that will create a window and render a spinning Gouraud-shaded square.

The *EAGLView* object subclasses the *UIView* object and provides most of the routines that an OpenGL ES application would need to run. The *EAGLView* object usually needs only minimal modification to have the application's custom rendering code added to it. One change from the template that is necessary is to specifically request an OpenGL ES 2.0 context rather than the default OpenGL ES 1.1 context. Unlike many other platforms, the iPhone SDK will allow a program to compile and link with calls to both OpenGL ES 1.1 and OpenGL ES 2.0 functions. However, in order for these calls to actually be able to execute, one must request the appropriate context. To request an OpenGL ES 2.0 context in the *EAGLView* class that is generated, we use the following code:

```
context = [[EAGLContext alloc] initWithAPI:kEAGLRenderingAPIOpenGLES2];
```

This line is different from the default configuration provided in *EAGLView.m*, which provides an OpenGL ES 1.1 context.

In order to write an application that will safely run on either the iPhone 3G or iPhone 3GS, you must check the device's capabilities at application initialization. As OpenGL ES 2.0 is available only on the iPhone 3GS, it is necessary to have an OpenGL ES 1.1 fallback path to run on previous-generation iPhones. The call to initWithAPI will return nil on devices that do not support OpenGL ES 2.0. In those cases, an OpenGL ES 1.1 context can be created and a fallback rendering path executed.

In addition to creating an OpenGL ES 2.0 context, the application will also need to include the OpenGL ES 2.0 header files (rather than the OpenGL ES 1.1 headers provided by default in *EAGLView.h*):

```
#import <OpenGLES/ES2/gl.h>
#import <OpenGLES/ES2/glext.h>
```

One final change that is required is modifying the default `drawView` method that draws a spinning square using OpenGL ES 1.1. You should replace those routines with the OpenGL ES 2.0 rendering code of your application. That was the approach taken when creating the samples in the book. The default *EAGLView* class was modified to create an OpenGL ES 2.0 context and call the sample code from the book.

Using a Framebuffer Object for Rendering

One other unique aspect of the iPhone is that all rendering is done to an off-screen framebuffer object. The full details of creating and rendering with framebuffer objects are covered in Chapter 12. On most platforms, one creates a displayable window surface using EGL and then uses `eglSwapBuffers` to present the surface to the screen. This was the approach that we took in the sample code in this book. However, on the iPhone an off-screen renderbuffer is used for all rendering and then presented to the screen using the *EAGLContext* `presentRenderbuffer` method. It was a small change in our examples to convert the call to `eglSwapBuffers` and to wrap our main drawing function to bind and present the renderbuffer.

Discussion of a Complete Example

Figure E.1 shows the output from the iPhone simulator for our example MipMap2D from Chapter 9. In this section we'll show all of the modified source code for that example, including the modified *EAGLView.m* file that forms the framework of OpenGL ES applications on the iPhone, and reiterate explicitly the steps required to port the application to the iPhone 3GS. In order to simplify the changes we made, we've numbered the lines of the original source files that Xcode creates when you start a project. Our modifications are described and presented as the unnumbered lines, usually with a reference to the lines affected in the original file.

EAGLView.h Header File

When you start with the default OpenGL ES application framework in the iPhone SDK, two files are created on your behalf: *EAGLView.h* and *EAGLView.m*. The *EAGLView.h* file provides the Objective C interface definition, including the prototypes of the methods of the *EAGLView* object that is subclassed from the base *UIView* class. The modifications to the default *EAGLView.h* file are minimal, consisting of adding only a few items related to working with our ES Utility Framework.

```
1   //
2   //  EAGLView.h
3   //  MipMap2D
4   //
5   //  Created by __YourNameHere__ on 7/5/09.
6   //  Copyright __MyCompanyName__ 2009. All rights reserved.
7   //
8
9
10  #import <UIKit/UIKit.h>
11  #import <OpenGLES/EAGL.h>
12  #import <OpenGLES/ES1/gl.h>
13  #import <OpenGLES/ES1/glext.h>
14
```

The first modification is to convert from using the OpenGL ES 1.1 header files to using those for OpenGL ES 2.0. A simple replacement of the 1 with a 2 will bring in the right header files. We also include our *esUtil.h* header file in the definition for the *ESContext* type:

```
    #import <OpenGLES/ES2/gl.h>
    #import <OpenGLES/ES2/glext.h>
    #import "esUtil.h"
15
16  /*
17  This class wraps the CAEAGLLayer from CoreAnimation into a
18  convenient UIView subclass. The view content is basically an
19  EAGL surface you render your OpenGL scene into. Note that
20  setting the view non-opaque will work only if the EAGL surface
21  has an alpha channel.
22  */
23  @interface EAGLView : UIView {
24
25  @private
26      /* The pixel dimensions of the backbuffer */
27      GLint backingWidth;
28      GLint backingHeight;
29
30      EAGLContext *context;
31
32      /* OpenGL names for the renderbuffer and framebuffers used
33         to render to this view */
34      GLuint viewRenderbuffer, viewFramebuffer;
35
36      /* OpenGL name for the depth buffer that is attached to
37         viewFramebuffer, if it exists (0 if it does not exist) */
```

```
38       GLuint depthRenderbuffer;
39
40       NSTimer *animationTimer;
41       NSTimeInterval animationInterval;
```

We also added a member variable to record the time for the previous frame for use in updating our application's animation:

```
NSTimeInterval prevTick;
```

Our final modification to the *EAGLView.h* file is the declaration of an *ESContext* for use by our ES Utility Framework. We include it in the *EAGLView* class definition for easy access and encapsulation:

```
         // ES Programming Guide context
         ESContext esContext;
42  }
43
44  @property NSTimeInterval animationInterval;
45
46  - (void)startAnimation;
47  - (void)stopAnimation;
48  - (void)drawView;
49
50  @end
```

EAGLView.m Source File

The implementation file associated with the *EAGLView.h* header file, *EAGLView.m*, is where the heart of the application lives. This file contains the equivalent of the windowing and event-processing routines in our ES Utility Framework library. The initial contents of the file, containing the boilerplate (including comments), is provided below. We've added line numbers to the original Xcode generated to make it easier to reference and describe the changes.

```
 1  //
 2  //  EAGLView.m
 3  //  MipMap2D
 4  //
 5  //  Created by __YourNameHere__ on 7/5/09.
 6  //  Copyright __MyCompanyName__ 2009. All rights reserved.
 7  //
 8
 9
10
11  #import <QuartzCore/QuartzCore.h>
```

```
12   #import <OpenGLES/EAGLDrawable.h>
13
14   #import "EAGLView.h"
```

The first change required is adding our header file for our ES Utility Framework, *esUtil.h*, and function prototypes for the routines defined in our *MipMap2D.c* file:

```
#import "esUtil.h"

// Functions in MipMap2D.c
int Init(ESContext *esContext);
void Draw(ESContext *esContext);
void ShutDown(ESContext *esContext);
```

Our example doesn't require a depth buffer, but if your application does, you would redefine the following macro to be true, which would cause the later creation of a renderbuffer for use as a depth buffer. As we mentioned, the iPhone 3GS renders entirely into off-screen renderbuffers, which you need to manually set up at application initialization time. This is different from the operation of our ES Utility Framework, which would take care of buffer creation for you. If your application needs a stencil buffer, you would create a stencil renderbuffer in a manner almost identical to that for creating a depth buffer.

```
15   #define USE_DEPTH_BUFFER 0
16
17   // A class extension to declare private methods
18   @interface EAGLView ()
19
20   @property (nonatomic, retain) EAGLContext *context;
21   @property (nonatomic, assign) NSTimer *animationTimer;
22
23   - (BOOL) createFramebuffer;
24   - (void) destroyFramebuffer;
25
26   @end
27
28
29   @implementation EAGLView
30
31   @synthesize context;
32   @synthesize animationTimer;
33   @synthesize animationInterval;
34
35
36   // You must implement this method
37   + (Class)layerClass {
```

```
38      return [CAEAGLLayer class];
39  }
40
41
42  // The GL view is stored in the nib file. When it's unarchived
43      it's sent -initWithCoder:
44  - (id)initWithCoder:(NSCoder*)coder {
45
46      if ((self = [super initWithCoder:coder])) {
47          // Get the layer
48          CAEAGLLayer *eaglLayer = (CAEAGLLayer *)self.layer;
49
50          eaglLayer.opaque = YES;
51          eaglLayer.drawableProperties =
52              [NSDictionary dictionaryWithObjectsAndKeys:
53              [NSNumber numberWithBool:NO],
54              kEAGLDrawablePropertyRetainedBacking,
55              kEAGLColorFormatRGBA8,
56              kEAGLDrawablePropertyColorFormat, nil];
57
```

The following lines create the OpenGL ES rendering context, which is
another activity that occurred under the covers of our ES Utility
Framework:

```
58  context = [[EAGLContext alloc]
59              initWithAPI:kEAGLRenderingAPIOpenGLES1];
```

As we mentioned before, you will need to create the type of context that's
appropriate for your application. By default, the iPhone SDK creates an
OpenGL ES 1.1 rendering context, as specified by the 1 at the very end of the
Objective C function to allocate an OpenGL ES context. Changing the 1 to a
2 will request, as you might expect, an OpenGL ES 2.0 context. If your
application happens to be running on an iPhone device that doesn't support
OpenGL ES 2.0, no context will be allocated, and a nil value will be
returned. Successful context creation is verified on line 61, along with a
successful setting of the current context to the recently allocated one. It
would be at this point where your application would apply a fallback path to
render using OpenGL ES 1.1, if no OpenGL ES 2.0 context were available.

```
60
61  if (!context || ![EAGLContext setCurrentContext:context]) {
62      [self release];
63      return nil;
64  }
65
66  animationInterval = 1.0 / 60.0;
```

The final initialization change we need to make is to initialize our ES Utility Framework by calling our `Init` routine.

```
67          Init(&esContext);
68      }
69      return self;
70  }
71
72
73  - (void)drawView {
```

As the following comment suggests, here is where you would add your own rendering code. In our case, we have replaced lines 79 through 116 in the original file. Our new code is shown after line 113.

```
74
75  // Replace the implementation of this method to do your
76     own custom drawing
77
78     const GLfloat squareVertices[] = {
79         -0.5f, -0.5f,
80          0.5f, -0.5f,
81         -0.5f,  0.5f,
82          0.5f,  0.5f,
83     };
84     const GLubyte squareColors[] = {
85         255, 255,   0, 255,
86         0,   255, 255, 255,
87         0,     0,   0,   0,
88         255,   0, 255, 255,
89     };
90
91     [EAGLContext setCurrentContext:context];
92
93     glBindFramebufferOES(GL_FRAMEBUFFER_OES, viewFramebuffer);
94     glViewport(0, 0, backingWidth, backingHeight);
95
96     glMatrixMode(GL_PROJECTION);
97     glLoadIdentity();
98     glOrthof(-1.0f, 1.0f, -1.5f, 1.5f, -1.0f, 1.0f);
99     glMatrixMode(GL_MODELVIEW);
100    glRotatef(3.0f, 0.0f, 0.0f, 1.0f);
101
102    glClearColor(0.5f, 0.5f, 0.5f, 1.0f);
103    glClear(GL_COLOR_BUFFER_BIT);
104
105    glVertexPointer(2, GL_FLOAT, 0, squareVertices);
106    glEnableClientState(GL_VERTEX_ARRAY);
107    glColorPointer(4, GL_UNSIGNED_BYTE, 0, squareColors);
```

```
108      glEnableClientState(GL_COLOR_ARRAY);
109
110      glDrawArrays(GL_TRIANGLE_STRIP, 0, 4);
111
112      glBindRenderbufferOES(GL_RENDERBUFFER_OES,
113                            viewRenderbuffer);
114      [context presentRenderbuffer:GL_RENDERBUFFER_OES];
115
```

The code we include for our example does several operations: updating the animation time; setting the current context; binding our framebuffer object for rendering, including its width and height, which our ES Utility Framework routine uses to set the viewport; and finally rendering. The lines following the call to the Draw function (defined in *MipMap2D.c*) signal the iPhone that our rendered frame should be shown on the display.

```
// Compute time delta
NSTimeInterval curTick = [NSDate
        timeIntervalSinceReferenceDate];
NSTimeInterval deltaTime = curTick - prevTick;
prevTick = curTick;

[EAGLContext setCurrentContext:context];

glBindFramebuffer(GL_FRAMEBUFFER, viewFramebuffer);
esContext.width = backingWidth;
esContext.height = backingHeight;

Draw(&esContext);

glBindRenderbuffer(GL_RENDERBUFFER, viewRenderbuffer);
[context presentRenderbuffer:GL_RENDERBUFFER];
```

```
116  }
117
118
119  -  (void)layoutSubviews {
120      [EAGLContext setCurrentContext:context];
121      [self destroyFramebuffer];
122      [self createFramebuffer];
123      [self drawView];
124  }
125
126
```

The following method, createFramebuffer, requires the same change applied numerous times. While framebuffer objects are part of the core OpenGL ES 2.0 API, they were an extension to OpenGL ES 1.1, which you can infer from the copious OES suffixes to the routines and tokens in the following routine. In order to use the OpenGL ES 2.0 versions of those routines, we merely removed all of the OES suffixes on lines 129 through 160, with our version shown after line 163.

```
127   - (BOOL)createFramebuffer {
128
129       glGenFramebuffersOES(1, &viewFramebuffer);
130       glGenRenderbuffersOES(1, &viewRenderbuffer);
131
132       glBindFramebufferOES(GL_FRAMEBUFFER_OES, viewFramebuffer);
133       glBindRenderbufferOES(GL_RENDERBUFFER_OES,
134          viewRenderbuffer);
135       [context renderbufferStorage:GL_RENDERBUFFER_OES
136          fromDrawable:(CAEAGLLayer*)self.layer];
137       glFramebufferRenderbufferOES(GL_FRAMEBUFFER_OES,
138          GL_COLOR_ATTACHMENT0_OES, GL_RENDERBUFFER_OES,
139          viewRenderbuffer);
140
141       glGetRenderbufferParameterivOES(GL_RENDERBUFFER_OES,
142          GL_RENDERBUFFER_WIDTH_OES, &backingWidth);
143       glGetRenderbufferParameterivOES(GL_RENDERBUFFER_OES,
144          GL_RENDERBUFFER_HEIGHT_OES, &backingHeight);
145
146       if (USE_DEPTH_BUFFER) {
147          glGenRenderbuffersOES(1, &depthRenderbuffer);
148          glBindRenderbufferOES(GL_RENDERBUFFER_OES,
149             depthRenderbuffer);
150          glRenderbufferStorageOES(GL_RENDERBUFFER_OES,
151             GL_DEPTH_COMPONENT16_OES, backingWidth, backingHeight);
152          glFramebufferRenderbufferOES(GL_FRAMEBUFFER_OES,
153             GL_DEPTH_ATTACHMENT_OES, GL_RENDERBUFFER_OES,
154             depthRenderbuffer);
155       }
156
157       if(glCheckFramebufferStatusOES(GL_FRAMEBUFFER_OES) !=
158             GL_FRAMEBUFFER_COMPLETE_OES) {
159          NSLog(@"failed to make complete framebuffer object %x",
160             glCheckFramebufferStatusOES(GL_FRAMEBUFFER_OES));
161          return NO;
162       }
163
          glGenFramebuffers(1, &viewFramebuffer);
          glGenRenderbuffers(1, &viewRenderbuffer);

          glBindFramebuffer(GL_FRAMEBUFFER, viewFramebuffer);
          glBindRenderbuffer(GL_RENDERBUFFER, viewRenderbuffer);
```

```
[context renderbufferStorage:GL_RENDERBUFFER
    fromDrawable:(CAEAGLLayer*)self.layer];
glFramebufferRenderbuffer(GL_FRAMEBUFFER,
    GL_COLOR_ATTACHMENT0, GL_RENDERBUFFER, viewRenderbuffer);

glGetRenderbufferParameteriv(GL_RENDERBUFFER,
    GL_RENDERBUFFER_WIDTH, &backingWidth);
glGetRenderbufferParameteriv(GL_RENDERBUFFER,
    GL_RENDERBUFFER_HEIGHT, &backingHeight);
```

If your application requires a stencil buffer, you would repeat the same operation for creating a depth buffer, as demonstrated below, to create a stencil buffer (making suitable replacements, of course).

```
if (USE_DEPTH_BUFFER) {
    glGenRenderbuffers(1, &depthRenderbuffer);
    glBindRenderbuffer(GL_RENDERBUFFER, depthRenderbuffer);
    glRenderbufferStorage(GL_RENDERBUFFER,
        GL_DEPTH_COMPONENT16, backingWidth, backingHeight);
    glFramebufferRenderbuffer(GL_FRAMEBUFFER,
        GL_DEPTH_ATTACHMENT, GL_RENDERBUFFER,
        depthRenderbuffer);
}

if(glCheckFramebufferStatus(GL_FRAMEBUFFER) !=
    GL_FRAMEBUFFER_COMPLETE) {
        NSLog(@"failed to make complete framebuffer object %x",
            glCheckFramebufferStatus(GL_FRAMEBUFFER));
        return NO;
}
164
165     return YES;
166 }
167
168
```

Similarly for the next routine, destroyFramebuffer, we once again needed to port from the OpenGL ES 1.1 extension version of framebuffer objects to the core version by removing the OES suffixes.

```
169 - (void)destroyFramebuffer {
170
171     glDeleteFramebuffersOES(1, &viewFramebuffer);
172     viewFramebuffer = 0;
173     glDeleteRenderbuffersOES(1, &viewRenderbuffer);
174     viewRenderbuffer = 0;
175
176     if(depthRenderbuffer) {
```

```
177          glDeleteRenderbuffersOES(1, &depthRenderbuffer);
178          depthRenderbuffer = 0;
179      }

         glDeleteFramebuffers(1, &viewFramebuffer);
         viewFramebuffer = 0;
         glDeleteRenderbuffers(1, &viewRenderbuffer);
         viewRenderbuffer = 0;

         if(depthRenderbuffer) {
             glDeleteRenderbuffers(1, &depthRenderbuffer);
             depthRenderbuffer = 0;
         }
180
181  }
182
183
184  - (void)startAnimation {
185      self.animationTimer =
186          [NSTimer scheduledTimerWithTimeInterval:animationInterval
187          target:self selector:@selector(drawView) userInfo:nil
188          repeats:YES];
189  }
190
191
192  - (void)stopAnimation {
193      self.animationTimer = nil;
194  }
195
196
197  - (void)setAnimationTimer:(NSTimer *)newTimer {
198      [animationTimer invalidate];
199      animationTimer = newTimer;
200  }
201
202
203  - (void)setAnimationInterval:(NSTimeInterval)interval {
204
205      animationInterval = interval;
206      if (animationTimer) {
207          [self stopAnimation];
208          [self startAnimation];
209      }
210  }
211
212
213  - (void)dealloc {
214
215      [self stopAnimation];
```

Our final change occurs in the `dealloc` method where we close down the ES Utility library by calling our `ShutDown` routine:

```
        ShutDown(&esContext);
216
217     if ([EAGLContext currentContext] == context) {
218         [EAGLContext setCurrentContext:nil];
219     }
220
221     [context release];
222     [super dealloc];
223 }
224
225 @end
```

That summarizes all of the modifications required to the OpenGL ES framework that are provided by the iPhone SDK. The remainder of the MipMap2D example is identical to what's provided in our source code, available at our Web site.

Transitioning from OpenGL ES 1.1 to OpenGL ES 2.0

For developers who are currently writing applications that target OpenGL ES 1.1 on the iPhone 3G, the move to OpenGL ES 2.0 may be a bit difficult at first. While OpenGL ES 2.0 is significantly more powerful than OpenGL ES 1.1, it also pushes the responsibility to the developer to implement the vertex transformation and fragment shading pipeline. This means becoming intimately familiar with how the fixed-function vertex and fragment pipelines in OpenGL ES 1.1 work and translating those pipelines into OpenGL ES 2.0 shaders.

The OpenGL ES 2.0 Programming Guide was written with this type of developer in mind. In Chapter 8, Vertex Shaders, we provide a shader that implements the entire OpenGL ES 1.1 fixed-function pipeline (Example 8-8). This includes vertex transformation, texture coordinate generation, lighting, and vertex fog. In Example 8-6, we also show how to implement matrix palette skinning in a vertex shader. In Chapter 10, Fragment Shaders, we show how fixed-function state from OpenGL ES 1.1 can be translated into fragment shader code. In particular, we cover the texture environment, multi-texturing, fog, alpha test, and clipping using user-defined clipping planes.

In addition to these chapters, the ES Utility Framework provides functions that do the equivalent of `glRotate`, `glTranslate`, and `glScale`. It also contains functions for generating the perspective transformation matrix and the model-view matrix. These functions should be helpful to a developer who has relied on the fixed-function API of OpenGL ES 1.1 for generating transformation matrices.

Conclusion

The iPhone 3GS brings OpenGL ES 2.0–programmable hardware into millions of consumers' hands. *The OpenGL ES 2.0 Programming Guide* covers everything in the API to help you render efficient shader-based 3D graphics on the iPhone 3GS. In this appendix we covered the basics of how to begin developing OpenGL ES 2.0 applications for the iPhone 3GS. Throughout the book we developed a number of C-based samples to demonstrate the use of various features of the API. In order to help you use the content of the book on the iPhone, we ported these samples to the iPhone SDK, which you can download from the book's Web site. In addition, we covered some of the unique aspects of programming with OpenGL ES 2.0 on the iPhone.

Index

array subscripting, 81
artifacts
    avoiding, 143, 144
    multisampling prone to, 250
    produced by nearest sampling, 189
attachment points, 262
attachments
    to a framebuffer, 338
    minimum of one valid, 268
attenuation, 163
attribute(s)
    associated with an `EGLConfig`, 39
    binding, 31
    getting and setting, 72
    in the OpenGL ES Shading
        Language, 89–90
    for a vertex shader, 4, 5, 148, 149
attribute index, 113
`attribute` qualifier, 110
attribute variable name, 115
attribute variables, 89
automatic mipmap generation,
        193–194

B

`b` argument data type, 15
back buffer, 34, 234
back-facing triangles, 142
backward compatibility, of OpenGL ES
        2.0 and OpenGL ES 1.x, 11–12
backward differencing, 372
bias matrix, 303, 304
bias parameter, 369
bilinear filtering, 193
binary compilation tools, 351
binary fragment shader, 75
binary operators, 84
binary shader format, 74, 351
binary shaders
    loading, 74–75
    supporting, 73
binary vertex shader, 75
BinaryShader.lib, 351
binding, 115
bit test, stencil test as, 240
bitmask, specifying, 54
bits, in color buffer, 43

blending
    enabling, 333
    in per-fragment operations, 10
    pixel colors, 246–248
blending coefficients, 247–248
blending equation, 246, 248
Bloom effect, 298
blur fragment shader, 297–298
Boolean-based vector types, 79
bottom clip plane, 138
bound texture objects, 193
box filtering technique, 189
BREW operating system, 339
buffer(s), 234–235
    clearing, 235–236
    involved in drawing, 32
    requesting additional, 235
    size of, 234
    swapping of, 234
    types of, 234
    unmapping previously mapped, 125
buffer object data store, 119
buffer object names, 117
buffer objects
    deleting, 124
    for each vertex attribute, 122–123
    mapping, 124–126
    state associated with, 118
    types supported, 116
    usage of, 118
buffer write mask, 236
built-in constants, 150, 220–221
built-in functions, 357–373
    in applications, 358
    categories of, 357
    in the OpenGL ES Shading
        Language, 86–87
    overloading, 358
built-in special variables, 149–150,
        219–220
built-in uniform state, 150
built-in variables, of a vertex shader,
        149

C

C code, syntax compared to shaders, 78
C compiler, generating object code, 57–58

Windows Mobile 6 SDK, downloading, 341

Windows Mobile Developer Center, 341

Windows Mobile operating system, 340

Windows/Linux developers, development environment for, 340

wispy fog effect, 313, 315

world space, 287–288

world-space normal vector, 281

world-space reflection vector, 288

wrap modes, 194, 307

writable static global variables, 340

write masks, 10

X

x argument data type, 15

Z

Z fighting, 98, 143